SPEED RACER™

Vol. 2

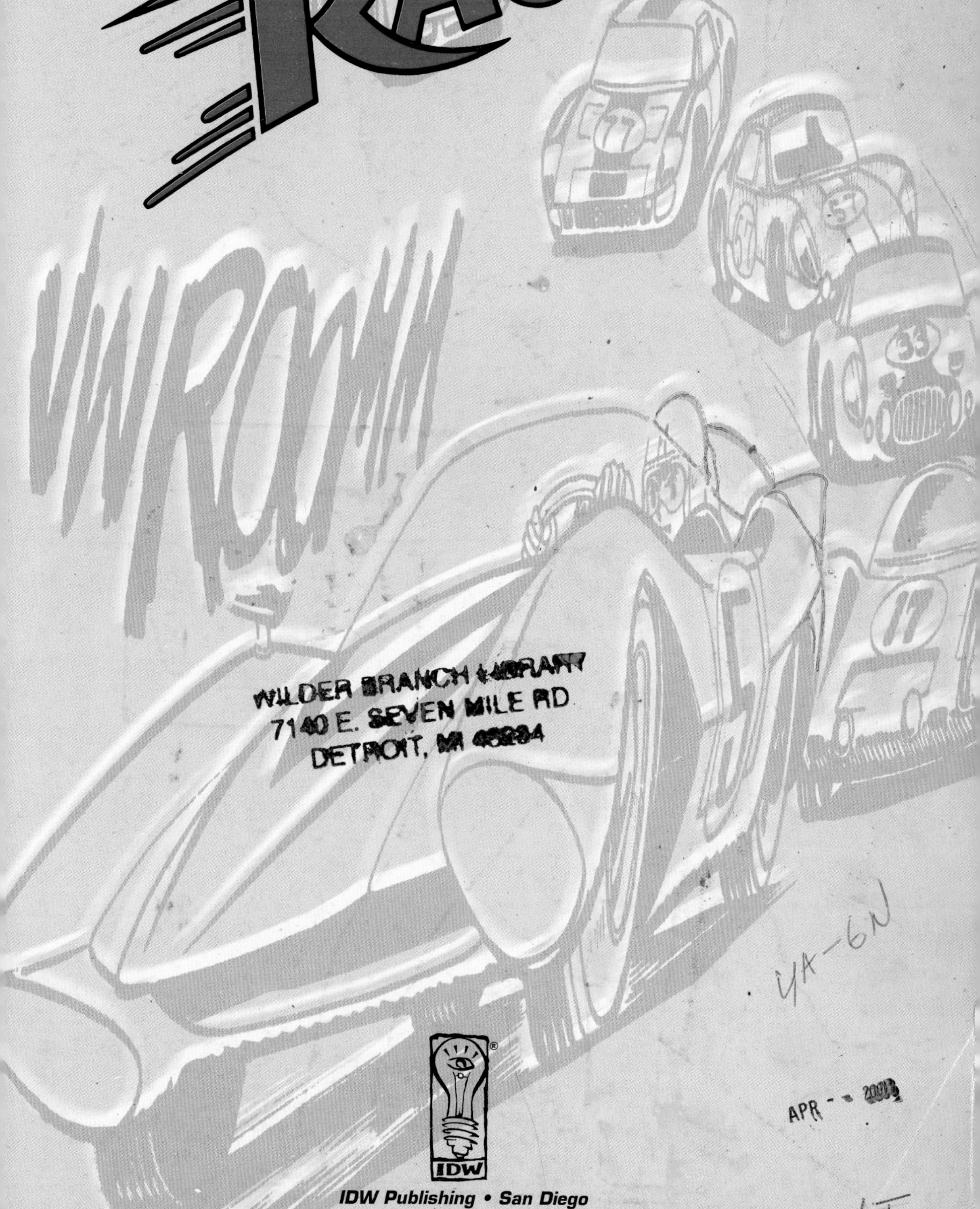

IDW

IDW Publishing • San Diego

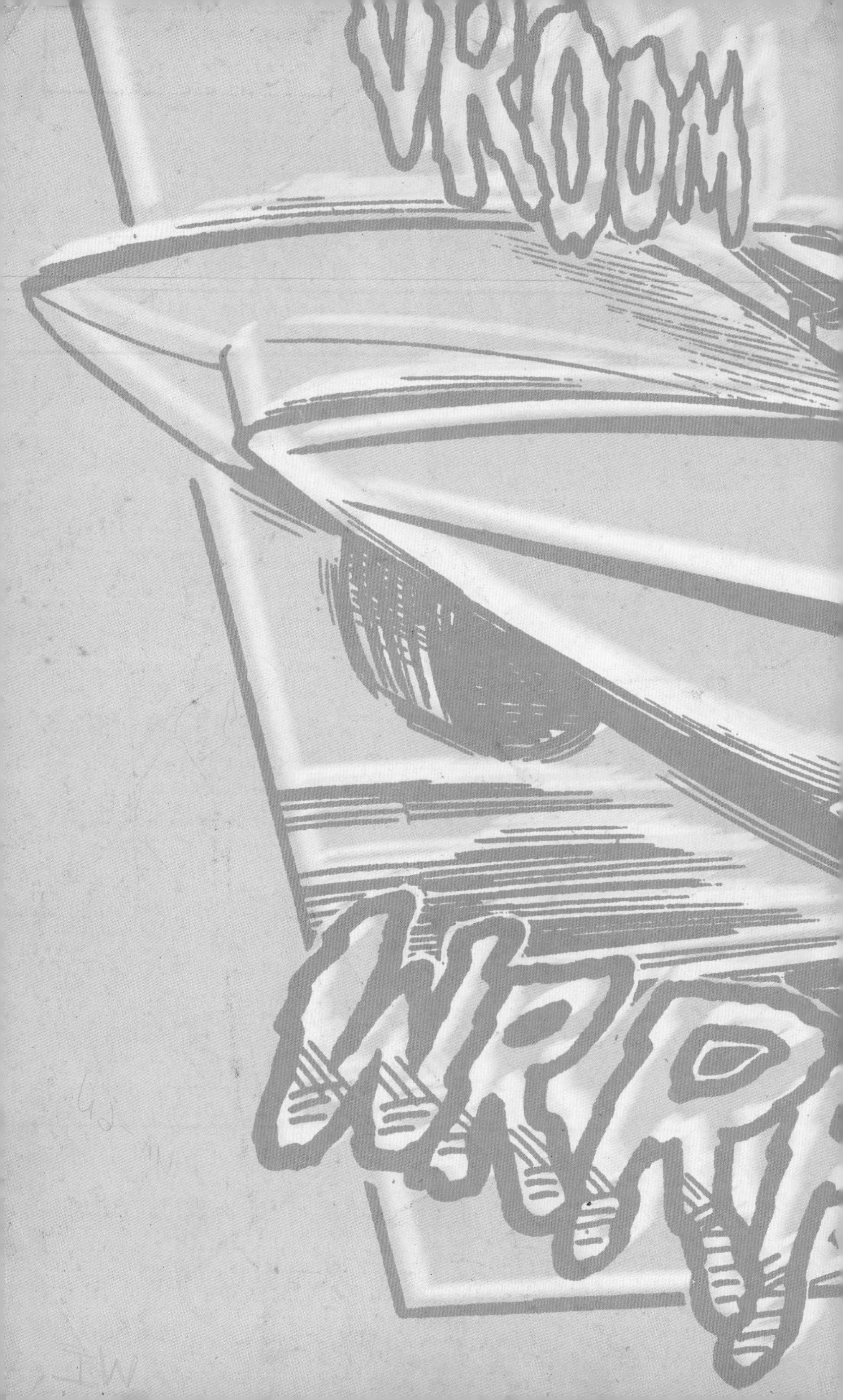
VROOM

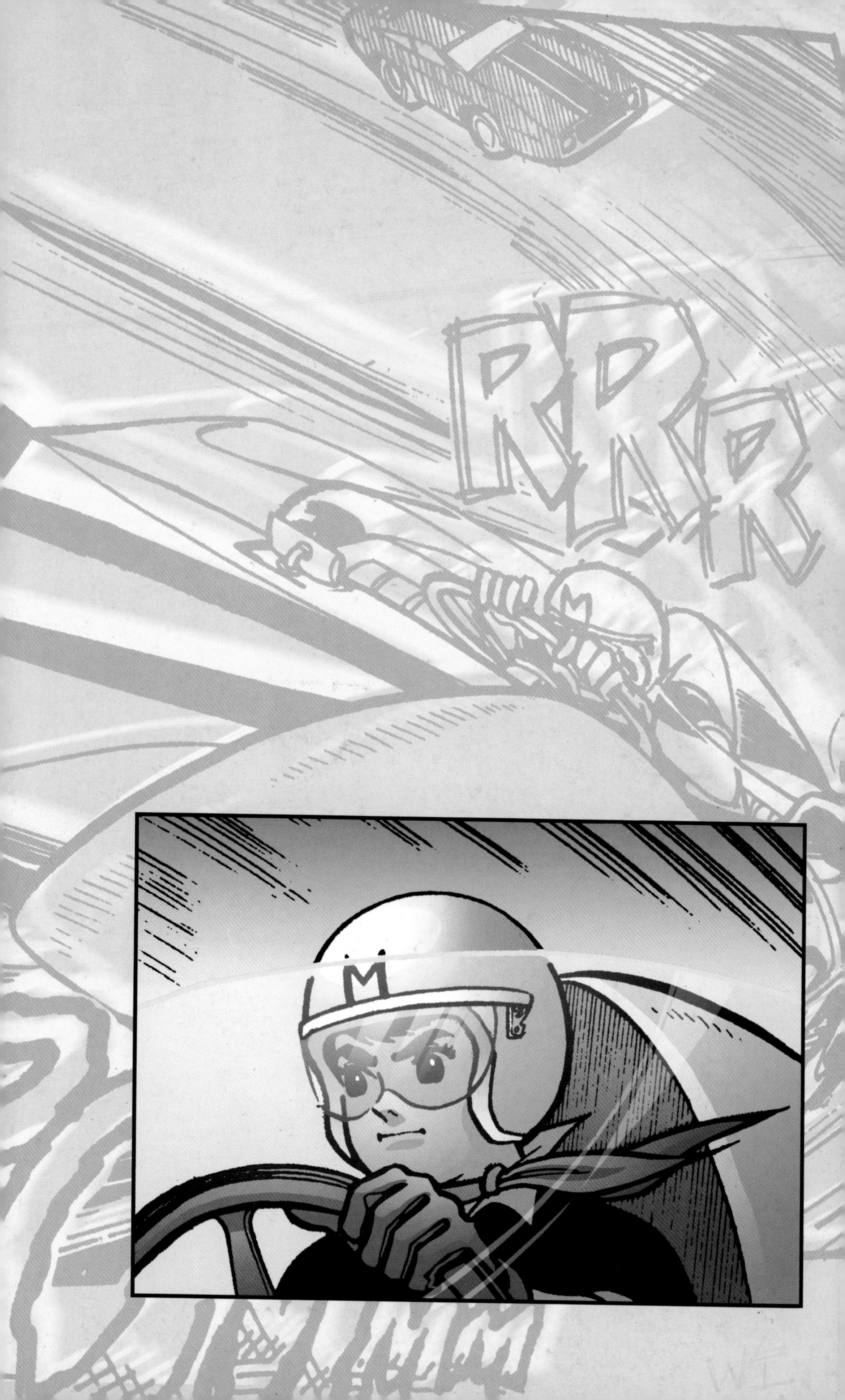
RRR

IDW Publishing is:
Ted Adams, *President*
Robbie Robbins, *EVP/Sr. Graphic Artist*
Chris Ryall, *Publisher/Editor-in-Chief*
Clifford Meth, *EVP of Strategies/Editorial*
Alan Payne, *VP of Sales*
Neil Uyetake, *Art Director*
Tom Waltz, *Editor*
Andrew Steven Harris, *Editor*
Chris Mowry, *Graphic Artist*
Amauri Osorio, *Graphic Artist*
Dene Nee, *Graphic Artist/Editor*
Matthew Ruzicka, *CPA, Controller*
Alonzo Simon, *Shipping Manager*
Kris Oprisko, *Editor/Foreign Lic. Rep*

www.idwpublishing.com
www.speedracer.com

ISBN: 978-1-60010-175-5
11 10 09 08   1 2 3 4 5

Speed Racer #6
page 7
Written by ***Lamar Waldron***
Pencilled by ***Jill Thompson***
Inked by ***Brian Thomas***
Lettered and Colored by
Ken Holewczynski
Edited by ***Tony Caputo***

Speed Racer #7
page 27
Written by ***Lamar Waldron***
Pencilled by ***Jill Thompson***
Inked by ***Brian Thomas*** & ***Jim Nelson***
Lettered and Colored by
Ken Holewczynski

Speed Racer #8
page 47
Written by ***Lamar Waldron***
Pencilled by ***George Booker***
Inked by ***Brian Thomas***
Lettered and Colored by
Ken Holewczynski

Speed Racer #9
page 67
Written by ***Lamar Waldron***
Pencilled by ***George Booker***
Inked by ***Brian Thomas***
Lettered by ***Ken Holewczynski***
Colored by ***Cygnet Ash***

Speed Racer #10
page 87
Written by ***Lamar Waldron***
Pencilled by ***Tom Morgan***
Inked by ***Brian Thomas***
Lettered by ***Ken Holewczynski***
Colored by ***Cygnet Ash***

Speed Racer #11
page 107
Written by ***Fred Schiller***
Pencilled by ***George Booker***
Inked by ***Brian Thomas***
Lettered by ***Ken Holewczynski***
Colored by ***Rich Powers***

Speed Racer #12
page 127
Written by ***Lamar Waldron***
Pencilled by ***Joe Phillips***
Inked by ***Jim Brozman***
Lettered by ***Ken Holewczynski***

Speed Racer #13
page 147
Written by ***Lamar Waldron***
Pencilled by ***Joe Phillips***
Inked by ***John Bell III***

Speed Racer Vol. 2 TPB

Cover by ***Ken Steacy***
Edited by ***Dene Nee***
Design and Remaster by ***Tom B. Long***

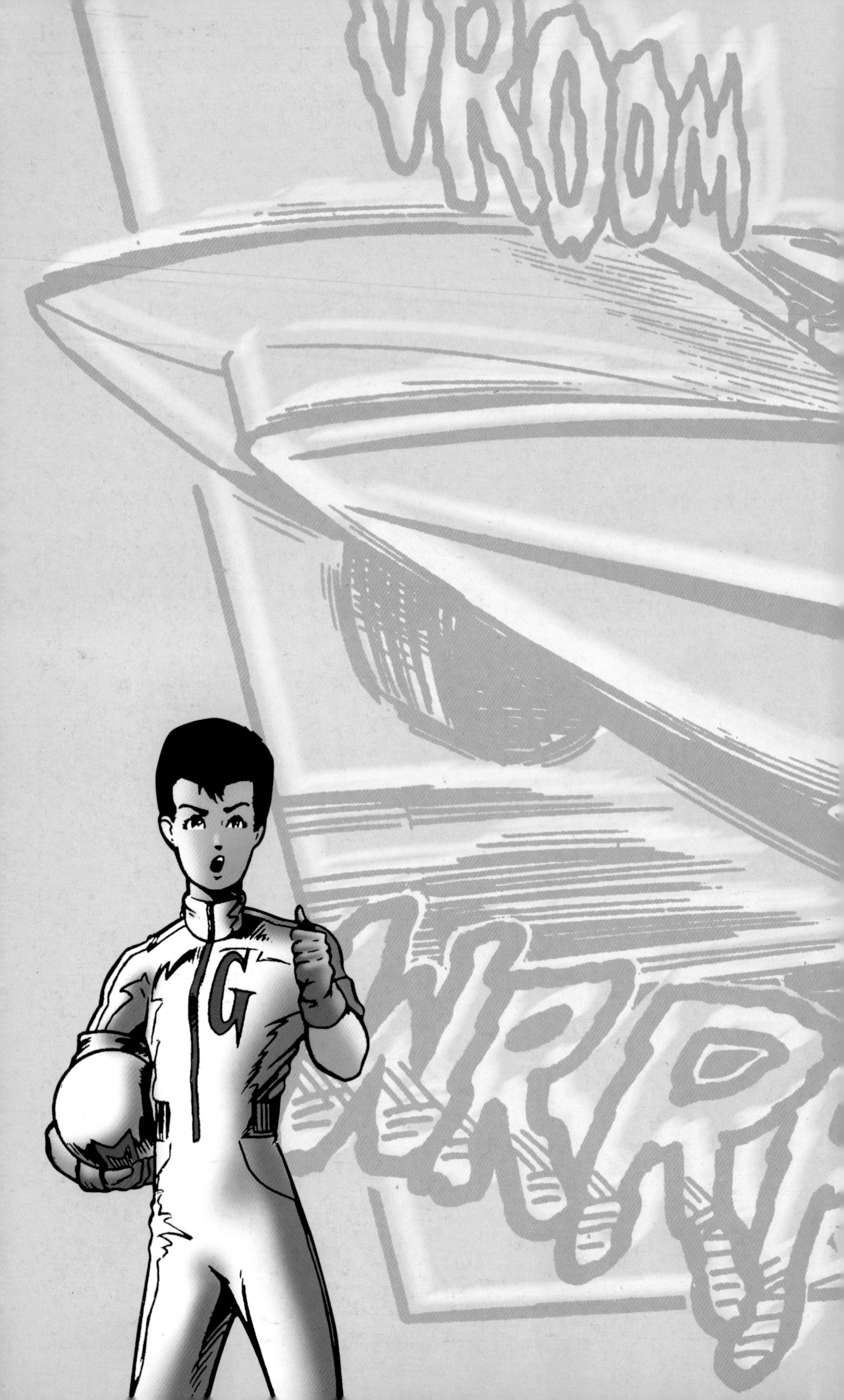
VROOM

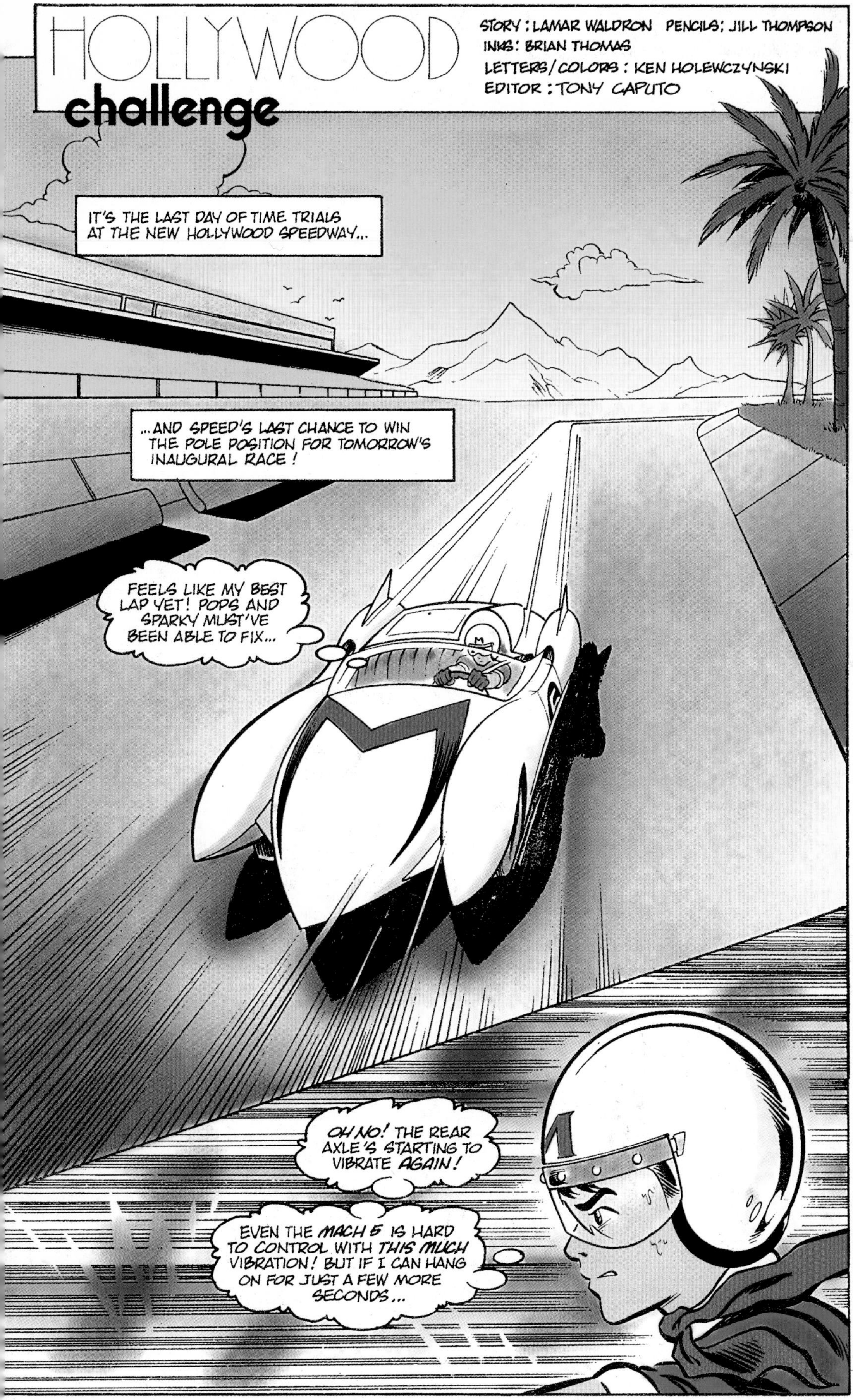
HOLLYWOOD challenge
STORY: LAMAR WALDRON PENCILS: JILL THOMPSON
INKS: BRIAN THOMAS
LETTERS/COLORS: KEN HOLEWCZYNSKI
EDITOR: TONY CAPUTO
IT'S THE LAST DAY OF TIME TRIALS AT THE NEW HOLLYWOOD SPEEDWAY...
...AND SPEED'S LAST CHANCE TO WIN THE POLE POSITION FOR TOMORROW'S INAUGURAL RACE!
FEELS LIKE MY BEST LAP YET! POPS AND SPARKY MUST'VE BEEN ABLE TO FIX...
OH NO! THE REAR AXLE'S STARTING TO VIBRATE AGAIN!
EVEN THE MACH 5 IS HARD TO CONTROL WITH THIS MUCH VIBRATION! BUT IF I CAN HANG ON FOR JUST A FEW MORE SECONDS...

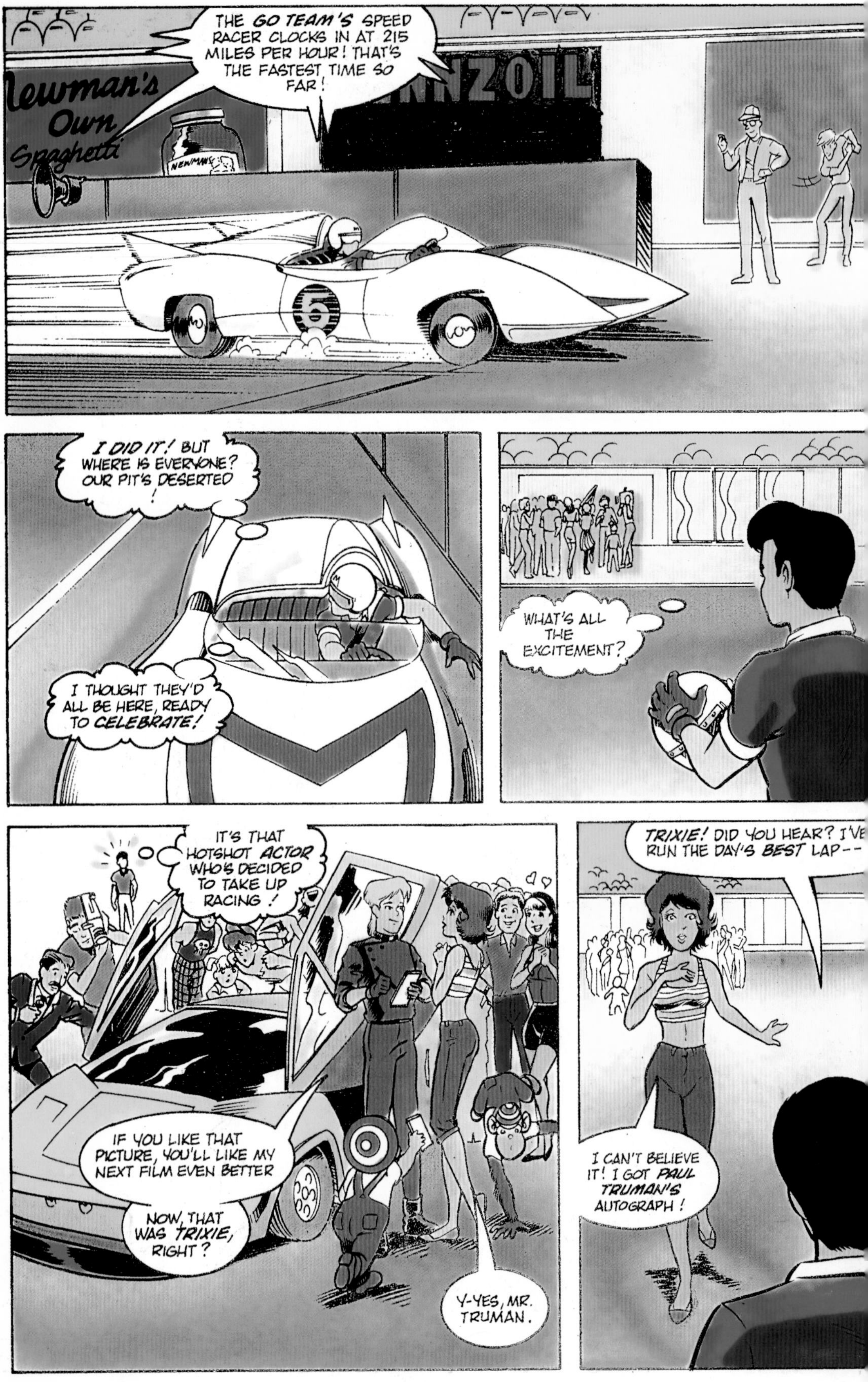
THE GO TEAM'S SPEED RACER CLOCKS IN AT 215 MILES PER HOUR! THAT'S THE FASTEST TIME SO FAR!
Newman's Own Spaghetti
NZOIL
I DID IT! BUT WHERE IS EVERYONE? OUR PIT'S DESERTED!
I THOUGHT THEY'D ALL BE HERE, READY TO CELEBRATE!
WHAT'S ALL THE EXCITEMENT?
IT'S THAT HOTSHOT ACTOR WHO'S DECIDED TO TAKE UP RACING!
IF YOU LIKE THAT PICTURE, YOU'LL LIKE MY NEXT FILM EVEN BETTER
NOW, THAT WAS TRIXIE, RIGHT?
Y-YES, MR. TRUMAN.
TRIXIE! DID YOU HEAR? I'VE RUN THE DAY'S BEST LAP--
I CAN'T BELIEVE IT! I GOT PAUL TRUMAN'S AUTOGRAPH!

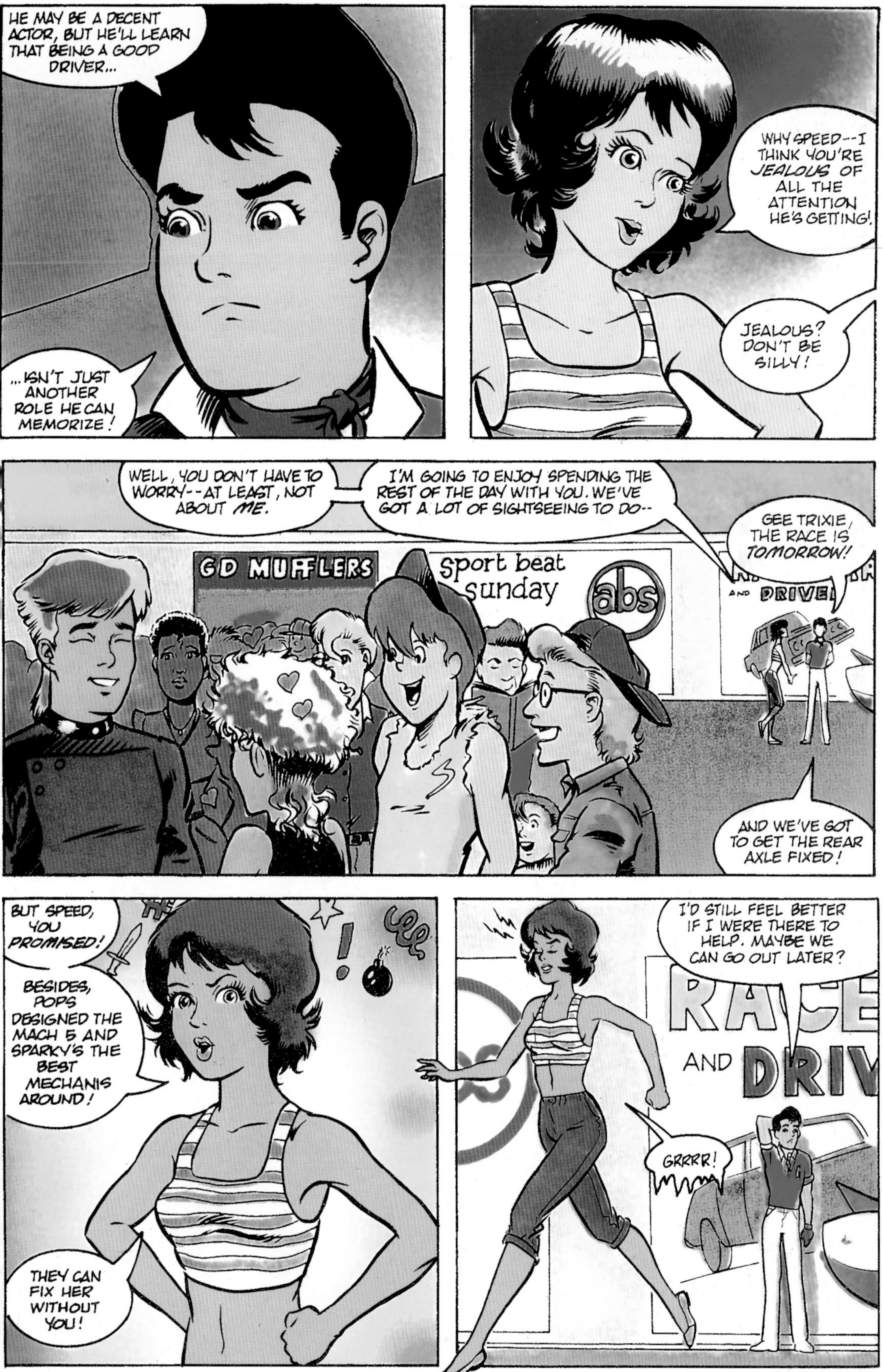

HE MAY BE A DECENT ACTOR, BUT HE'LL LEARN THAT BEING A GOOD DRIVER...
...ISN'T JUST ANOTHER ROLE HE CAN MEMORIZE!
WHY SPEED--I THINK YOU'RE JEALOUS OF ALL THE ATTENTION HE'S GETTING!
JEALOUS? DON'T BE SILLY!
WELL, YOU DON'T HAVE TO WORRY--AT LEAST, NOT ABOUT ME.
I'M GOING TO ENJOY SPENDING THE REST OF THE DAY WITH YOU. WE'VE GOT A LOT OF SIGHTSEEING TO DO--
GD MUFFLERS
sport beat sunday
abs
GEE TRIXIE, THE RACE IS TOMORROW!
AND WE'VE GOT TO GET THE REAR AXLE FIXED!
BUT SPEED, YOU PROMISED!
BESIDES, POPS DESIGNED THE MACH 5 AND SPARKY'S THE BEST MECHANIS AROUND!
THEY CAN FIX HER WITHOUT YOU!
I'D STILL FEEL BETTER IF I WERE THERE TO HELP. MAYBE WE CAN GO OUT LATER?
AND
GRRRR!

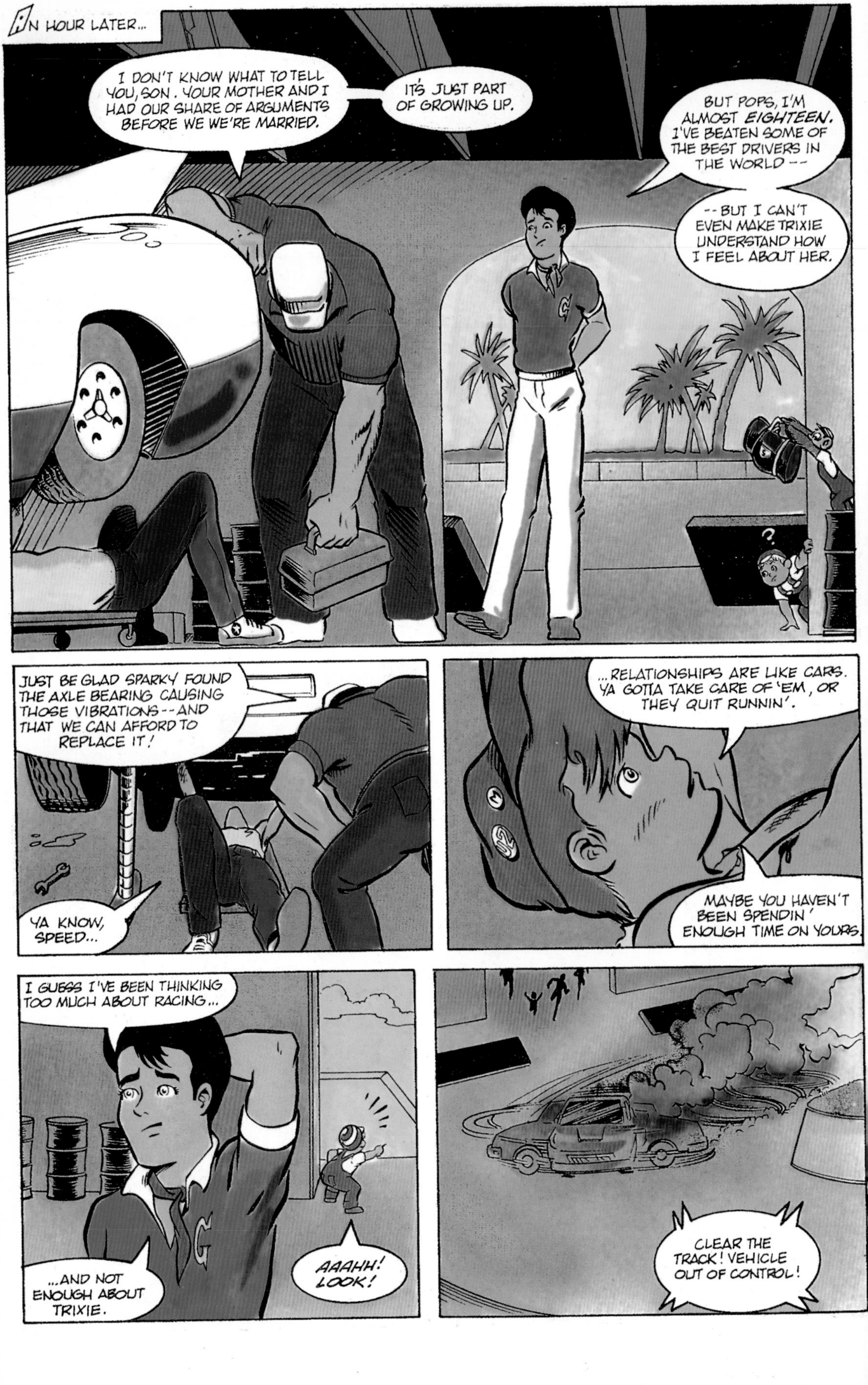
AN HOUR LATER...
I DON'T KNOW WHAT TO TELL YOU, SON. YOUR MOTHER AND I HAD OUR SHARE OF ARGUMENTS BEFORE WE WE'RE MARRIED.
IT'S JUST PART OF GROWING UP.
BUT POPS, I'M ALMOST EIGHTEEN. I'VE BEATEN SOME OF THE BEST DRIVERS IN THE WORLD --
-- BUT I CAN'T EVEN MAKE TRIXIE UNDERSTAND HOW I FEEL ABOUT HER.
?
JUST BE GLAD SPARKY FOUND THE AXLE BEARING CAUSING THOSE VIBRATIONS -- AND THAT WE CAN AFFORD TO REPLACE IT!
YA KNOW, SPEED...
...RELATIONSHIPS ARE LIKE CARS. YA GOTTA TAKE CARE OF 'EM, OR THEY QUIT RUNNIN'.
MAYBE YOU HAVEN'T BEEN SPENDIN' ENOUGH TIME ON YOURS.
I GUESS I'VE BEEN THINKING TOO MUCH ABOUT RACING...
...AND NOT ENOUGH ABOUT TRIXIE.
AAAHH! LOOK!
CLEAR THE TRACK! VEHICLE OUT OF CONTROL!

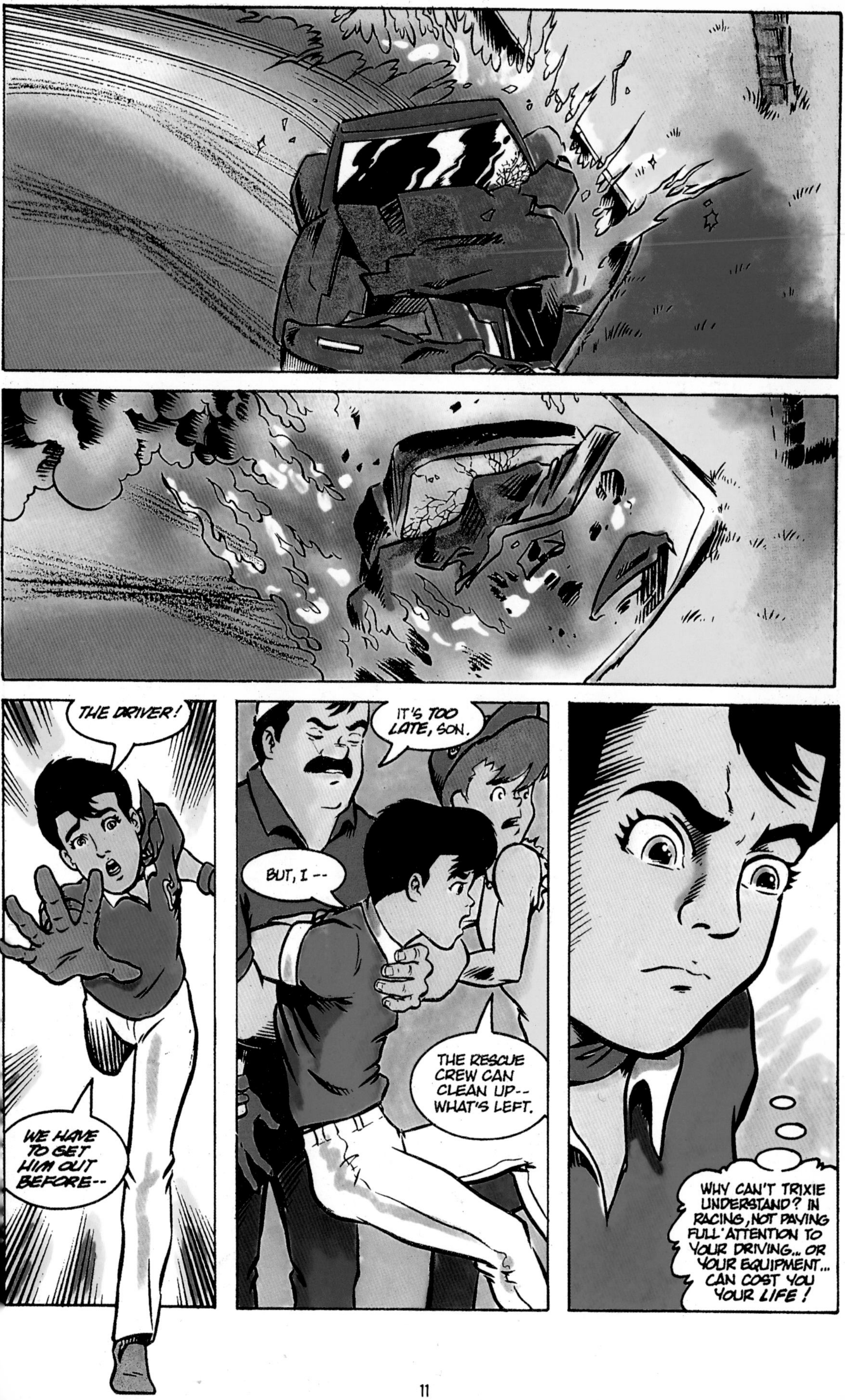
THE DRIVER!
WE HAVE TO GET HIM OUT BEFORE--
IT'S TOO LATE, SON.
BUT, I --
THE RESCUE CREW CAN CLEAN UP-- WHAT'S LEFT.
WHY CAN'T TRIXIE UNDERSTAND? IN RACING, NOT PAYING FULL ATTENTION TO YOUR DRIVING... OR YOUR EQUIPMENT... CAN COST YOU YOUR LIFE!

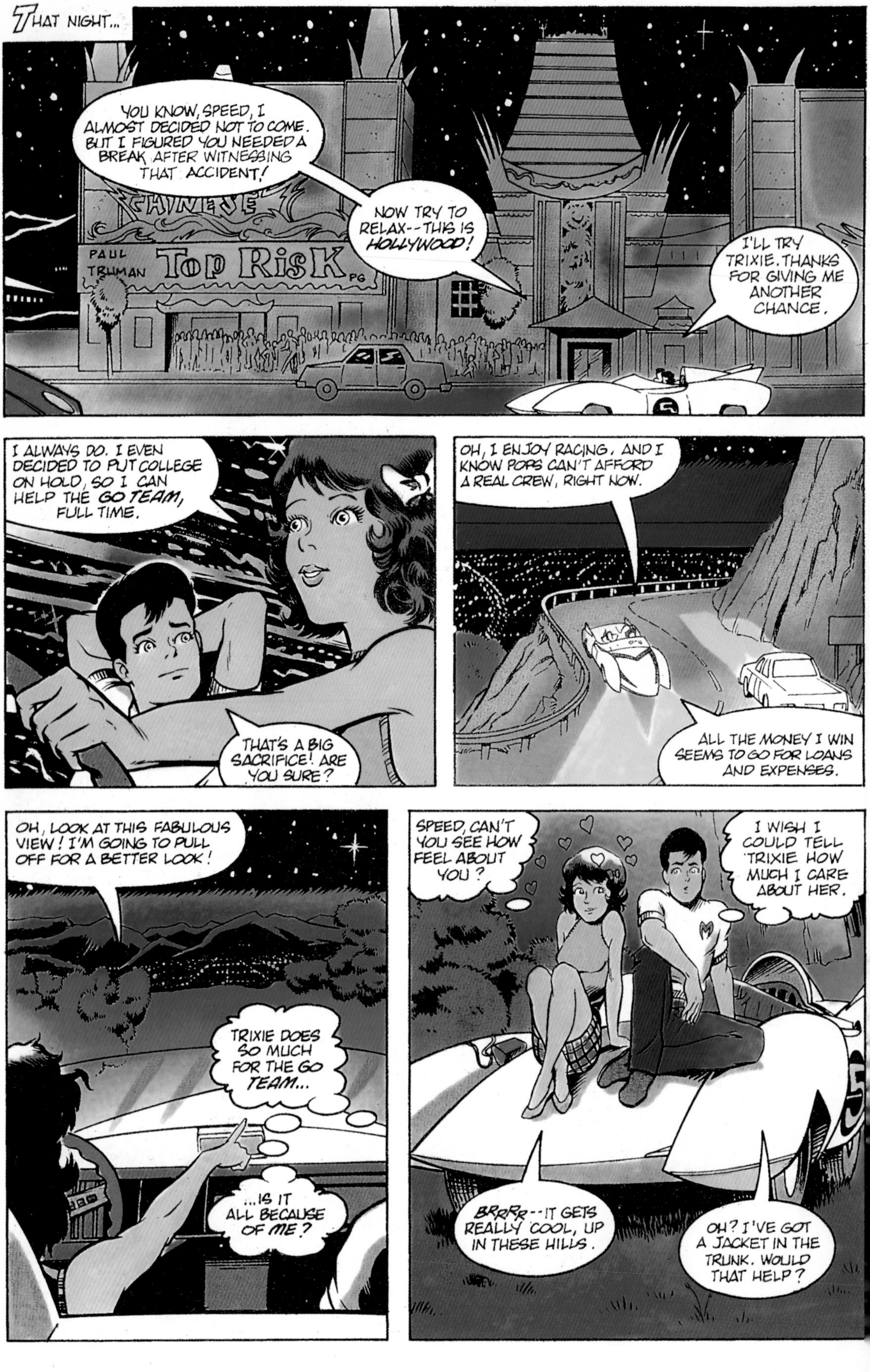
THAT NIGHT...
YOU KNOW, SPEED, I ALMOST DECIDED NOT TO COME. BUT I FIGURED YOU NEEDED A BREAK AFTER WITNESSING THAT ACCIDENT!
NOW TRY TO RELAX--THIS IS HOLLYWOOD!
CHINESE
PAUL TRUMAN
Top Risk
PG
I'LL TRY TRIXIE. THANKS FOR GIVING ME ANOTHER CHANCE.
I ALWAYS DO. I EVEN DECIDED TO PUT COLLEGE ON HOLD, SO I CAN HELP THE GO TEAM, FULL TIME.
THAT'S A BIG SACRIFICE! ARE YOU SURE?
OH, I ENJOY RACING. AND I KNOW POPS CAN'T AFFORD A REAL CREW, RIGHT NOW.
ALL THE MONEY I WIN SEEMS TO GO FOR LOANS AND EXPENSES.
OH, LOOK AT THIS FABULOUS VIEW! I'M GOING TO PULL OFF FOR A BETTER LOOK!
TRIXIE DOES SO MUCH FOR THE GO TEAM...
...IS IT ALL BECAUSE OF ME?
SPEED, CAN'T YOU SEE HOW FEEL ABOUT YOU?
I WISH I COULD TELL TRIXIE HOW MUCH I CARE ABOUT HER.
BRRRR--IT GETS REALLY COOL, UP IN THESE HILLS.
OH? I'VE GOT A JACKET IN THE TRUNK. WOULD THAT HELP?

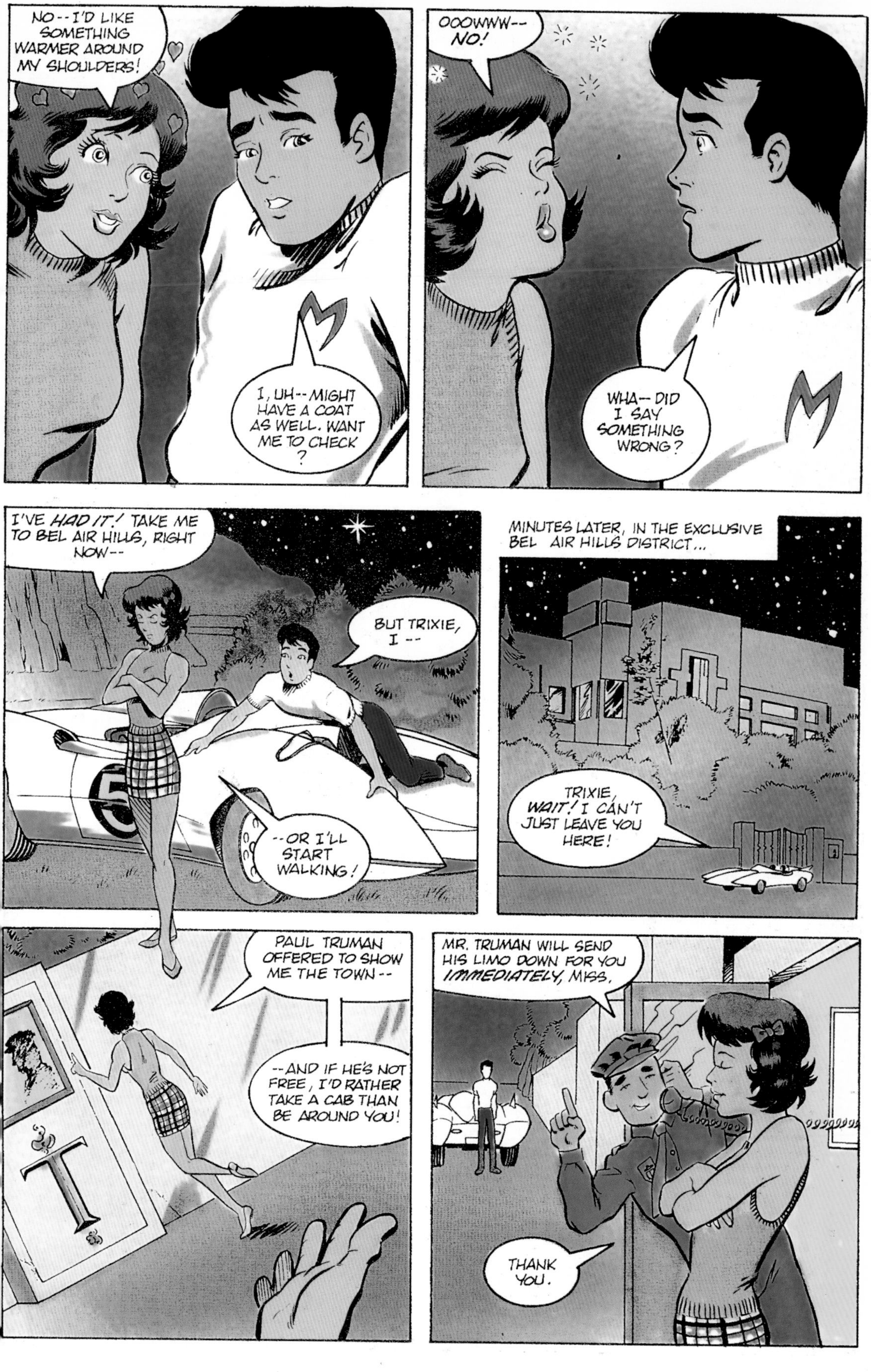

NO--I'D LIKE SOMETHING WARMER AROUND MY SHOULDERS!
I, UH--MIGHT HAVE A COAT AS WELL. WANT ME TO CHECK?
OOOWWW-- NO!
WHA-- DID I SAY SOMETHING WRONG?
I'VE HAD IT! TAKE ME TO BEL AIR HILLS, RIGHT NOW--
BUT TRIXIE, I --
--OR I'LL START WALKING!
MINUTES LATER, IN THE EXCLUSIVE BEL AIR HILLS DISTRICT...
TRIXIE, WAIT! I CAN'T JUST LEAVE YOU HERE!
PAUL TRUMAN OFFERED TO SHOW ME THE TOWN--
--AND IF HE'S NOT FREE, I'D RATHER TAKE A CAB THAN BE AROUND YOU!
T
MR. TRUMAN WILL SEND HIS LIMO DOWN FOR YOU IMMEDIATELY, MISS.
THANK YOU.

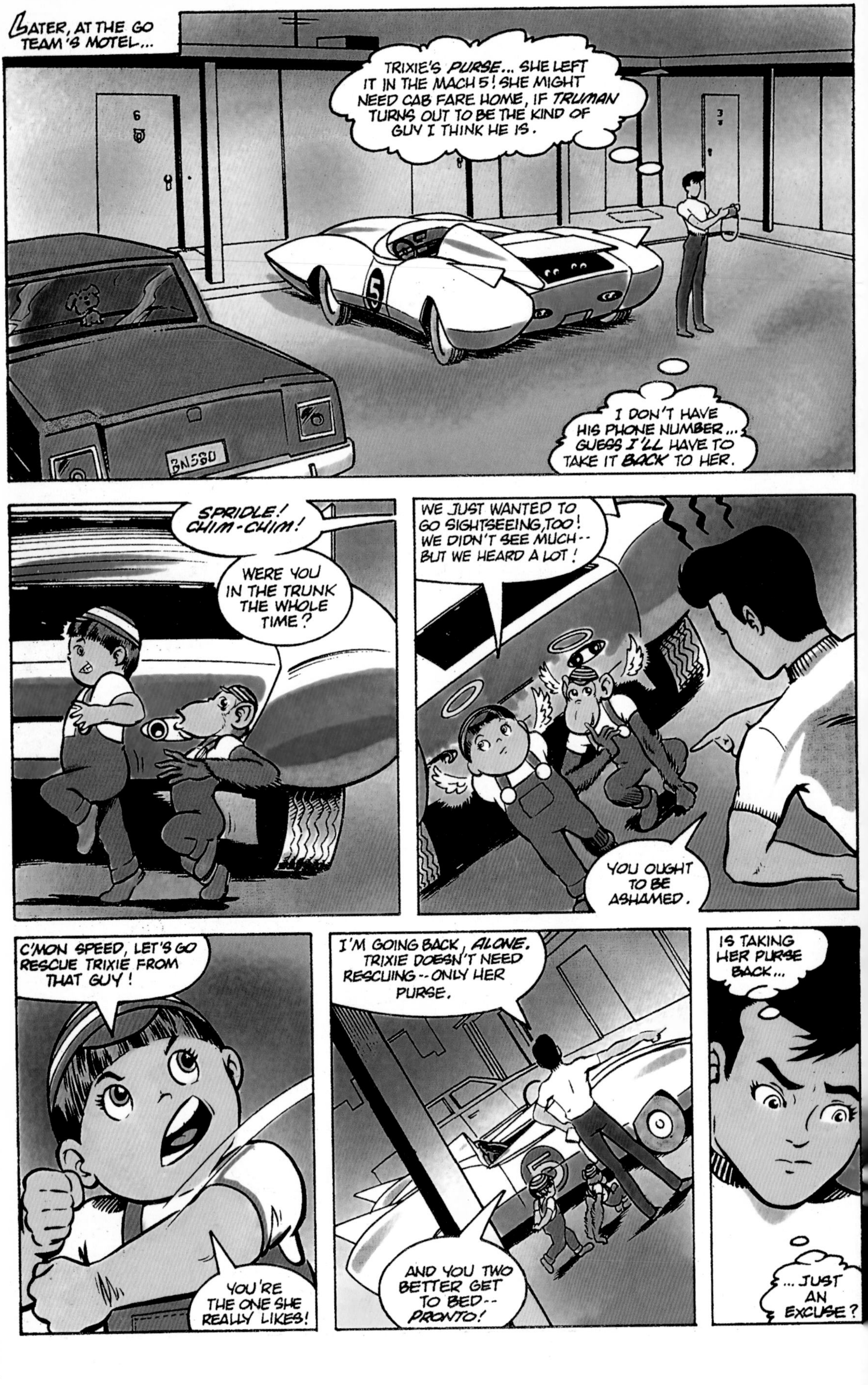
LATER, AT THE GO TEAM'S MOTEL...
TRIXIE'S PURSE... SHE LEFT IT IN THE MACH 5! SHE MIGHT NEED CAB FARE HOME, IF TRUMAN TURNS OUT TO BE THE KIND OF GUY I THINK HE IS.
I DON'T HAVE HIS PHONE NUMBER... GUESS I'LL HAVE TO TAKE IT BACK TO HER.
SPRIDLE! CHIM-CHIM!
WERE YOU IN THE TRUNK THE WHOLE TIME?
WE JUST WANTED TO GO SIGHTSEEING, TOO! WE DIDN'T SEE MUCH-- BUT WE HEARD A LOT!
YOU OUGHT TO BE ASHAMED.
C'MON SPEED, LET'S GO RESCUE TRIXIE FROM THAT GUY!
YOU'RE THE ONE SHE REALLY LIKES!
I'M GOING BACK, ALONE. TRIXIE DOESN'T NEED RESCUING--ONLY HER PURSE.
AND YOU TWO BETTER GET TO BED-- PRONTO!
IS TAKING HER PURSE BACK...
...JUST AN EXCUSE?

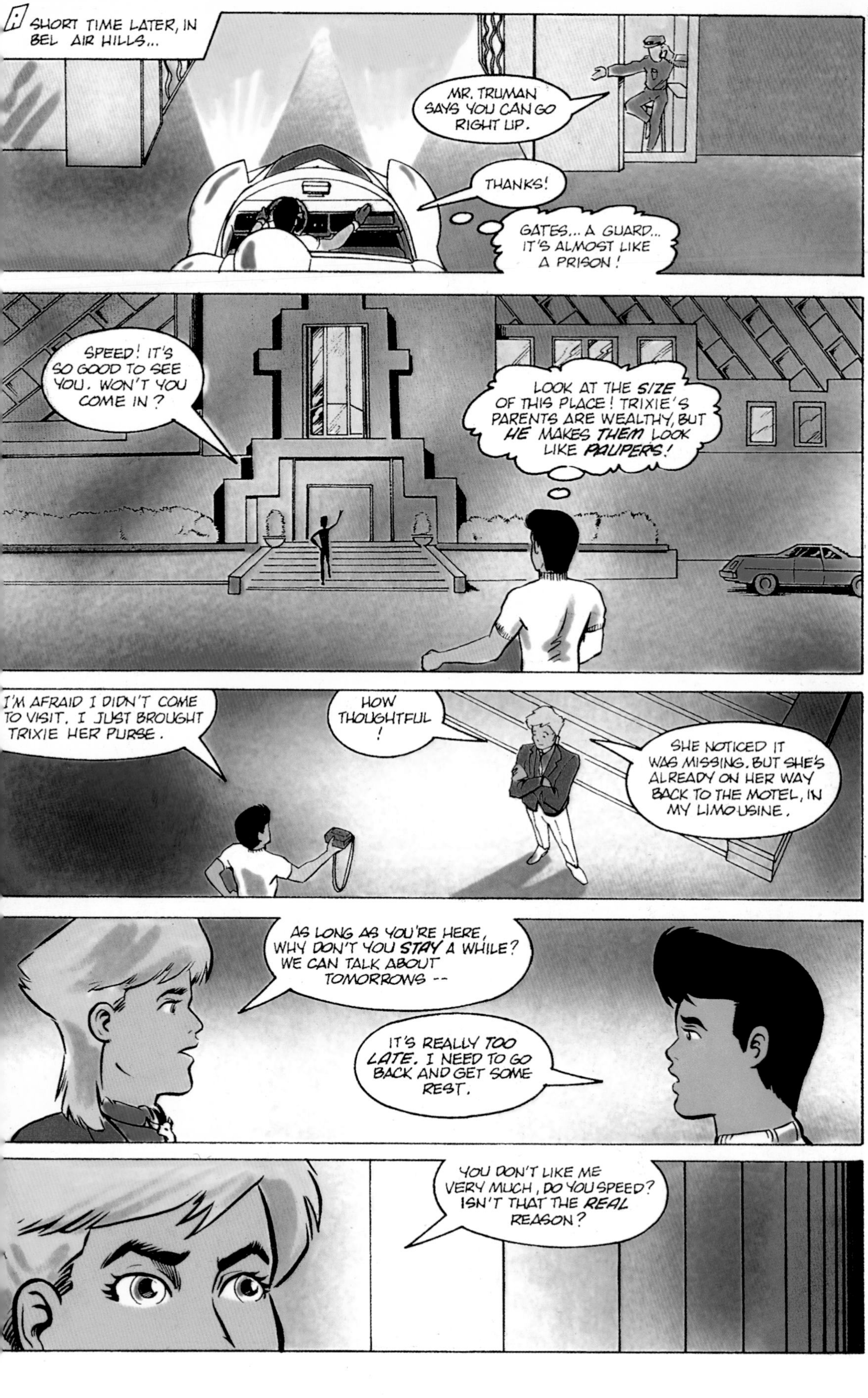
A SHORT TIME LATER, IN BEL AIR HILLS...
MR. TRUMAN SAYS YOU CAN GO RIGHT UP.
THANKS!
GATES... A GUARD... IT'S ALMOST LIKE A PRISON!
SPEED! IT'S SO GOOD TO SEE YOU. WON'T YOU COME IN?
LOOK AT THE SIZE OF THIS PLACE! TRIXIE'S PARENTS ARE WEALTHY, BUT HE MAKES THEM LOOK LIKE PAUPERS!
I'M AFRAID I DIDN'T COME TO VISIT. I JUST BROUGHT TRIXIE HER PURSE.
HOW THOUGHTFUL!
SHE NOTICED IT WAS MISSING. BUT SHE'S ALREADY ON HER WAY BACK TO THE MOTEL, IN MY LIMOUSINE.
AS LONG AS YOU'RE HERE, WHY DON'T YOU STAY A WHILE? WE CAN TALK ABOUT TOMORROWS --
IT'S REALLY TOO LATE. I NEED TO GO BACK AND GET SOME REST.
YOU DON'T LIKE ME VERY MUCH, DO YOU SPEED? ISN'T THAT THE REAL REASON?

I JUST THINK YOU MIGHT NOT BE *SERIOUS* ABOUT RACING, THAT'S ALL.

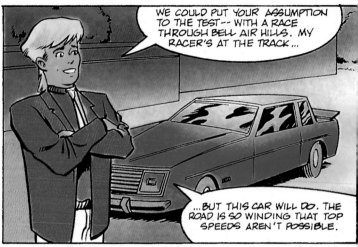

WE COULD PUT YOUR ASSUMPTION TO THE TEST -- WITH A RACE THROUGH BELL AIR HILLS. MY RACER'S AT THE TRACK...

...BUT THIS CAR WILL DO. THE ROAD IS SO WINDING THAT TOP SPEEDS AREN'T POSSIBLE.

RACING ON ROADS IS DANGEROUS *AND ILLEGAL*!

ALL ROADS IN BEL AIR HILLS ARE *PRIVATE* PROPERTY, WITH NO *SPEED LIMITS*. BESIDES, THERE'S NO TRAFFIC THIS LATE.

AND EVERY HOUSE IS PROTECTED BY A WALL. I'LL EVEN GIVE YOU A *HEAD START*, SINCE YOU'RE NOT FAMILIAR WITH THE ROAD!

THAT WON'T BE NECESSARY! *LET'S GO!*

JUST STAY ON THIS ROAD -- IT CIRCLES THE ENTIRE SUBDIVISION. ARE YOU READY?

YOU CALL THE START!

ALL RIGHT! 5-4-3-2-1 -- *GO!*

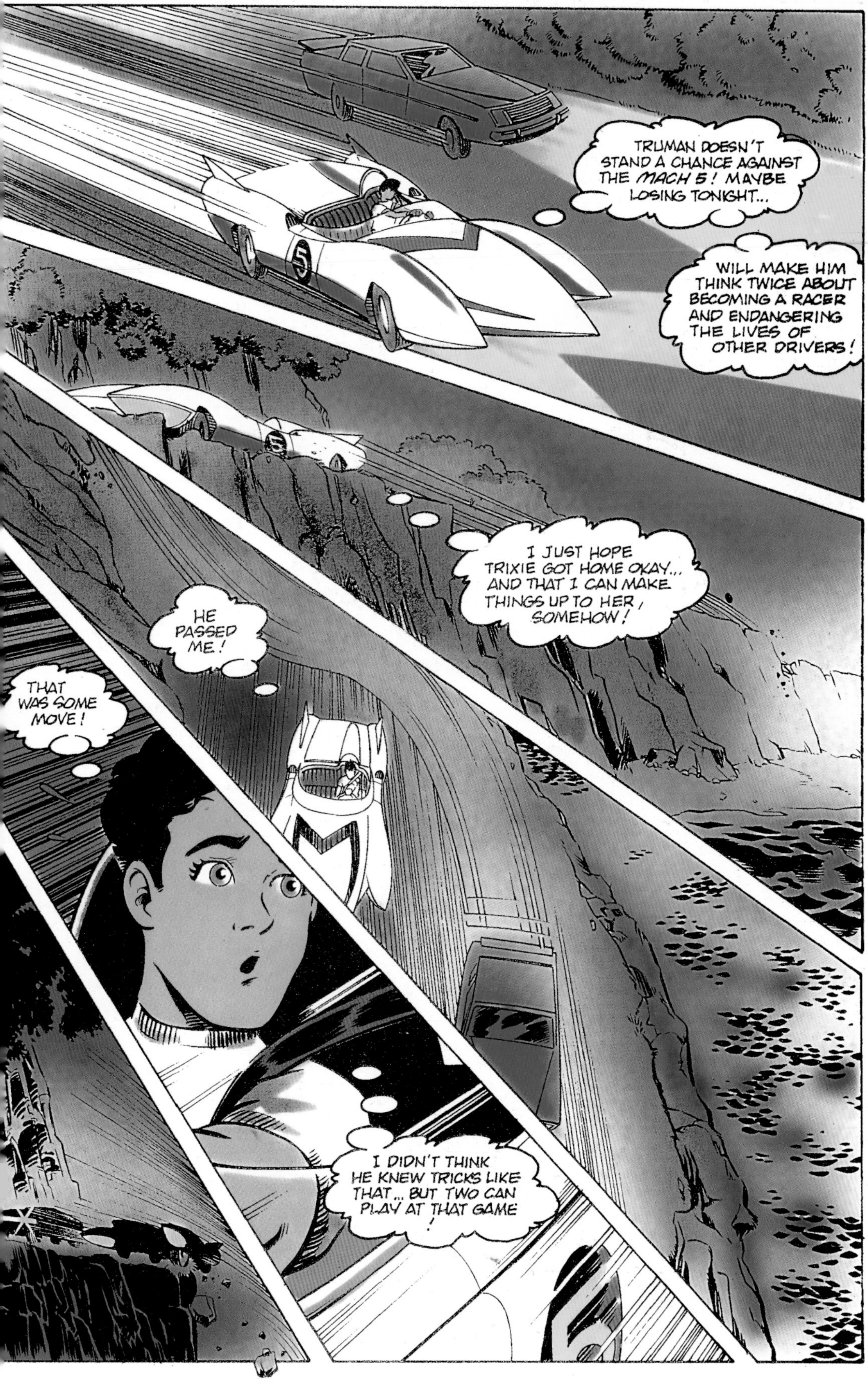
TRUMAN DOESN'T STAND A CHANCE AGAINST THE *MACH 5*! MAYBE LOSING TONIGHT...
WILL MAKE HIM THINK TWICE ABOUT BECOMING A RACER AND ENDANGERING THE LIVES OF OTHER DRIVERS!
I JUST HOPE TRIXIE GOT HOME OKAY... AND THAT I CAN MAKE THINGS UP TO HER, SOMEHOW!
HE PASSED ME!
THAT WAS SOME MOVE!
I DIDN'T THINK HE KNEW TRICKS LIKE THAT... BUT TWO CAN PLAY AT THAT GAME!

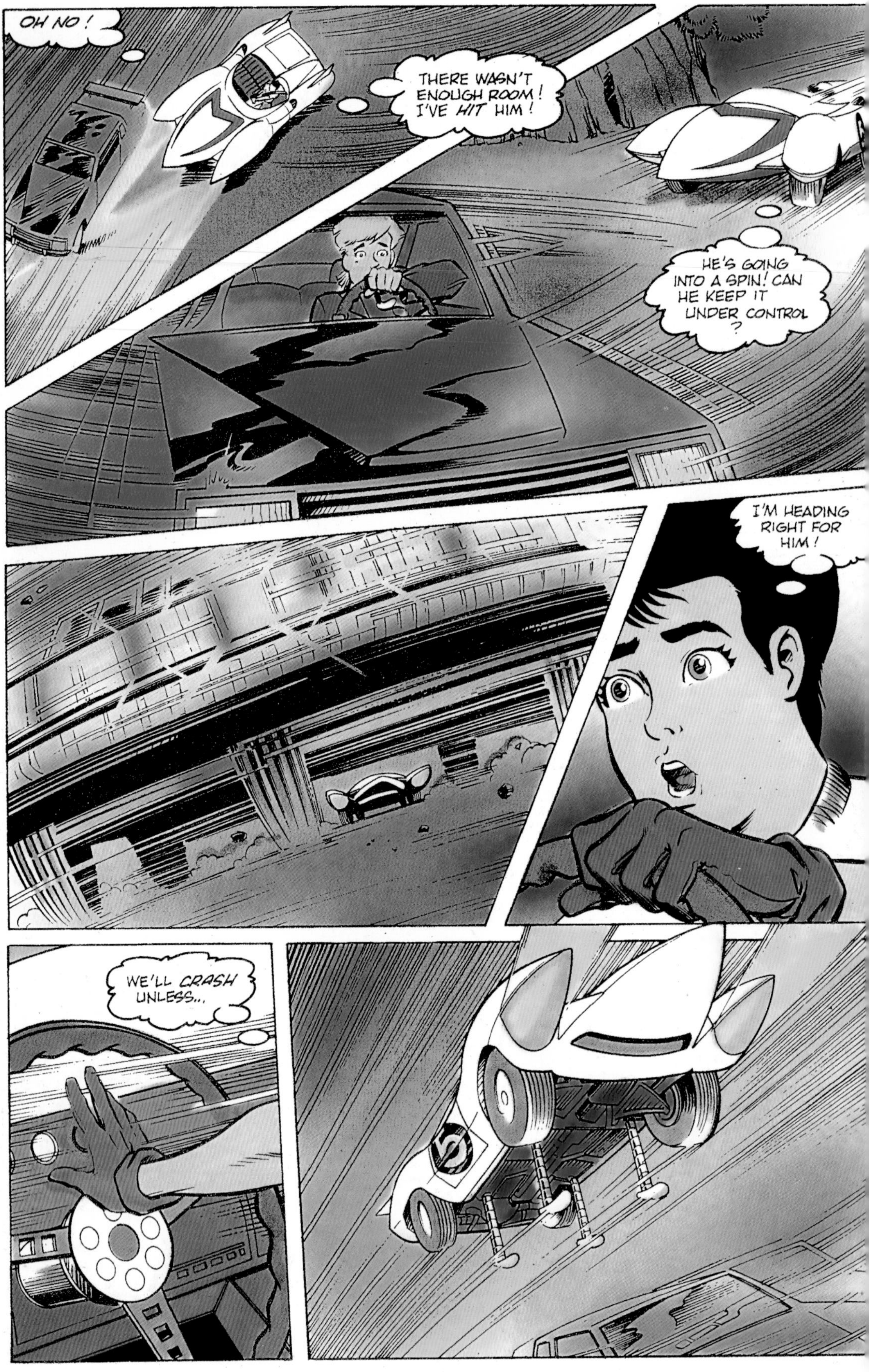
OH NO!
THERE WASN'T ENOUGH ROOM! I'VE HIT HIM!
HE'S GOING INTO A SPIN! CAN HE KEEP IT UNDER CONTROL?
I'M HEADING RIGHT FOR HIM!
WE'LL CRASH UNLESS...

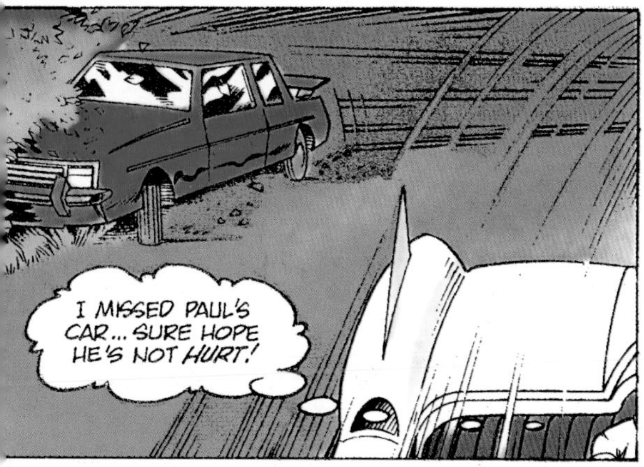
I MISSED PAUL'S CAR... SURE HOPE HE'S NOT *HURT*!

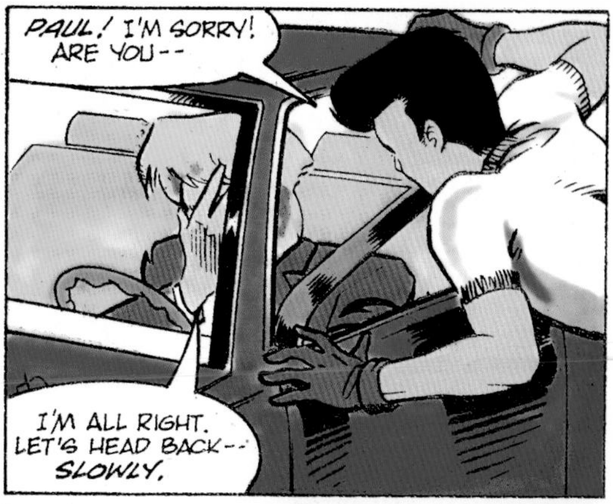
PAUL! I'M SORRY! ARE YOU--
I'M ALL RIGHT. LET'S HEAD BACK-- *SLOWLY.*

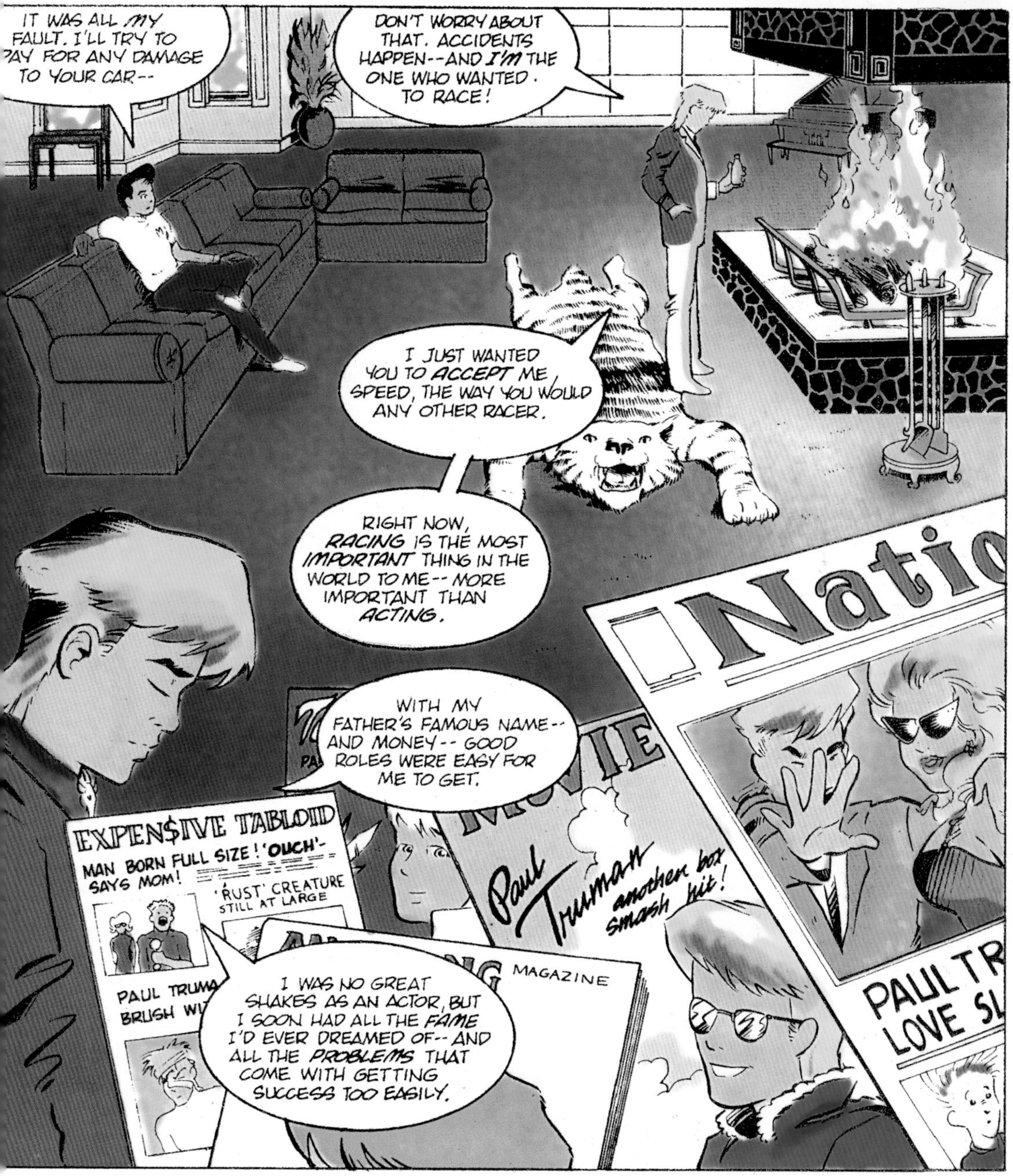
IT WAS ALL *MY* FAULT. I'LL TRY TO PAY FOR ANY DAMAGE TO YOUR CAR--
DON'T WORRY ABOUT THAT. ACCIDENTS HAPPEN--AND *I'M* THE ONE WHO WANTED TO RACE!
I JUST WANTED YOU TO *ACCEPT* ME SPEED, THE WAY YOU WOULD ANY OTHER RACER.
RIGHT NOW, *RACING* IS THE MOST *IMPORTANT* THING IN THE WORLD TO ME-- MORE IMPORTANT THAN *ACTING.*
WITH MY FATHER'S FAMOUS NAME-- AND MONEY-- GOOD ROLES WERE EASY FOR ME TO GET.
EXPEN$IVE TABLOID
MAN BORN FULL SIZE! 'OUCH'- SAYS MOM!
'RUST' CREATURE STILL AT LARGE
PAUL TRUMA
MOVIE
Paul Truman another box smash hit!
MAGAZINE
I WAS NO GREAT SHAKES AS AN ACTOR, BUT I SOON HAD ALL THE *FAME* I'D EVER DREAMED OF-- AND ALL THE *PROBLEMS* THAT COME WITH GETTING SUCCESS TOO EASILY.

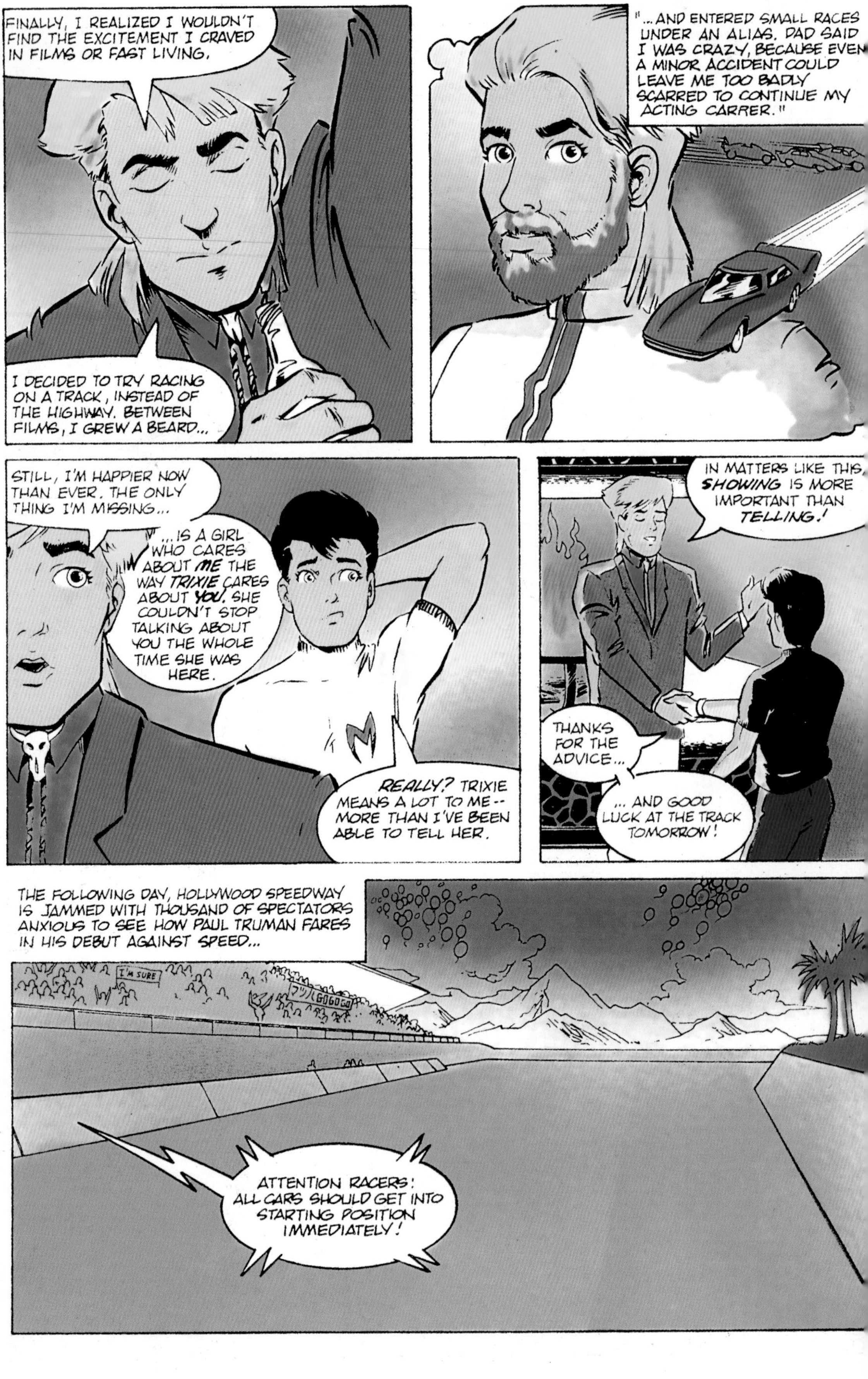
FINALLY, I REALIZED I WOULDN'T FIND THE EXCITEMENT I CRAVED IN FILMS OR FAST LIVING.
I DECIDED TO TRY RACING ON A TRACK, INSTEAD OF THE HIGHWAY. BETWEEN FILMS, I GREW A BEARD...
"...AND ENTERED SMALL RACES UNDER AN ALIAS. DAD SAID I WAS CRAZY, BECAUSE EVEN A MINOR ACCIDENT COULD LEAVE ME TOO BADLY SCARRED TO CONTINUE MY ACTING CARRER."
STILL, I'M HAPPIER NOW THAN EVER. THE ONLY THING I'M MISSING...
...IS A GIRL WHO CARES ABOUT ME THE WAY TRIXIE CARES ABOUT YOU. SHE COULDN'T STOP TALKING ABOUT YOU THE WHOLE TIME SHE WAS HERE.
REALLY? TRIXIE MEANS A LOT TO ME -- MORE THAN I'VE BEEN ABLE TO TELL HER.
IN MATTERS LIKE THIS, SHOWING IS MORE IMPORTANT THAN TELLING!
THANKS FOR THE ADVICE...
... AND GOOD LUCK AT THE TRACK TOMORROW!
THE FOLLOWING DAY, HOLLYWOOD SPEEDWAY IS JAMMED WITH THOUSAND OF SPECTATORS ANXIOUS TO SEE HOW PAUL TRUMAN FARES IN HIS DEBUT AGAINST SPEED...
I'M SURE
GOGOGO
ATTENTION RACERS: ALL CARS SHOULD GET INTO STARTING POSITION IMMEDIATELY!

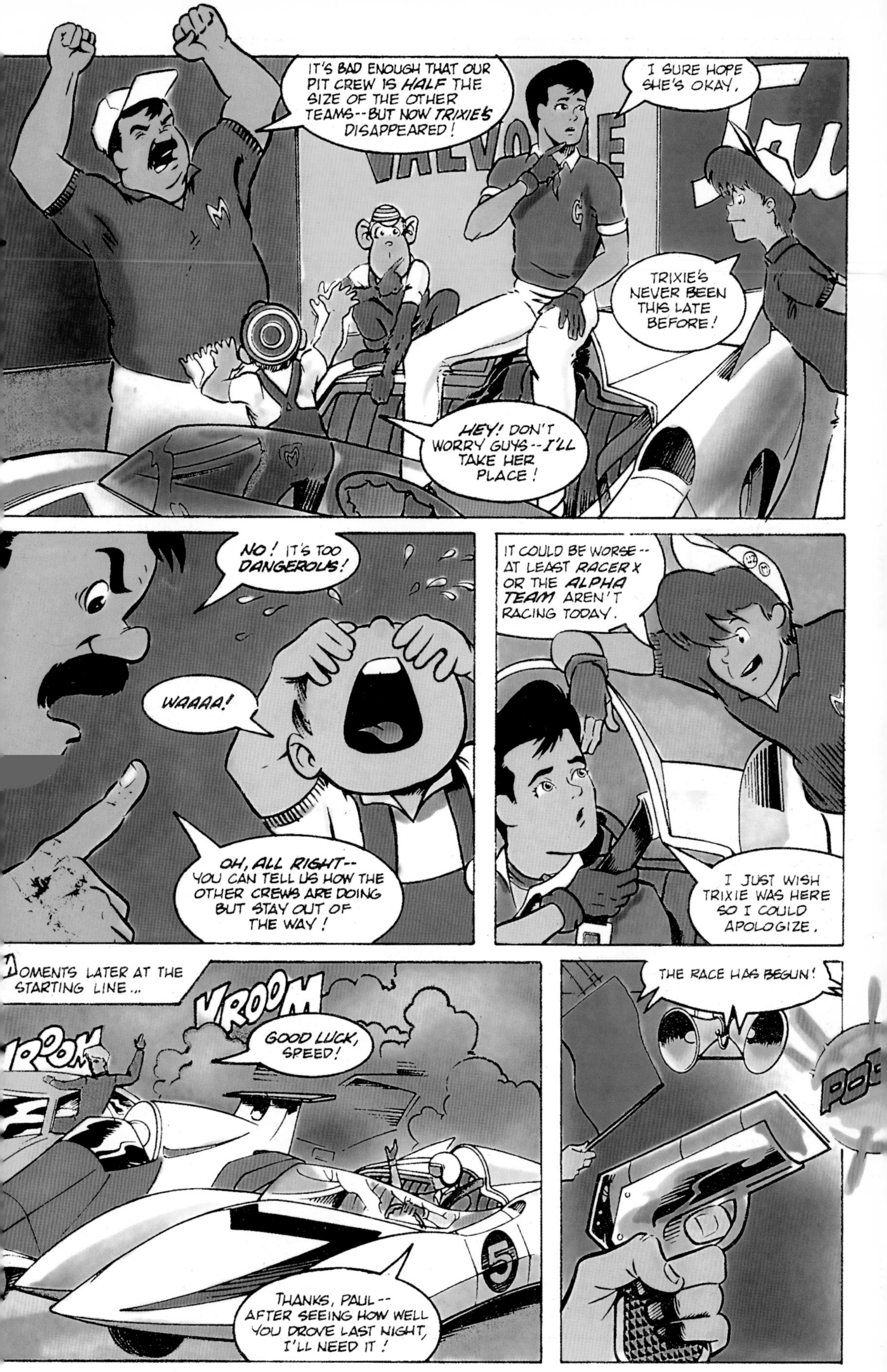
IT'S BAD ENOUGH THAT OUR PIT CREW IS HALF THE SIZE OF THE OTHER TEAMS--BUT NOW TRIXIE'S DISAPPEARED!
I SURE HOPE SHE'S OKAY.
TRIXIE'S NEVER BEEN THIS LATE BEFORE!
HEY! DON'T WORRY GUYS--I'LL TAKE HER PLACE!
NO! IT'S TOO DANGEROUS!
WAAAA!
OH, ALL RIGHT-- YOU CAN TELL US HOW THE OTHER CREWS ARE DOING BUT STAY OUT OF THE WAY!
IT COULD BE WORSE-- AT LEAST RACER X OR THE ALPHA TEAM AREN'T RACING TODAY.
I JUST WISH TRIXIE WAS HERE SO I COULD APOLOGIZE.
MOMENTS LATER AT THE STARTING LINE...
VROOM
VROOM
GOOD LUCK, SPEED!
THANKS, PAUL-- AFTER SEEING HOW WELL YOU DROVE LAST NIGHT, I'LL NEED IT!
THE RACE HAS BEGUN!

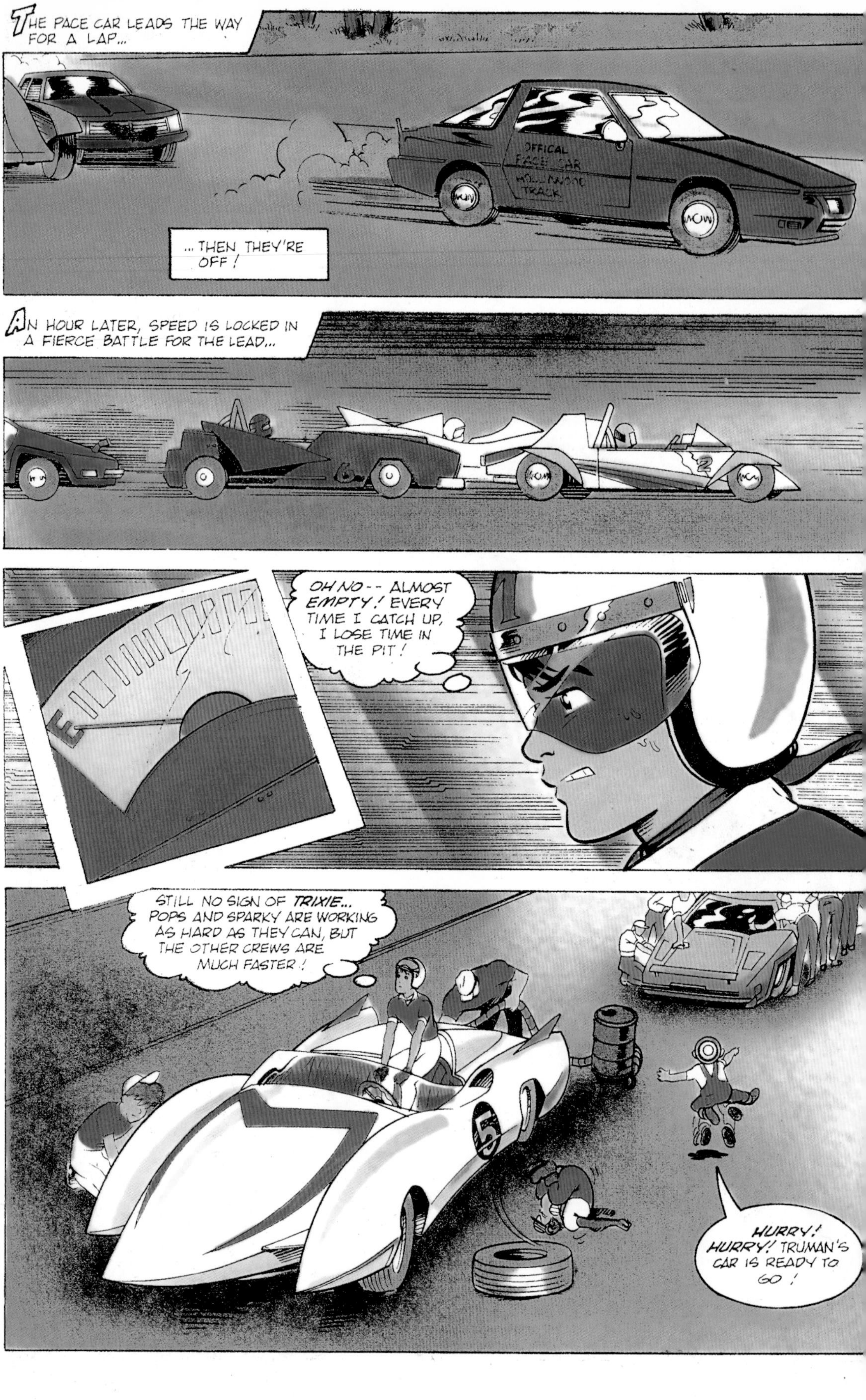
THE PACE CAR LEADS THE WAY FOR A LAP...
OFFICAL PACE CAR HOLLYWOOD TRACK
...THEN THEY'RE OFF!
AN HOUR LATER, SPEED IS LOCKED IN A FIERCE BATTLE FOR THE LEAD...
OH NO-- ALMOST EMPTY! EVERY TIME I CATCH UP, I LOSE TIME IN THE PIT!
STILL NO SIGN OF TRIXIE... POPS AND SPARKY ARE WORKING AS HARD AS THEY CAN, BUT THE OTHER CREWS ARE MUCH FASTER!
HURRY! HURRY! TRUMAN'S CAR IS READY TO GO!

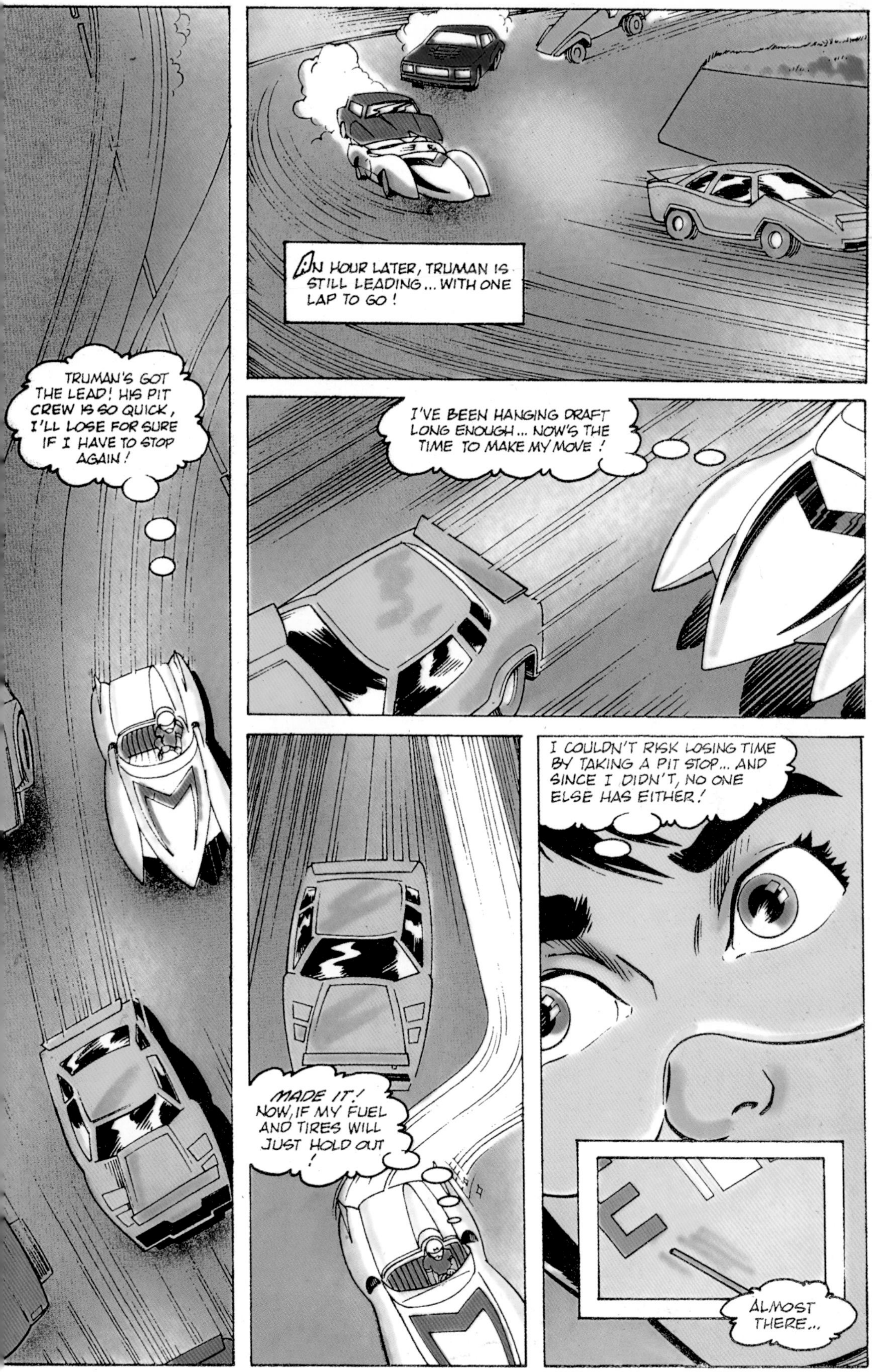
AN HOUR LATER, TRUMAN IS STILL LEADING... WITH ONE LAP TO GO!
TRUMAN'S GOT THE LEAD! HIS PIT CREW IS SO QUICK, I'LL LOSE FOR SURE IF I HAVE TO STOP AGAIN!
I'VE BEEN HANGING DRAFT LONG ENOUGH... NOW'S THE TIME TO MAKE MY MOVE!
MADE IT! NOW, IF MY FUEL AND TIRES WILL JUST HOLD OUT!
I COULDN'T RISK LOSING TIME BY TAKING A PIT STOP... AND SINCE I DIDN'T, NO ONE ELSE HAS EITHER!
ALMOST THERE...

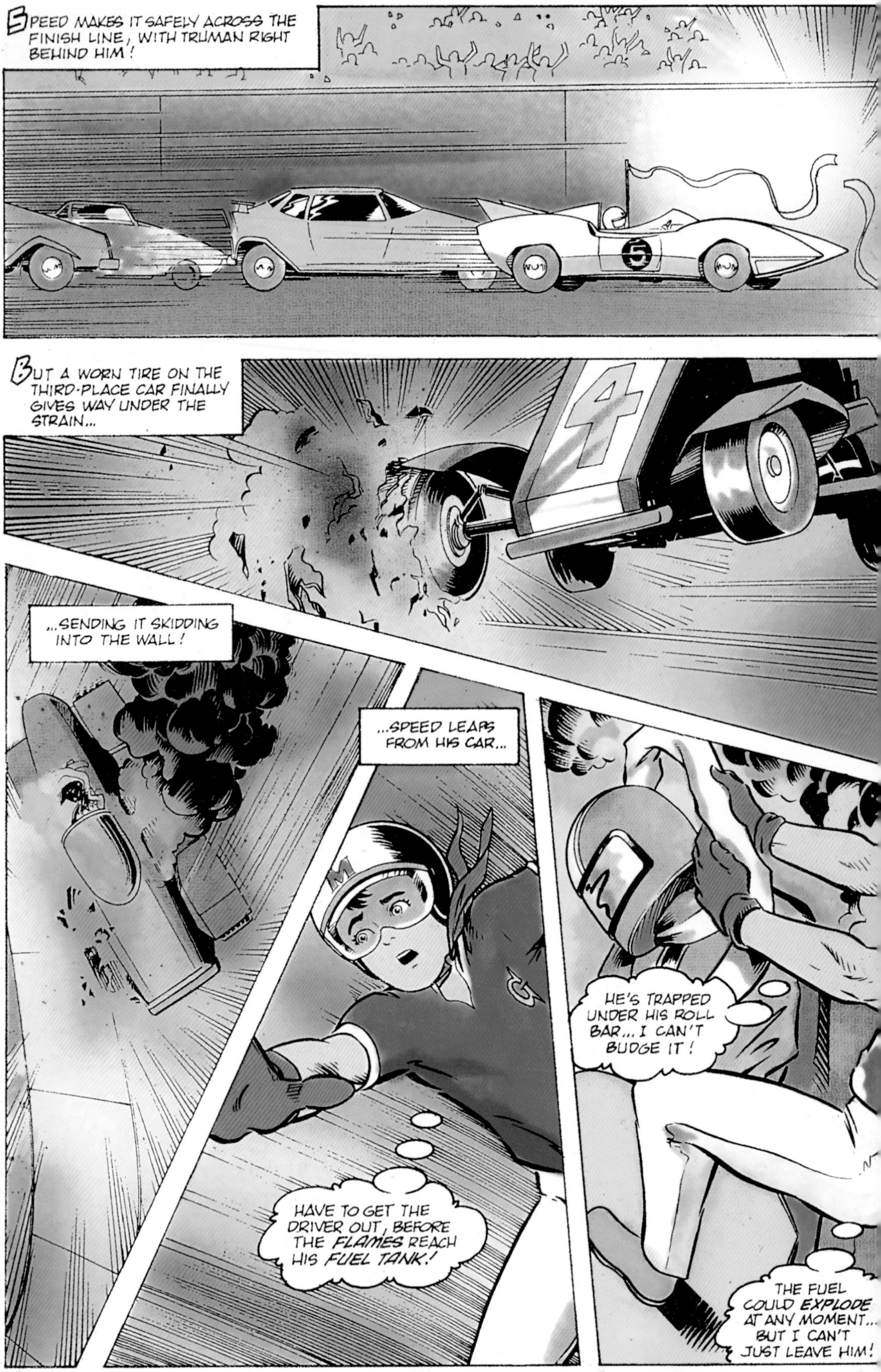
SPEED MAKES IT SAFELY ACROSS THE FINISH LINE, WITH TRUMAN RIGHT BEHIND HIM!
BUT A WORN TIRE ON THE THIRD-PLACE CAR FINALLY GIVES WAY UNDER THE STRAIN...
...SENDING IT SKIDDING INTO THE WALL!
...SPEED LEAPS FROM HIS CAR...
HAVE TO GET THE DRIVER OUT, BEFORE THE FLAMES REACH HIS FUEL TANK!
HE'S TRAPPED UNDER HIS ROLL BAR... I CAN'T BUDGE IT!
THE FUEL COULD EXPLODE AT ANY MOMENT... BUT I CAN'T JUST LEAVE HIM!

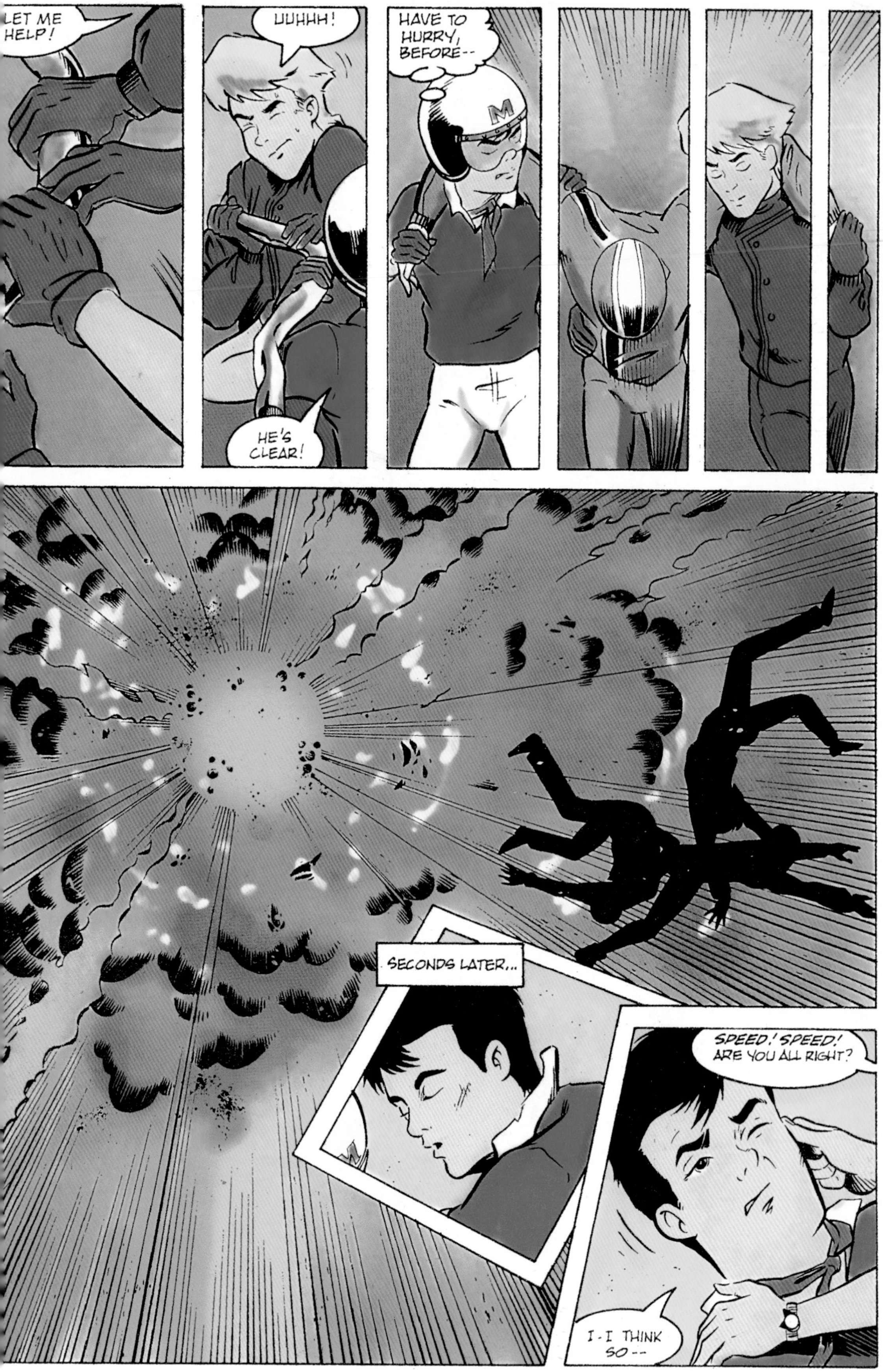
LET ME HELP!
UUHHH!
HE'S CLEAR!
HAVE TO HURRY, BEFORE--
SECONDS LATER...
SPEED! SPEED! ARE YOU ALL RIGHT?
I-I THINK SO--

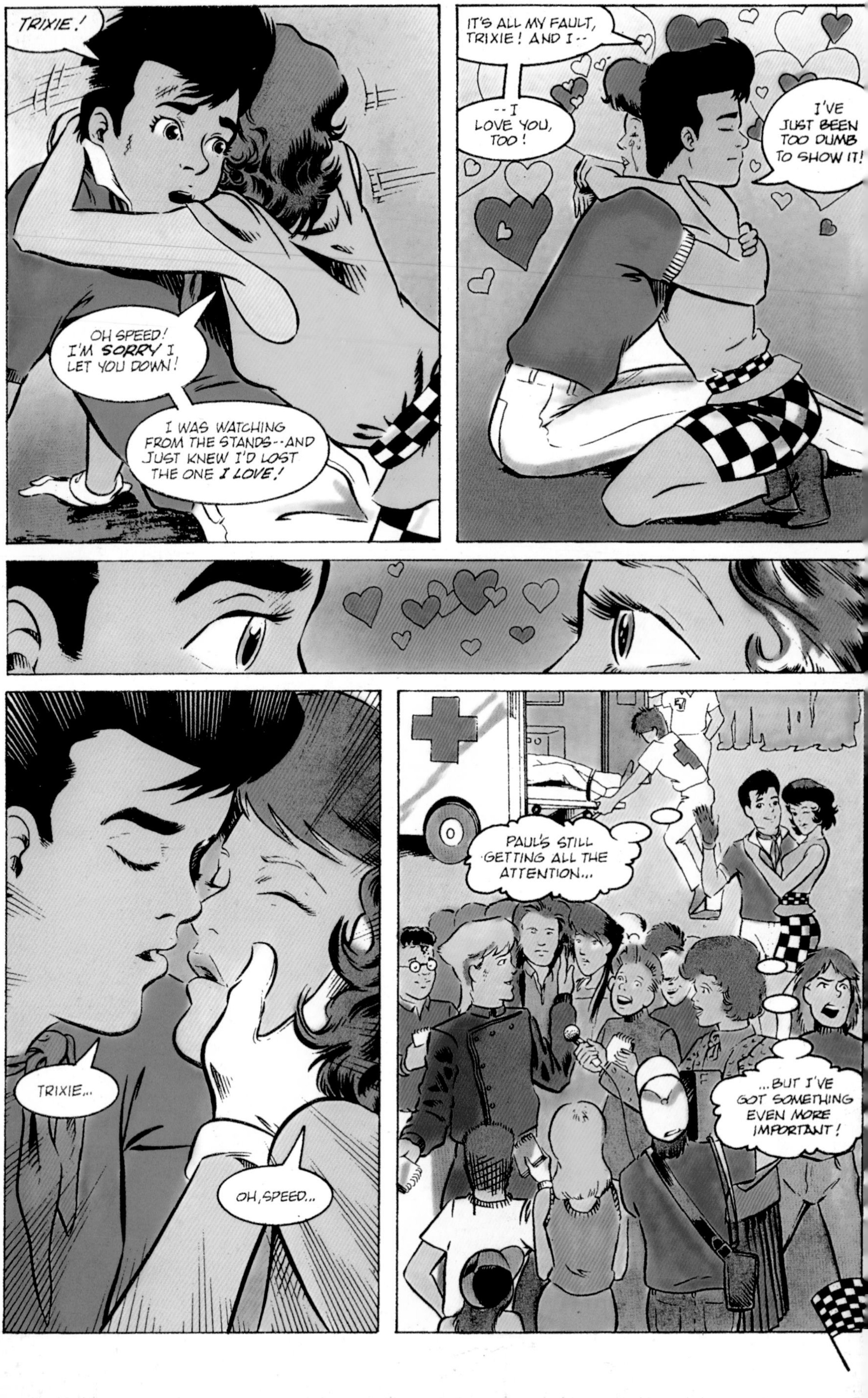

TRIXIE!
OH SPEED! I'M SORRY I LET YOU DOWN!
I WAS WATCHING FROM THE STANDS--AND JUST KNEW I'D LOST THE ONE I LOVE!
IT'S ALL MY FAULT, TRIXIE! AND I--
--I LOVE YOU, TOO!
I'VE JUST BEEN TOO DUMB TO SHOW IT!
TRIXIE...
OH, SPEED...
PAUL'S STILL GETTING ALL THE ATTENTION...
...BUT I'VE GOT SOMETHING EVEN MORE IMPORTANT!

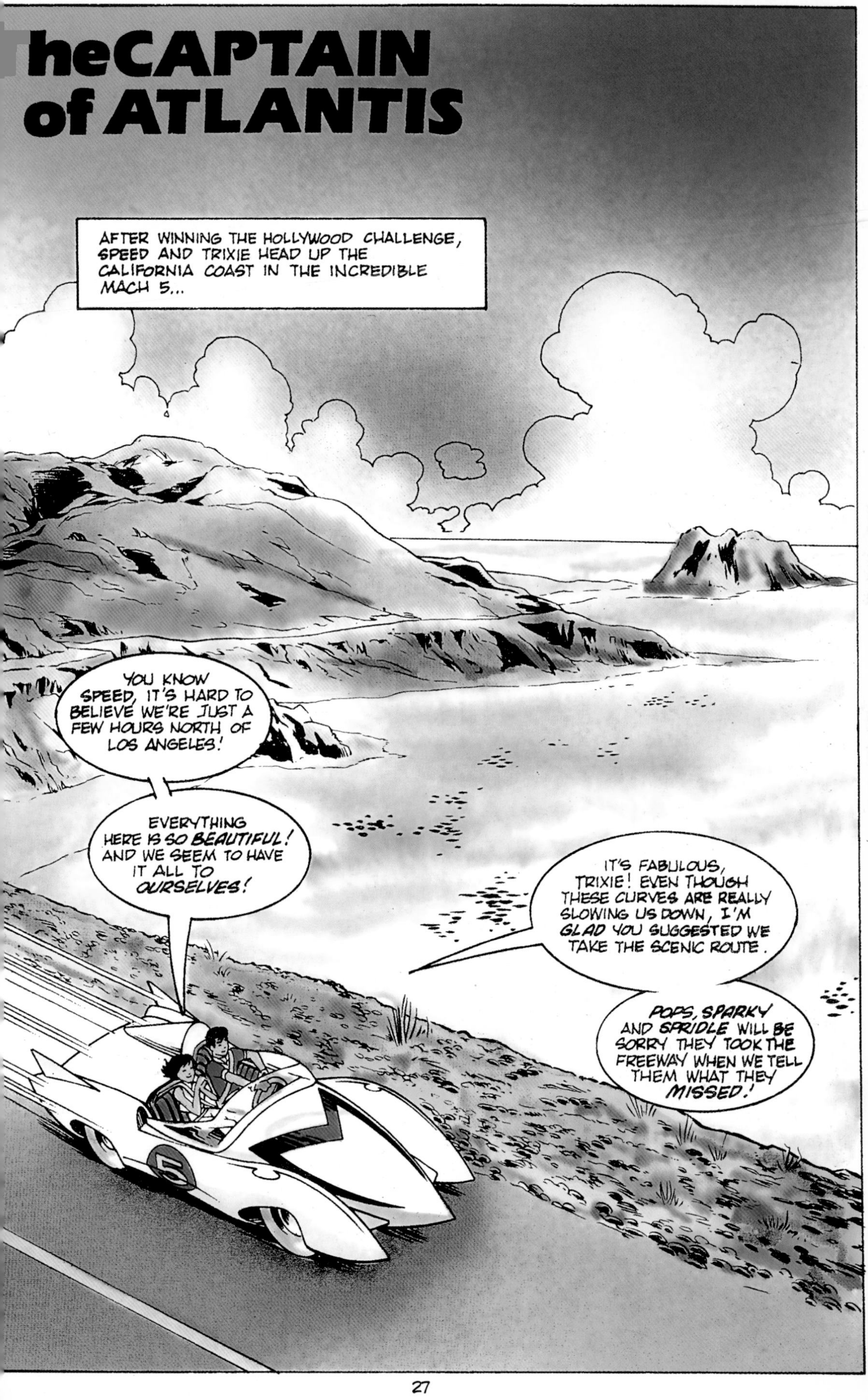

The CAPTAIN of ATLANTIS
AFTER WINNING THE HOLLYWOOD CHALLENGE, SPEED AND TRIXIE HEAD UP THE CALIFORNIA COAST IN THE INCREDIBLE MACH 5...
YOU KNOW SPEED, IT'S HARD TO BELIEVE WE'RE JUST A FEW HOURS NORTH OF LOS ANGELES!
EVERYTHING HERE IS SO BEAUTIFUL! AND WE SEEM TO HAVE IT ALL TO OURSELVES!
IT'S FABULOUS, TRIXIE! EVEN THOUGH THESE CURVES ARE REALLY SLOWING US DOWN, I'M GLAD YOU SUGGESTED WE TAKE THE SCENIC ROUTE.
POPS, SPARKY AND SPRIDLE WILL BE SORRY THEY TOOK THE FREEWAY WHEN WE TELL THEM WHAT THEY MISSED!

TO TELL THE TRUTH, I'M GLAD THEY DIDN'T COME ALONG. AFTER EVERYTHING WE WENT THROUGH IN HOLLYWOOD, THIS GIVES US A CHANCE TO RELAX WITH EACH OTHER--ALONE!

AND I DON'T MIND ALL THE CURVES IN THE ROAD-- IT GIVES US MORE TIME *TOGETHER!*

WELL, FOR ONCE, I'M HAPPY *NOT* TO BE GOING AS FAST AS I CAN!

OF COURSE, I HOPE POPS AND THE REST AREN'T *TOO* BORED!

I COULD CALL THEM ON THE RADIO--

BUT *THIS* WILL BE MORE FUN!

THIS SHOULD REALLY SURPRISE THEM!

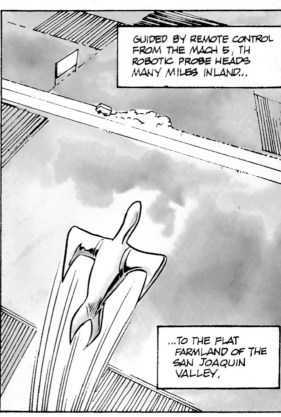

GUIDED BY REMOTE CONTROL FROM THE MACH 5, TH ROBOTIC PROBE HEADS MANY MILES INLAND...

...TO THE FLAT FARMLAND OF THE SAN JOAQUIN VALLEY.

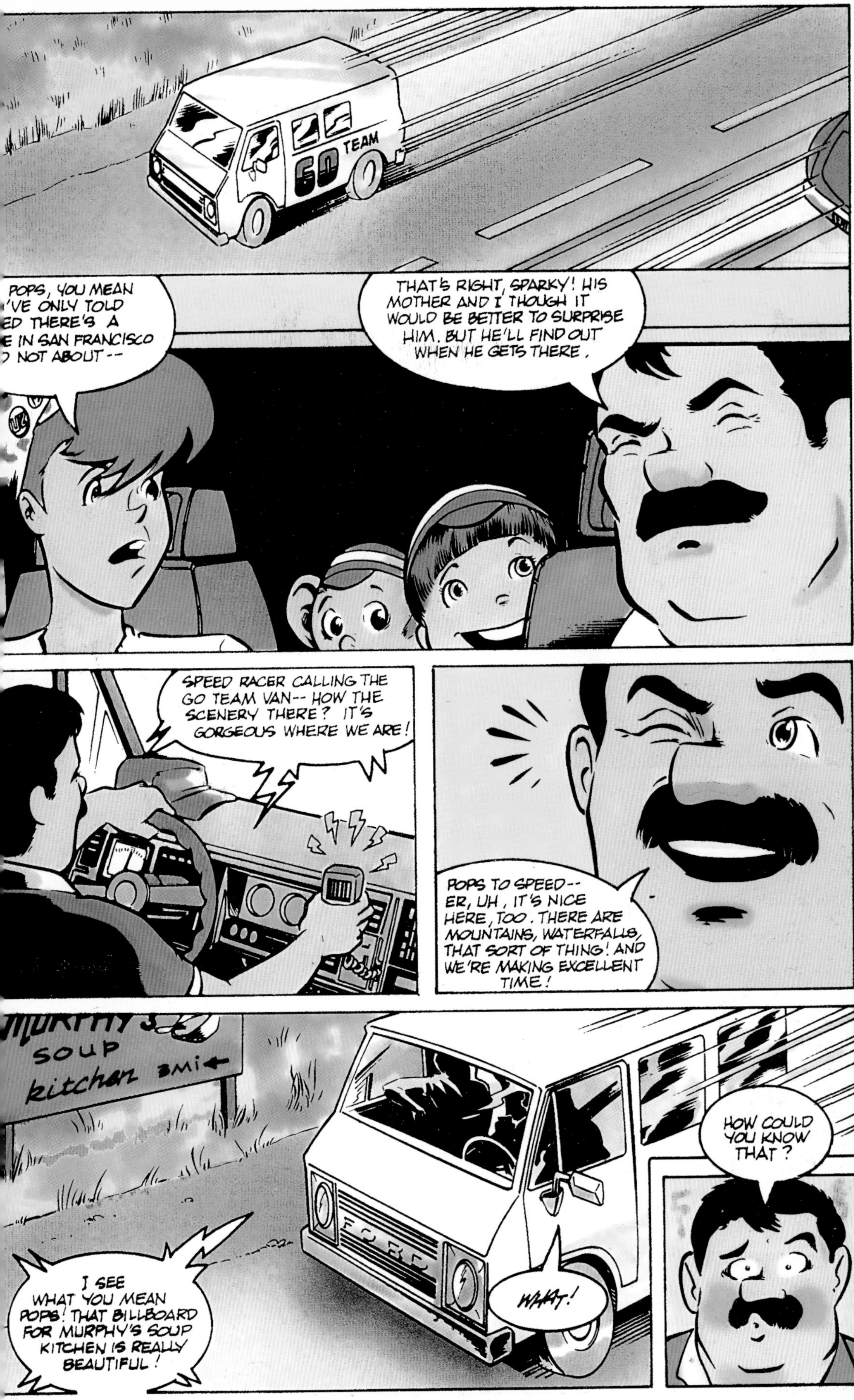
POPS, YOU MEAN
'VE ONLY TOLD
ED THERE'S A
E IN SAN FRANCISCO
NOT ABOUT--
THAT'S RIGHT, SPARKY! HIS MOTHER AND I THOUGH IT WOULD BE BETTER TO SURPRISE HIM. BUT HE'LL FIND OUT WHEN HE GETS THERE.
SPEED RACER CALLING THE GO TEAM VAN-- HOW THE SCENERY THERE? IT'S GORGEOUS WHERE WE ARE!
POPS TO SPEED-- ER, UH, IT'S NICE HERE, TOO. THERE ARE MOUNTAINS, WATERFALLS, THAT SORT OF THING! AND WE'RE MAKING EXCELLENT TIME!
MURPHY'S SOUP kitchen 3MI←
I SEE WHAT YOU MEAN POPS! THAT BILLBOARD FOR MURPHY'S SOUP KITCHEN IS REALLY BEAUTIFUL!
WHAT!
HOW COULD YOU KNOW THAT?

HEY, POPS-- THERE'S THE ROBOTIC PROBE! THAT'S HOW HE KNEW!

THANKS, SPARKY.

AS FOR YOU, SPEED, JUST BE SURE TO HAVE THE MACH 5 AT THE TRACK IN SAN FRANCISCO BY 7:00--

--FOR INSPECTION BY THE RACE OFFICIALS!

BACK AT THE MACH 5, SPEED AND TRIXIE WATCH THE VAN ON A MONITOR AS POPS FINISHES...

IF YOU'RE NOT THERE ON TIME, WE WON'T BE ALLOWED TO RACE-- AND YOU KNOW HOW BADLY WE NEED THE PRIZE MONEY!

DON'T WORRY, I WON' LET YO DOW

OVER AND OUT

SPEED THAT VAN-- IT'S COMING UP AWFUL FAST

IF THEY DON'T SLOW DOWN, THEY'LL--

-- HIT US WHAT'S WR WITH THEM?

30

GET US [A]Y FROM [?] LUNATIC !

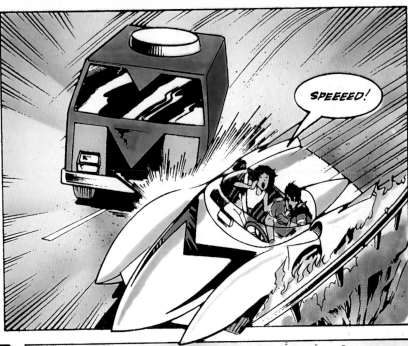

SPEEEED!

Y'RE DELIBERATELY TRYING TO --

-- RUN US OFF THE ROAD !

[S]PEED -- I [T]HINK THEY'RE [T]RYING TO [KI]LL US !

·BUT WHY?

HOLD ON TIGHT, TRIXIE!

THE MACH 5 IS STARTING TO SKID OFF THE ROAD !

I CAN'T HIT THE BRAKES WITHOUT MAKING US GO INTO A SPIN !

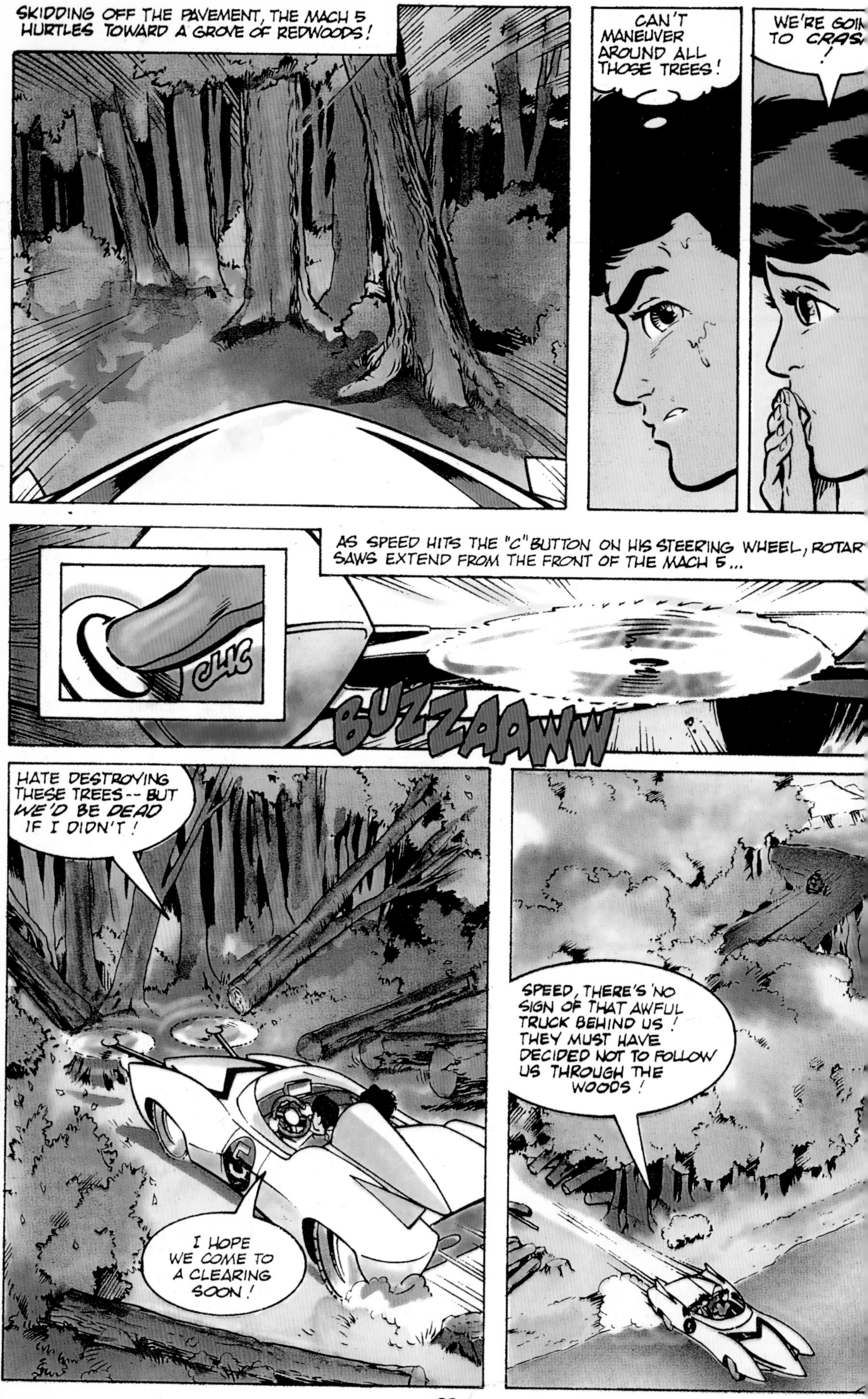
SKIDDING OFF THE PAVEMENT, THE MACH 5 HURTLES TOWARD A GROVE OF REDWOODS!
CAN'T MANEUVER AROUND ALL THOSE TREES!
WE'RE GOI
TO CRAS
!
AS SPEED HITS THE "C" BUTTON ON HIS STEERING WHEEL, ROTAR
SAWS EXTEND FROM THE FRONT OF THE MACH 5...
CLIK
BUZZAAWW
HATE DESTROYING THESE TREES-- BUT WE'D BE DEAD IF I DIDN'T!
I HOPE WE COME TO A CLEARING SOON!
SPEED, THERE'S NO SIGN OF THAT AWFUL TRUCK BEHIND US! THEY MUST HAVE DECIDED NOT TO FOLLOW US THROUGH THE WOODS!

BUT MOMENTS LATER...

OH NO! HERE IT COMES AGAIN! AND IT'S GAINING ON US!

IF THE ROAD'S NOT SAFE, THERE'S ONLY ONE PLACE LEFT TO GO!

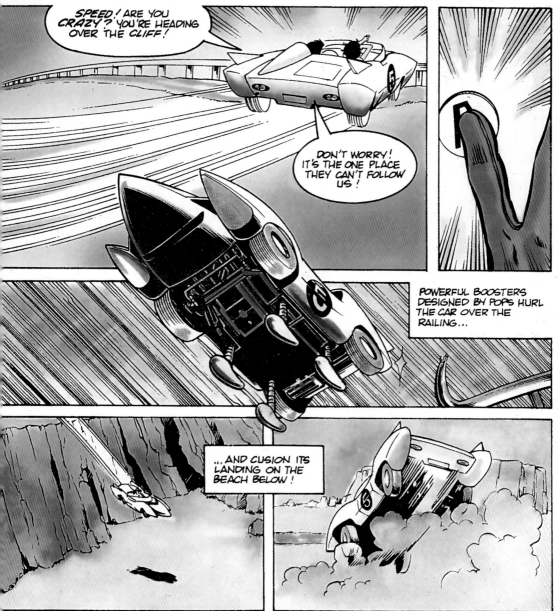

SPEED! ARE YOU CRAZY? YOU'RE HEADING OVER THE CLIFF!

DON'T WORRY! IT'S THE ONE PLACE THEY CAN'T FOLLOW US!

POWERFUL BOOSTERS DESIGNED BY POPS HURL THE CAR OVER THE RAILING...

...AND CUSION ITS LANDING ON THE BEACH BELOW!

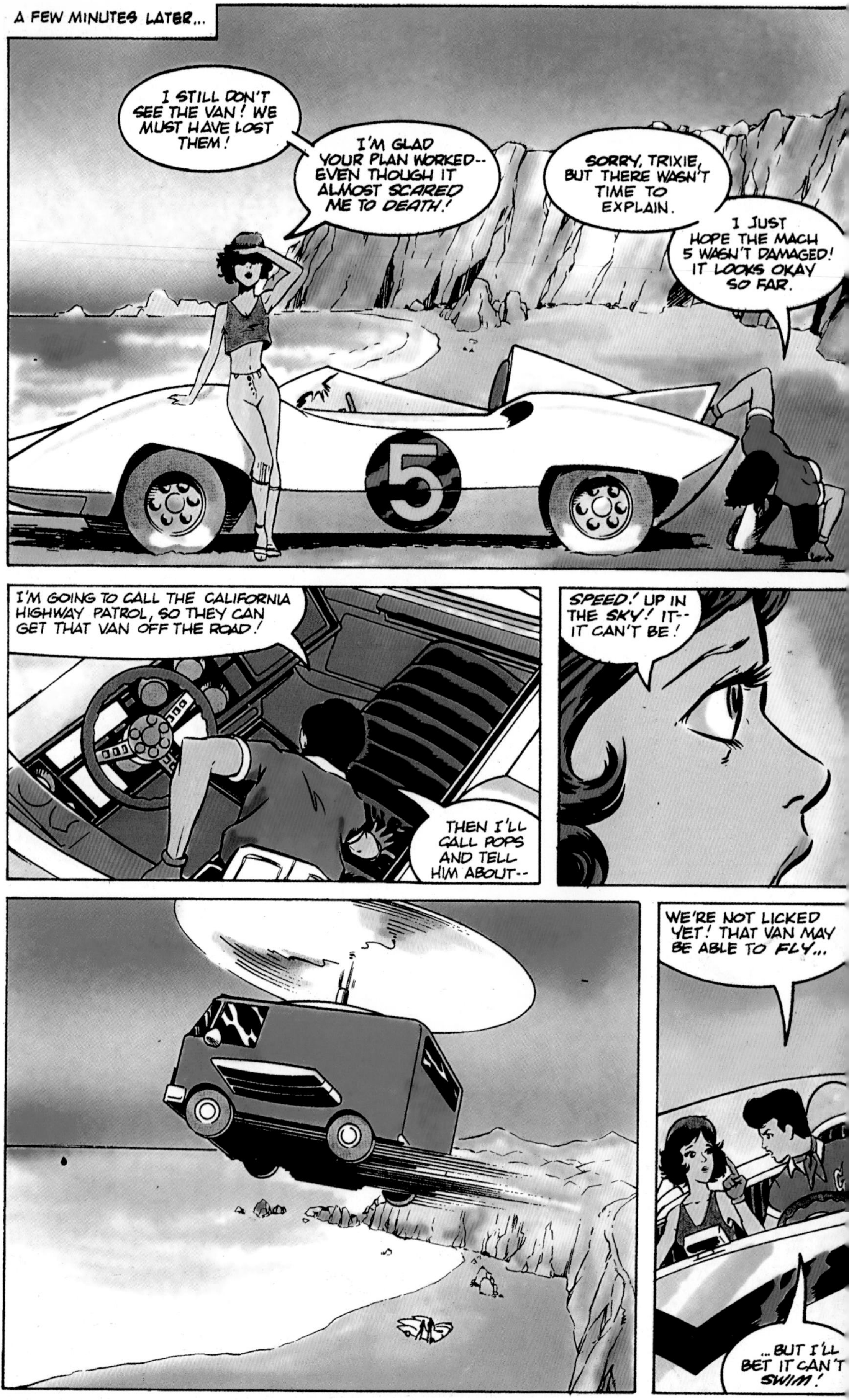
A FEW MINUTES LATER...
I STILL DON'T SEE THE VAN! WE MUST HAVE LOST THEM!
I'M GLAD YOUR PLAN WORKED-- EVEN THOUGH IT ALMOST SCARED ME TO DEATH!
SORRY, TRIXIE, BUT THERE WASN'T TIME TO EXPLAIN.
I JUST HOPE THE MACH 5 WASN'T DAMAGED! IT LOOKS OKAY SO FAR.
5
I'M GOING TO CALL THE CALIFORNIA HIGHWAY PATROL, SO THEY CAN GET THAT VAN OFF THE ROAD!
THEN I'LL CALL POPS AND TELL HIM ABOUT--
SPEED! UP IN THE SKY! IT-- IT CAN'T BE!
WE'RE NOT LICKED YET! THAT VAN MAY BE ABLE TO FLY...
...BUT I'LL BET IT CAN'T SWIM!

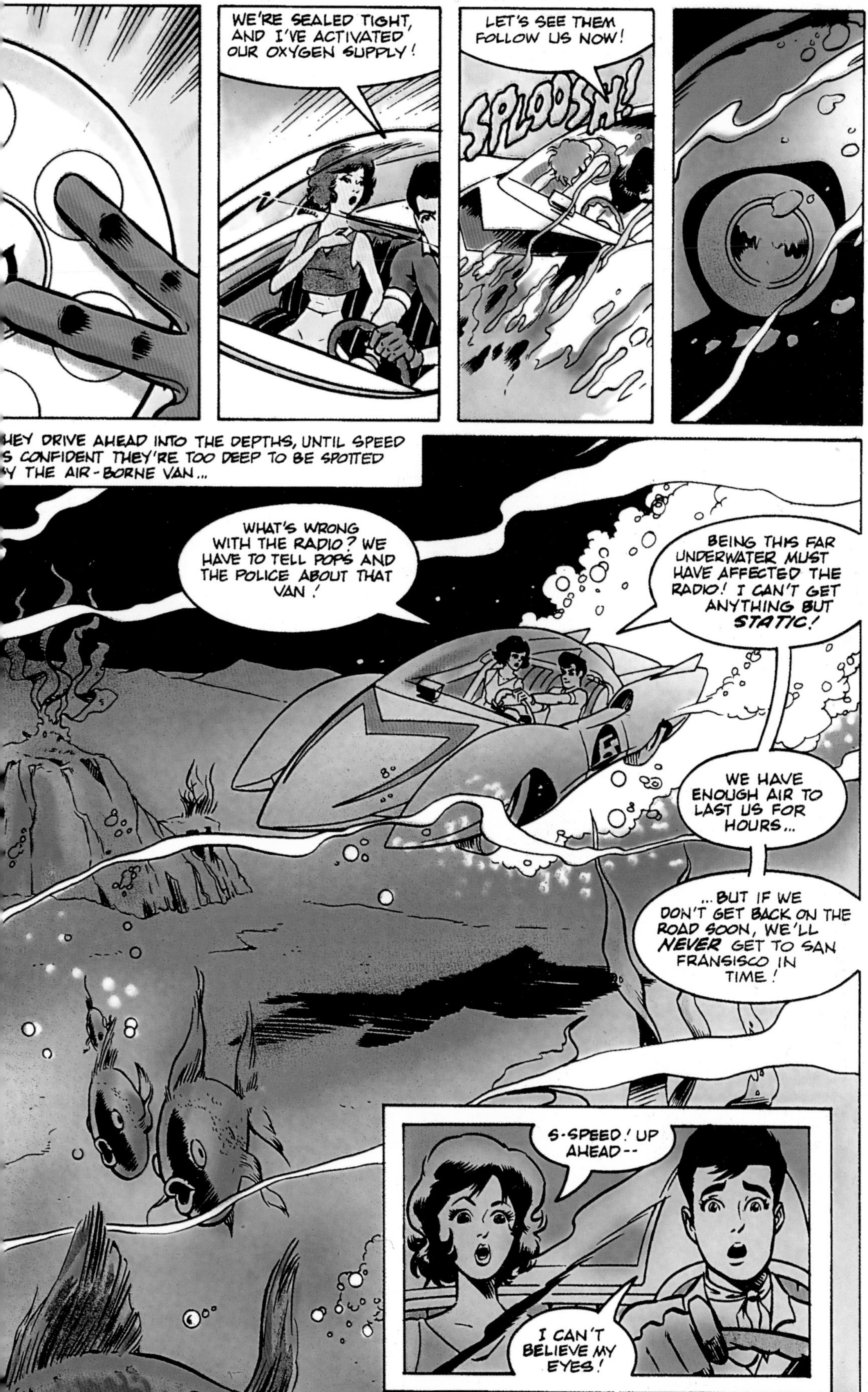
WE'RE SEALED TIGHT, AND I'VE ACTIVATED OUR OXYGEN SUPPLY!
LET'S SEE THEM FOLLOW US NOW!
SPLOOSH!
HEY DRIVE AHEAD INTO THE DEPTHS, UNTIL SPEED S CONFIDENT THEY'RE TOO DEEP TO BE SPOTTED Y THE AIR-BORNE VAN...
WHAT'S WRONG WITH THE RADIO? WE HAVE TO TELL POPS AND THE POLICE ABOUT THAT VAN!
BEING THIS FAR UNDERWATER MUST HAVE AFFECTED THE RADIO! I CAN'T GET ANYTHING BUT STATIC!
WE HAVE ENOUGH AIR TO LAST US FOR HOURS...
...BUT IF WE DON'T GET BACK ON THE ROAD SOON, WE'LL NEVER GET TO SAN FRANSISCO IN TIME!
S-SPEED! UP AHEAD--
I CAN'T BELIEVE MY EYES!

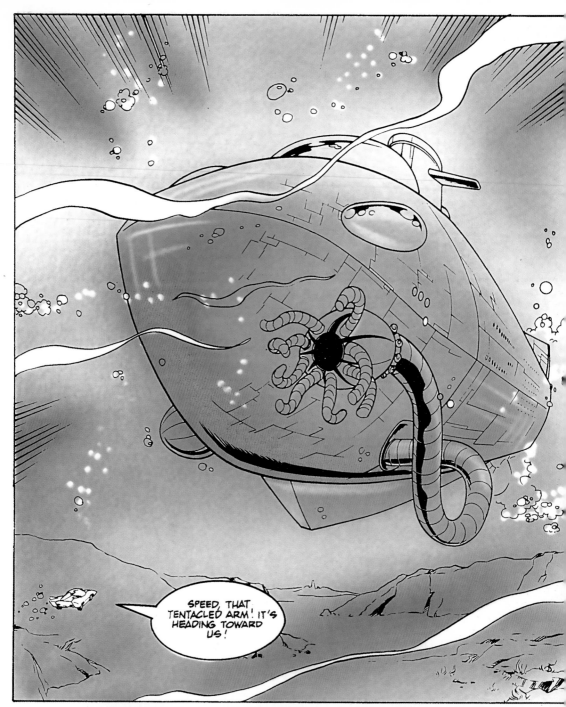

SPEED, THAT TENTACLED ARM! IT'S HEADING TOWARD US!

DON'T WORRY, I'LL --

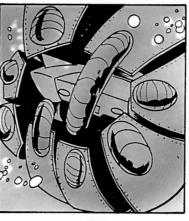

AS THE TENTACLES CLOSE AROUND THE MACH 5, SPEED AND TRIXIE ARE ENGULFED BY A WAVE OF DARKNESS...

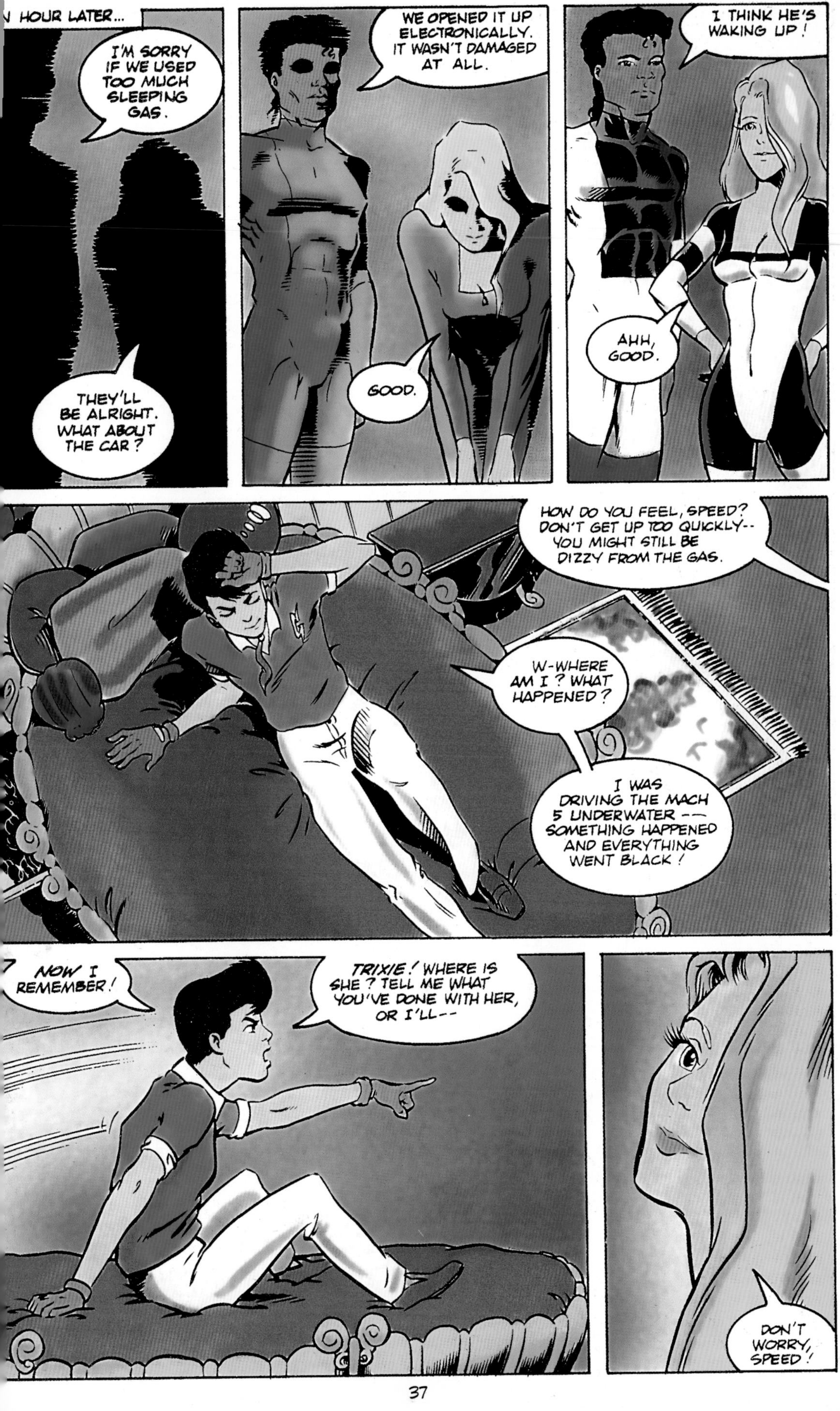

N HOUR LATER...
I'M SORRY IF WE USED TOO MUCH SLEEPING GAS.
THEY'LL BE ALRIGHT. WHAT ABOUT THE CAR?
WE OPENED IT UP ELECTRONICALLY. IT WASN'T DAMAGED AT ALL.
GOOD.
I THINK HE'S WAKING UP!
AHH, GOOD.
HOW DO YOU FEEL, SPEED? DON'T GET UP TOO QUICKLY-- YOU MIGHT STILL BE DIZZY FROM THE GAS.
W-WHERE AM I? WHAT HAPPENED?
I WAS DRIVING THE MACH 5 UNDERWATER -- SOMETHING HAPPENED AND EVERYTHING WENT BLACK!
NOW I REMEMBER!
TRIXIE! WHERE IS SHE? TELL ME WHAT YOU'VE DONE WITH HER, OR I'LL--
DON'T WORRY, SPEED!

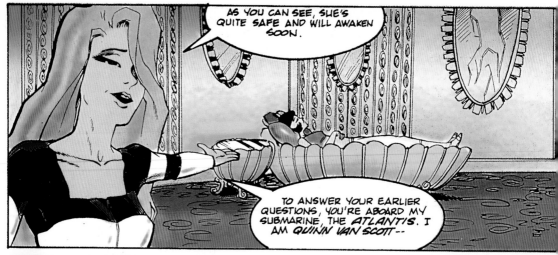

AS YOU CAN SEE, SHE'S QUITE SAFE AND WILL AWAKEN SOON.

TO ANSWER YOUR EARLIER QUESTIONS, YOU'RE ABOARD MY SUBMARINE, THE *ATLANTIS*. I AM *QUINN VAN SCOTT*--

--BUT YOU WILL CALL ME *CAPTAIN*.

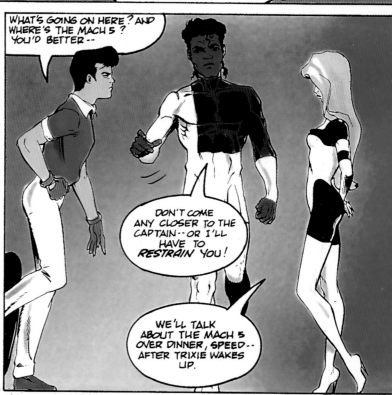

WHAT'S GOING ON HERE? AND WHERE'S THE MACH 5? YOU'D BETTER--

DON'T COME ANY CLOSER TO THE CAPTAIN--OR I'LL HAVE TO *RESTRAIN* YOU!

WE'LL TALK ABOUT THE MACH 5 OVER DINNER, SPEED-- AFTER TRIXIE WAKES UP.

MEANWHILE...

San Francisc 15 miles

THIS IS SPARKY CALLING THE MACH 5!

DO YOU READ ME? REPEAT-- DO YOU READ ME?

IT'S NO USE, POPS-- STILL NO ANSWER!

I HOPE THEY'RE ALL RIGHT!

IT'LL SPOIL THE SURPRISE IF THEY'RE LATE--BUT IF THEY MISS THE INSPECTION--IT'LL COST US THE RACE!

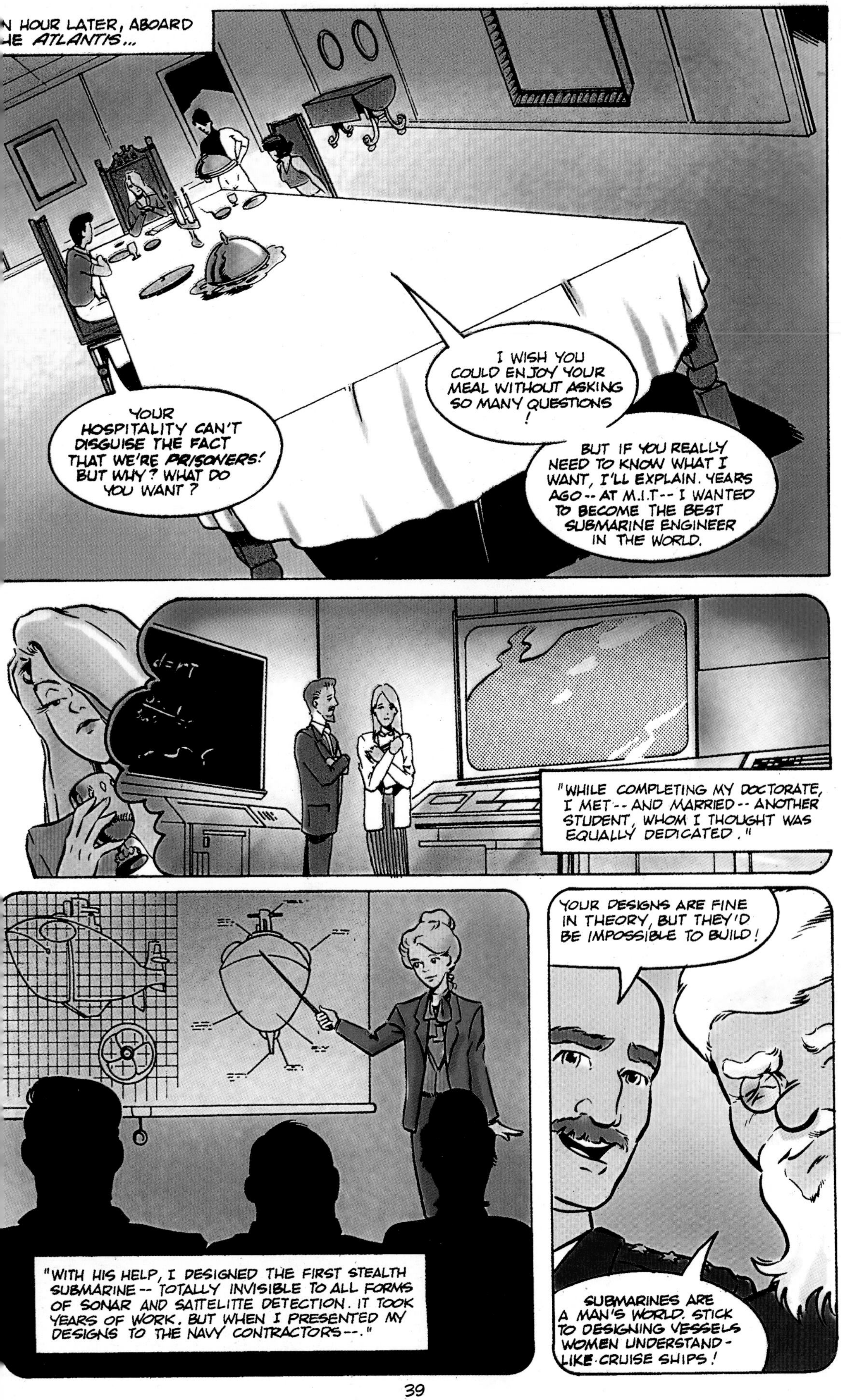
N HOUR LATER, ABOARD
HE *ATLANTIS*...
YOUR HOSPITALITY CAN'T DISGUISE THE FACT THAT WE'RE ***PRISONERS!*** BUT WHY? WHAT DO YOU WANT?
I WISH YOU COULD ENJOY YOUR MEAL WITHOUT ASKING SO MANY QUESTIONS!
BUT IF YOU REALLY NEED TO KNOW WHAT I WANT, I'LL EXPLAIN. YEARS AGO -- AT M.I.T -- I WANTED TO BECOME THE BEST SUBMARINE ENGINEER IN THE WORLD.
d=rT
"WHILE COMPLETING MY DOCTORATE, I MET -- AND MARRIED -- ANOTHER STUDENT, WHOM I THOUGHT WAS EQUALLY DEDICATED."
"WITH HIS HELP, I DESIGNED THE FIRST STEALTH SUBMARINE -- TOTALLY INVISIBLE TO ALL FORMS OF SONAR AND SATTELITTE DETECTION. IT TOOK YEARS OF WORK. BUT WHEN I PRESENTED MY DESIGNS TO THE NAVY CONTRACTORS --."
YOUR DESIGNS ARE FINE IN THEORY, BUT THEY'D BE IMPOSSIBLE TO BUILD!
SUBMARINES ARE A MAN'S WORLD. STICK TO DESIGNING VESSELS WOMEN UNDERSTAND - LIKE CRUISE SHIPS!

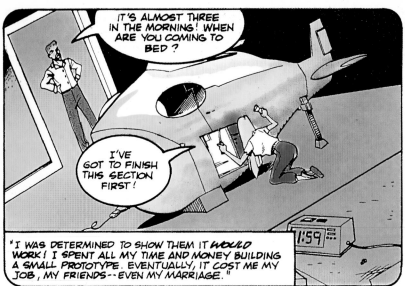

IT'S ALMOST THREE IN THE MORNING! WHEN ARE YOU COMING TO BED?

I'VE GOT TO FINISH THIS SECTION FIRST!

BUT WHEN THE SUB WAS FINISHED--THE NAVY WOULDN'T EVEN LOOK AT IT.

"I WAS DETERMINED TO SHOW THEM IT *WOULD* WORK! I SPENT ALL MY TIME AND MONEY BUILDING A SMALL PROTOTYPE. EVENTUALLY, IT COST ME MY JOB, MY FRIENDS--EVEN MY MARRIAGE."

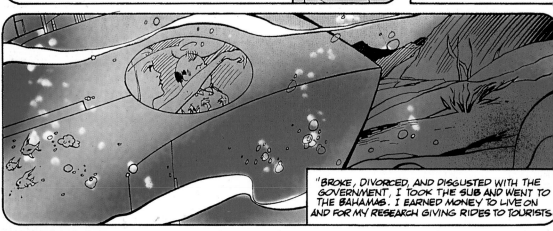

"BROKE, DIVORCED, AND DISGUSTED WITH THE GOVERNMENT, I TOOK THE SUB AND WENT TO THE BAHAMAS. I EARNED MONEY TO LIVE ON AND FOR MY RESEARCH GIVING RIDES TO TOURISTS."

'I WAS NEAR THE STONE *RUINS* OFF THE COAST OF *BIMINI* ...

...WHEN AN EARTHQUAKE STARTING THROWING THE SUB AROUND LIKE A TOY."

"THE SUB WAS WRECKED AND HAD TO BE ABANDONED. IT WAS ALL I HAD--AND I ALMOST FELT LIKE STAYING DOWN WITH IT, BUT THEN I NOTICED A STRANGE *GLOW* COMING FROM A CRACK IN THE *RUINS.*"

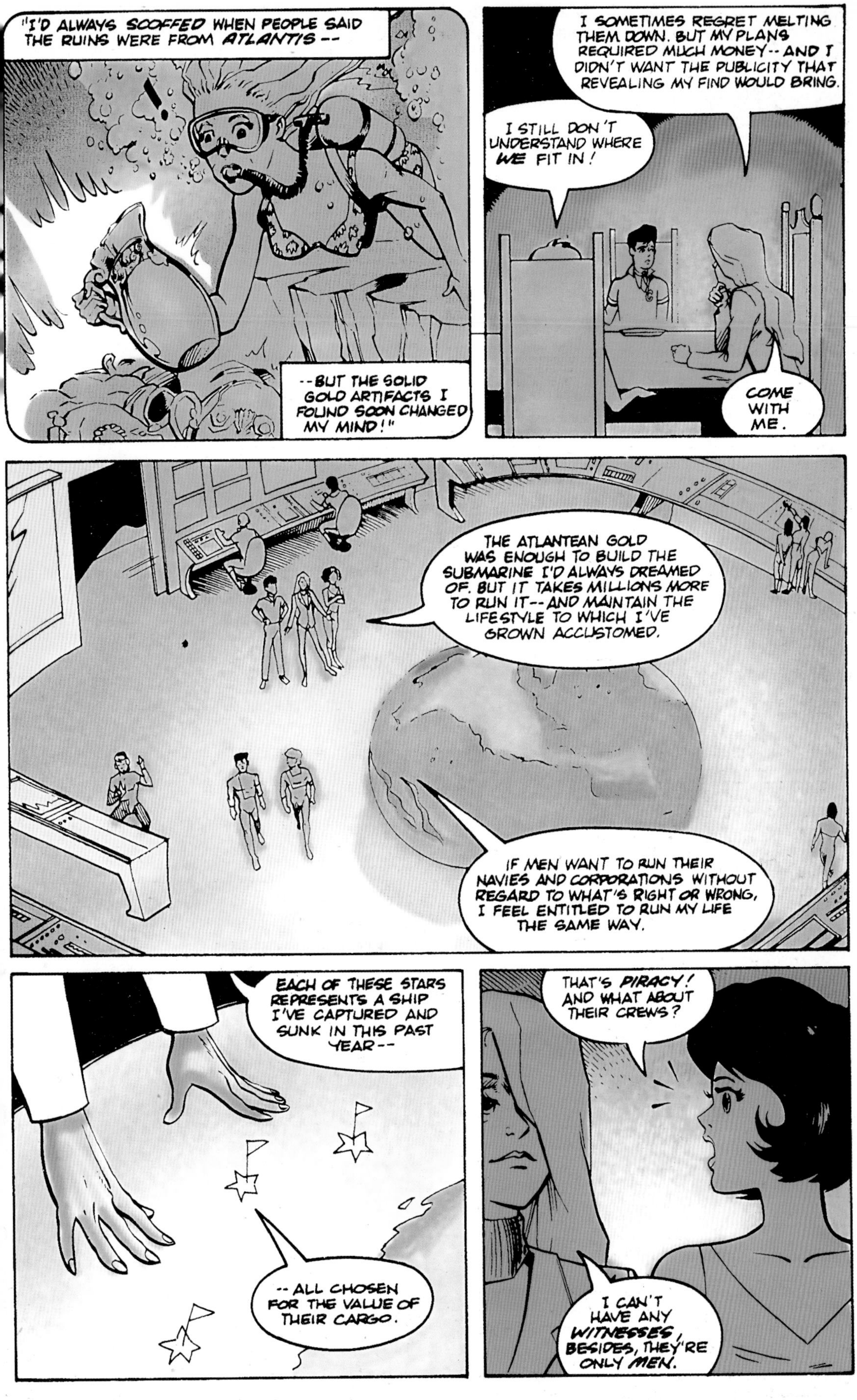
"I'D ALWAYS SCOFFED WHEN PEOPLE SAID THE RUINS WERE FROM ATLANTIS --
--BUT THE SOLID GOLD ARTIFACTS I FOUND SOON CHANGED MY MIND!"
I SOMETIMES REGRET MELTING THEM DOWN. BUT MY PLANS REQUIRED MUCH MONEY-- AND I DIDN'T WANT THE PUBLICITY THAT REVEALING MY FIND WOULD BRING.
I STILL DON'T UNDERSTAND WHERE WE FIT IN!
COME WITH ME.
THE ATLANTEAN GOLD WAS ENOUGH TO BUILD THE SUBMARINE I'D ALWAYS DREAMED OF. BUT IT TAKES MILLIONS MORE TO RUN IT--AND MAINTAIN THE LIFESTYLE TO WHICH I'VE GROWN ACCUSTOMED.
IF MEN WANT TO RUN THEIR NAVIES AND CORPORATIONS WITHOUT REGARD TO WHAT'S RIGHT OR WRONG, I FEEL ENTITLED TO RUN MY LIFE THE SAME WAY.
EACH OF THESE STARS REPRESENTS A SHIP I'VE CAPTURED AND SUNK IN THIS PAST YEAR--
--ALL CHOSEN FOR THE VALUE OF THEIR CARGO.
THAT'S PIRACY! AND WHAT ABOUT THEIR CREWS?
I CAN'T HAVE ANY WITNESSES, BESIDES, THEY'RE ONLY MEN.

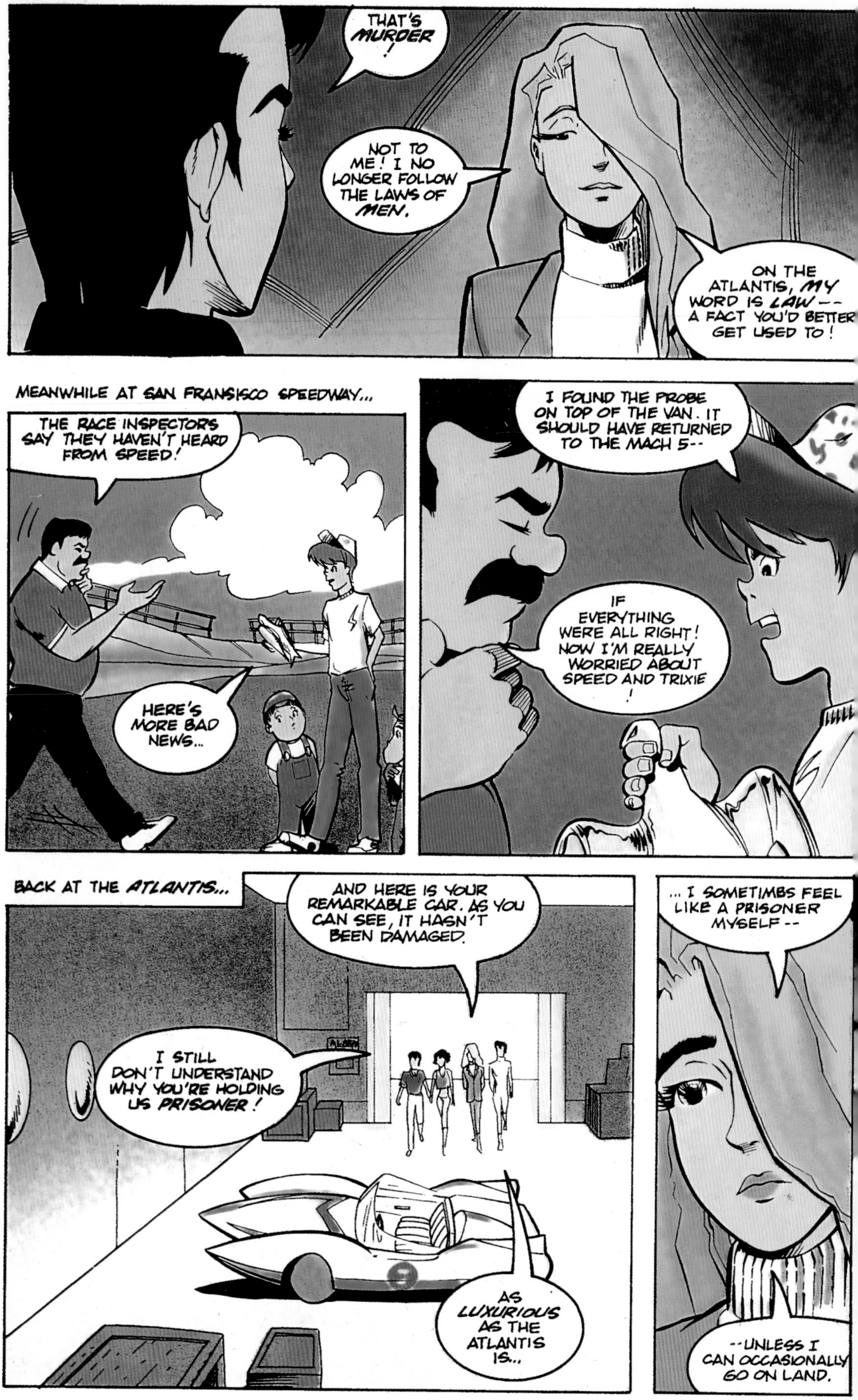
THAT'S MURDER!
NOT TO ME! I NO LONGER FOLLOW THE LAWS OF MEN.
ON THE ATLANTIS, MY WORD IS LAW -- A FACT YOU'D BETTER GET USED TO!
MEANWHILE AT SAN FRANSISCO SPEEDWAY...
THE RACE INSPECTORS SAY THEY HAVEN'T HEARD FROM SPEED!
HERE'S MORE BAD NEWS...
I FOUND THE PROBE ON TOP OF THE VAN. IT SHOULD HAVE RETURNED TO THE MACH 5--
IF EVERYTHING WERE ALL RIGHT! NOW I'M REALLY WORRIED ABOUT SPEED AND TRIXIE!
BACK AT THE ATLANTIS...
AND HERE IS YOUR REMARKABLE CAR. AS YOU CAN SEE, IT HASN'T BEEN DAMAGED.
I STILL DON'T UNDERSTAND WHY YOU'RE HOLDING US PRISONER!
AS LUXURIOUS AS THE ATLANTIS IS...
... I SOMETIMBS FEEL LIKE A PRISONER MYSELF --
--UNLESS I CAN OCCASIONALLY GO ON LAND.

IN THE MACH 5, I COULD TRAVEL ON LAND...

SECURE IN THE KNOWLEDGE THAT I COULD EASILY *ELUDE* THE MEN OF THE F.B.I. OR INTERPOL.

WHEN I GIVE THE WORD TRIXIE, GO FOR THE CAPTAIN, THEN HOP IN THE CAR!

NOW!

KRAK

UUGGHH!

YOU'RE CRAZY TO THINK YOU CAN GET AWAY!

ALARM

ONCE MY MEN HEAR THE ALARM--

WHAT NOW SPEED?

SHE DIDN'T THINK I COULD START THE MACH 5 WITHOUT THE KEYS--

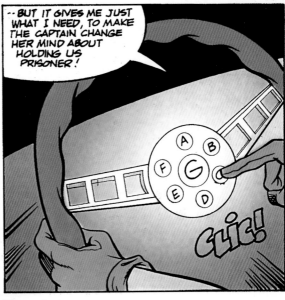

--BUT IT GIVES ME JUST WHAT I NEED, TO MAKE THE CAPTAIN CHANGE HER MIND ABOUT HOLDING US PRISONER!

CLIC!

43

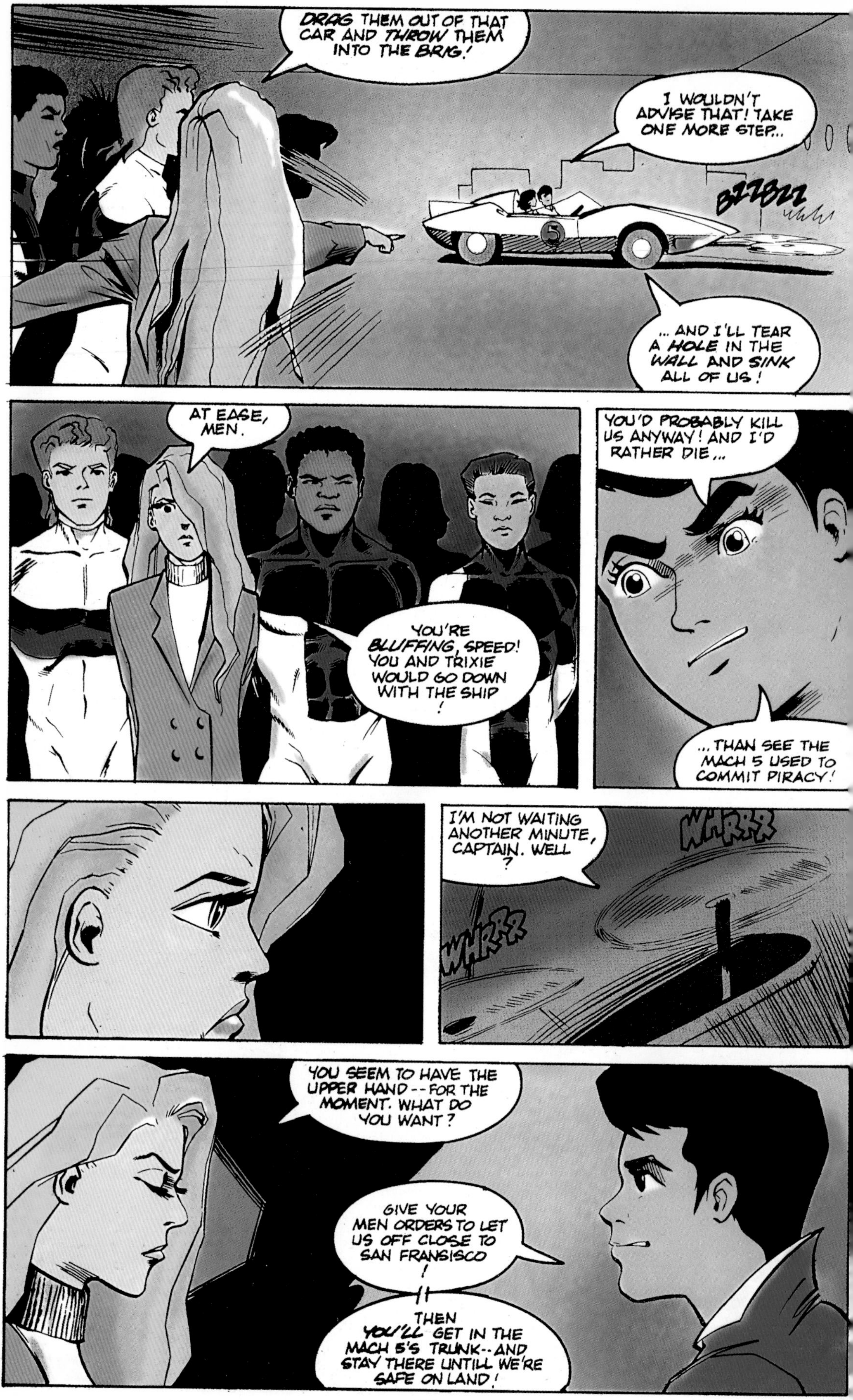
DRAG THEM OUT OF THAT CAR AND THROW THEM INTO THE BRIG!
I WOULDN'T ADVISE THAT! TAKE ONE MORE STEP...
BZZBZZ
... AND I'LL TEAR A HOLE IN THE WALL AND SINK ALL OF US!
AT EASE, MEN.
YOU'RE BLUFFING, SPEED! YOU AND TRIXIE WOULD GO DOWN WITH THE SHIP!
YOU'D PROBABLY KILL US ANYWAY! AND I'D RATHER DIE...
...THAN SEE THE MACH 5 USED TO COMMIT PIRACY!
I'M NOT WAITING ANOTHER MINUTE, CAPTAIN. WELL?
WHRRR
WHRRR
YOU SEEM TO HAVE THE UPPER HAND--FOR THE MOMENT. WHAT DO YOU WANT?
GIVE YOUR MEN ORDERS TO LET US OFF CLOSE TO SAN FRANSISCO!
THEN YOU'LL GET IN THE MACH 5'S TRUNK--AND STAY THERE UNTILL WE'RE SAFE ON LAND!

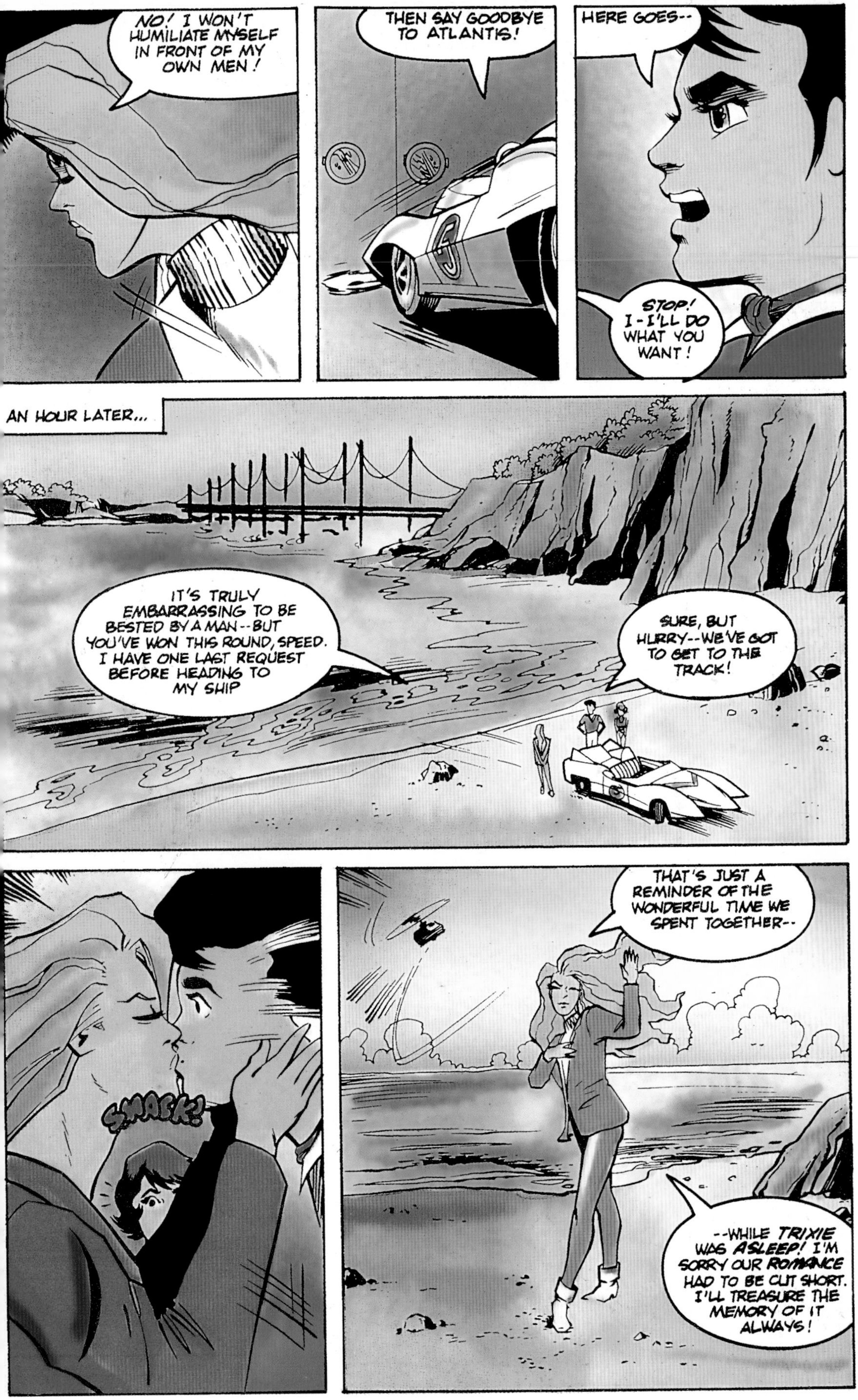
NO! I WON'T HUMILIATE MYSELF IN FRONT OF MY OWN MEN!
THEN SAY GOODBYE TO ATLANTIS!
HERE GOES--
STOP! I-I'LL DO WHAT YOU WANT!
AN HOUR LATER...
IT'S TRULY EMBARRASSING TO BE BESTED BY A MAN--BUT YOU'VE WON THIS ROUND, SPEED. I HAVE ONE LAST REQUEST BEFORE HEADING TO MY SHIP
SURE, BUT HURRY--WE'VE GOT TO GET TO THE TRACK!
SMACK!
THAT'S JUST A REMINDER OF THE WONDERFUL TIME WE SPENT TOGETHER--
--WHILE TRIXIE WAS ASLEEP! I'M SORRY OUR ROMANCE HAD TO BE CUT SHORT. I'LL TREASURE THE MEMORY OF IT ALWAYS!

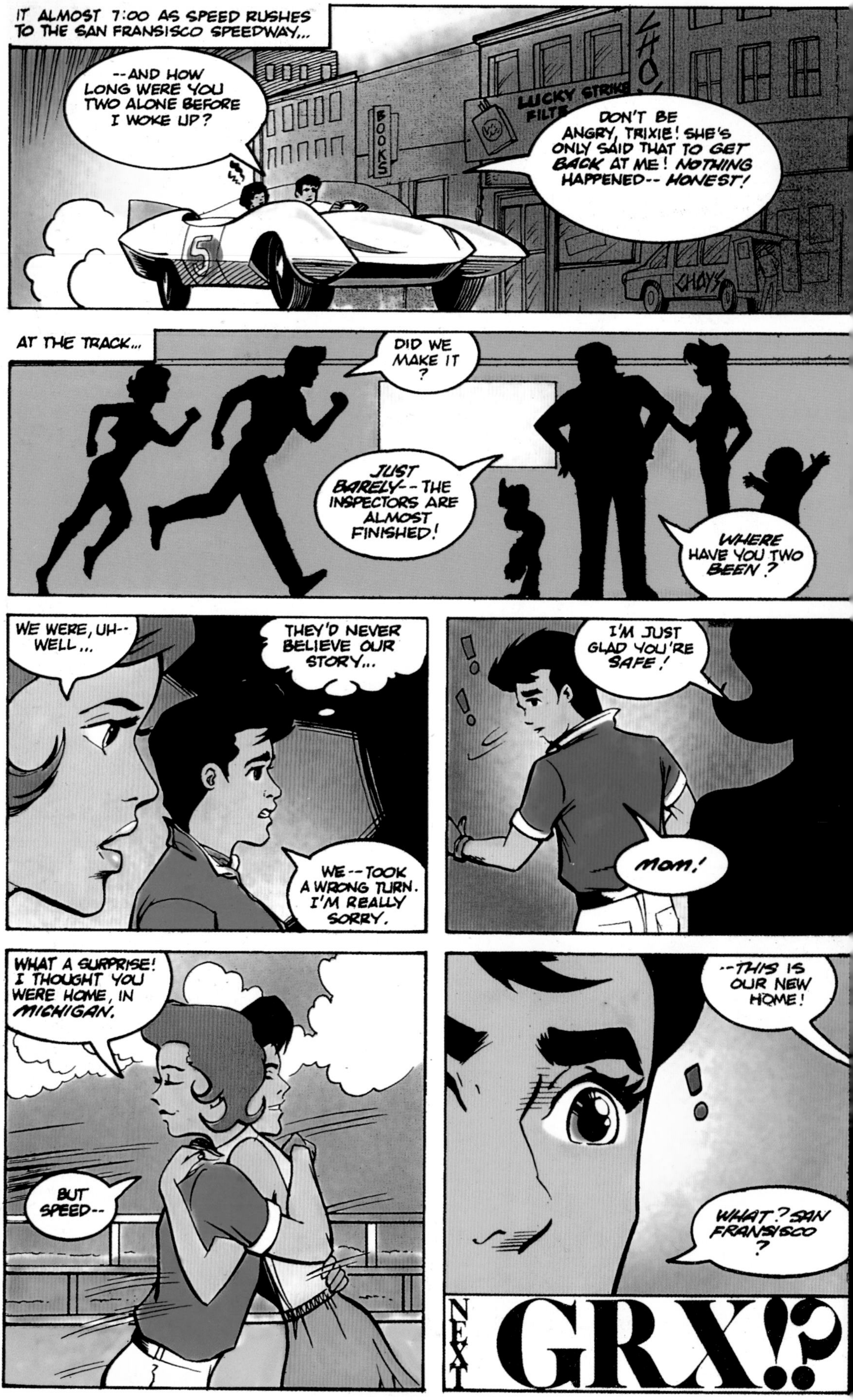
IT ALMOST 7:00 AS SPEED RUSHES TO THE SAN FRANSISCO SPEEDWAY...
--AND HOW LONG WERE YOU TWO ALONE BEFORE I WOKE UP?
BOOKS
LUCKY STRIKE
FILTE
DON'T BE ANGRY, TRIXIE! SHE'S ONLY SAID THAT TO *GET BACK* AT ME! *NOTHING* HAPPENED-- *HONEST!*
AT THE TRACK...
DID WE MAKE IT?
JUST BARELY-- THE INSPECTORS ARE ALMOST FINISHED!
WHERE HAVE YOU TWO *BEEN*?
WE WERE, UH-- WELL...
THEY'D NEVER BELIEVE OUR STORY...
WE--TOOK A WRONG TURN. I'M REALLY SORRY.
I'M JUST GLAD YOU'RE *SAFE*!
MOM!
WHAT A SURPRISE! I THOUGHT YOU WERE HOME, IN *MICHIGAN.*
BUT SPEED--
--*THIS* IS OUR NEW HOME!
WHAT? SAN FRANSISCO?
NEXT
GRX!?

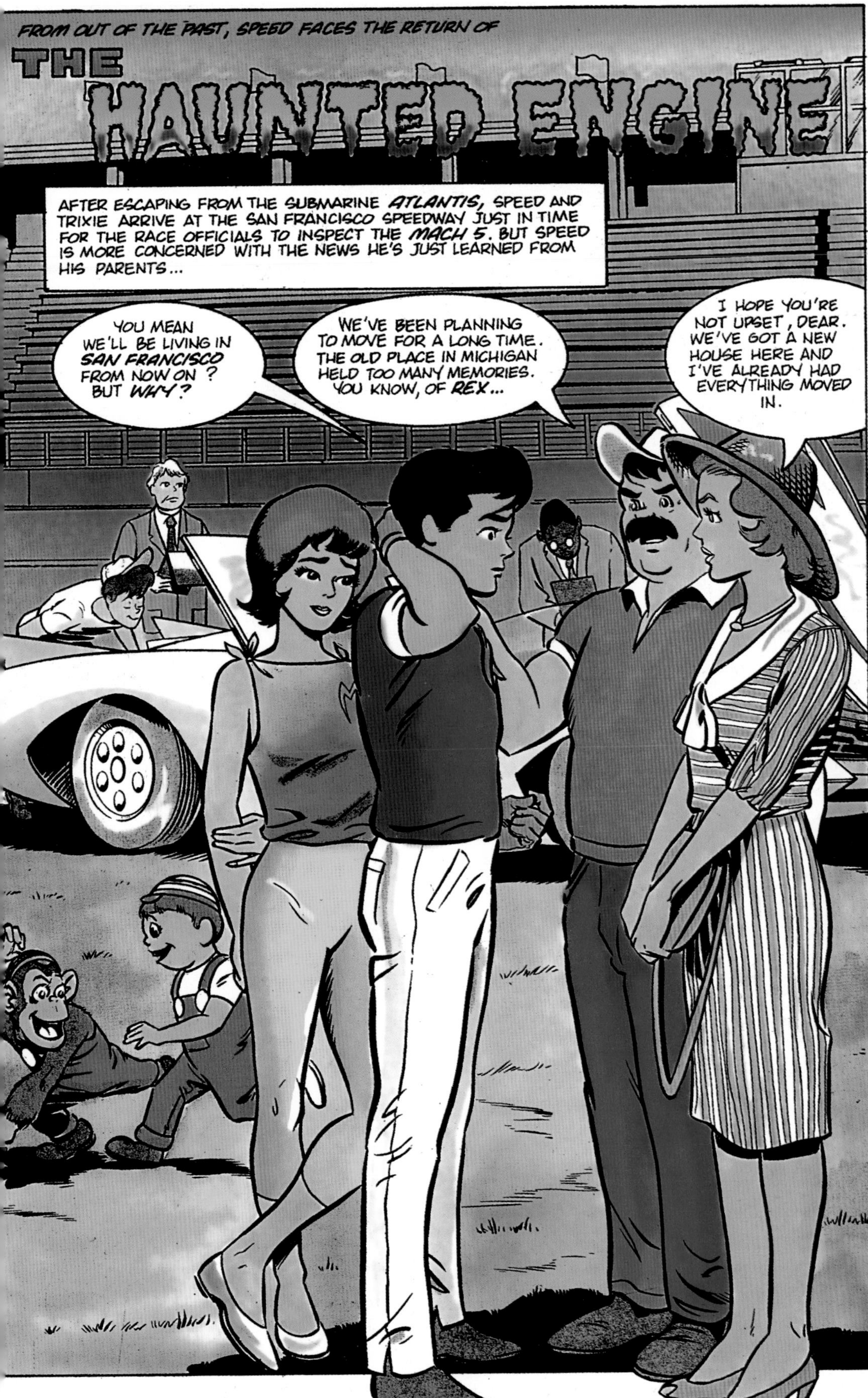
FROM OUT OF THE PAST, SPEED FACES THE RETURN OF
THE HAUNTED ENGINE
AFTER ESCAPING FROM THE SUBMARINE ATLANTIS, SPEED AND TRIXIE ARRIVE AT THE SAN FRANCISCO SPEEDWAY JUST IN TIME FOR THE RACE OFFICIALS TO INSPECT THE MACH 5. BUT SPEED IS MORE CONCERNED WITH THE NEWS HE'S JUST LEARNED FROM HIS PARENTS...
YOU MEAN WE'LL BE LIVING IN SAN FRANCISCO FROM NOW ON ? BUT WHY ?
WE'VE BEEN PLANNING TO MOVE FOR A LONG TIME. THE OLD PLACE IN MICHIGAN HELD TOO MANY MEMORIES. YOU KNOW, OF REX...
I HOPE YOU'RE NOT UPSET, DEAR. WE'VE GOT A NEW HOUSE HERE AND I'VE ALREADY HAD EVERYTHING MOVED IN.

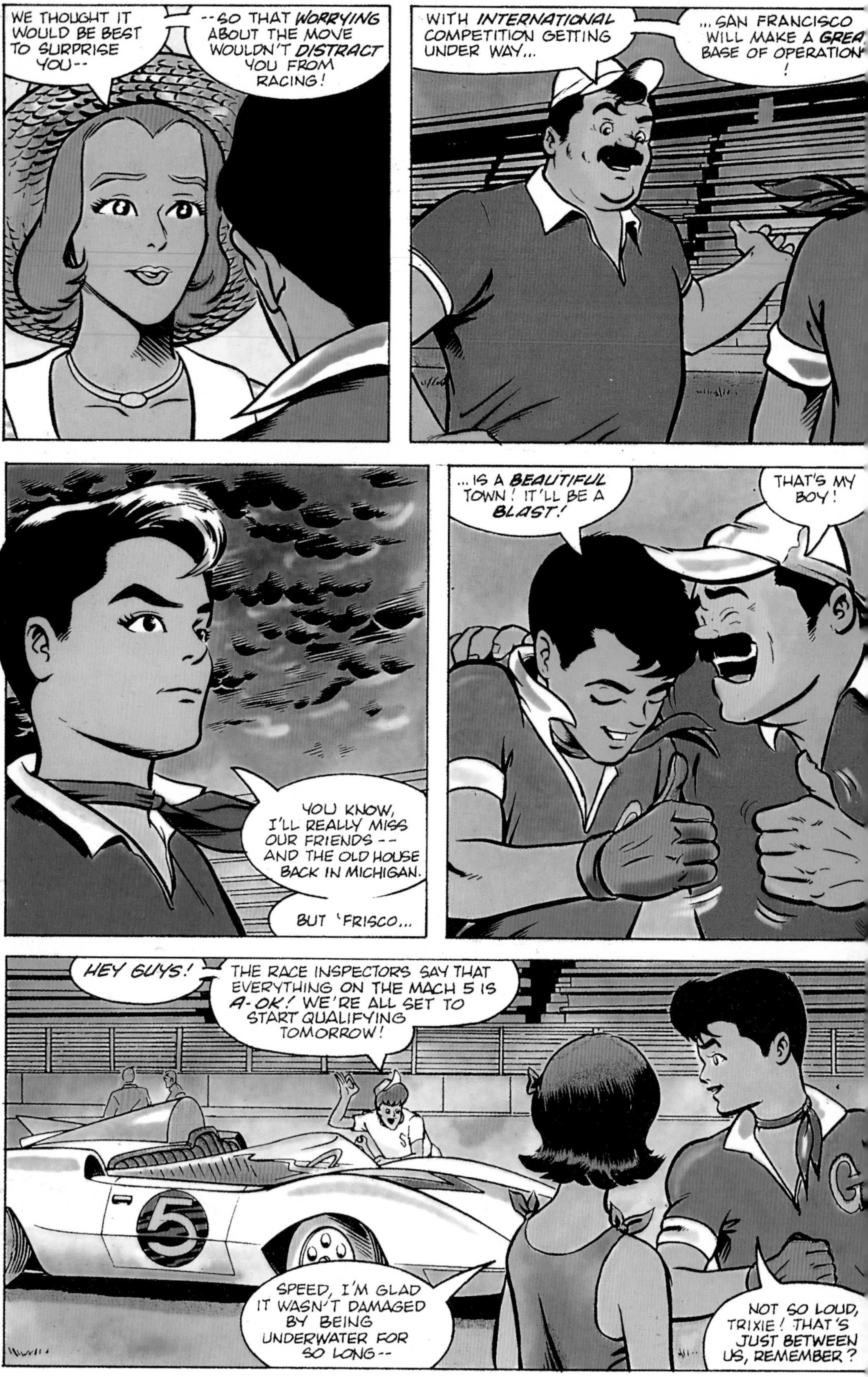
WE THOUGHT IT WOULD BE BEST TO SURPRISE YOU--
--SO THAT WORRYING ABOUT THE MOVE WOULDN'T DISTRACT YOU FROM RACING!
WITH INTERNATIONAL COMPETITION GETTING UNDER WAY...
...SAN FRANCISCO WILL MAKE A GREA BASE OF OPERATION !
YOU KNOW, I'LL REALLY MISS OUR FRIENDS -- AND THE OLD HOUSE BACK IN MICHIGAN.
BUT 'FRISCO...
...IS A BEAUTIFUL TOWN! IT'LL BE A BLAST!
THAT'S MY BOY!
HEY GUYS!
THE RACE INSPECTORS SAY THAT EVERYTHING ON THE MACH 5 IS A-OK! WE'RE ALL SET TO START QUALIFYING TOMORROW!
SPEED, I'M GLAD IT WASN'T DAMAGED BY BEING UNDERWATER FOR SO LONG--
NOT SO LOUD, TRIXIE! THAT'S JUST BETWEEN US, REMEMBER?

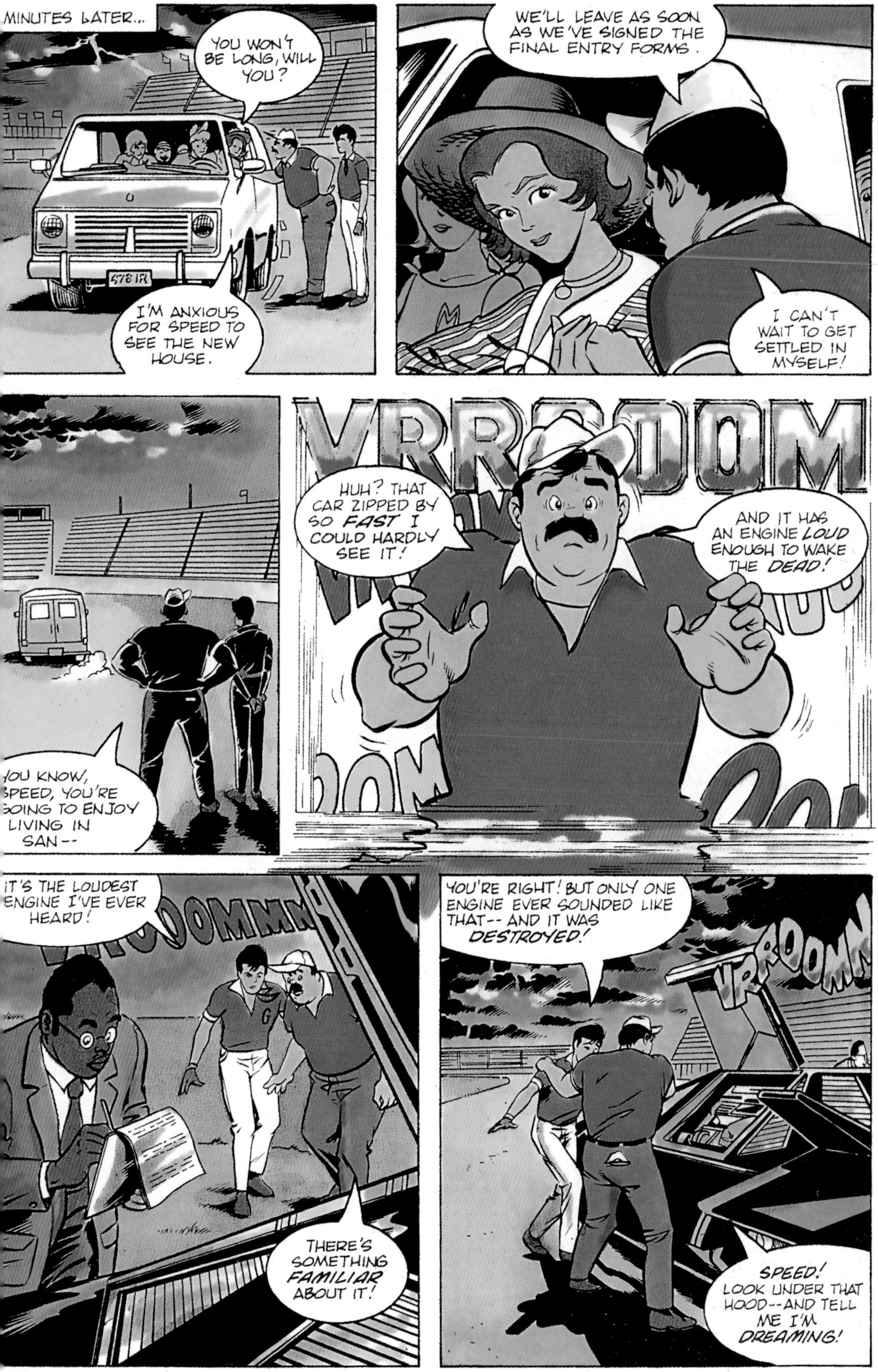
MINUTES LATER...
YOU WON'T BE LONG, WILL YOU?
I'M ANXIOUS FOR SPEED TO SEE THE NEW HOUSE.
WE'LL LEAVE AS SOON AS WE'VE SIGNED THE FINAL ENTRY FORMS.
I CAN'T WAIT TO GET SETTLED IN MYSELF!
YOU KNOW, SPEED, YOU'RE GOING TO ENJOY LIVING IN SAN--
VRROOOM
HUH? THAT CAR ZIPPED BY SO FAST I COULD HARDLY SEE IT!
AND IT HAS AN ENGINE LOUD ENOUGH TO WAKE THE DEAD!
IT'S THE LOUDEST ENGINE I'VE EVER HEARD!
VROOOMMM
THERE'S SOMETHING FAMILIAR ABOUT IT!
YOU'RE RIGHT! BUT ONLY ONE ENGINE EVER SOUNDED LIKE THAT-- AND IT WAS DESTROYED!
VRROOMM
SPEED! LOOK UNDER THAT HOOD--AND TELL ME I'M DREAMING!

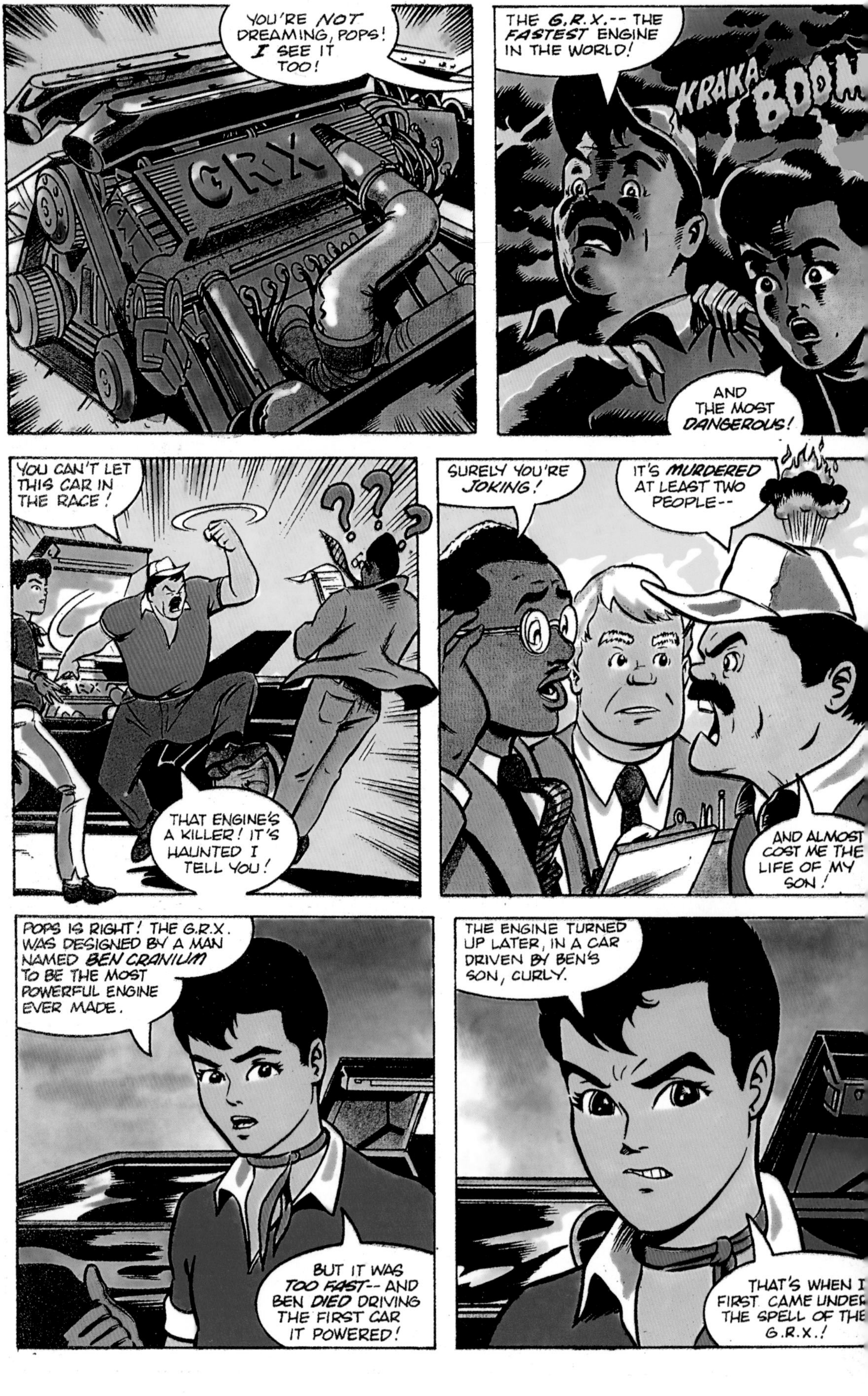
YOU'RE NOT DREAMING, POPS! I SEE IT TOO!
GRX
THE G.R.X.-- THE FASTEST ENGINE IN THE WORLD!
KRAKA BOOM
AND THE MOST DANGEROUS!
YOU CAN'T LET THIS CAR IN THE RACE!
THAT ENGINE'S A KILLER! IT'S HAUNTED I TELL YOU!
SURELY YOU'RE JOKING!
IT'S MURDERED AT LEAST TWO PEOPLE--
AND ALMOST COST ME THE LIFE OF MY SON!
POPS IS RIGHT! THE G.R.X. WAS DESIGNED BY A MAN NAMED BEN CRANIUM TO BE THE MOST POWERFUL ENGINE EVER MADE.
BUT IT WAS TOO FAST-- AND BEN DIED DRIVING THE FIRST CAR IT POWERED!
THE ENGINE TURNED UP LATER, IN A CAR DRIVEN BY BEN'S SON, CURLY.
THAT'S WHEN I FIRST CAME UNDER THE SPELL OF THE G.R.X.!

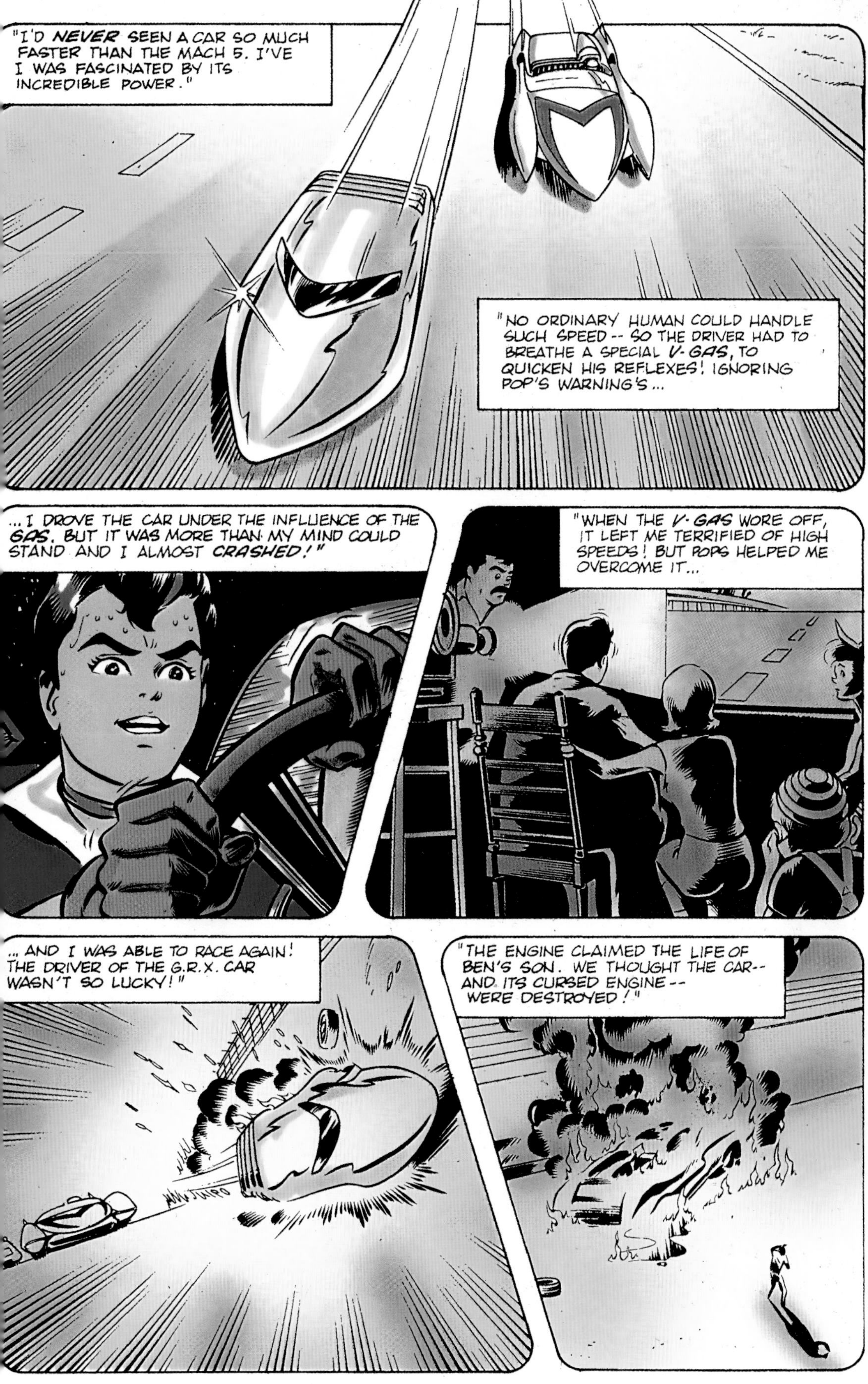
"I'D NEVER SEEN A CAR SO MUCH FASTER THAN THE MACH 5. I'VE I WAS FASCINATED BY ITS INCREDIBLE POWER."
"NO ORDINARY HUMAN COULD HANDLE SUCH SPEED -- SO THE DRIVER HAD TO BREATHE A SPECIAL V-GAS, TO QUICKEN HIS REFLEXES! IGNORING POP'S WARNING'S...
...I DROVE THE CAR UNDER THE INFLUENCE OF THE GAS. BUT IT WAS MORE THAN MY MIND COULD STAND AND I ALMOST CRASHED!"
"WHEN THE V-GAS WORE OFF, IT LEFT ME TERRIFIED OF HIGH SPEEDS! BUT POPS HELPED ME OVERCOME IT...
...AND I WAS ABLE TO RACE AGAIN! THE DRIVER OF THE G.R.X. CAR WASN'T SO LUCKY!"
"THE ENGINE CLAIMED THE LIFE OF BEN'S SON. WE THOUGHT THE CAR-- AND ITS CURSED ENGINE -- WERE DESTROYED!"

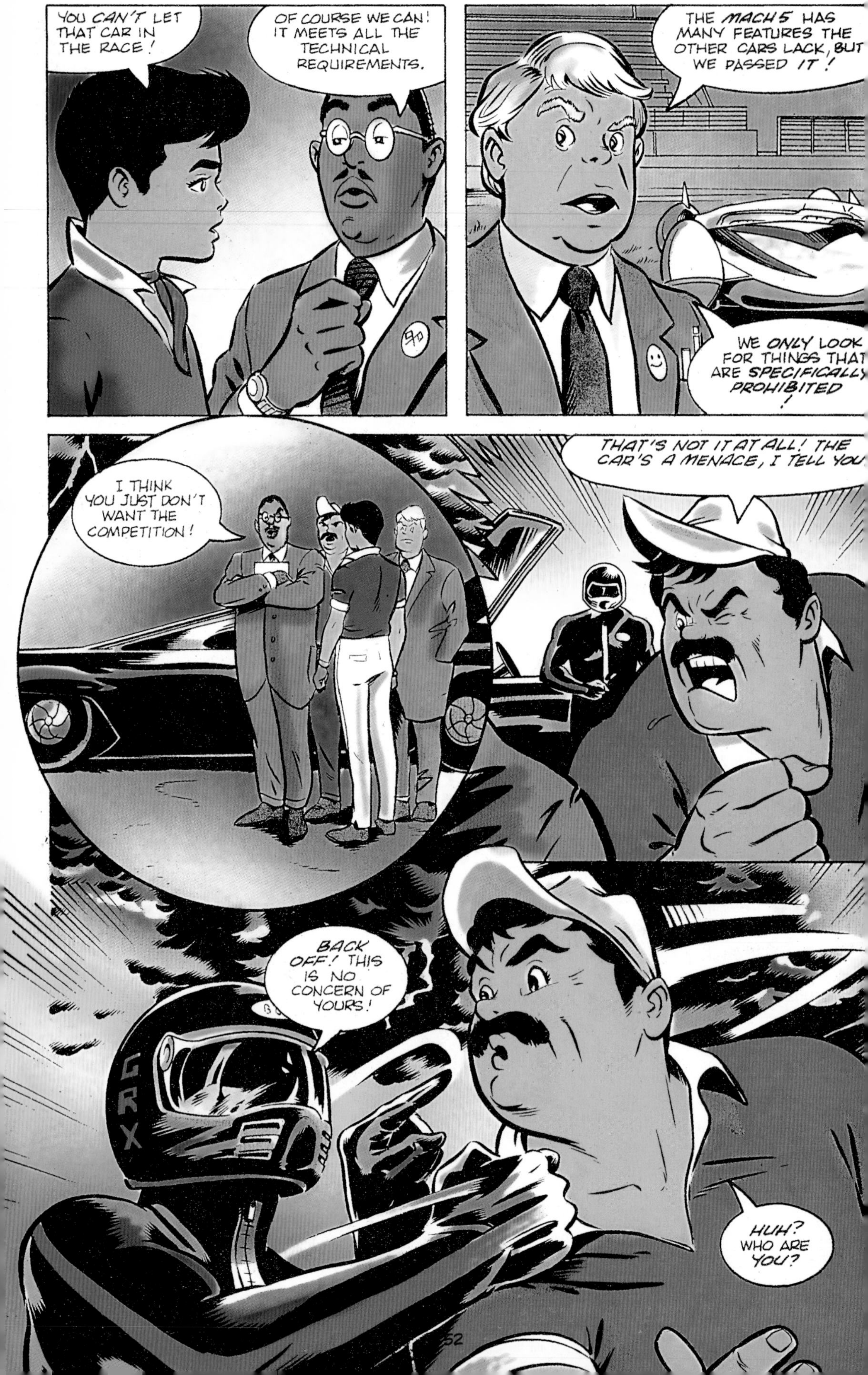

YOU CAN'T LET THAT CAR IN THE RACE!
OF COURSE WE CAN! IT MEETS ALL THE TECHNICAL REQUIREMENTS.
THE MACH 5 HAS MANY FEATURES THE OTHER CARS LACK, BUT WE PASSED IT!
WE ONLY LOOK FOR THINGS THAT ARE SPECIFICALLY PROHIBITED!
I THINK YOU JUST DON'T WANT THE COMPETITION!
THAT'S NOT IT AT ALL! THE CAR'S A MENACE, I TELL YOU
BACK OFF! THIS IS NO CONCERN OF YOURS!
HUH? WHO ARE YOU?

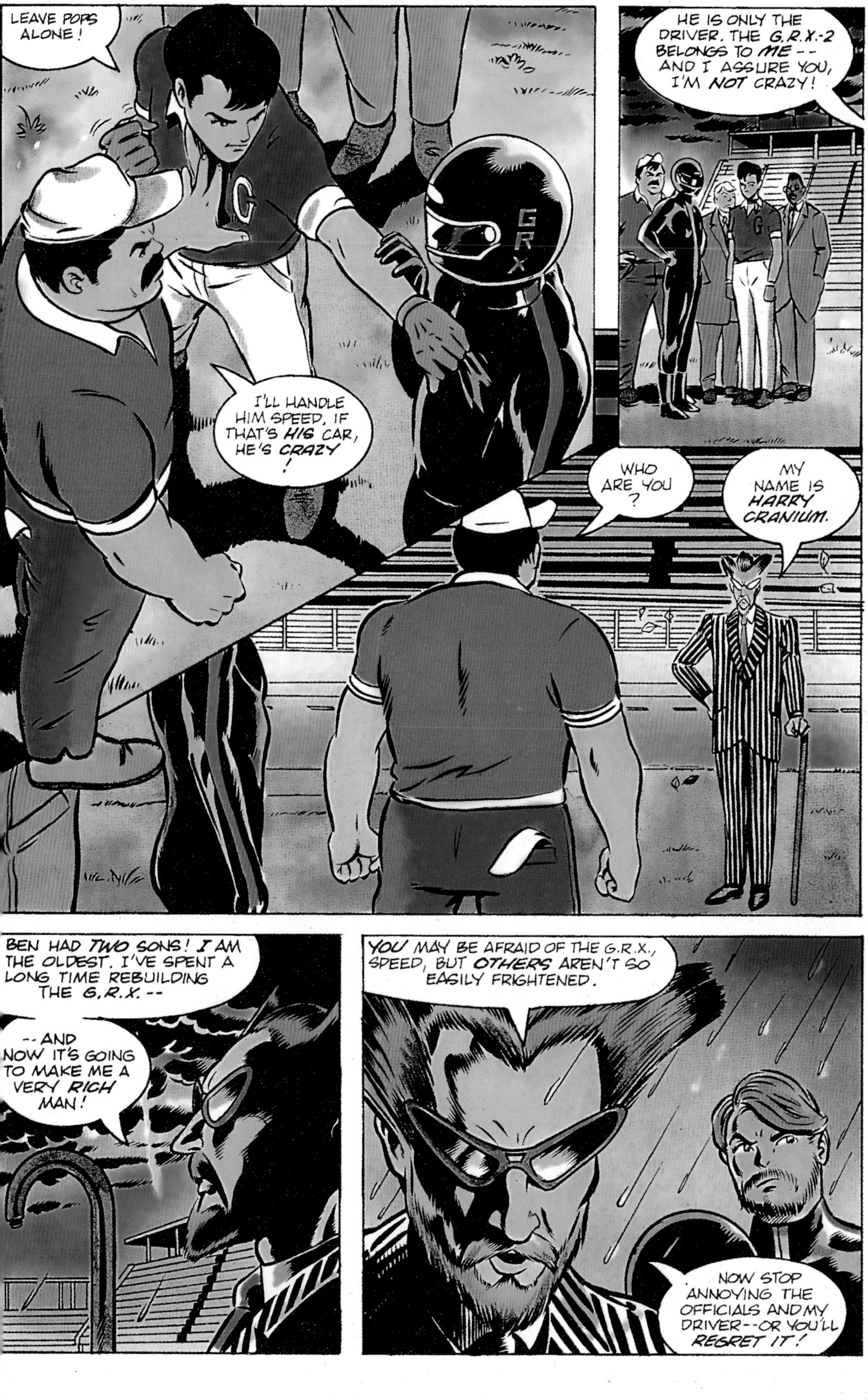
LEAVE POPS ALONE!
I'LL HANDLE HIM SPEED. IF THAT'S HIS CAR, HE'S CRAZY!
HE IS ONLY THE DRIVER. THE G.R.X.-2 BELONGS TO ME -- AND I ASSURE YOU, I'M NOT CRAZY!
WHO ARE YOU?
MY NAME IS HARRY CRANIUM.
BEN HAD TWO SONS! I AM THE OLDEST. I'VE SPENT A LONG TIME REBUILDING THE G.R.X. --
-- AND NOW IT'S GOING TO MAKE ME A VERY RICH MAN!
YOU MAY BE AFRAID OF THE G.R.X., SPEED, BUT OTHERS AREN'T SO EASILY FRIGHTENED.
NOW STOP ANNOYING THE OFFICIALS AND MY DRIVER--OR YOU'LL REGRET IT!

LATER THAT EVENING AS POPS AND SPEED FINALLY ARRIVE AT THEIR NEW HOME...

LET'S NOT MENTION THE G.R.X. TO YOUR MOTHER JUST YET, SPEED, SHE'S BEEN THROUGH A LOT, ARRANGING THE MOVE.

SURE, POPS!

IT LOOKS *HUGE!*

ONLY THE *BEST* FOR *MY* FAMILY!

WELL? WHAT DO YOU THINK?

IT'S *FANTASTIC!* LIKE SOMETHING OUT OF A MAGAZINE!

I WAS GETTING *WORRIED* ABOUT YOU TWO!

HAVE SOME LEMONADE AND I'LL GIVE YOU THE *GRAND TOUR!*

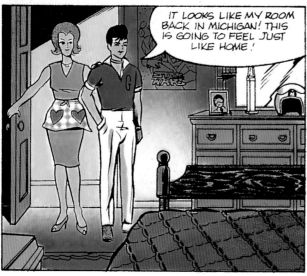

IT LOOKS LIKE MY ROOM BACK IN MICHIGAN! THIS IS GOING TO FEEL JUST LIKE HOME!

I ONLY WISH REX COULD BE HERE -- TO SEE OUR NEW PLACE!

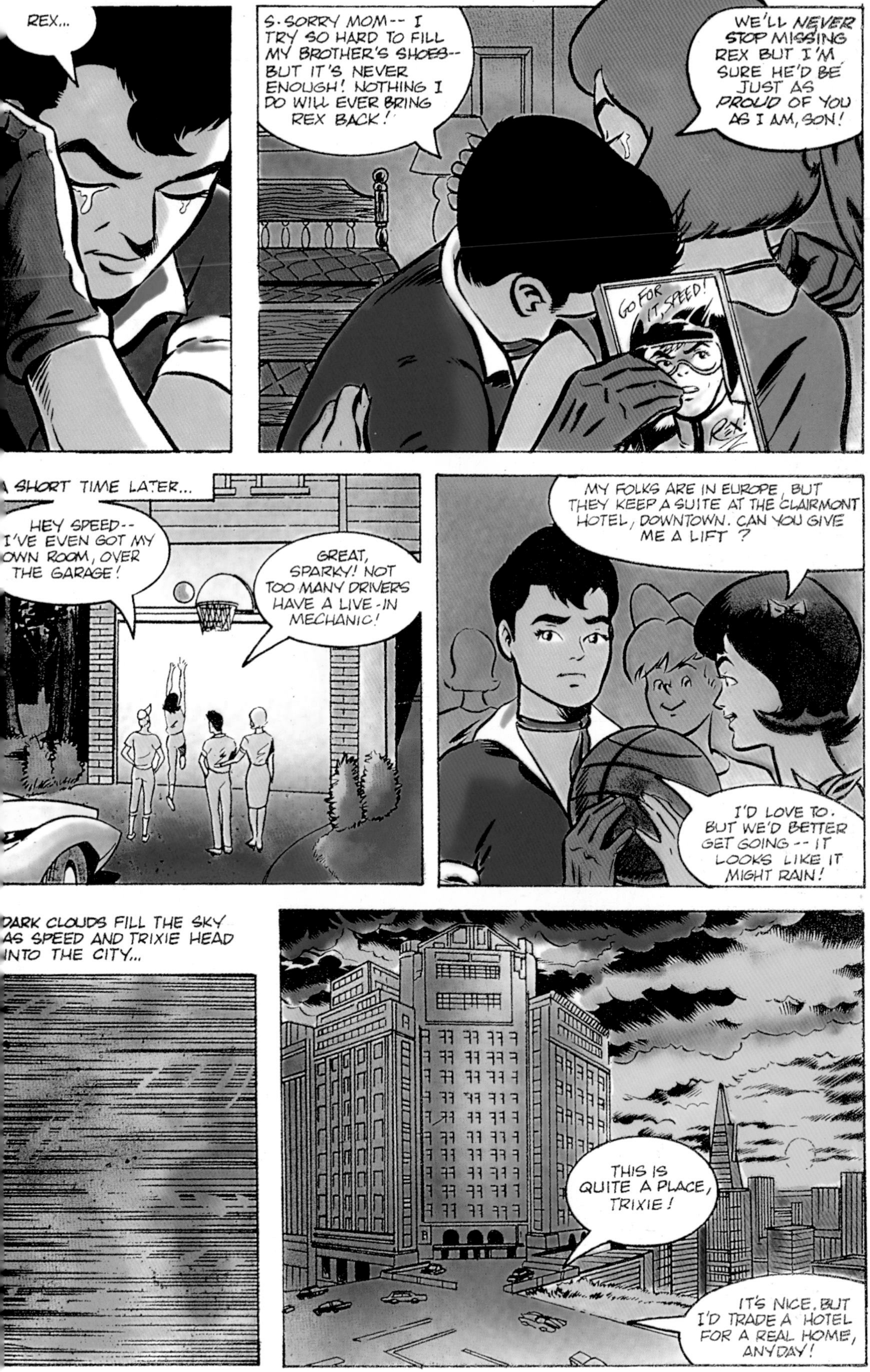
REX...
S-SORRY MOM-- I TRY SO HARD TO FILL MY BROTHER'S SHOES-- BUT IT'S NEVER ENOUGH! NOTHING I DO WILL EVER BRING REX BACK!
WE'LL NEVER STOP MISSING REX BUT I'M SURE HE'D BE JUST AS PROUD OF YOU AS I AM, SON!
GO FOR IT, SPEED!
REX
A SHORT TIME LATER...
HEY SPEED-- I'VE EVEN GOT MY OWN ROOM, OVER THE GARAGE!
GREAT, SPARKY! NOT TOO MANY DRIVERS HAVE A LIVE-IN MECHANIC!
MY FOLKS ARE IN EUROPE, BUT THEY KEEP A SUITE AT THE CLAIRMONT HOTEL, DOWNTOWN. CAN YOU GIVE ME A LIFT ?
I'D LOVE TO. BUT WE'D BETTER GET GOING -- IT LOOKS LIKE IT MIGHT RAIN!
DARK CLOUDS FILL THE SKY AS SPEED AND TRIXIE HEAD INTO THE CITY...
THIS IS QUITE A PLACE, TRIXIE!
IT'S NICE, BUT I'D TRADE A HOTEL FOR A REAL HOME, ANYDAY!

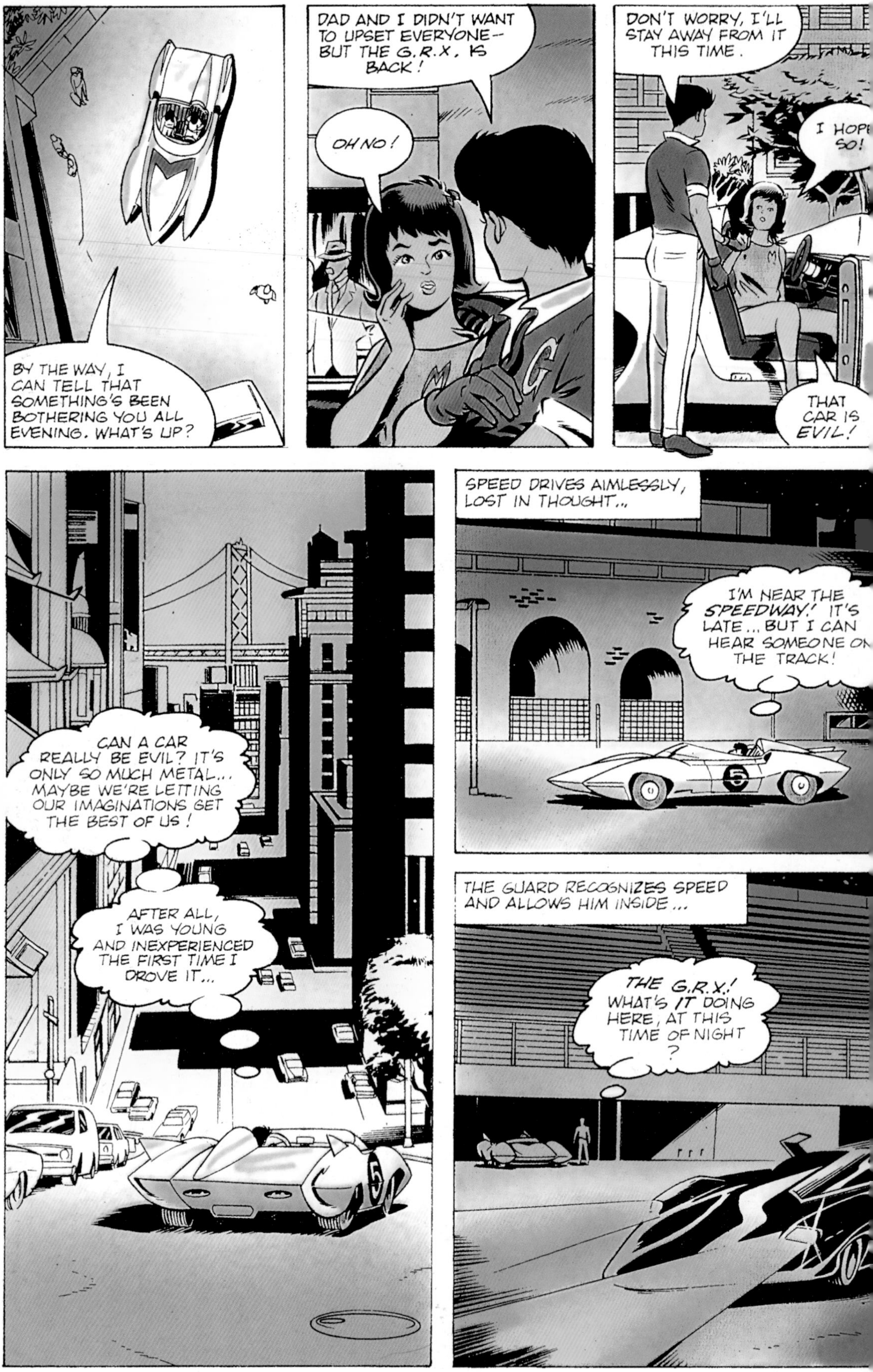
BY THE WAY, I CAN TELL THAT SOMETHING'S BEEN BOTHERING YOU ALL EVENING. WHAT'S UP?
DAD AND I DIDN'T WANT TO UPSET EVERYONE-- BUT THE G.R.X. IS BACK!
OH NO!
DON'T WORRY, I'LL STAY AWAY FROM IT THIS TIME.
I HOPE SO!
THAT CAR IS EVIL!
CAN A CAR REALLY BE EVIL? IT'S ONLY SO MUCH METAL... MAYBE WE'RE LETTING OUR IMAGINATIONS GET THE BEST OF US!
AFTER ALL, I WAS YOUNG AND INEXPERIENCED THE FIRST TIME I DROVE IT...
SPEED DRIVES AIMLESSLY, LOST IN THOUGHT...
I'M NEAR THE SPEEDWAY! IT'S LATE... BUT I CAN HEAR SOMEONE ON THE TRACK!
THE GUARD RECOGNIZES SPEED AND ALLOWS HIM INSIDE...
THE G.R.X.! WHAT'S IT DOING HERE, AT THIS TIME OF NIGHT?

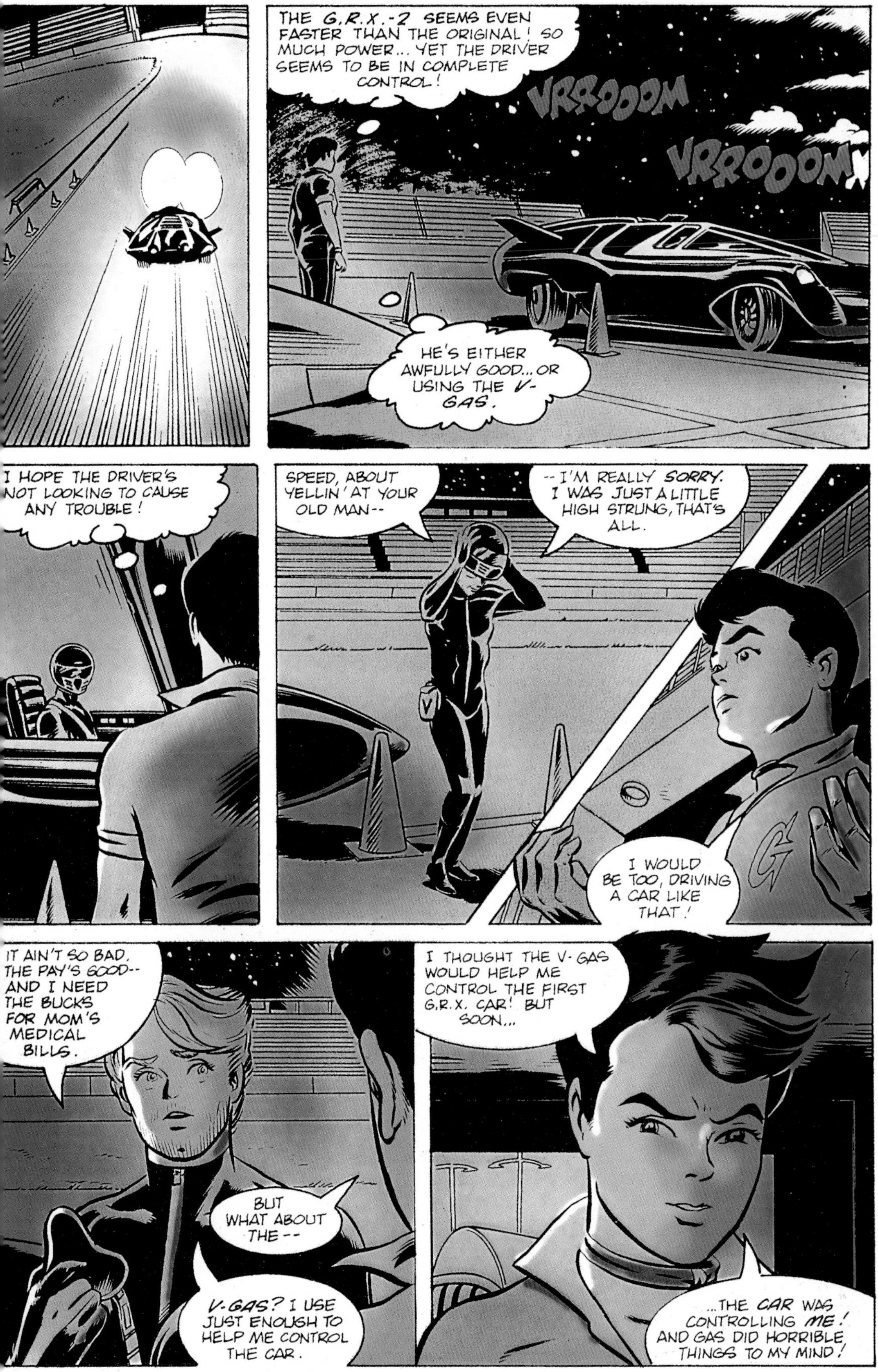
THE G.R.X.-2 SEEMS EVEN FASTER THAN THE ORIGINAL! SO MUCH POWER... YET THE DRIVER SEEMS TO BE IN COMPLETE CONTROL!
VRROOOM
VRROOOM
HE'S EITHER AWFULLY GOOD... OR USING THE V-GAS.
I HOPE THE DRIVER'S NOT LOOKING TO CAUSE ANY TROUBLE!
SPEED, ABOUT YELLIN' AT YOUR OLD MAN--
--I'M REALLY SORRY. I WAS JUST A LITTLE HIGH STRUNG, THAT'S ALL.
I WOULD BE TOO, DRIVING A CAR LIKE THAT!
IT AIN'T SO BAD. THE PAY'S GOOD-- AND I NEED THE BUCKS FOR MOM'S MEDICAL BILLS.
BUT WHAT ABOUT THE--
V-GAS? I USE JUST ENOUGH TO HELP ME CONTROL THE CAR.
I THOUGHT THE V-GAS WOULD HELP ME CONTROL THE FIRST G.R.X. CAR! BUT SOON...
...THE CAR WAS CONTROLLING ME! AND GAS DID HORRIBLE THINGS TO MY MIND!

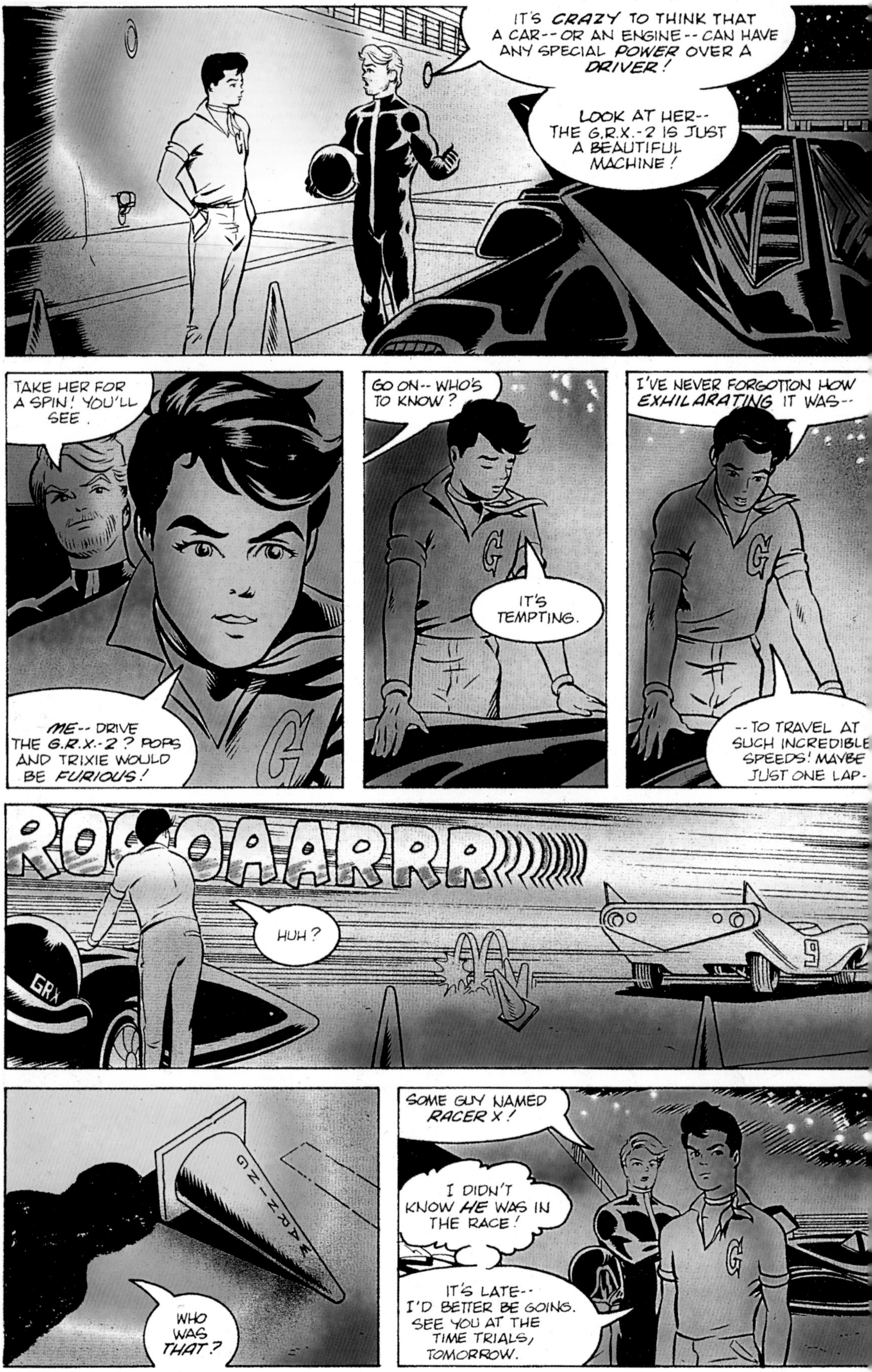
IT'S CRAZY TO THINK THAT A CAR-- OR AN ENGINE -- CAN HAVE ANY SPECIAL POWER OVER A DRIVER!
LOOK AT HER-- THE G.R.X.-2 IS JUST A BEAUTIFUL MACHINE!
TAKE HER FOR A SPIN! YOU'LL SEE.
ME-- DRIVE THE G.R.X.-2? POPS AND TRIXIE WOULD BE FURIOUS!
GO ON-- WHO'S TO KNOW?
IT'S TEMPTING.
I'VE NEVER FORGOTTON HOW EXHILARATING IT WAS--
--TO TRAVEL AT SUCH INCREDIBLE SPEEDS! MAYBE JUST ONE LAP-
ROOOAARRR
HUH?
GRX
WHO WAS THAT?
SOME GUY NAMED RACER X!
I DIDN'T KNOW HE WAS IN THE RACE!
IT'S LATE-- I'D BETTER BE GOING. SEE YOU AT THE TIME TRIALS, TOMORROW.

LATER... GOING AGAINST THE G.R.X.-2 *AND* RACER X COULD MAKE THIS THE *TOUGHEST* RACE OF MY CAREER!

BUT IF *RACER X* HADN'T SHOWN UP WHEN HE DID,...

...I MIGHT HAVE SUCCUMBED TO THE G.R.X. AGAIN!

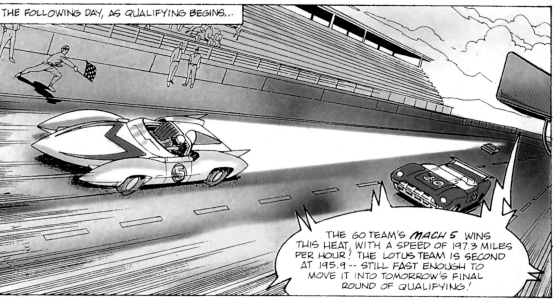

THE FOLLOWING DAY, AS QUALIFYING BEGINS,...

THE GO TEAM'S *MACH 5* WINS THIS HEAT, WITH A SPEED OF 197.3 MILES PER HOUR! THE LOTUS TEAM IS SECOND AT 195.9 -- STILL FAST ENOUGH TO MOVE IT INTO TOMORROW'S FINAL ROUND OF QUALIFYING!

HOW'D I DO?

WONDERFUL, SPEED!

YOU'LL HAVE TO GO *FASTER* TO BEAT RACER X AND THE G.R.X-2!

WE'LL NEED MORE THAN THE EXTRA *PIT CREW* I'VE HIRED TO BEAT THOSE TWO!

59

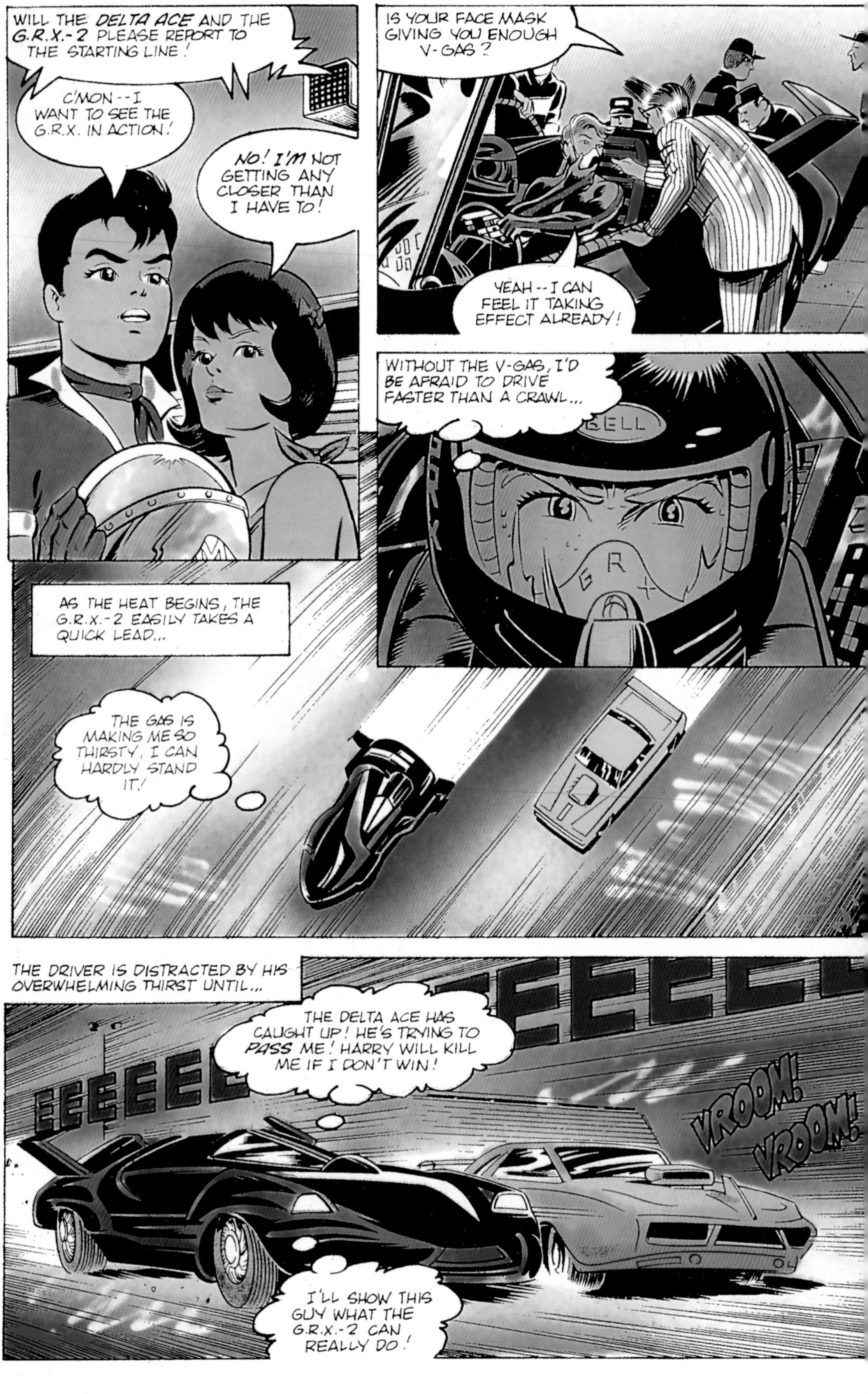

WILL THE DELTA ACE AND THE G.R.X.-2 PLEASE REPORT TO THE STARTING LINE!
C'MON--I WANT TO SEE THE G.R.X. IN ACTION!
NO! I'M NOT GETTING ANY CLOSER THAN I HAVE TO!
IS YOUR FACE MASK GIVING YOU ENOUGH V-GAS?
YEAH--I CAN FEEL IT TAKING EFFECT ALREADY!
WITHOUT THE V-GAS, I'D BE AFRAID TO DRIVE FASTER THAN A CRAWL...
BELL
G R X
AS THE HEAT BEGINS, THE G.R.X.-2 EASILY TAKES A QUICK LEAD...
THE GAS IS MAKING ME SO THIRSTY, I CAN HARDLY STAND IT!
THE DRIVER IS DISTRACTED BY HIS OVERWHELMING THIRST UNTIL...
THE DELTA ACE HAS CAUGHT UP! HE'S TRYING TO PASS ME! HARRY WILL KILL ME IF I DON'T WIN!
VROOM! VROOM!
I'LL SHOW THIS GUY WHAT THE G.R.X.-2 CAN REALLY DO!

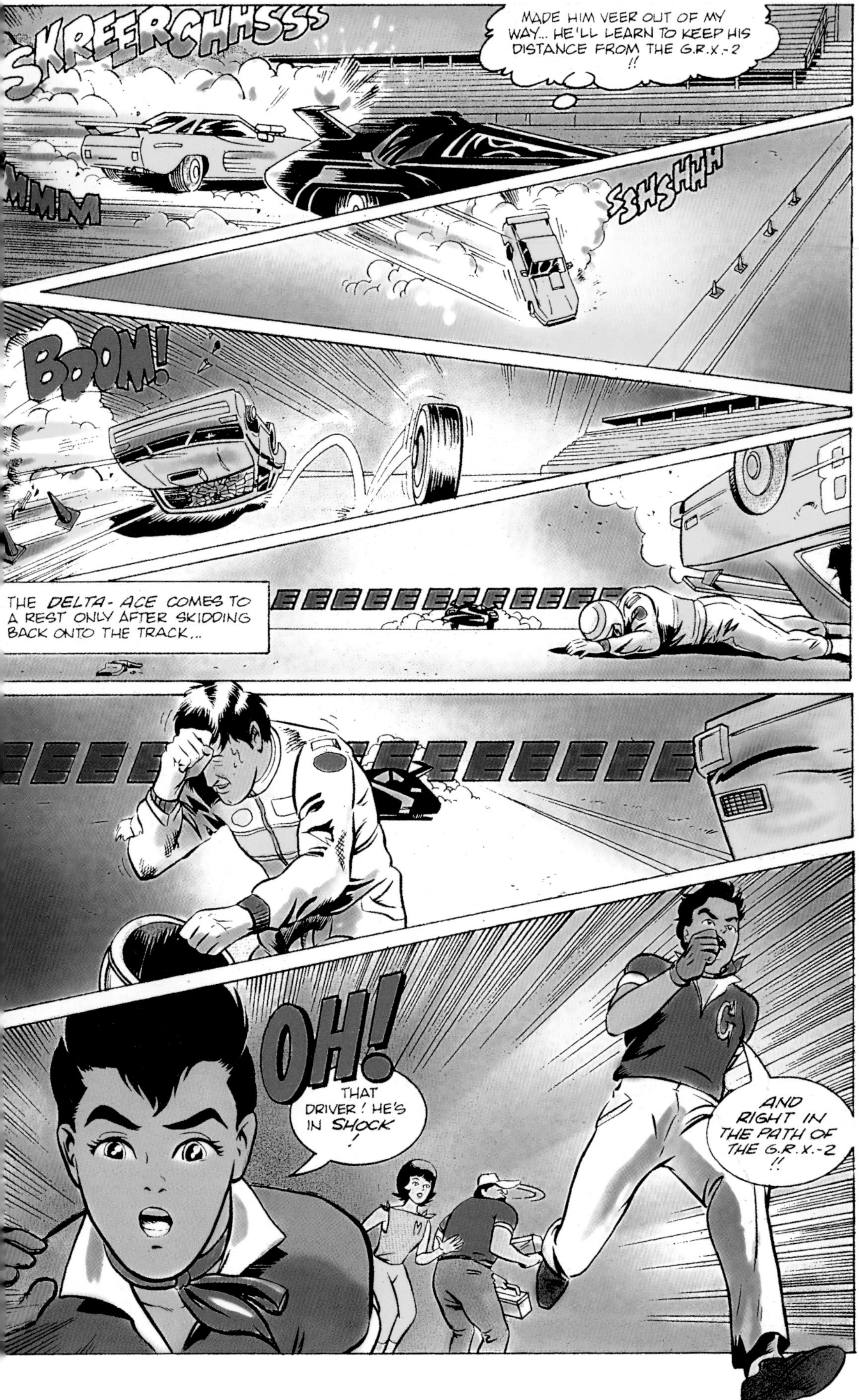
SKREERCHHSSS
MADE HIM VEER OUT OF MY WAY... HE'LL LEARN TO KEEP HIS DISTANCE FROM THE G.R.X.-2 !!
MMMM
SSHSHHH
BOOM!
THE DELTA-ACE COMES TO A REST ONLY AFTER SKIDDING BACK ONTO THE TRACK...
EEEEEEEEEEEE
EEEEEEEEEEEEEEEE
OH!
THAT DRIVER! HE'S IN SHOCK!
AND RIGHT IN THE PATH OF THE G.R.X.-2 !!

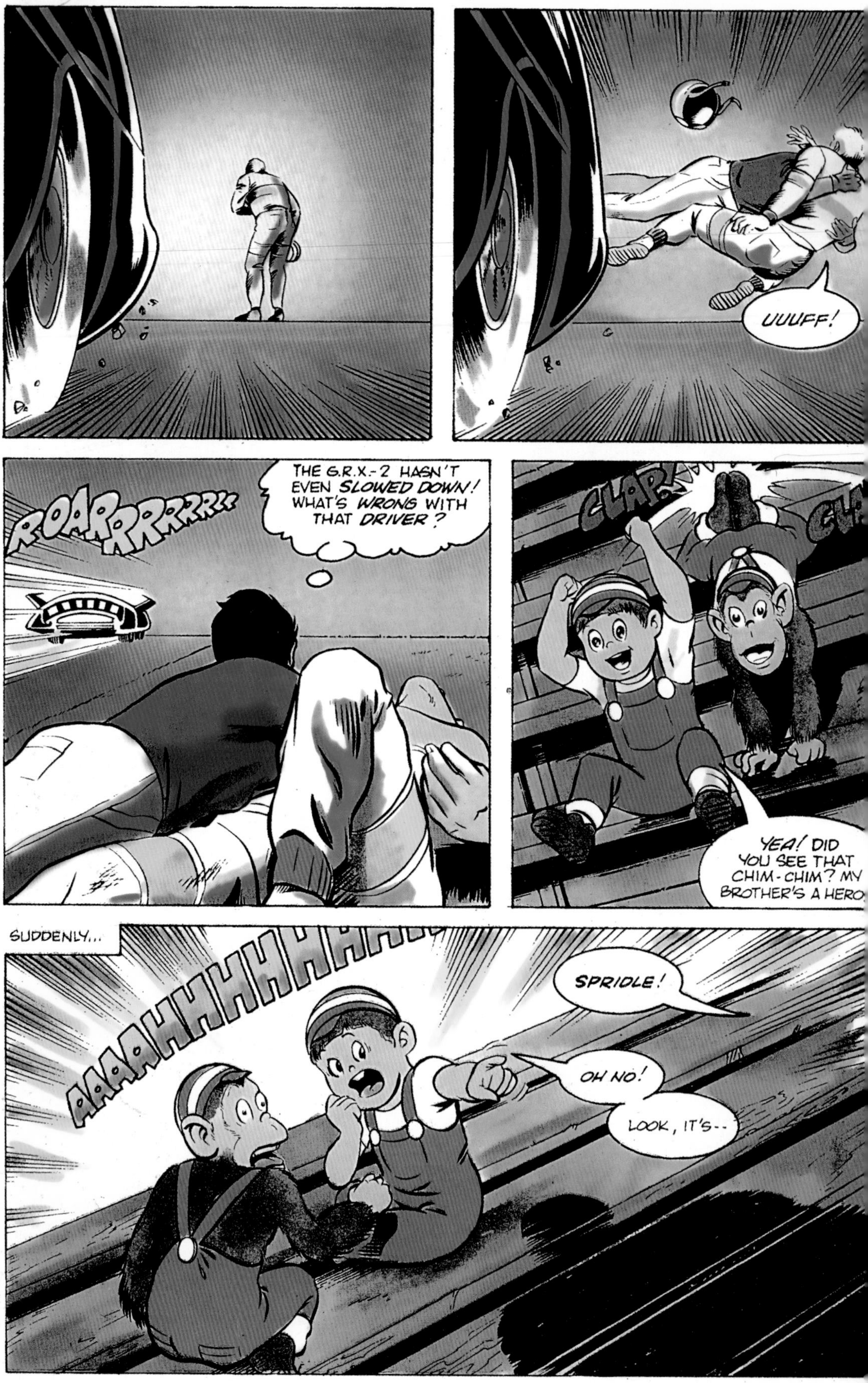
UUUFF!
ROARRRRRRR
THE G.R.X.-2 HASN'T EVEN SLOWED DOWN! WHAT'S WRONG WITH THAT DRIVER?
CLAP!
YEA! DID YOU SEE THAT CHIM-CHIM? MY BROTHER'S A HERO
SUDDENLY...
AAAAHHHHHHHHH
SPRIDLE!
OH NO!
LOOK, IT'S--

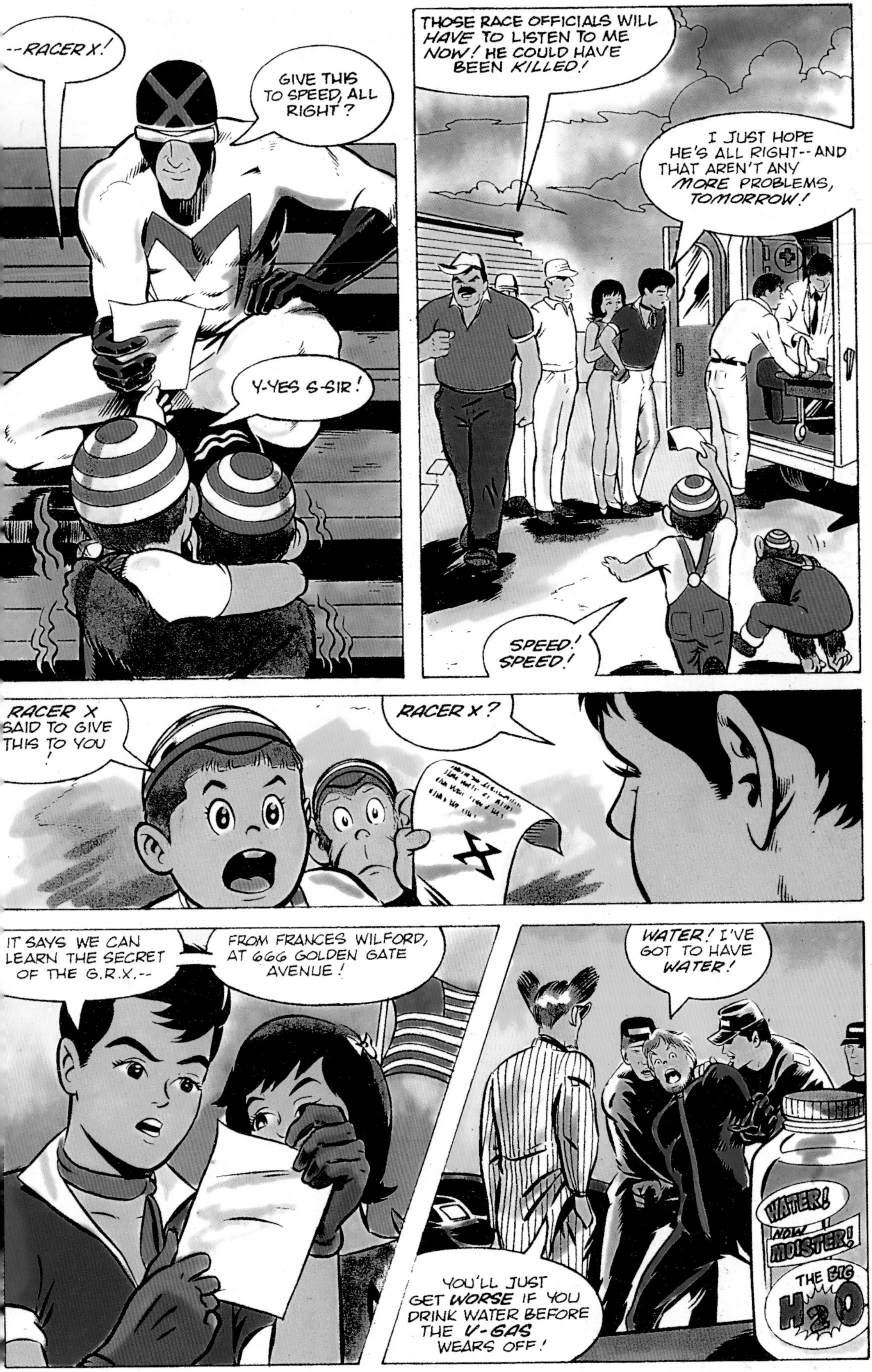
--RACER X!
GIVE THIS TO SPEED, ALL RIGHT?
Y-YES S-SIR!
THOSE RACE OFFICIALS WILL HAVE TO LISTEN TO ME NOW! HE COULD HAVE BEEN KILLED!
I JUST HOPE HE'S ALL RIGHT-- AND THAT AREN'T ANY MORE PROBLEMS, TOMORROW!
SPEED! SPEED!
RACER X SAID TO GIVE THIS TO YOU!
RACER X?
IT SAYS WE CAN LEARN THE SECRET OF THE G.R.X.--
FROM FRANCES WILFORD, AT 666 GOLDEN GATE AVENUE!
WATER! I'VE GOT TO HAVE WATER!
YOU'LL JUST GET WORSE IF YOU DRINK WATER BEFORE THE V-GAS WEARS OFF!
WATER!
NOW MOISTER!
THE BIG H2O

THAT EVENING,,,

NO ONE SEEMS TO BE HOME, SPEED.

LET'S WAIT A FEW MORE MINUTES! THIS HOUSE IS SO BIG, IT MIGHT TAKE THEM A WHILE TO ANSWER THE BELL!

QUIET, CHIM-CHIM!

I WISH THE CURTAINS WEREN'T CLOSED, SO WE COULD SEE INSIDE--

BUT AS THE CURTAINS PART...

BONK!

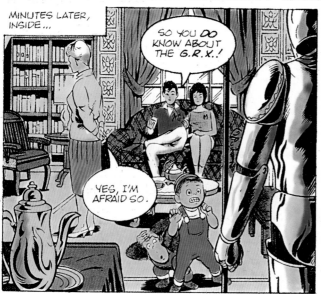

MINUTES LATER, INSIDE...

SO YOU DO KNOW ABOUT THE G.R.X.!

YES, I'M AFRAID SO.

IT ALL BEGAN YEARS AGO, WHEN MY SISTER FELL IN LOVE WITH A BRILLIANT AUTOMOTIVE ENGINEER NAMED BEN CRANIUM.

HOWEVER, BEN... FORGOT TO TELL HER THAT HE WAS ALREADY MARRIED!

64

WHEN MY SISTER FOUND OUT, BEN LEFT HER-- AND SHE DECIDED TO *KILL* HERSELF!

BUT FIRST, SHE *CURSED* BEN'S FAMILY *AND* HIS MOST PRIZED CREATION-- THE *G.R.X.*!

SO FAR, THE ENGINE HAS KILLED *BEN* AND HIS YOUNGEST *SON*! NOW, IT'S *HARRY'S* TURN-- AND *NOTHING* CAN SAVE HIM FROM MY SISTER'S *CURSE*!

THANK YOU FOR YOUR TIME. THAT'S A VERY INTERESTING STORY! BUT I'M TOO OLD TO BELIEVE IN WITCHES!

THAT'S WHAT *BEN* SAID-- THE LAST TIME I SAW HIM *ALIVE*.

STAY AWAY FROM THAT CURSED ENGINE, YOUNG MAN, ...

...OR YOU MAY FIND YOURSELF TRAPPED BY FORCES BEYOND YOUR CONTROL!

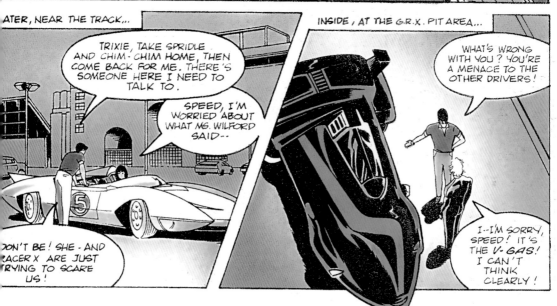

LATER, NEAR THE TRACK...

TRIXIE, TAKE SPRIDLE AND CHIM-CHIM HOME, THEN COME BACK FOR ME. THERE'S SOMEONE HERE I NEED TO TALK TO.

SPEED, I'M WORRIED ABOUT WHAT MS. WILFORD SAID--

DON'T BE! SHE - AND RACER X ARE JUST TRYING TO SCARE US!

INSIDE, AT THE G.R.X. PIT AREA...

WHAT'S WRONG WITH YOU? YOU'RE A MENACE TO THE OTHER DRIVERS!

I--I'M SORRY, SPEED! IT'S THE *V-GAS*! I CAN'T THINK CLEARLY!

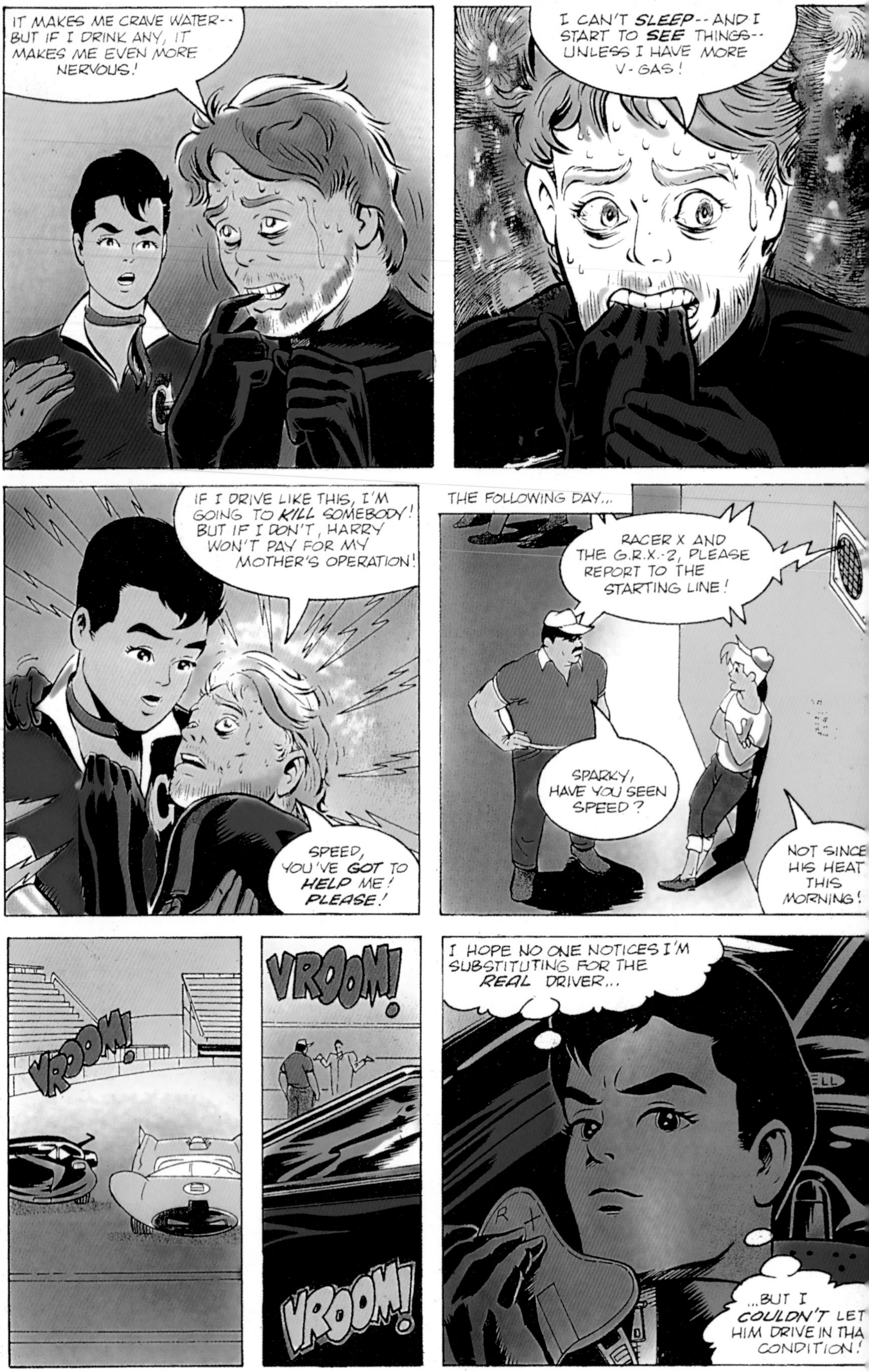

IT MAKES ME CRAVE WATER-- BUT IF I DRINK ANY, IT MAKES ME EVEN MORE NERVOUS!
I CAN'T SLEEP-- AND I START TO SEE THINGS-- UNLESS I HAVE MORE V-GAS!
IF I DRIVE LIKE THIS, I'M GOING TO KILL SOMEBODY! BUT IF I DON'T, HARRY WON'T PAY FOR MY MOTHER'S OPERATION!
SPEED, YOU'VE GOT TO HELP ME! PLEASE!
THE FOLLOWING DAY...
RACER X AND THE G.R.X.-2, PLEASE REPORT TO THE STARTING LINE!
SPARKY, HAVE YOU SEEN SPEED?
NOT SINCE HIS HEAT THIS MORNING!
VROOM!
VROOM!
VROOM!
I HOPE NO ONE NOTICES I'M SUBSTITUTING FOR THE REAL DRIVER...
...BUT I COULDN'T LET HIM DRIVE IN THA CONDITION!

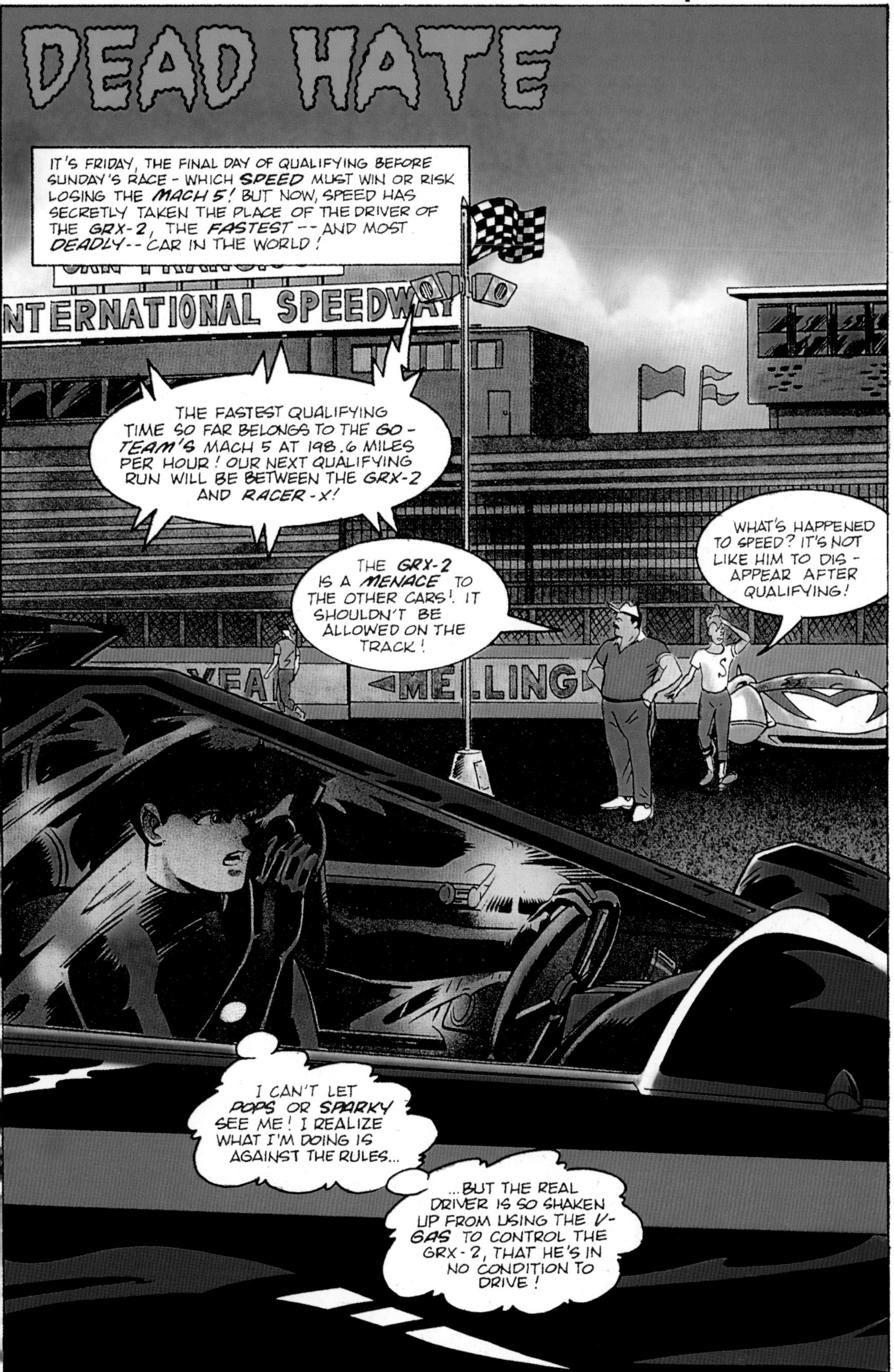
DEAD HATE
IT'S FRIDAY, THE FINAL DAY OF QUALIFYING BEFORE SUNDAY'S RACE - WHICH SPEED MUST WIN OR RISK LOSING THE MACH 5! BUT NOW, SPEED HAS SECRETLY TAKEN THE PLACE OF THE DRIVER OF THE GRX-2, THE FASTEST -- AND MOST DEADLY -- CAR IN THE WORLD!
NTERNATIONAL SPEEDWAY
THE FASTEST QUALIFYING TIME SO FAR BELONGS TO THE GO-TEAM'S MACH 5 AT 198.6 MILES PER HOUR! OUR NEXT QUALIFYING RUN WILL BE BETWEEN THE GRX-2 AND RACER-X!
THE GRX-2 IS A MENACE TO THE OTHER CARS! IT SHOULDN'T BE ALLOWED ON THE TRACK!
WHAT'S HAPPENED TO SPEED? IT'S NOT LIKE HIM TO DIS-APPEAR AFTER QUALIFYING!
I CAN'T LET POPS OR SPARKY SEE ME! I REALIZE WHAT I'M DOING IS AGAINST THE RULES...
...BUT THE REAL DRIVER IS SO SHAKEN UP FROM USING THE V-GAS TO CONTROL THE GRX-2, THAT HE'S IN NO CONDITION TO DRIVE!

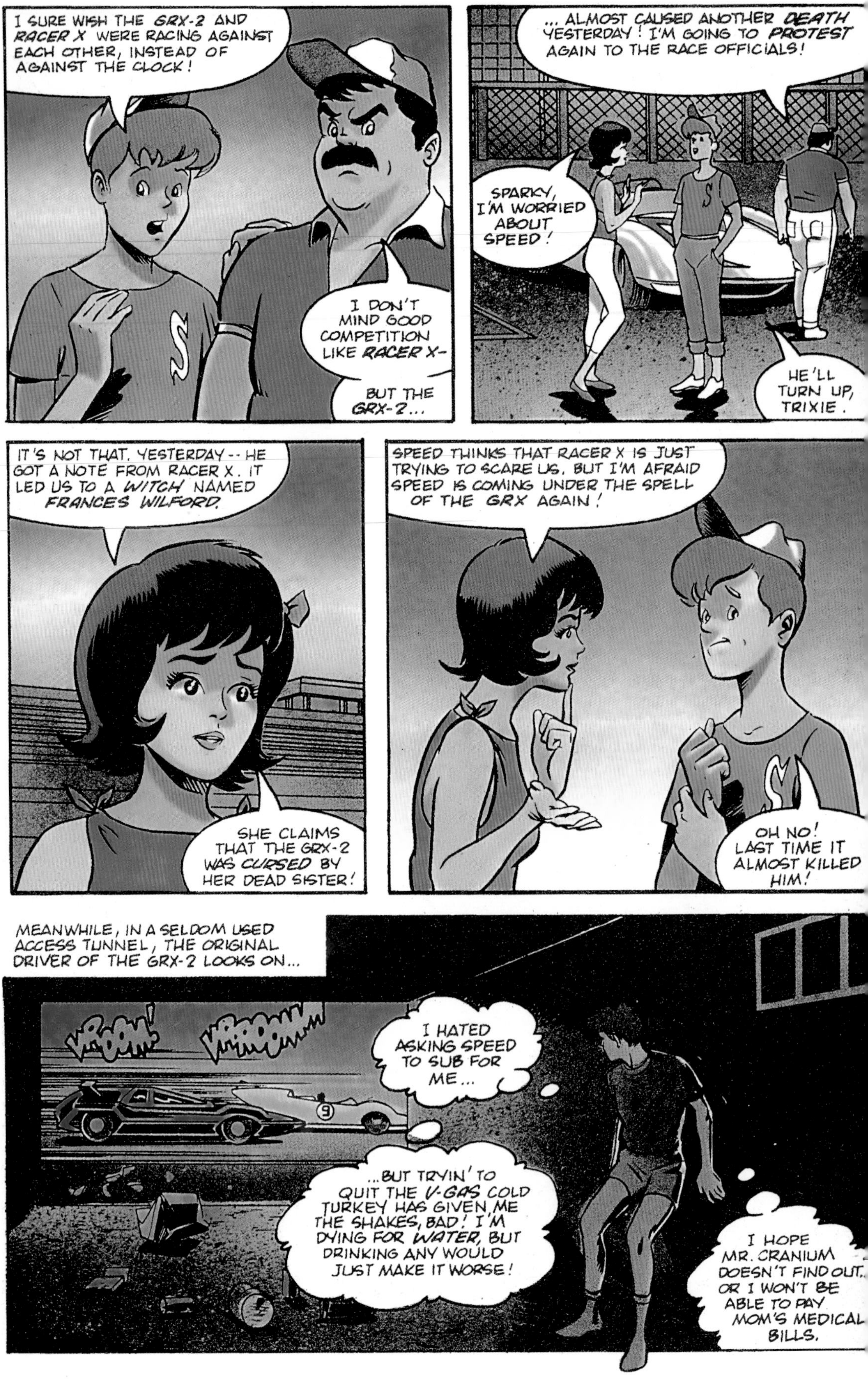

I SURE WISH THE GRX-2 AND RACER X WERE RACING AGAINST EACH OTHER, INSTEAD OF AGAINST THE CLOCK!
I DON'T MIND GOOD COMPETITION LIKE RACER X-
BUT THE GRX-2...
...ALMOST CAUSED ANOTHER DEATH YESTERDAY! I'M GOING TO PROTEST AGAIN TO THE RACE OFFICIALS!
SPARKY, I'M WORRIED ABOUT SPEED!
HE'LL TURN UP, TRIXIE.
IT'S NOT THAT. YESTERDAY-- HE GOT A NOTE FROM RACER X. IT LED US TO A WITCH NAMED FRANCES WILFORD.
SHE CLAIMS THAT THE GRX-2 WAS CURSED BY HER DEAD SISTER!
SPEED THINKS THAT RACER X IS JUST TRYING TO SCARE US, BUT I'M AFRAID SPEED IS COMING UNDER THE SPELL OF THE GRX AGAIN!
OH NO! LAST TIME IT ALMOST KILLED HIM!
MEANWHILE, IN A SELDOM USED ACCESS TUNNEL, THE ORIGINAL DRIVER OF THE GRX-2 LOOKS ON...
VROOM!
VRROOM
I HATED ASKING SPEED TO SUB FOR ME...
...BUT TRYIN' TO QUIT THE V-GAS COLD TURKEY HAS GIVEN ME THE SHAKES, BAD! I'M DYING FOR WATER, BUT DRINKING ANY WOULD JUST MAKE IT WORSE!
I HOPE MR. CRANIUM DOESN'T FIND OUT, OR I WON'T BE ABLE TO PAY MOM'S MEDICAL BILLS.

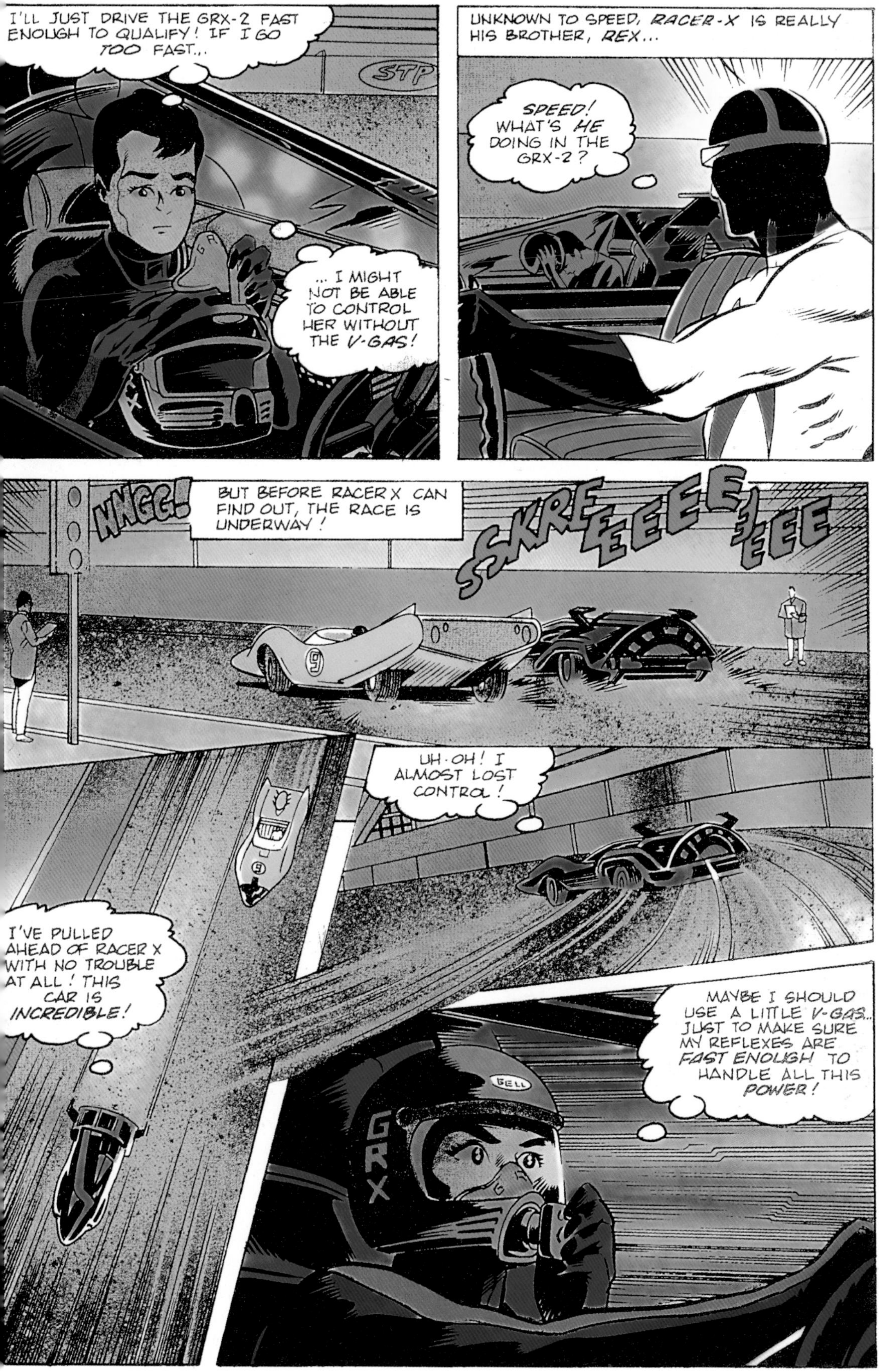

I'LL JUST DRIVE THE GRX-2 FAST ENOUGH TO QUALIFY! IF I GO TOO FAST...
... I MIGHT NOT BE ABLE TO CONTROL HER WITHOUT THE V-GAS!
UNKNOWN TO SPEED, RACER-X IS REALLY HIS BROTHER, REX...
SPEED! WHAT'S HE DOING IN THE GRX-2?
NNGG!
BUT BEFORE RACER X CAN FIND OUT, THE RACE IS UNDERWAY!
SSKREEEEEEEEEEE
UH-OH! I ALMOST LOST CONTROL!
I'VE PULLED AHEAD OF RACER X WITH NO TROUBLE AT ALL! THIS CAR IS INCREDIBLE!
MAYBE I SHOULD USE A LITTLE V-GAS... JUST TO MAKE SURE MY REFLEXES ARE FAST ENOUGH TO HANDLE ALL THIS POWER!

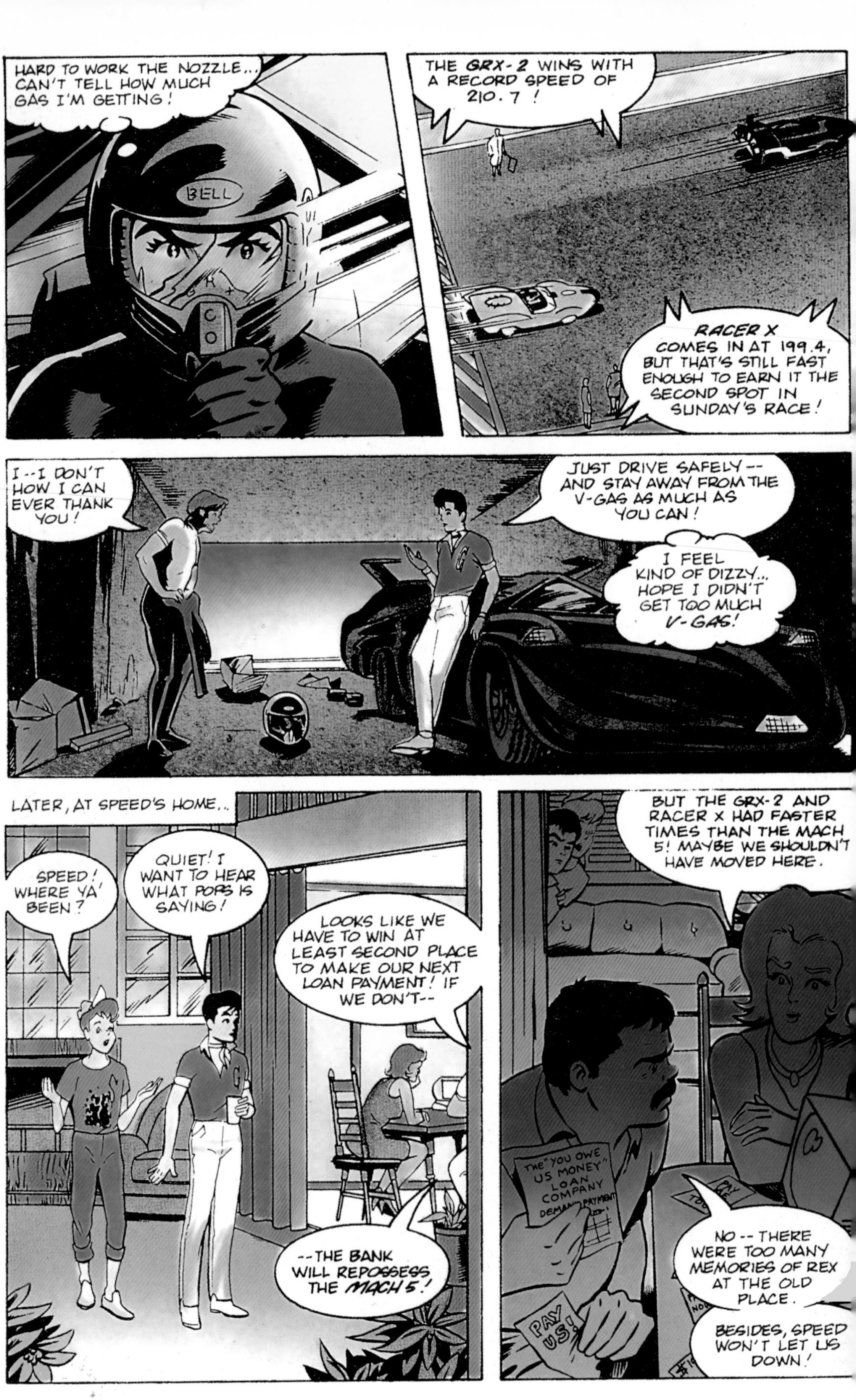

HARD TO WORK THE NOZZLE... CAN'T TELL HOW MUCH GAS I'M GETTING!
BELL
THE GRX-2 WINS WITH A RECORD SPEED OF 210.7!
RACER X COMES IN AT 199.4, BUT THAT'S STILL FAST ENOUGH TO EARN IT THE SECOND SPOT IN SUNDAY'S RACE!
I--I DON'T HOW I CAN EVER THANK YOU!
JUST DRIVE SAFELY--AND STAY AWAY FROM THE V-GAS AS MUCH AS YOU CAN!
I FEEL KIND OF DIZZY... HOPE I DIDN'T GET TOO MUCH V-GAS!
LATER, AT SPEED'S HOME...
SPEED! WHERE YA' BEEN?
QUIET! I WANT TO HEAR WHAT POPS IS SAYING!
LOOKS LIKE WE HAVE TO WIN AT LEAST SECOND PLACE TO MAKE OUR NEXT LOAN PAYMENT! IF WE DON'T--
--THE BANK WILL REPOSSESS THE MACH 5!
BUT THE GRX-2 AND RACER X HAD FASTER TIMES THAN THE MACH 5! MAYBE WE SHOULDN'T HAVE MOVED HERE.
THE "YOU OWE US MONEY" LOAN COMPANY
PAY US!
NO--THERE WERE TOO MANY MEMORIES OF REX AT THE OLD PLACE.
BESIDES, SPEED WON'T LET US DOWN!

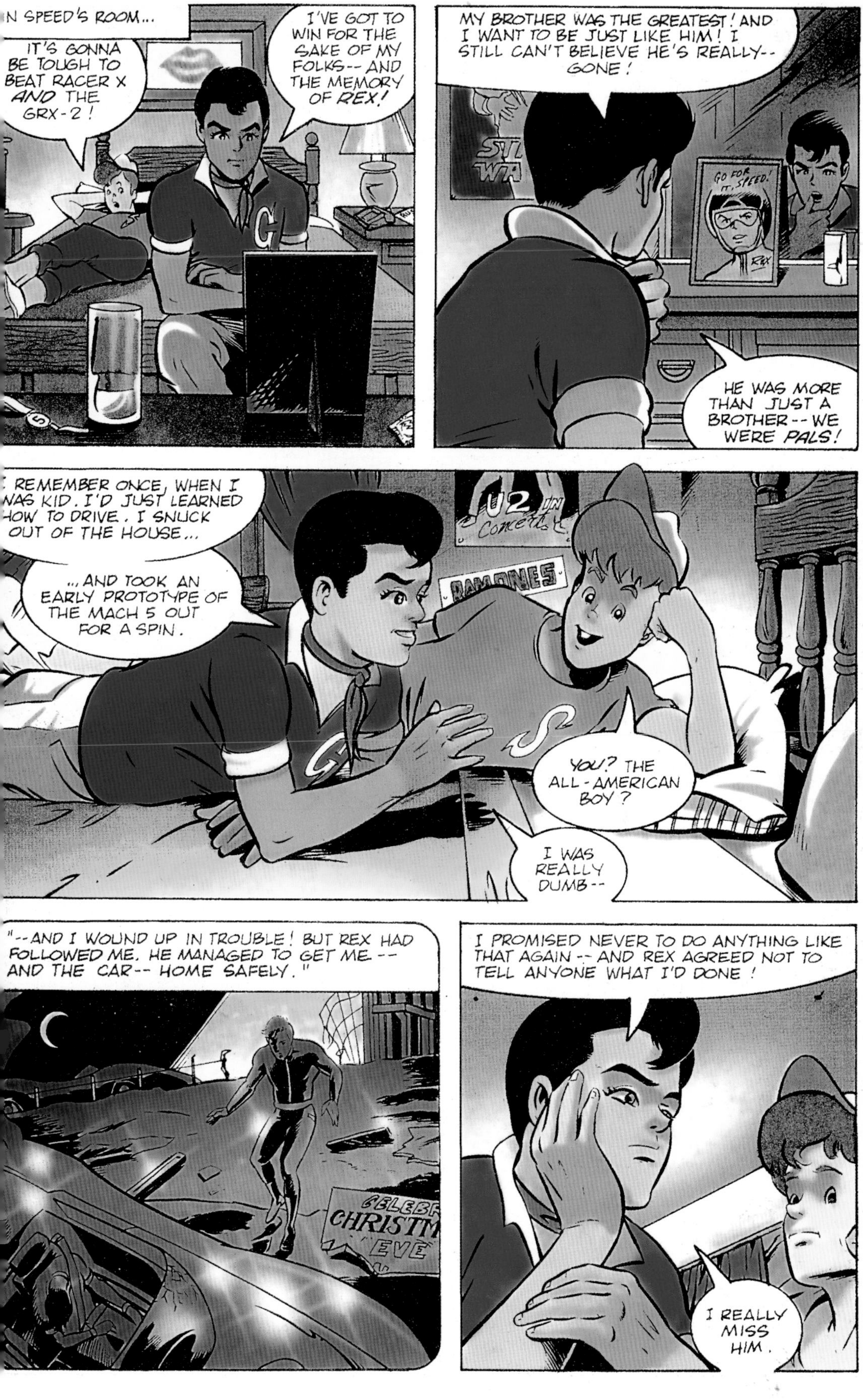

N SPEED'S ROOM...
IT'S GONNA BE TOUGH TO BEAT RACER X AND THE GRX-2!
I'VE GOT TO WIN FOR THE SAKE OF MY FOLKS-- AND THE MEMORY OF REX!
MY BROTHER WAS THE GREATEST! AND I WANT TO BE JUST LIKE HIM! I STILL CAN'T BELIEVE HE'S REALLY-- GONE!
GO FOR IT, SPEED!
REX
HE WAS MORE THAN JUST A BROTHER-- WE WERE PALS!
REMEMBER ONCE, WHEN I WAS KID. I'D JUST LEARNED HOW TO DRIVE. I SNUCK OUT OF THE HOUSE...
...AND TOOK AN EARLY PROTOTYPE OF THE MACH 5 OUT FOR A SPIN.
U2 IN Concert
RAMONES
YOU? THE ALL-AMERICAN BOY?
I WAS REALLY DUMB--
"--AND I WOUND UP IN TROUBLE! BUT REX HAD FOLLOWED ME. HE MANAGED TO GET ME-- AND THE CAR-- HOME SAFELY."
CHRISTM EVE
I PROMISED NEVER TO DO ANYTHING LIKE THAT AGAIN -- AND REX AGREED NOT TO TELL ANYONE WHAT I'D DONE!
I REALLY MISS HIM.

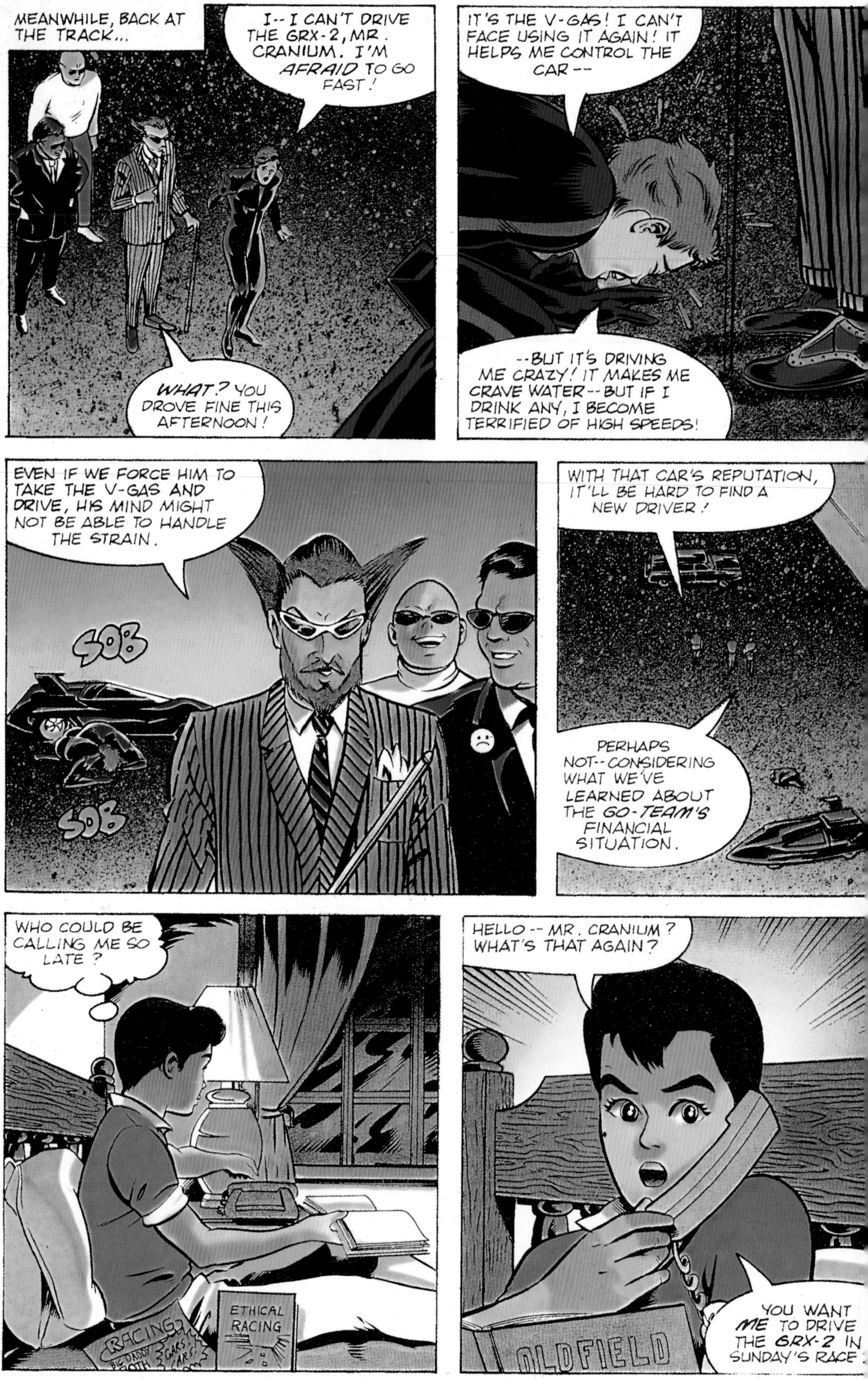
MEANWHILE, BACK AT THE TRACK...
I-- I CAN'T DRIVE THE GRX-2, MR. CRANIUM. I'M AFRAID TO GO FAST!
WHAT? YOU DROVE FINE THIS AFTERNOON!
IT'S THE V-GAS! I CAN'T FACE USING IT AGAIN! IT HELPS ME CONTROL THE CAR --
--BUT IT'S DRIVING ME CRAZY! IT MAKES ME CRAVE WATER--BUT IF I DRINK ANY, I BECOME TERRIFIED OF HIGH SPEEDS!
EVEN IF WE FORCE HIM TO TAKE THE V-GAS AND DRIVE, HIS MIND MIGHT NOT BE ABLE TO HANDLE THE STRAIN.
SOB
SOB
WITH THAT CAR'S REPUTATION, IT'LL BE HARD TO FIND A NEW DRIVER!
PERHAPS NOT--CONSIDERING WHAT WE'VE LEARNED ABOUT THE GO-TEAM'S FINANCIAL SITUATION.
WHO COULD BE CALLING ME SO LATE?
ETHICAL RACING
RACING
HELLO -- MR. CRANIUM? WHAT'S THAT AGAIN?
OLDFIELD
YOU WANT ME TO DRIVE THE GRX-2 IN SUNDAY'S RACE?

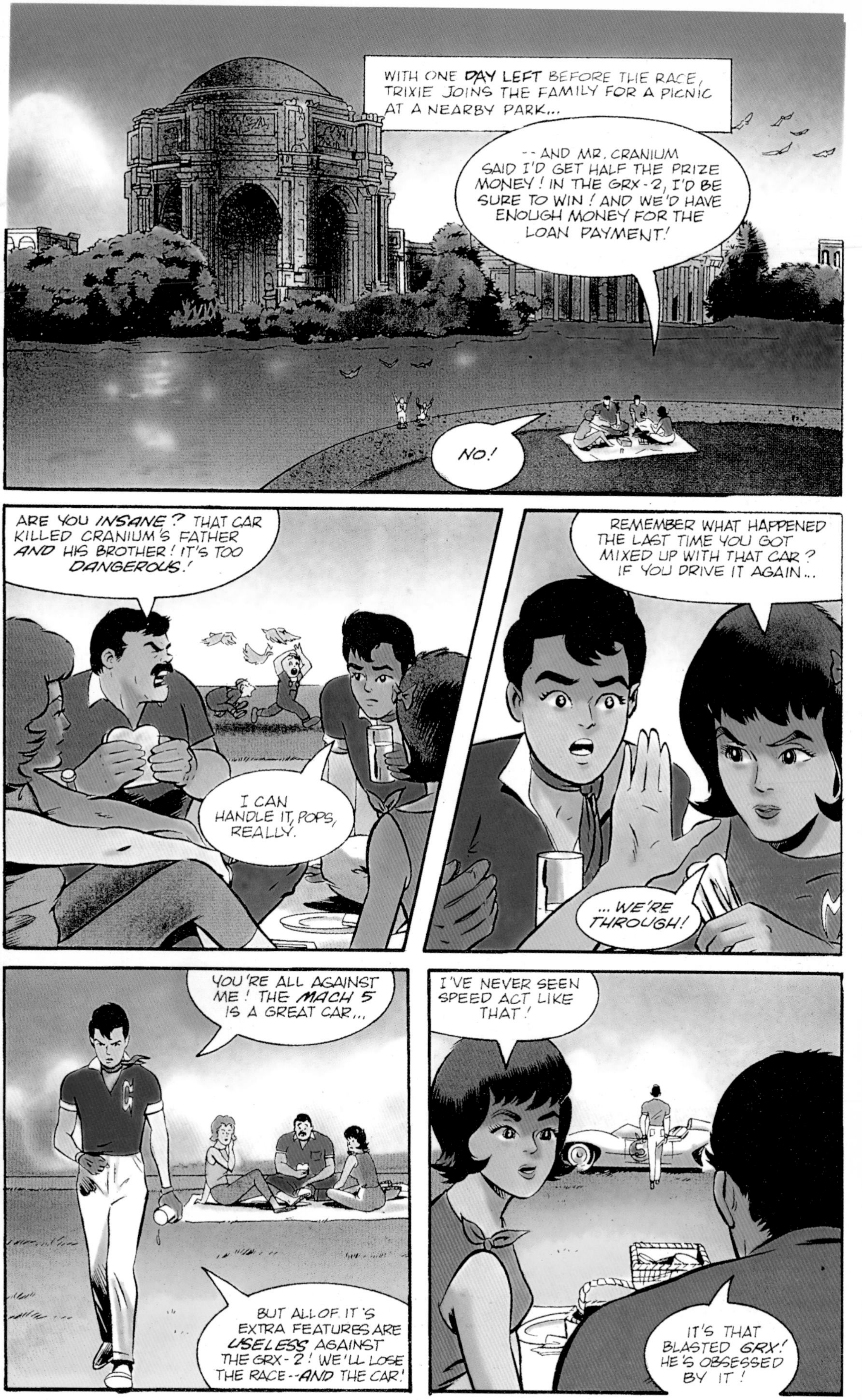

WITH ONE DAY LEFT BEFORE THE RACE, TRIXIE JOINS THE FAMILY FOR A PICNIC AT A NEARBY PARK...
-- AND MR. CRANIUM SAID I'D GET HALF THE PRIZE MONEY! IN THE GRX-2, I'D BE SURE TO WIN! AND WE'D HAVE ENOUGH MONEY FOR THE LOAN PAYMENT!
NO!
ARE YOU INSANE? THAT CAR KILLED CRANIUM'S FATHER AND HIS BROTHER! IT'S TOO DANGEROUS!
I CAN HANDLE IT, POPS, REALLY.
REMEMBER WHAT HAPPENED THE LAST TIME YOU GOT MIXED UP WITH THAT CAR? IF YOU DRIVE IT AGAIN...
...WE'RE THROUGH!
YOU'RE ALL AGAINST ME! THE MACH 5 IS A GREAT CAR...
BUT ALL OF IT'S EXTRA FEATURES ARE USELESS AGAINST THE GRX-2! WE'LL LOSE THE RACE--AND THE CAR!
I'VE NEVER SEEN SPEED ACT LIKE THAT!
IT'S THAT BLASTED GRX! HE'S OBSESSED BY IT!

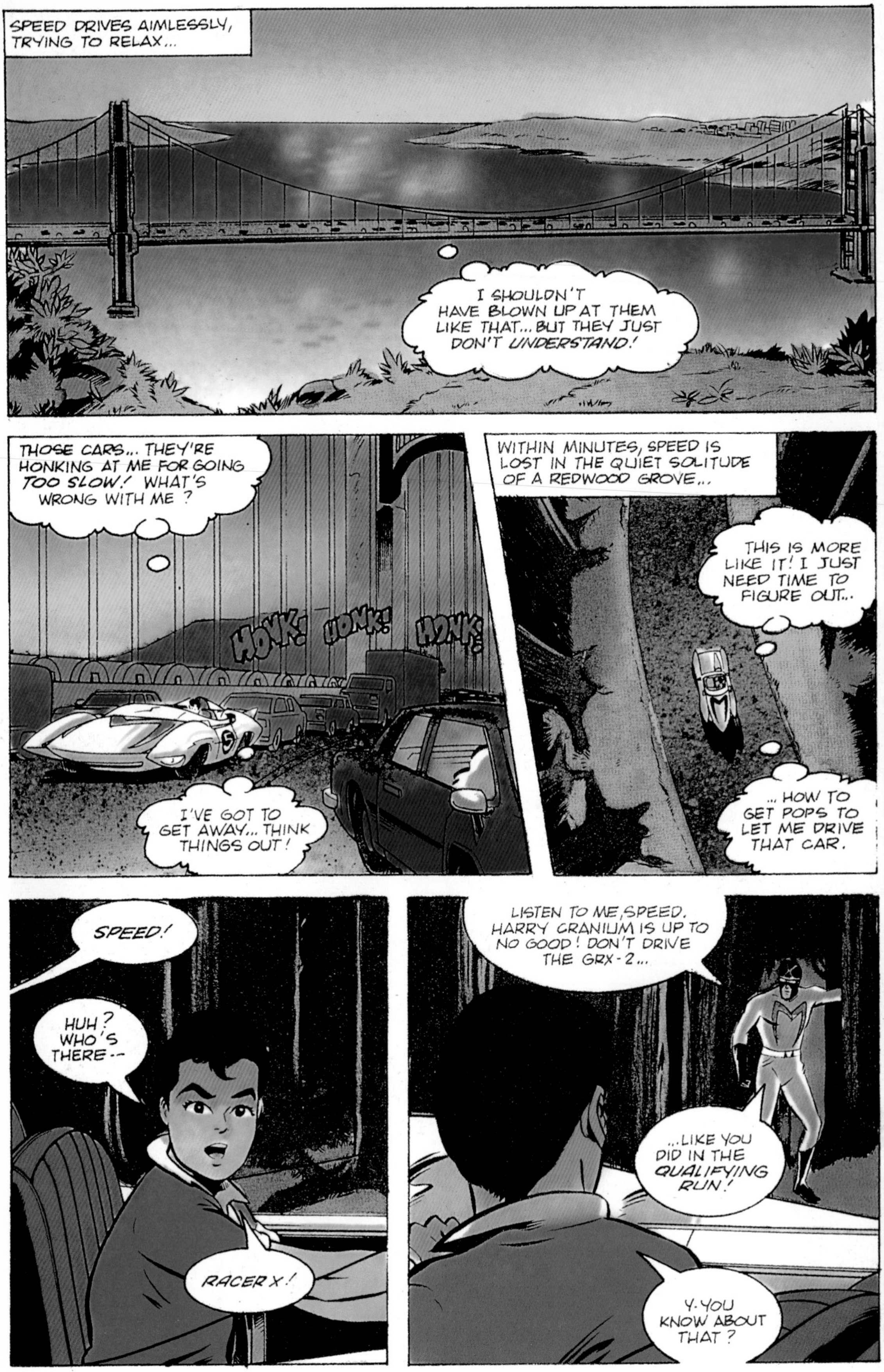
SPEED DRIVES AIMLESSLY, TRYING TO RELAX...
I SHOULDN'T HAVE BLOWN UP AT THEM LIKE THAT... BUT THEY JUST DON'T *UNDERSTAND!*
THOSE CARS... THEY'RE HONKING AT ME FOR GOING *TOO SLOW!* WHAT'S WRONG WITH ME ?
HONK! HONK! HONK!
I'VE GOT TO GET AWAY... THINK THINGS OUT!
WITHIN MINUTES, SPEED IS LOST IN THE QUIET SOLITUDE OF A REDWOOD GROVE...
THIS IS MORE LIKE IT! I JUST NEED TIME TO FIGURE OUT...
... HOW TO GET POPS TO LET ME DRIVE THAT CAR.
SPEED!
HUH? WHO'S THERE--
RACER X!
LISTEN TO ME, SPEED. HARRY CRANIUM IS UP TO NO GOOD! DON'T DRIVE THE GRX-2...
...LIKE YOU DID IN THE *QUALIFYING RUN!*
Y-YOU KNOW ABOUT THAT?

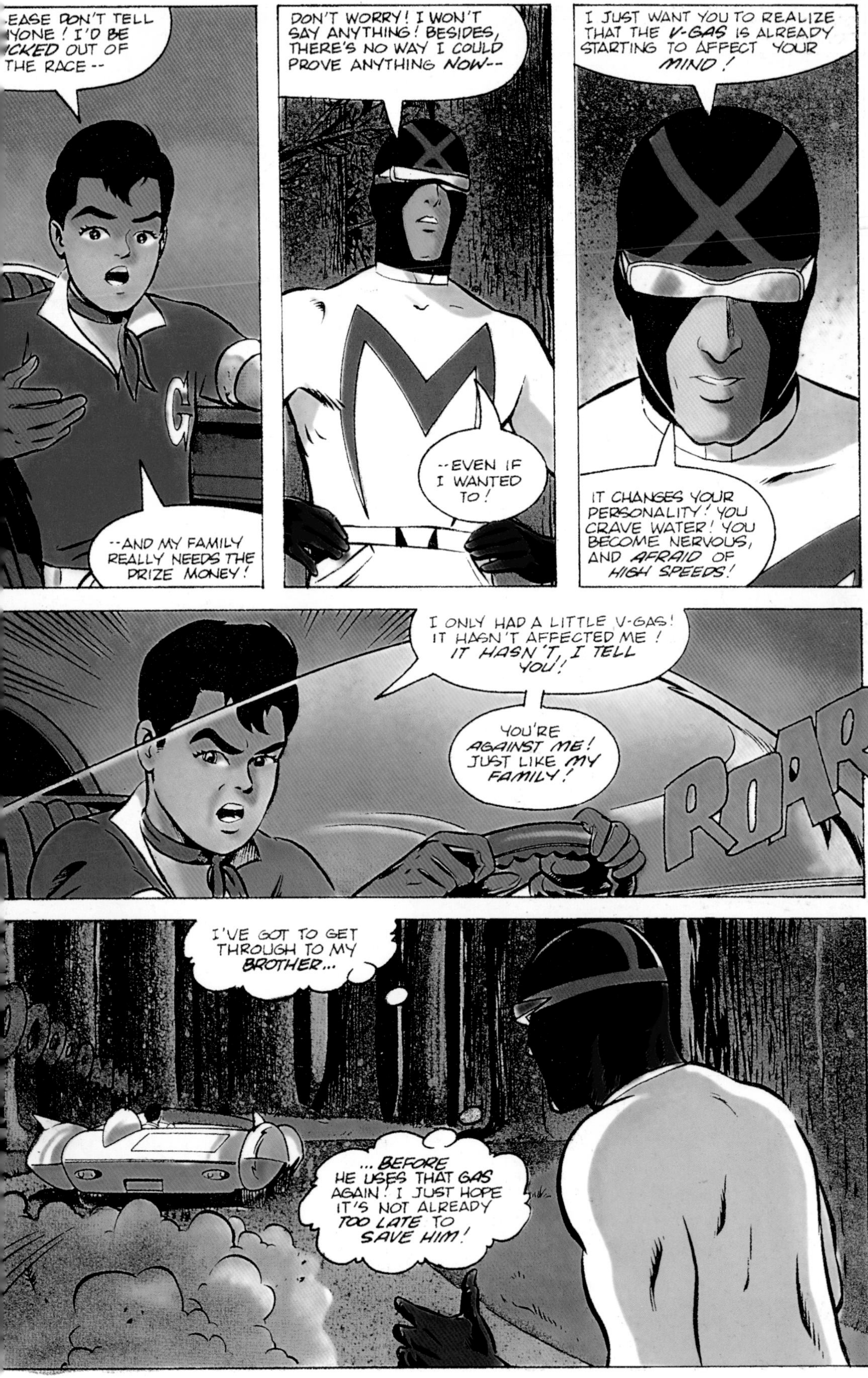

-EASE DON'T TELL
NYONE! I'D BE
ICKED OUT OF
THE RACE--
--AND MY FAMILY REALLY NEEDS THE PRIZE MONEY!
DON'T WORRY! I WON'T SAY ANYTHING! BESIDES, THERE'S NO WAY I COULD PROVE ANYTHING NOW--
--EVEN IF I WANTED TO!
I JUST WANT YOU TO REALIZE THAT THE V-GAS IS ALREADY STARTING TO AFFECT YOUR MIND!
IT CHANGES YOUR PERSONALITY! YOU CRAVE WATER! YOU BECOME NERVOUS, AND AFRAID OF HIGH SPEEDS!
I ONLY HAD A LITTLE V-GAS! IT HASN'T AFFECTED ME! IT HASN'T, I TELL YOU!
YOU'RE AGAINST ME! JUST LIKE MY FAMILY!
ROAR!
I'VE GOT TO GET THROUGH TO MY BROTHER...
...BEFORE HE USES THAT GAS AGAIN! I JUST HOPE IT'S NOT ALREADY TOO LATE TO SAVE HIM!

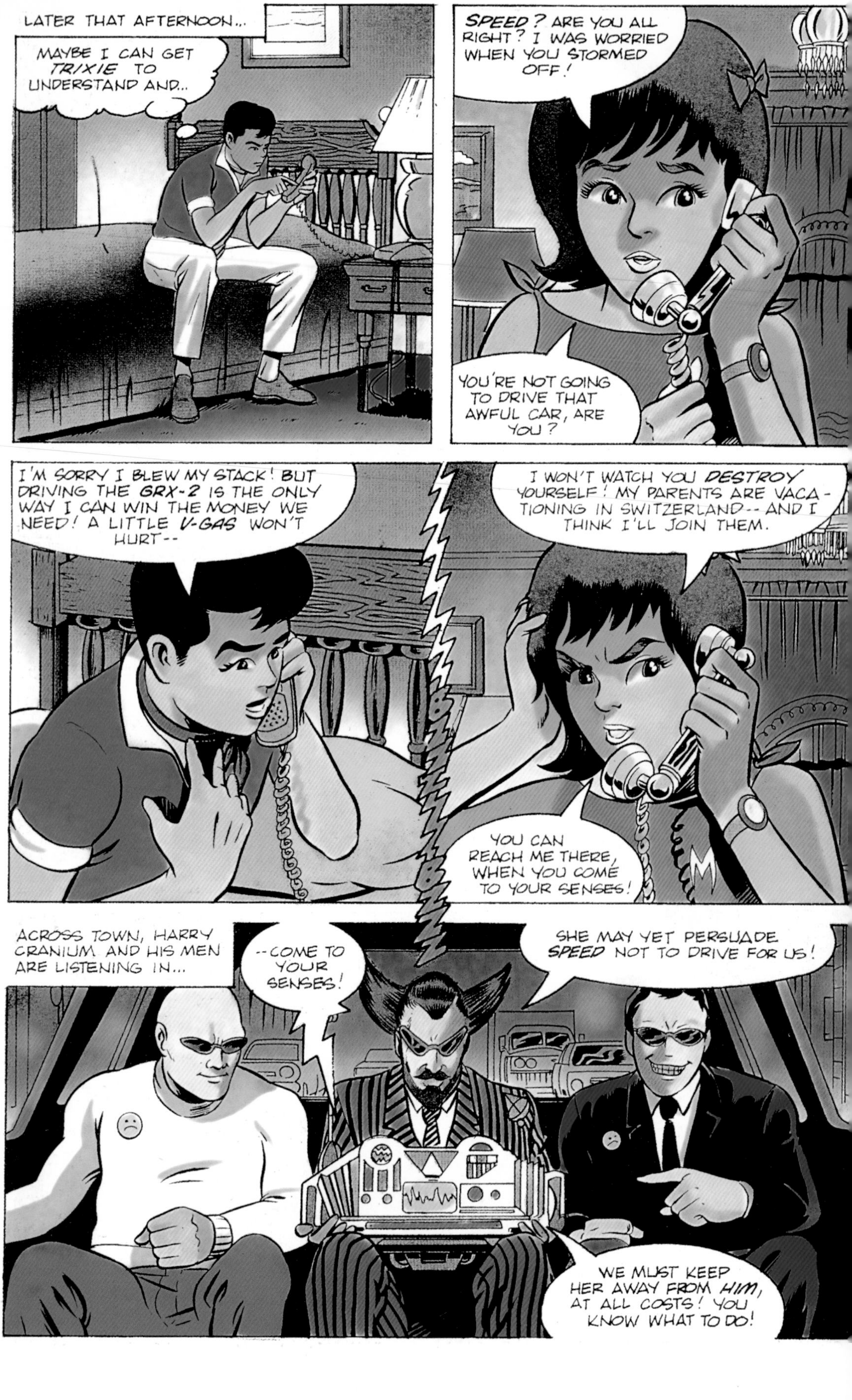
LATER THAT AFTERNOON...
MAYBE I CAN GET TRIXIE TO UNDERSTAND AND...
SPEED? ARE YOU ALL RIGHT? I WAS WORRIED WHEN YOU STORMED OFF!
YOU'RE NOT GOING TO DRIVE THAT AWFUL CAR, ARE YOU?
I'M SORRY I BLEW MY STACK! BUT DRIVING THE GRX-2 IS THE ONLY WAY I CAN WIN THE MONEY WE NEED! A LITTLE V-GAS WON'T HURT--
I WON'T WATCH YOU DESTROY YOURSELF! MY PARENTS ARE VACA-TIONING IN SWITZERLAND-- AND I THINK I'LL JOIN THEM.
YOU CAN REACH ME THERE, WHEN YOU COME TO YOUR SENSES!
ACROSS TOWN, HARRY CRANIUM AND HIS MEN ARE LISTENING IN...
--COME TO YOUR SENSES!
SHE MAY YET PERSUADE SPEED NOT TO DRIVE FOR US!
WE MUST KEEP HER AWAY FROM HIM, AT ALL COSTS! YOU KNOW WHAT TO DO!

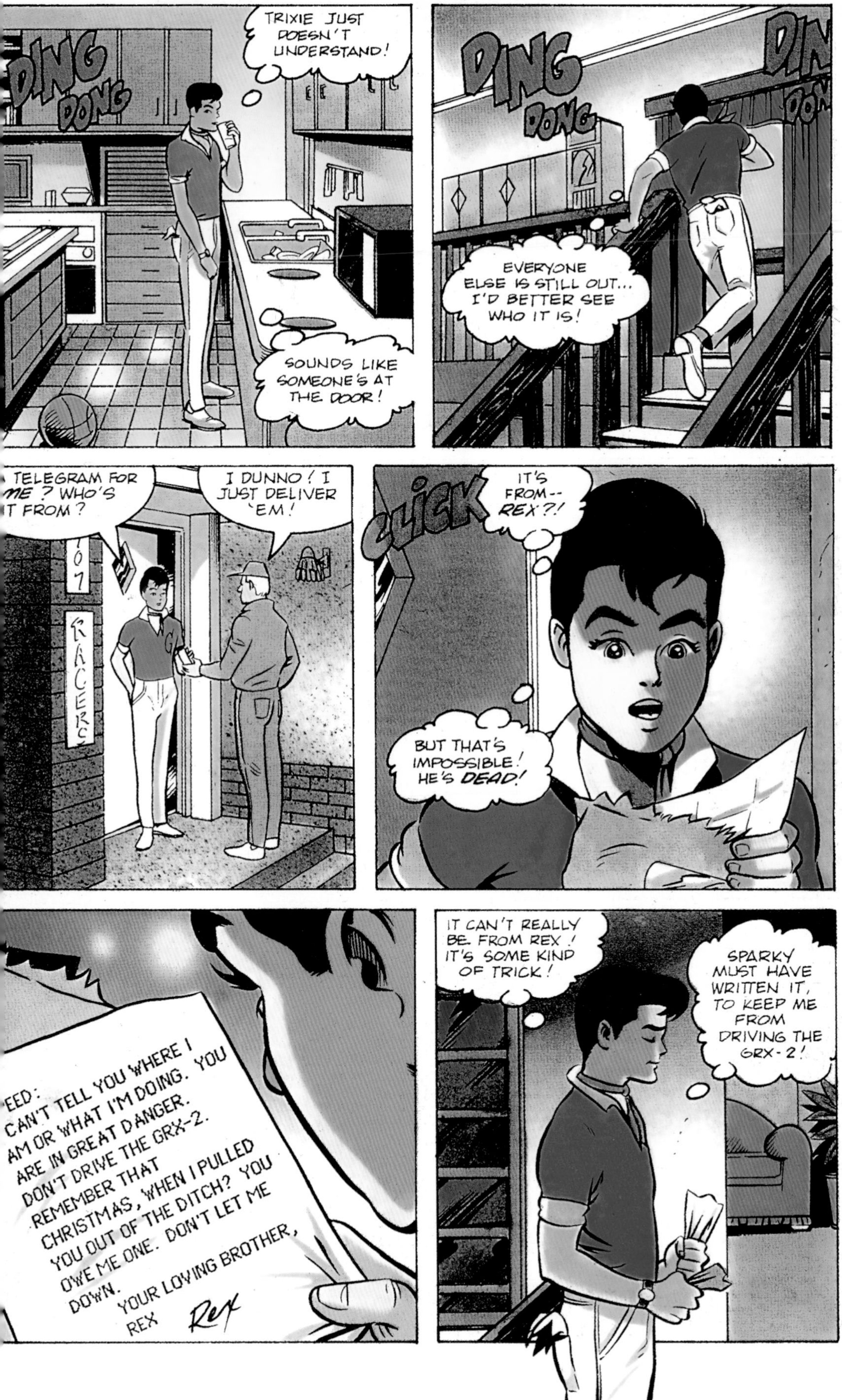
DING DONG
TRIXIE JUST DOESN'T UNDERSTAND!
SOUNDS LIKE SOMEONE'S AT THE DOOR!
DING DONG
DING DONG
EVERYONE ELSE IS STILL OUT... I'D BETTER SEE WHO IT IS!
TELEGRAM FOR ME? WHO'S IT FROM?
I DUNNO! I JUST DELIVER 'EM!
RACERS
CLICK
IT'S FROM-- REX?!
BUT THAT'S IMPOSSIBLE! HE'S DEAD!
EED:
CAN'T TELL YOU WHERE I
AM OR WHAT I'M DOING. YOU
ARE IN GREAT DANGER.
DON'T DRIVE THE GRX-2.
REMEMBER THAT
CHRISTMAS, WHEN I PULLED
YOU OUT OF THE DITCH? YOU
OWE ME ONE. DON'T LET ME
DOWN.
YOUR LOVING BROTHER,
REX Rex
IT CAN'T REALLY BE FROM REX! IT'S SOME KIND OF TRICK!
SPARKY MUST HAVE WRITTEN IT, TO KEEP ME FROM DRIVING THE GRX-2!

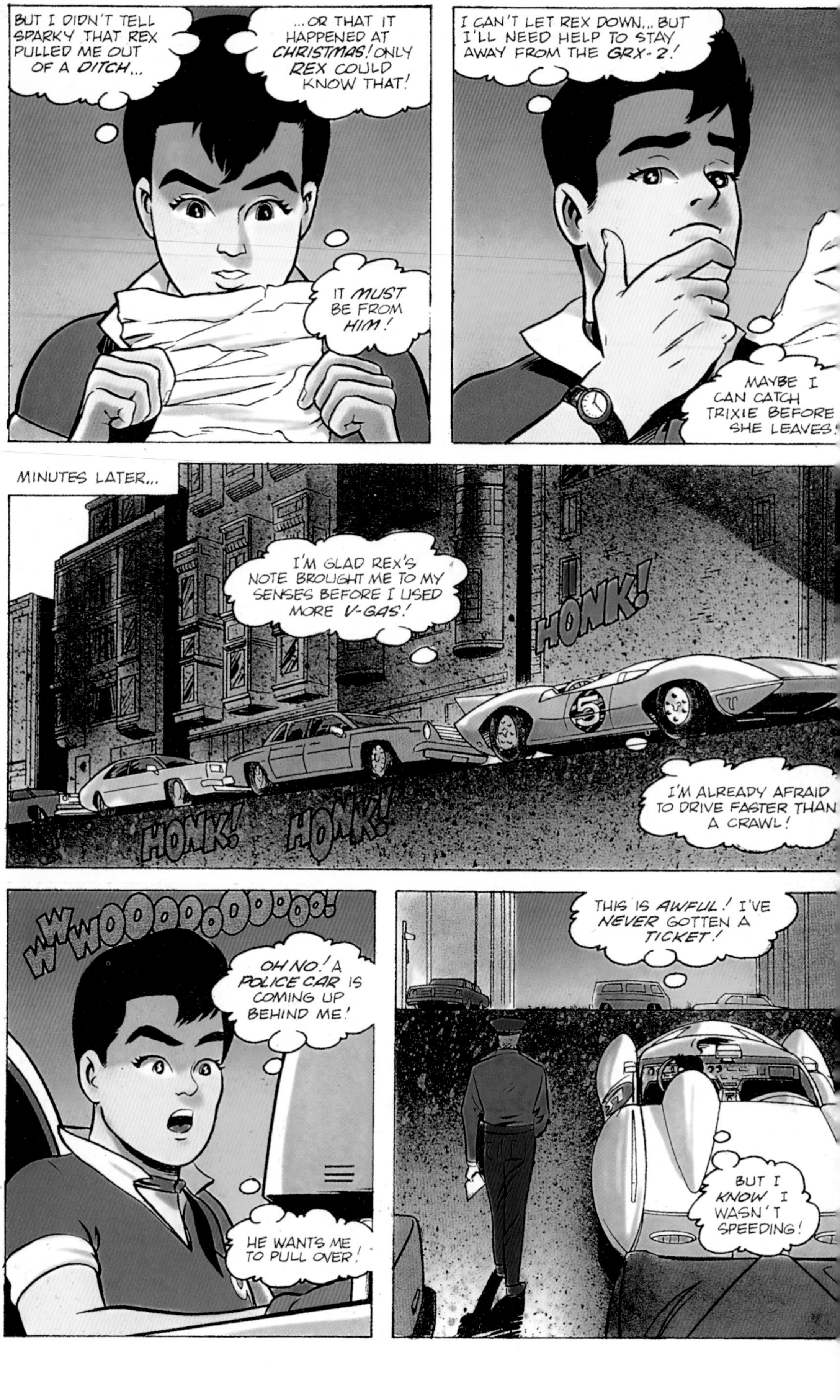

BUT I DIDN'T TELL SPARKY THAT REX PULLED ME OUT OF A *DITCH*...
...OR THAT IT HAPPENED AT *CHRISTMAS*! ONLY *REX* COULD KNOW THAT!
IT *MUST* BE FROM *HIM*!
I CAN'T LET REX DOWN... BUT I'LL NEED HELP TO STAY AWAY FROM THE *GRX-2*!
MAYBE I CAN CATCH TRIXIE BEFORE SHE LEAVES!
MINUTES LATER...
I'M GLAD REX'S NOTE BROUGHT ME TO MY SENSES BEFORE I USED MORE *V-GAS*!
HONK!
I'M ALREADY AFRAID TO DRIVE FASTER THAN A CRAWL!
HONK!
HONK!
WWWOOOOOOOOOOO!
OH NO! A *POLICE CAR* IS COMING UP BEHIND ME!
HE WANTS ME TO PULL OVER!
THIS IS *AWFUL*! I'VE *NEVER* GOTTEN A *TICKET*!
BUT I *KNOW* I WASN'T SPEEDING!

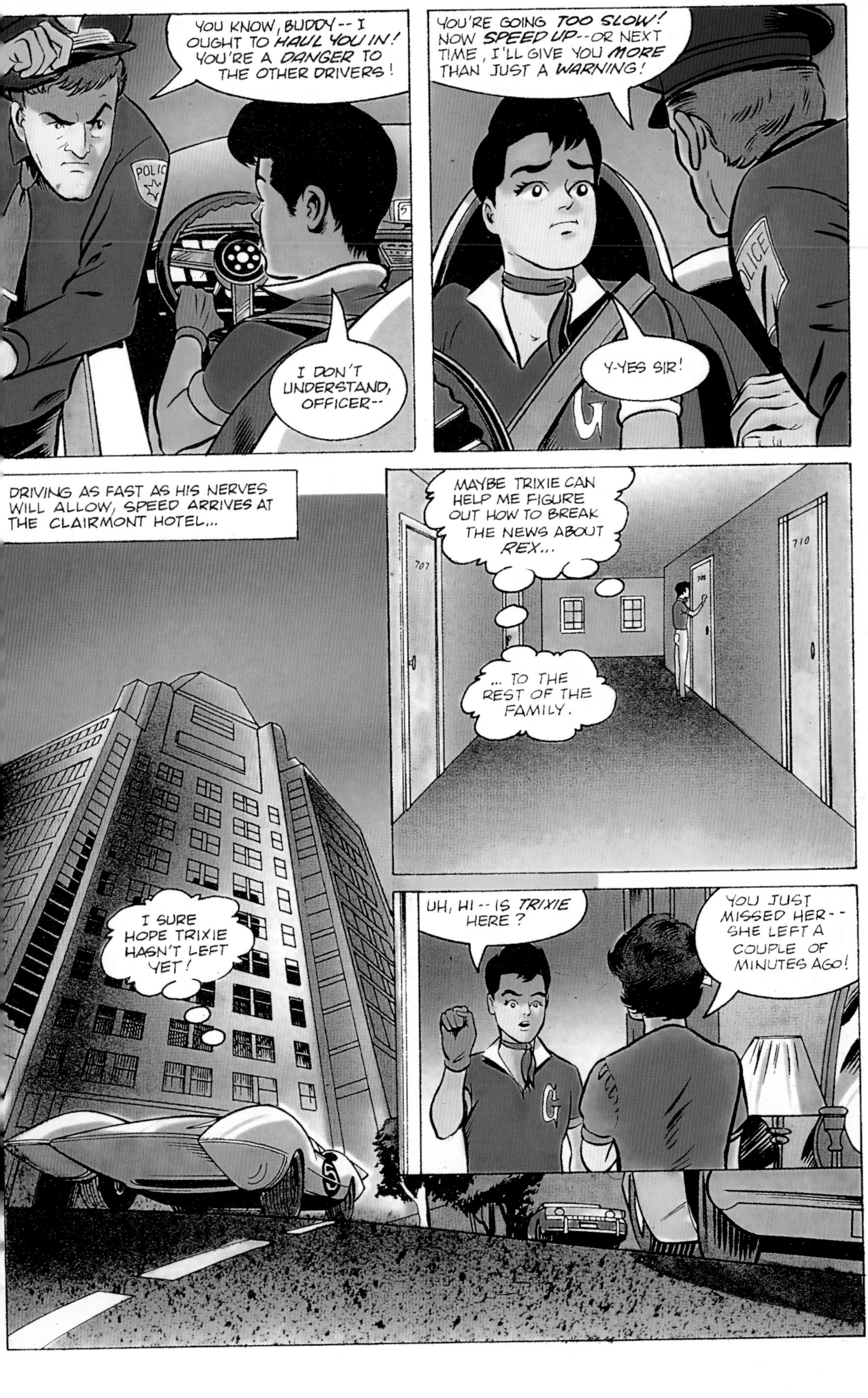
YOU KNOW, BUDDY -- I OUGHT TO HAUL YOU IN! YOU'RE A DANGER TO THE OTHER DRIVERS!
I DON'T UNDERSTAND, OFFICER--
YOU'RE GOING TOO SLOW! NOW SPEED UP--OR NEXT TIME, I'LL GIVE YOU MORE THAN JUST A WARNING!
Y-YES SIR!
DRIVING AS FAST AS HIS NERVES WILL ALLOW, SPEED ARRIVES AT THE CLAIRMONT HOTEL...
I SURE HOPE TRIXIE HASN'T LEFT YET!
MAYBE TRIXIE CAN HELP ME FIGURE OUT HOW TO BREAK THE NEWS ABOUT REX...
... TO THE REST OF THE FAMILY.
UH, HI -- IS TRIXIE HERE?
YOU JUST MISSED HER-- SHE LEFT A COUPLE OF MINUTES AGO!

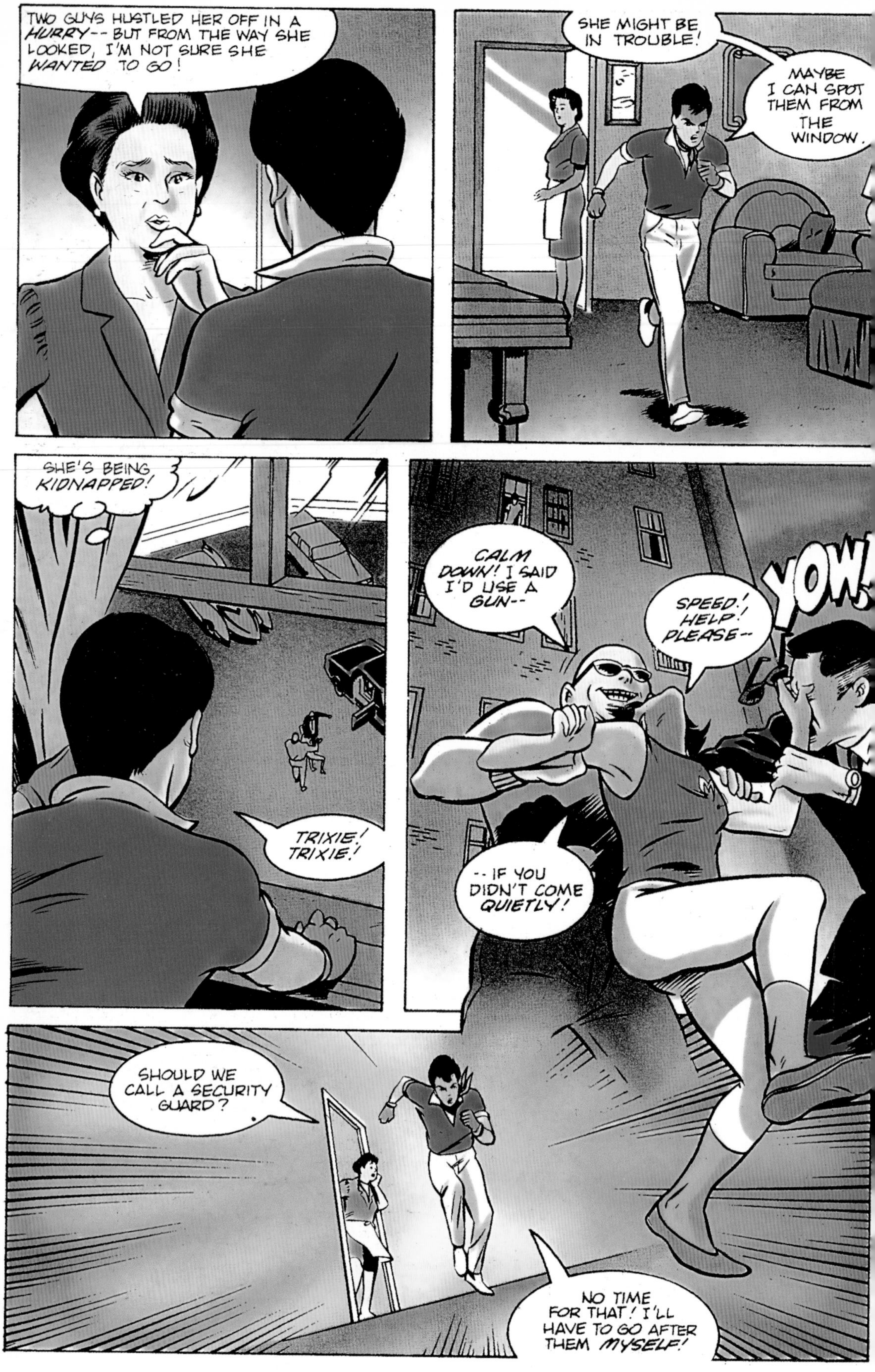

TWO GUYS HUSTLED HER OFF IN A *HURRY*-- BUT FROM THE WAY SHE LOOKED, I'M NOT SURE SHE *WANTED* TO GO!
SHE MIGHT BE IN TROUBLE!
MAYBE I CAN SPOT THEM FROM THE WINDOW.
SHE'S BEING *KIDNAPPED*!
TRIXIE! TRIXIE!
CALM DOWN! I SAID I'D USE A *GUN*--
SPEED! HELP! PLEASE--
YOW!
-- IF YOU DIDN'T COME *QUIETLY*!
SHOULD WE CALL A SECURITY GUARD?
NO TIME FOR THAT! I'LL HAVE TO GO AFTER THEM *MYSELF*!

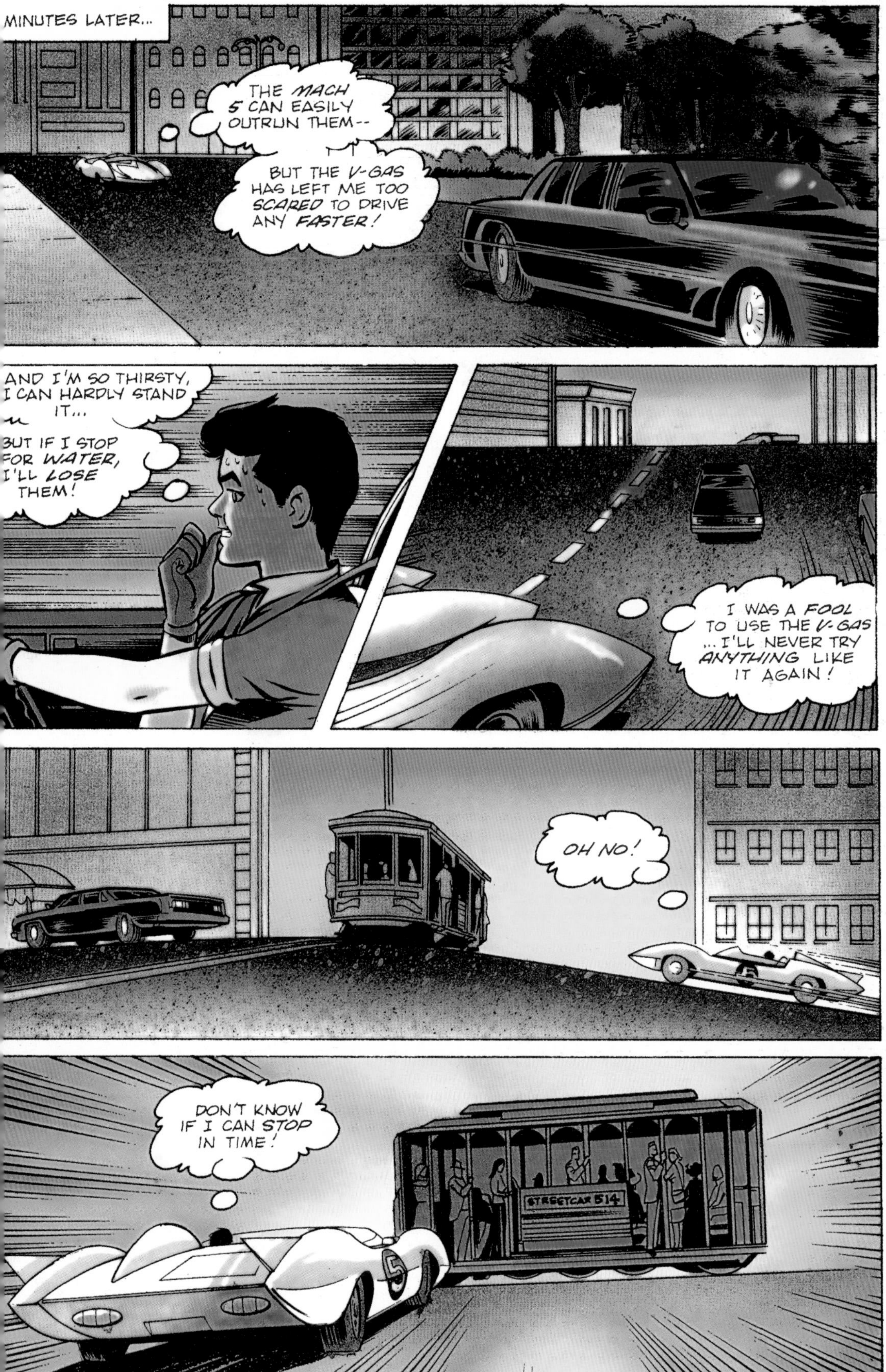
MINUTES LATER...
THE MACH 5 CAN EASILY OUTRUN THEM--
BUT THE V-GAS HAS LEFT ME TOO SCARED TO DRIVE ANY FASTER!
AND I'M SO THIRSTY, I CAN HARDLY STAND IT...
BUT IF I STOP FOR WATER, I'LL LOSE THEM!
I WAS A FOOL TO USE THE V-GAS ...I'LL NEVER TRY ANYTHING LIKE IT AGAIN!
OH NO!
DON'T KNOW IF I CAN STOP IN TIME!
STREETCAR 514

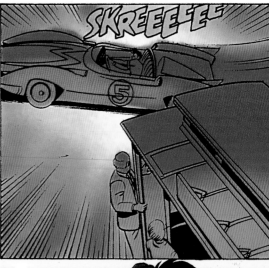

THAT WAS *TOO CLOSE!* MY HEART'S STILL POUNDING

AT LEAST THE RUSH OF *ADRENALINE...*

...SEEMS TO BE CLEARING MY MIND!

CHASING THEM THROUGH THE STREETS ENDANGERS TOO MANY PEOPLE...

...BUT I CAN'T RISK LOSING THEM! ONLY ONE THING TO DO...

CLICK!

EEEEEEEEEEEEE

SPEED ACTIVATES ONE OF THE SPECIAL FEATURES THAT *REX* AND *POPS* BUILT INTO THE *MACH 5...*

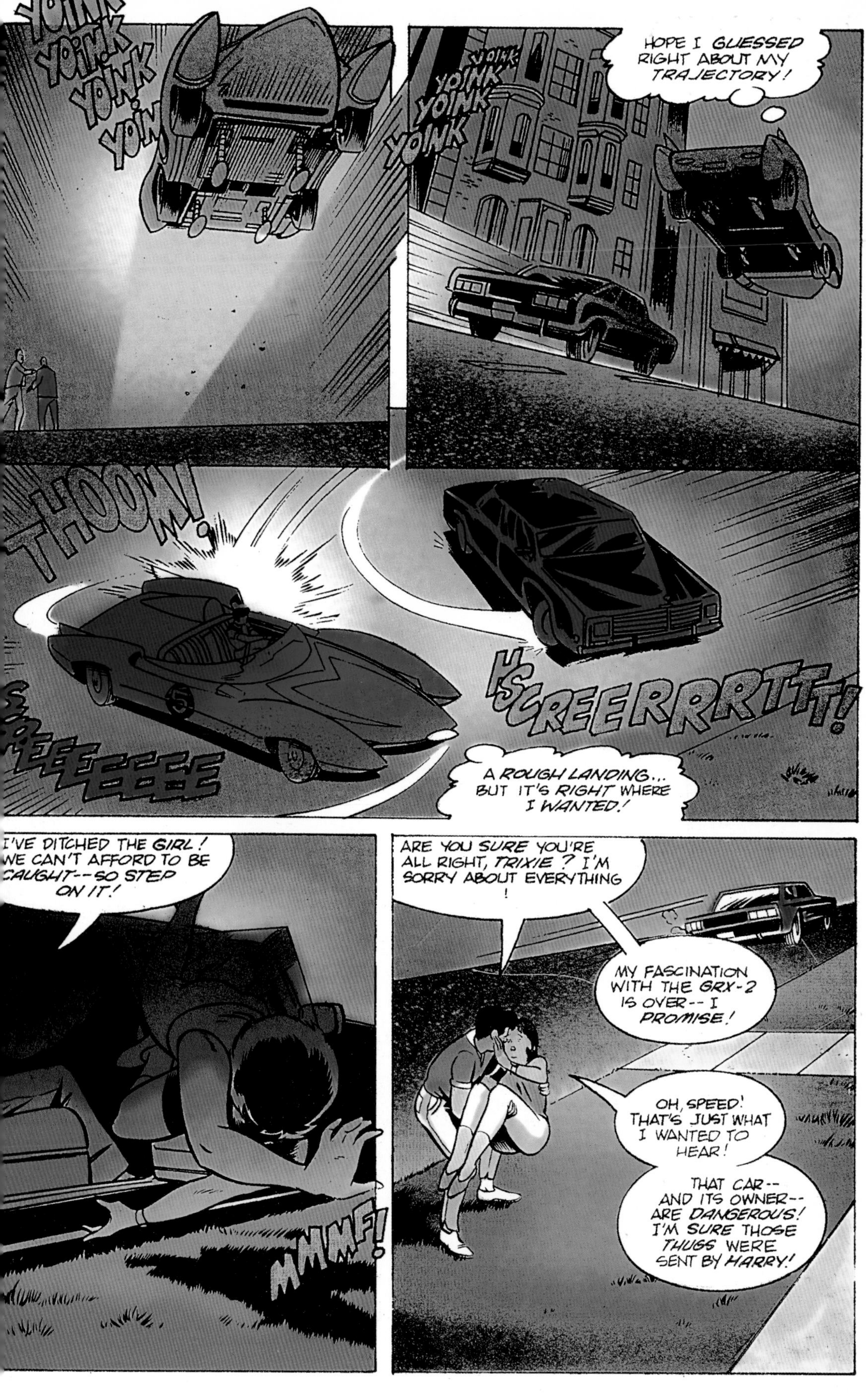
YOiNK YOiNK YOiNK YOiNK
YOINK YOINK YOINK YOINK
HOPE I GUESSED RIGHT ABOUT MY TRAJECTORY!
THOOM!
SCREEEEEEEE
HSCREERRRTTT!
A ROUGH LANDING... BUT IT'S RIGHT WHERE I WANTED!
I'VE DITCHED THE GIRL! WE CAN'T AFFORD TO BE CAUGHT--SO STEP ON IT!
MMMF!
ARE YOU SURE YOU'RE ALL RIGHT, TRIXIE? I'M SORRY ABOUT EVERYTHING!
MY FASCINATION WITH THE GRX-2 IS OVER-- I PROMISE!
OH, SPEED! THAT'S JUST WHAT I WANTED TO HEAR!
THAT CAR-- AND ITS OWNER-- ARE DANGEROUS! I'M SURE THOSE THUGS WERE SENT BY HARRY!

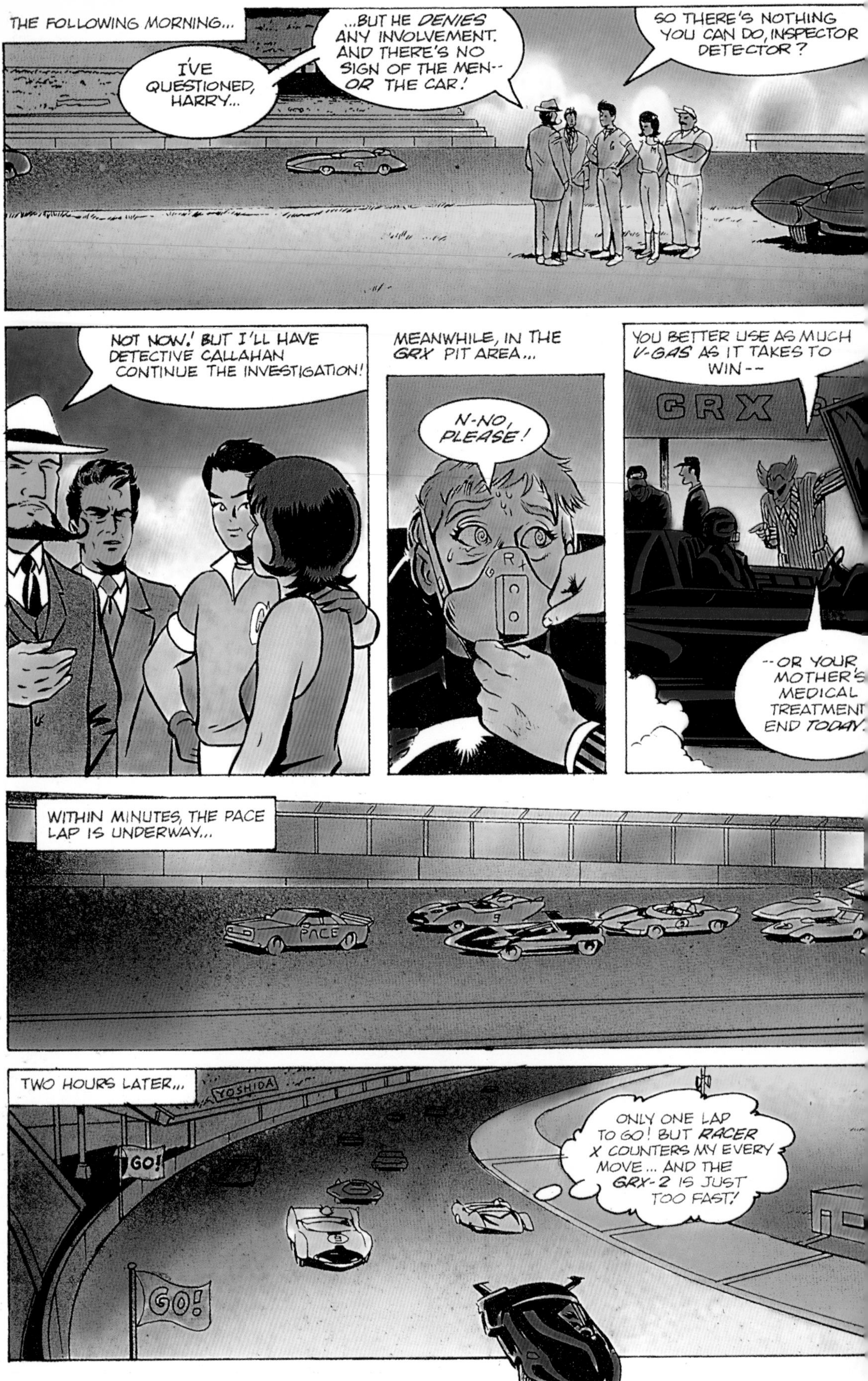
THE FOLLOWING MORNING...
I'VE QUESTIONED, HARRY...
...BUT HE DENIES ANY INVOLVEMENT. AND THERE'S NO SIGN OF THE MEN-- OR THE CAR!
SO THERE'S NOTHING YOU CAN DO, INSPECTOR DETECTOR?
NOT NOW! BUT I'LL HAVE DETECTIVE CALLAHAN CONTINUE THE INVESTIGATION!
MEANWHILE, IN THE GRX PIT AREA...
N-NO, PLEASE!
YOU BETTER USE AS MUCH V-GAS AS IT TAKES TO WIN--
GRX
--OR YOUR MOTHER'S MEDICAL TREATMENT END TODAY.
WITHIN MINUTES, THE PACE LAP IS UNDERWAY...
PACE
TWO HOURS LATER...
YOSHIDA
GO!
ONLY ONE LAP TO GO! BUT RACER X COUNTERS MY EVERY MOVE... AND THE GRX-2 IS JUST TOO FAST!
GO!

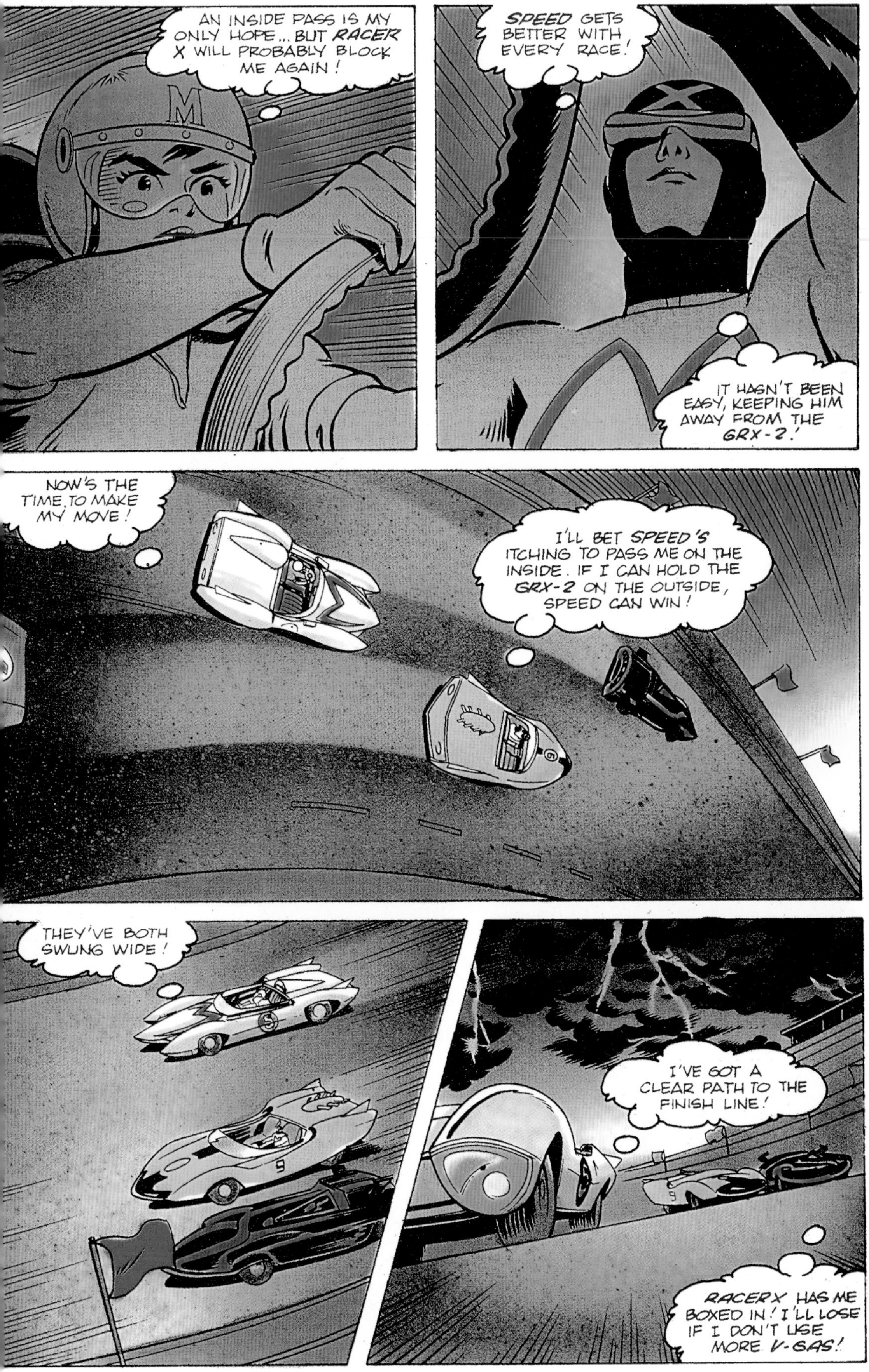

AN INSIDE PASS IS MY ONLY HOPE... BUT RACER X WILL PROBABLY BLOCK ME AGAIN!
SPEED GETS BETTER WITH EVERY RACE!
IT HASN'T BEEN EASY, KEEPING HIM AWAY FROM THE GRX-2!
NOW'S THE TIME TO MAKE MY MOVE!
I'LL BET SPEED'S ITCHING TO PASS ME ON THE INSIDE. IF I CAN HOLD THE GRX-2 ON THE OUTSIDE, SPEED CAN WIN!
THEY'VE BOTH SWUNG WIDE!
I'VE GOT A CLEAR PATH TO THE FINISH LINE!
RACER X HAS ME BOXED IN! I'LL LOSE IF I DON'T USE MORE V-GAS!

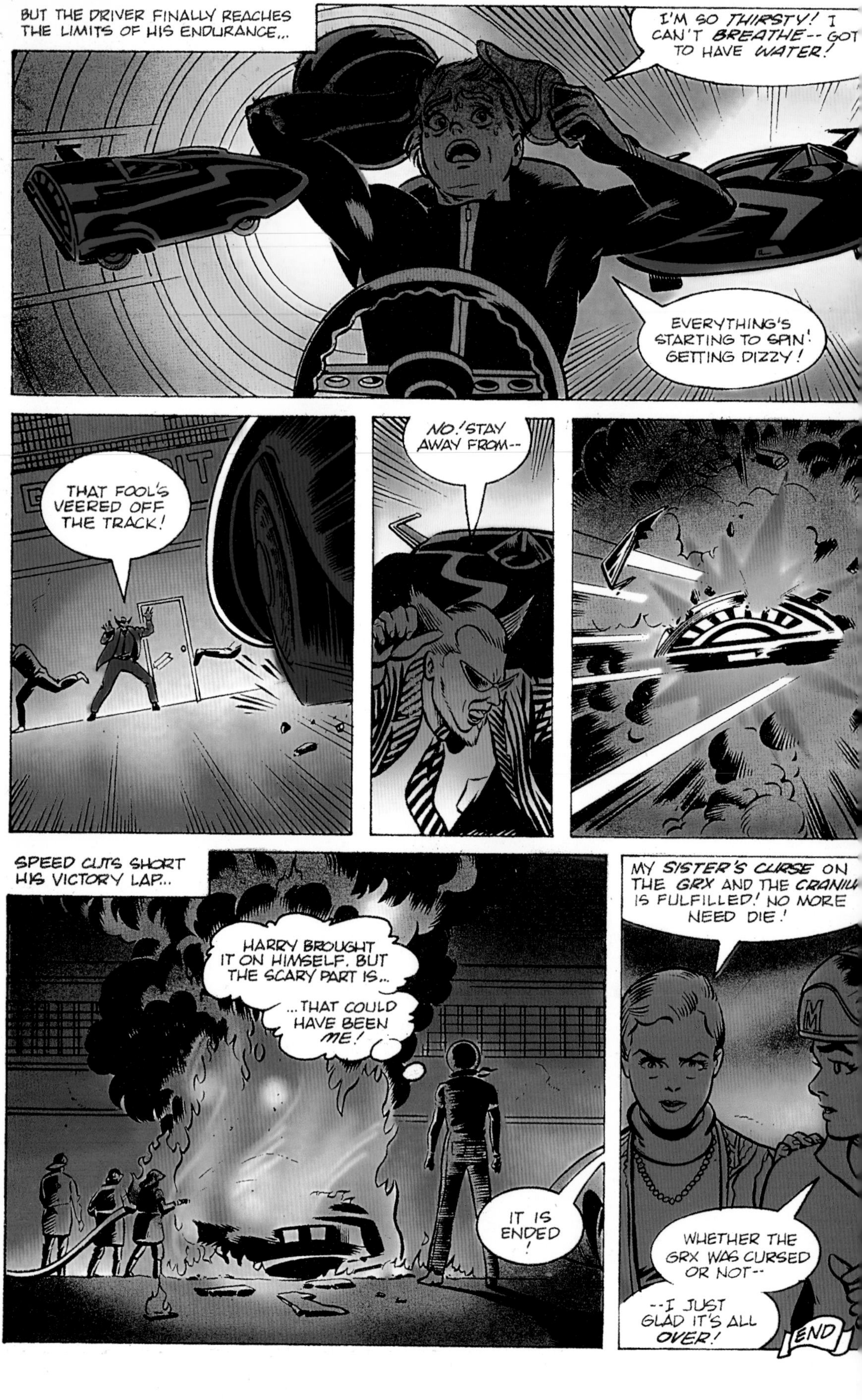

BUT THE DRIVER FINALLY REACHES THE LIMITS OF HIS ENDURANCE...
I'M SO THIRSTY! I CAN'T BREATHE-- GOT TO HAVE WATER!
EVERYTHING'S STARTING TO SPIN! GETTING DIZZY!
THAT FOOL'S VEERED OFF THE TRACK!
NO! STAY AWAY FROM--
SPEED CUTS SHORT HIS VICTORY LAP...
HARRY BROUGHT IT ON HIMSELF. BUT THE SCARY PART IS...
...THAT COULD HAVE BEEN ME!
IT IS ENDED!
MY SISTER'S CURSE ON THE GRX AND THE CRANIU
IS FULFILLED! NO MORE NEED DIE!
WHETHER THE GRX WAS CURSED OR NOT--
--I JUST GLAD IT'S ALL OVER!
END

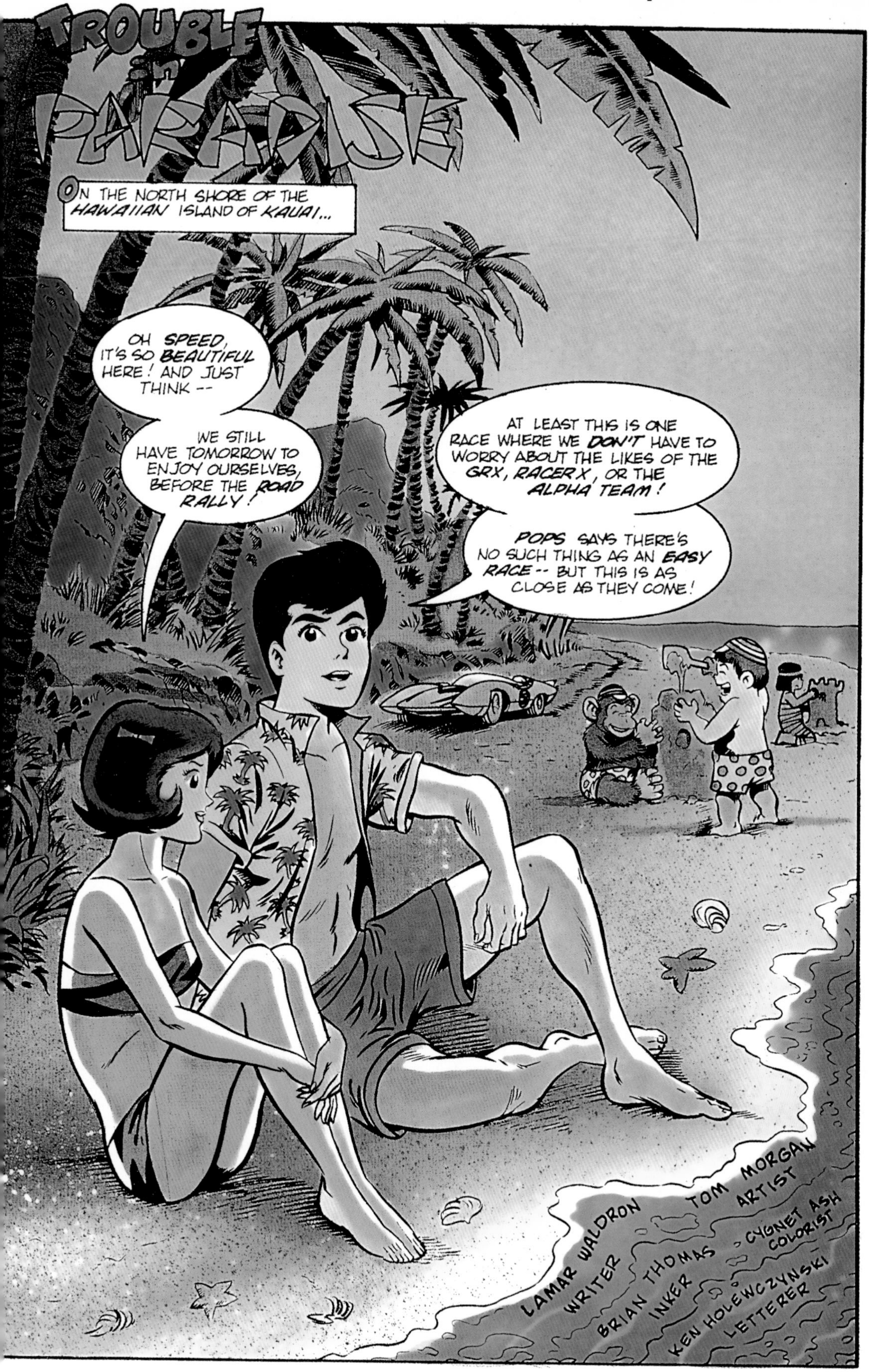
TROUBLE in PARADISE
ON THE NORTH SHORE OF THE HAWAIIAN ISLAND OF KAUAI...
OH SPEED, IT'S SO BEAUTIFUL HERE! AND JUST THINK --
WE STILL HAVE TOMORROW TO ENJOY OURSELVES, BEFORE THE ROAD RALLY!
AT LEAST THIS IS ONE RACE WHERE WE DON'T HAVE TO WORRY ABOUT THE LIKES OF THE GRX, RACER X, OR THE ALPHA TEAM!
POPS SAYS THERE'S NO SUCH THING AS AN EASY RACE -- BUT THIS IS AS CLOSE AS THEY COME!
LAMAR WALDRON WRITER
TOM MORGAN ARTIST
BRIAN THOMAS INKER
CYGNET ASH COLORIST
KEN HOLEWCZYNSKI LETTERER

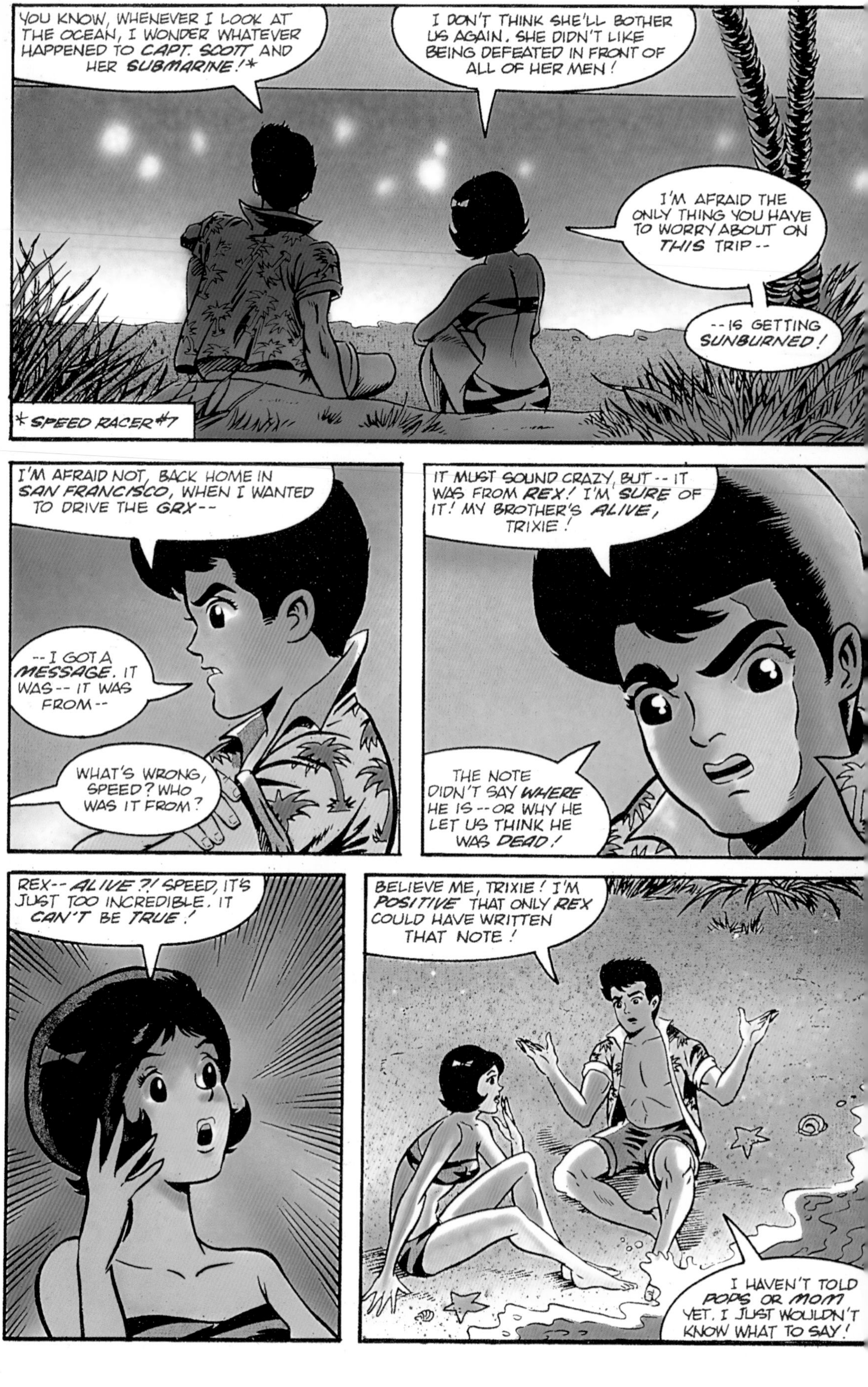
YOU KNOW, WHENEVER I LOOK AT THE OCEAN, I WONDER WHATEVER HAPPENED TO CAPT. SCOTT AND HER SUBMARINE!*
I DON'T THINK SHE'LL BOTHER US AGAIN. SHE DIDN'T LIKE BEING DEFEATED IN FRONT OF ALL OF HER MEN!
I'M AFRAID THE ONLY THING YOU HAVE TO WORRY ABOUT ON THIS TRIP--
--IS GETTING SUNBURNED!
*SPEED RACER #7
I'M AFRAID NOT. BACK HOME IN SAN FRANCISCO, WHEN I WANTED TO DRIVE THE GRX--
--I GOT A MESSAGE. IT WAS-- IT WAS FROM--
WHAT'S WRONG, SPEED? WHO WAS IT FROM?
IT MUST SOUND CRAZY, BUT-- IT WAS FROM REX! I'M SURE OF IT! MY BROTHER'S ALIVE, TRIXIE!
THE NOTE DIDN'T SAY WHERE HE IS--OR WHY HE LET US THINK HE WAS DEAD!
REX-- ALIVE?! SPEED, IT'S JUST TOO INCREDIBLE. IT CAN'T BE TRUE!
BELIEVE ME, TRIXIE! I'M POSITIVE THAT ONLY REX COULD HAVE WRITTEN THAT NOTE!
I HAVEN'T TOLD POPS OR MOM YET. I JUST WOULDN'T KNOW WHAT TO SAY!

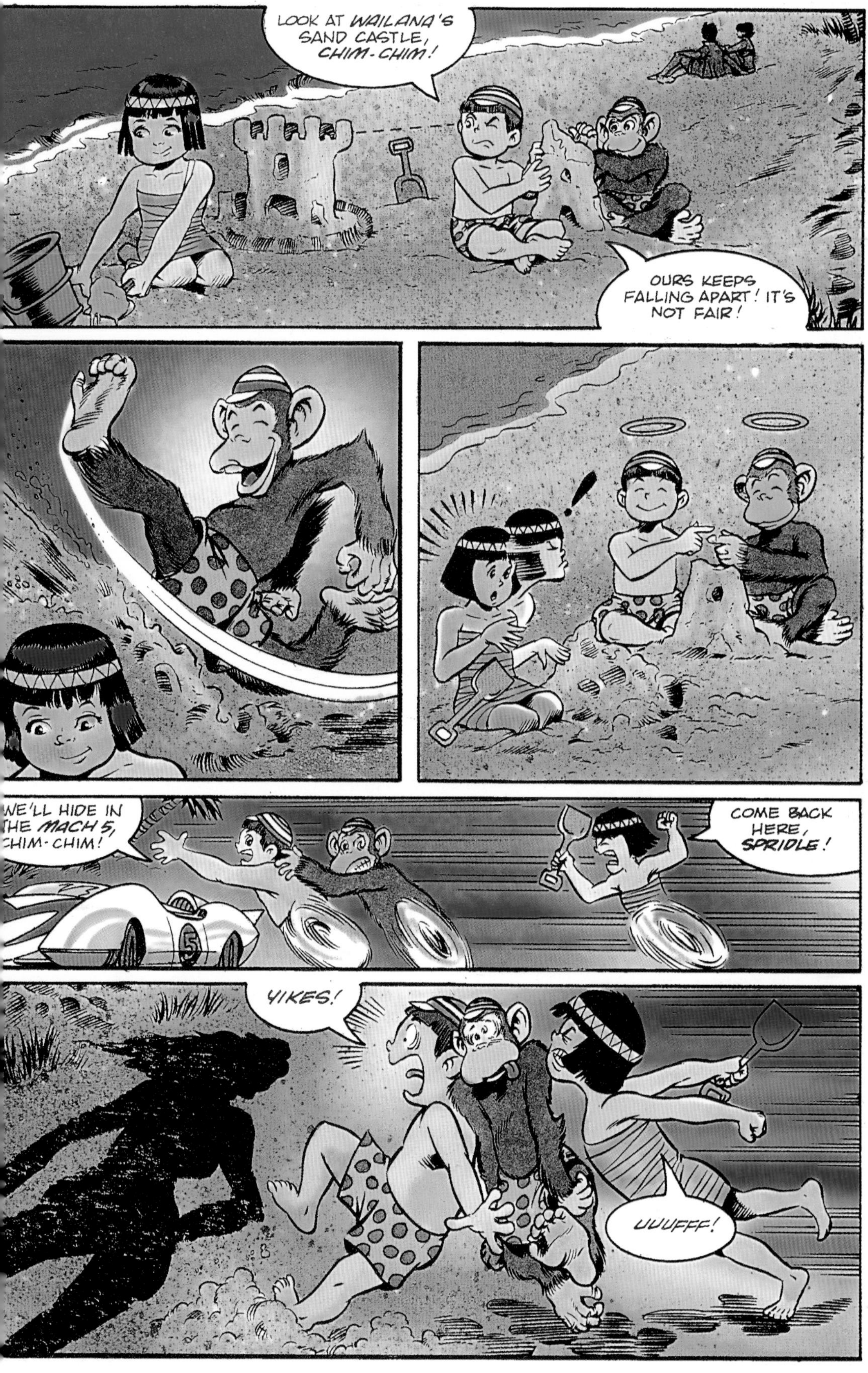
LOOK AT WAILANA'S SAND CASTLE, CHIM-CHIM!
OURS KEEPS FALLING APART! IT'S NOT FAIR!
WE'LL HIDE IN THE MACH 5, CHIM-CHIM!
COME BACK HERE, SPRIDLE!
YIKES!
UUUFFF!

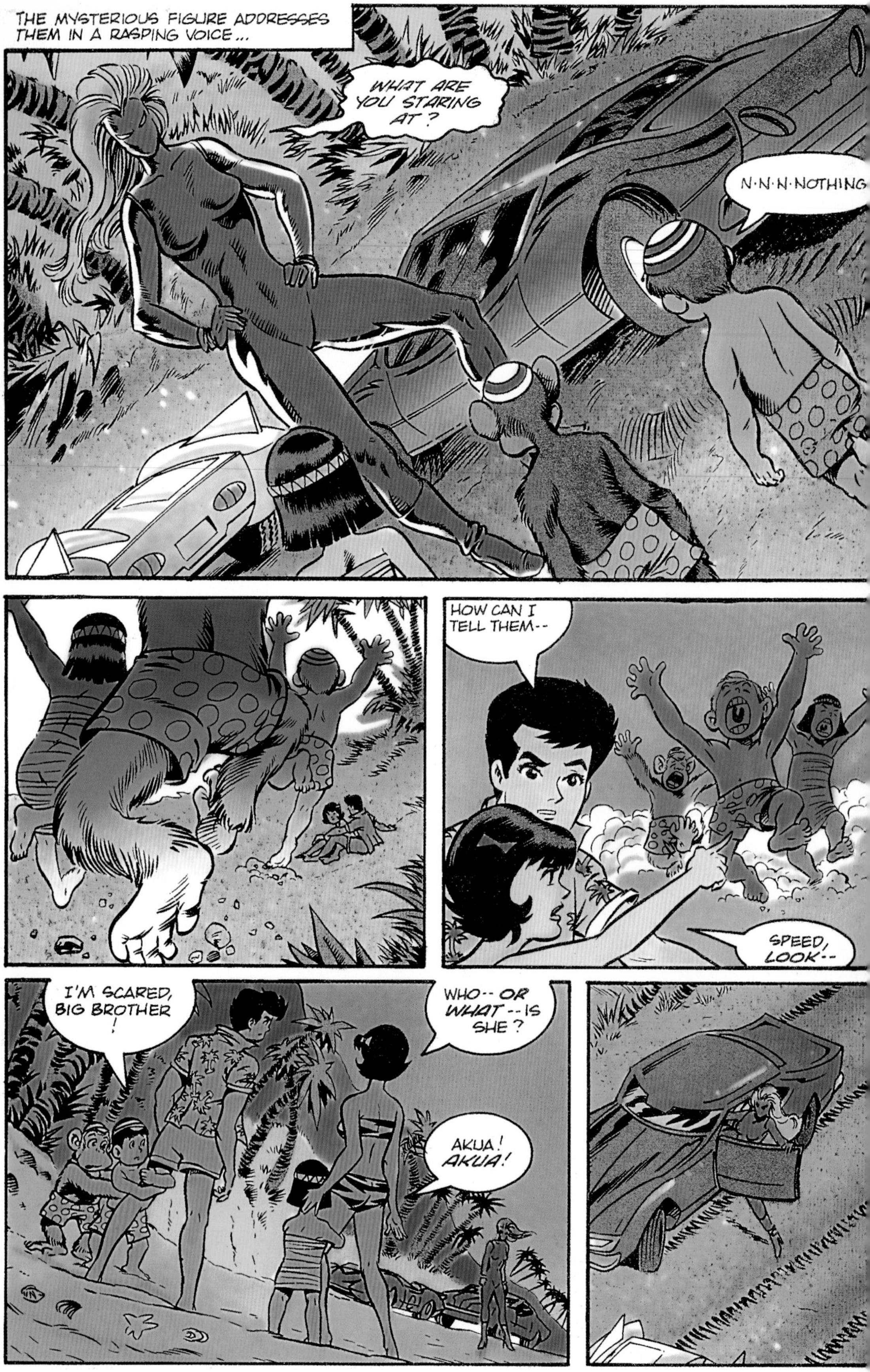
THE MYSTERIOUS FIGURE ADDRESSES THEM IN A RASPING VOICE...
WHAT ARE YOU STARING AT?
N·N·N·NOTHING
HOW CAN I TELL THEM--
SPEED, LOOK--
I'M SCARED, BIG BROTHER!
WHO-- OR WHAT --IS SHE?
AKUA! AKUA!

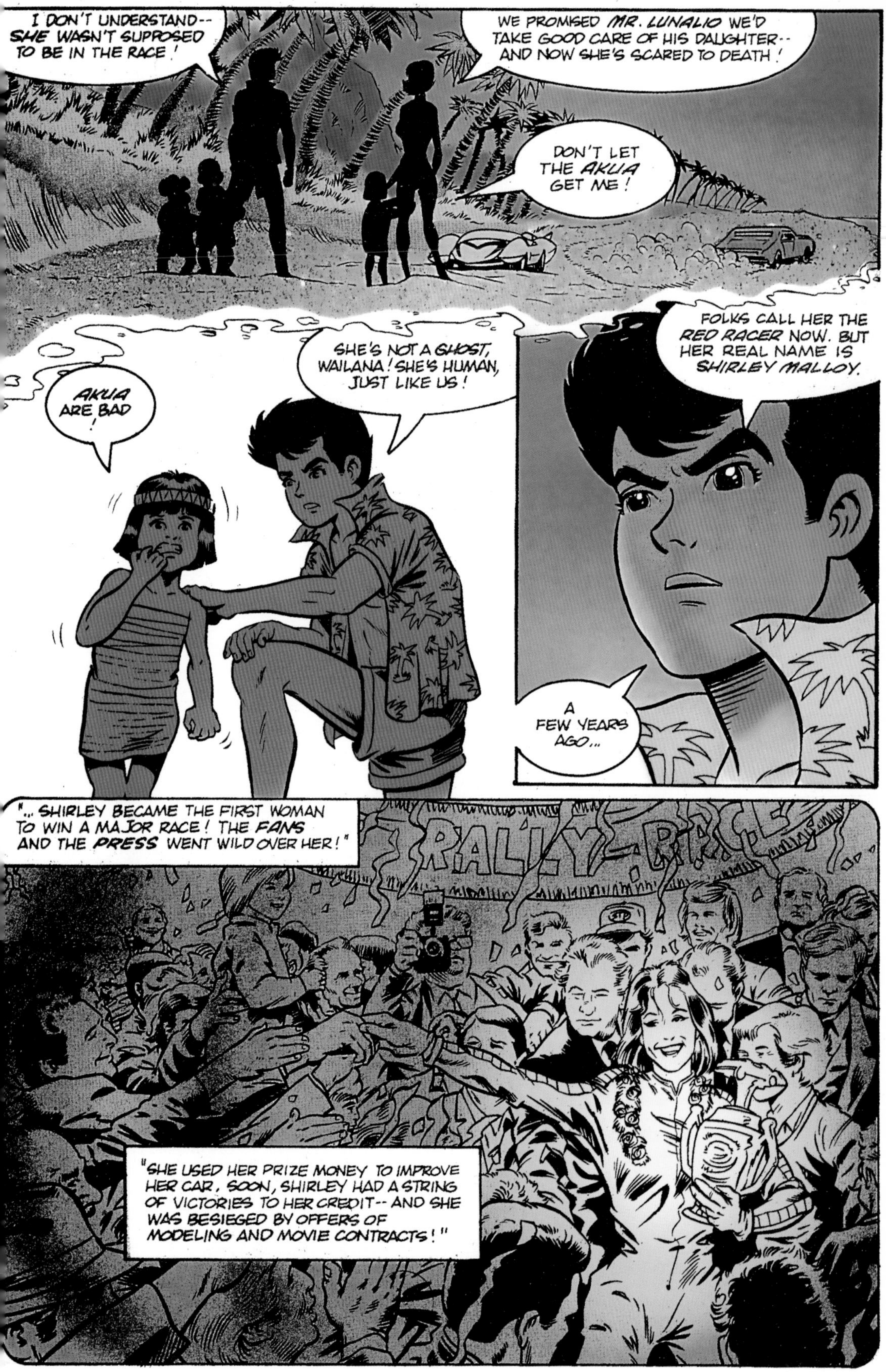

I DON'T UNDERSTAND-- SHE WASN'T SUPPOSED TO BE IN THE RACE!
WE PROMISED MR. LUNALIO WE'D TAKE GOOD CARE OF HIS DAUGHTER-- AND NOW SHE'S SCARED TO DEATH!
DON'T LET THE AKUA GET ME!
AKUA ARE BAD!
SHE'S NOT A GHOST, WAILANA! SHE'S HUMAN, JUST LIKE US!
FOLKS CALL HER THE RED RACER NOW. BUT HER REAL NAME IS SHIRLEY MALLOY.
A FEW YEARS AGO...
"...SHIRLEY BECAME THE FIRST WOMAN TO WIN A MAJOR RACE! THE FANS AND THE PRESS WENT WILD OVER HER!"
RALLY-RACE
"SHE USED HER PRIZE MONEY TO IMPROVE HER CAR. SOON, SHIRLEY HAD A STRING OF VICTORIES TO HER CREDIT-- AND SHE WAS BESIEGED BY OFFERS OF MODELING AND MOVIE CONTRACTS!"

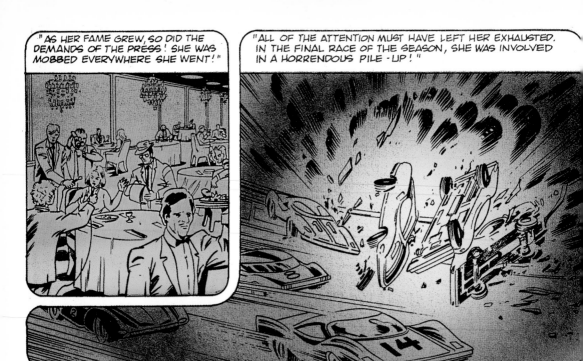

"AS HER FAME GREW, SO DID THE DEMANDS OF THE PRESS! SHE WAS MOBBED EVERYWHERE SHE WENT!"

"ALL OF THE ATTENTION MUST HAVE LEFT HER EXHAUSTED. IN THE FINAL RACE OF THE SEASON, SHE WAS INVOLVED IN A HORRENDOUS PILE-UP!"

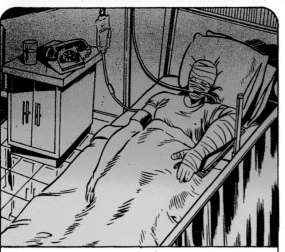

"I HEARD ALL SORTS OF STORIES ABOUT HOW HORRIBLY SHE'D BEEN *BURNED!* SHIRLEY SURVIVED-- BUT SHE WAS IN THE HOSPITAL FOR OVER A YEAR!"

"NO-ONE EXPECTED HER TO RACE AGAIN... BUT SHE DID!"

"SHE ALWAYS WEARS THAT RED SUIT... I GUESS TO HIDE THE SCARS. SHE'S A REAL LONER, NOW. EVERYONE KEEPS THEIR DISTANCE FROM HER!"

SO YOU SEE, YOU SHOULDN'T BE SCARED OF HER! MAYBE SHE JUST WANTED TO LOOK AT THE *MACH 5!*

OR TO SABOTAGE IT! SHE STILL GIVES ME THE *CREEPS!*

ANYWAY, WE'D BETTER HEAD BACK, IF WE'RE GOING TO GET READY FOR THE *PARTY!*

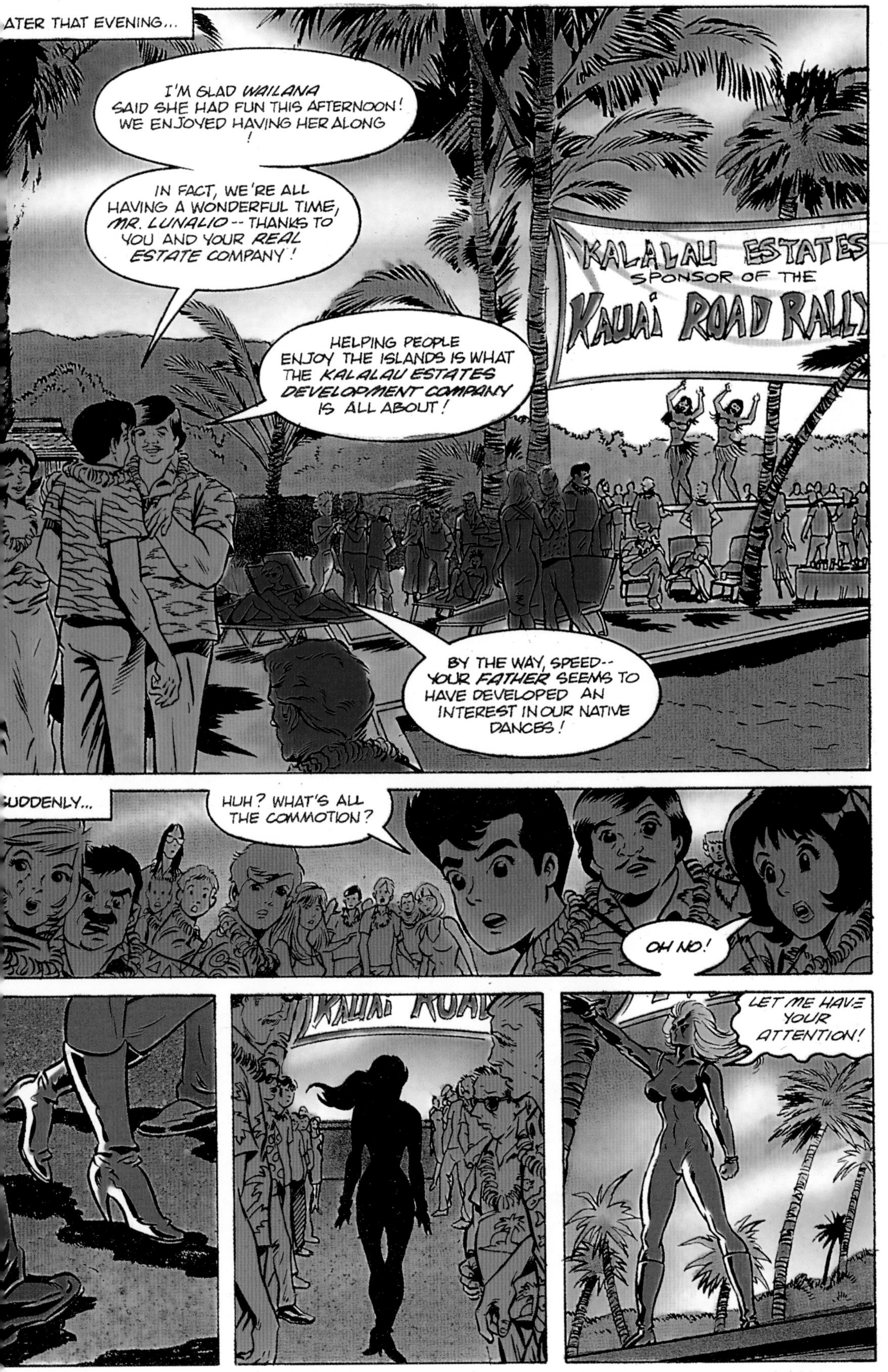
ATER THAT EVENING...
I'M GLAD WAILANA SAID SHE HAD FUN THIS AFTERNOON! WE ENJOYED HAVING HER ALONG!
IN FACT, WE'RE ALL HAVING A WONDERFUL TIME, MR. LUNALIO -- THANKS TO YOU AND YOUR REAL ESTATE COMPANY!
KALALAU ESTATES SPONSOR OF THE KAUAI ROAD RALLY
HELPING PEOPLE ENJOY THE ISLANDS IS WHAT THE KALALAU ESTATES DEVELOPMENT COMPANY IS ALL ABOUT!
BY THE WAY, SPEED-- YOUR FATHER SEEMS TO HAVE DEVELOPED AN INTEREST IN OUR NATIVE DANCES!
UDDENLY...
HUH? WHAT'S ALL THE COMMOTION?
OH NO!
KAUAI ROAD
LET ME HAVE YOUR ATTENTION!

KALALAU ESTATES
SPONSOR OF THE
KAUAI ROAD RALLY

KALALUA ESTATES WILL COVER AN UNSPOILED VALLEY WITH CONCRETE AND CONDOS! THEY'LL BE A MONUMENT TO THE GREED OF THE DEVELOPERS!

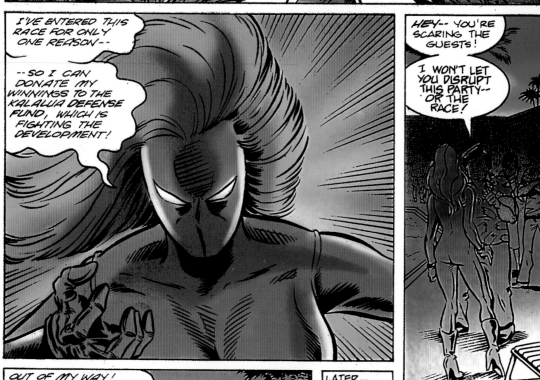

I'VE ENTERED THIS RACE FOR ONLY ONE REASON--

--SO I CAN DONATE MY WINNINGS TO THE KALALUA DEFENSE FUND, WHICH IS FIGHTING THE DEVELOPMENT!

HEY-- YOU'RE SCARING THE GUESTS!

I WON'T LET YOU DISRUPT THIS PARTY-- OR THE RACE!

OUT OF MY WAY! I'VE GOT A SIGNED CONTRACT TO RACE--

--AND THAT'S JUST WHAT I INTEND TO DO!

LATER...

THAT RED RACER IS SUCH A HORRIBLE PERSON!

DON'T JUDGE HER, UNTIL YOU HAVE ALL THE FACTS!

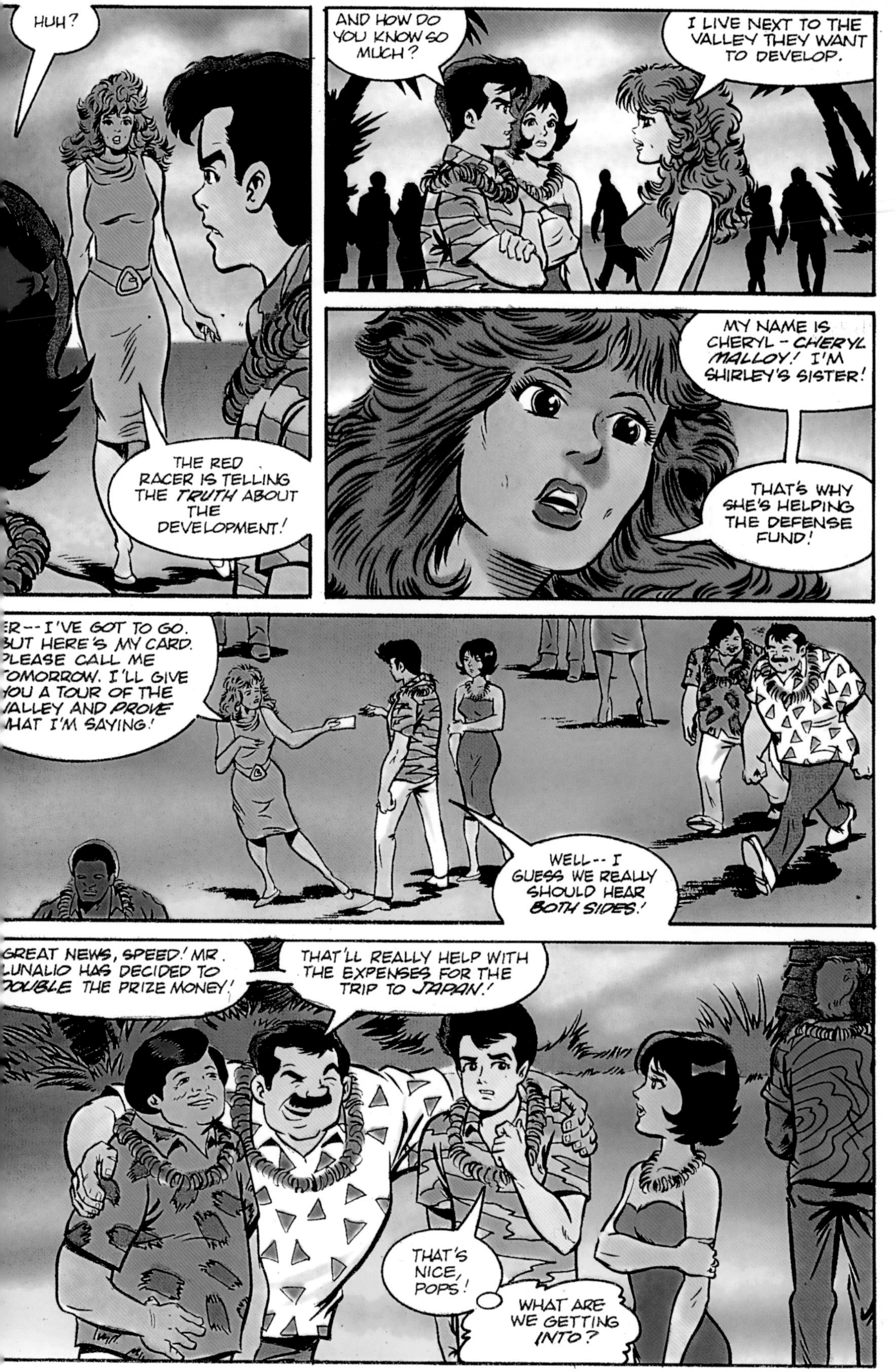
HUH?
AND HOW DO YOU KNOW SO MUCH?
I LIVE NEXT TO THE VALLEY THEY WANT TO DEVELOP.
THE RED RACER IS TELLING THE TRUTH ABOUT THE DEVELOPMENT!
MY NAME IS CHERYL - CHERYL MALLOY! I'M SHIRLEY'S SISTER!
THAT'S WHY SHE'S HELPING THE DEFENSE FUND!
ER-- I'VE GOT TO GO. BUT HERE'S MY CARD. PLEASE CALL ME TOMORROW. I'LL GIVE YOU A TOUR OF THE VALLEY AND PROVE WHAT I'M SAYING!
WELL-- I GUESS WE REALLY SHOULD HEAR BOTH SIDES!
GREAT NEWS, SPEED! MR. LUNALIO HAS DECIDED TO DOUBLE THE PRIZE MONEY!
THAT'LL REALLY HELP WITH THE EXPENSES FOR THE TRIP TO JAPAN!
THAT'S NICE, POPS!
WHAT ARE WE GETTING INTO?

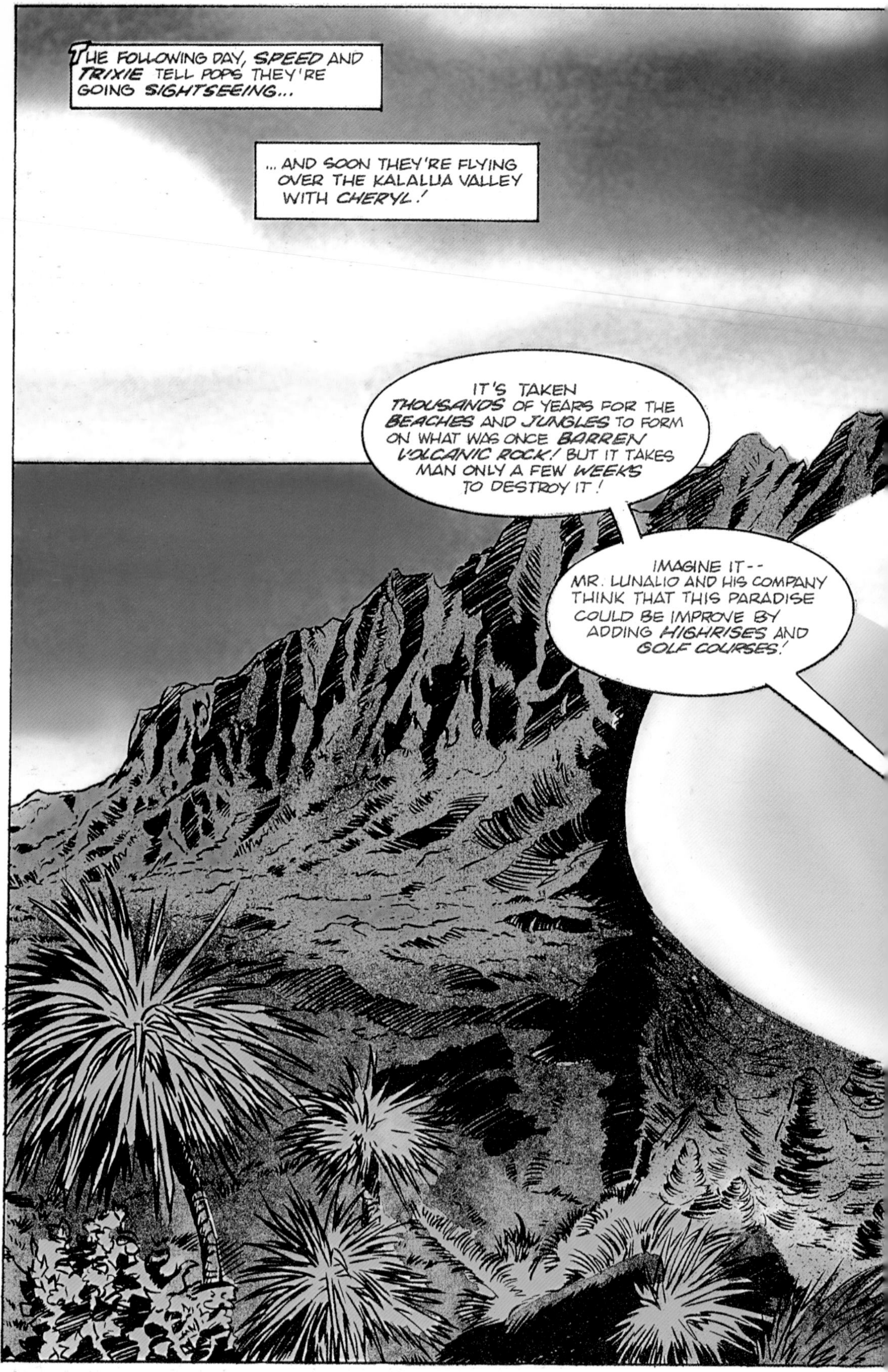
THE FOLLOWING DAY, SPEED AND TRIXIE TELL POPS THEY'RE GOING SIGHTSEEING...
...AND SOON THEY'RE FLYING OVER THE KALALUA VALLEY WITH CHERYL!
IT'S TAKEN THOUSANDS OF YEARS FOR THE BEACHES AND JUNGLES TO FORM ON WHAT WAS ONCE BARREN VOLCANIC ROCK! BUT IT TAKES MAN ONLY A FEW WEEKS TO DESTROY IT!
IMAGINE IT-- MR. LUNALIO AND HIS COMPANY THINK THAT THIS PARADISE COULD BE IMPROVE BY ADDING HIGHRISES AND GOLF COURSES!

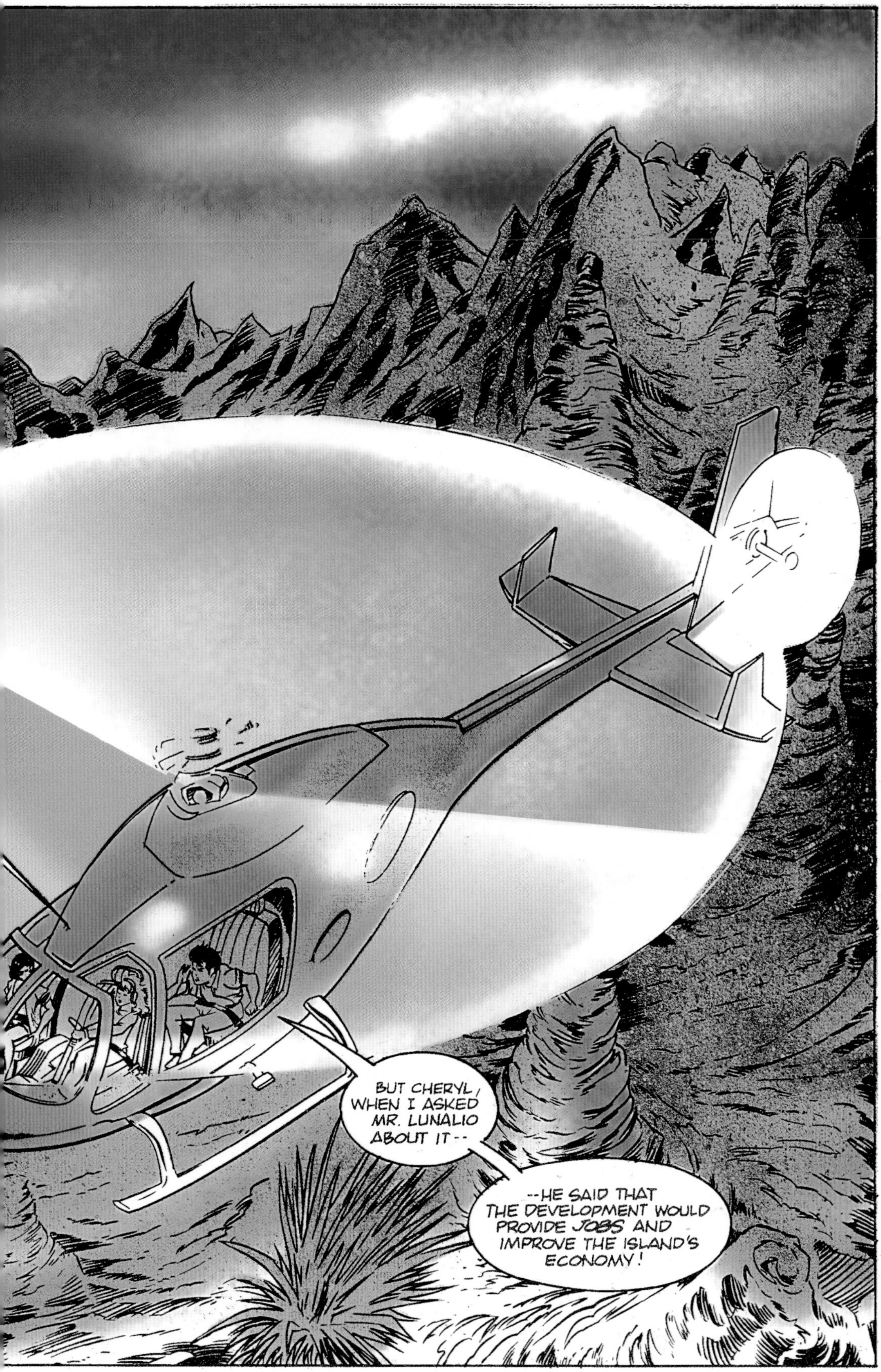
BUT CHERYL, WHEN I ASKED MR. LUNALIO ABOUT IT--
--HE SAID THAT THE DEVELOPMENT WOULD PROVIDE JOBS AND IMPROVE THE ISLAND'S ECONOMY!

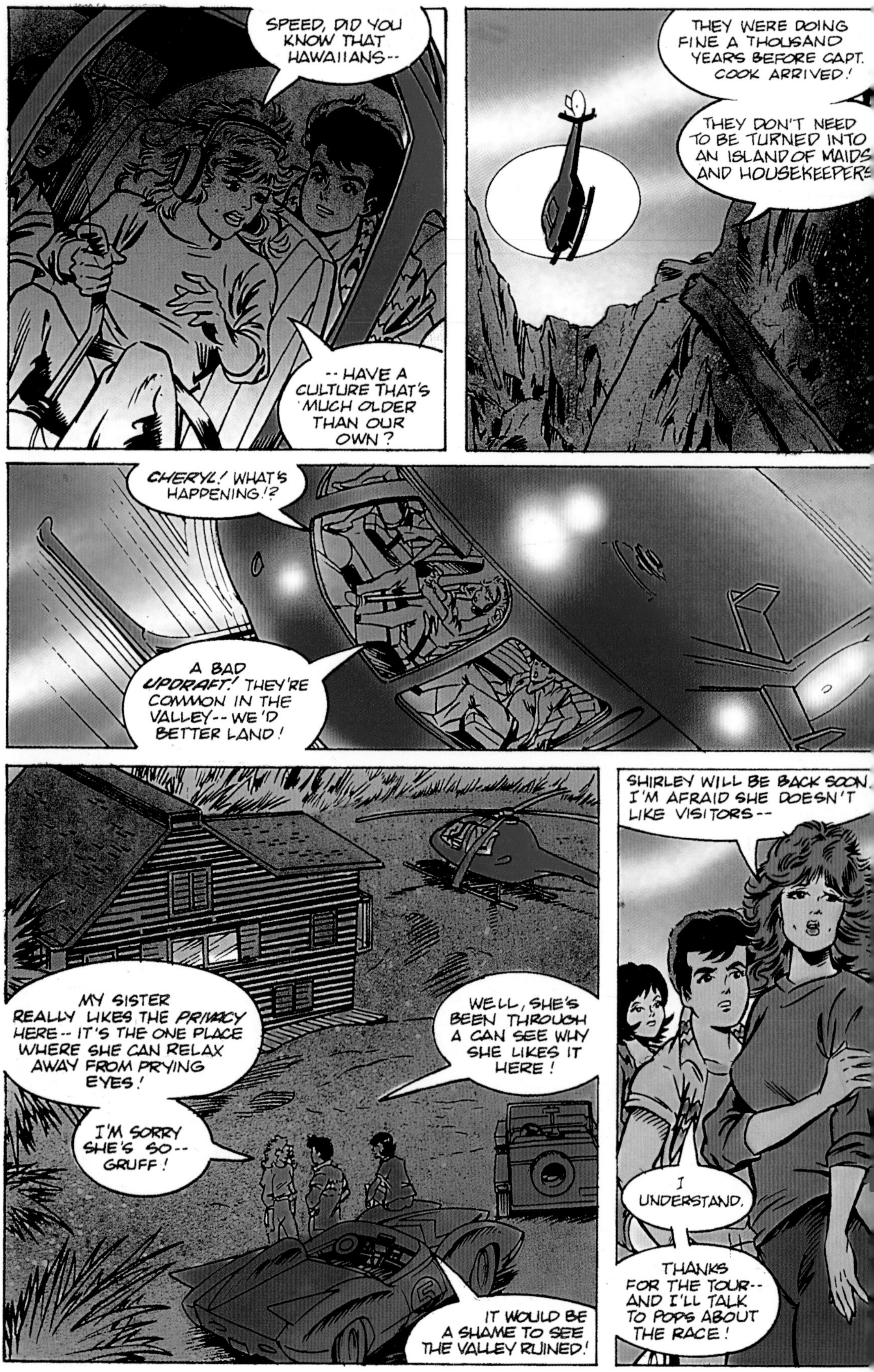
SPEED, DID YOU KNOW THAT HAWAIIANS--
--HAVE A CULTURE THAT'S MUCH OLDER THAN OUR OWN?
THEY WERE DOING FINE A THOUSAND YEARS BEFORE CAPT. COOK ARRIVED!
THEY DON'T NEED TO BE TURNED INTO AN ISLAND OF MAIDS AND HOUSEKEEPERS
CHERYL! WHAT'S HAPPENING!?
A BAD UPDRAFT! THEY'RE COMMON IN THE VALLEY--WE'D BETTER LAND!
MY SISTER REALLY LIKES THE PRIVACY HERE--IT'S THE ONE PLACE WHERE SHE CAN RELAX AWAY FROM PRYING EYES!
I'M SORRY SHE'S SO--GRUFF!
WELL, SHE'S BEEN THROUGH A CAN SEE WHY SHE LIKES IT HERE!
IT WOULD BE A SHAME TO SEE THE VALLEY RUINED!
SHIRLEY WILL BE BACK SOON. I'M AFRAID SHE DOESN'T LIKE VISITORS--
I UNDERSTAND.
THANKS FOR THE TOUR--AND I'LL TALK TO POPS ABOUT THE RACE!

THAT EVENING...

WHAT.!! ARE YOU CRAZY!!

UT POPS, THE ACE IS JUST TO ET PUBLICITY OR THE REAL STATE COMPANY !

GRRR-- SPEED, DON'T YOU REALIZE THAT RACING IS A BUSINESS--

-- A VERY EXPENSIVE BUSINESS?

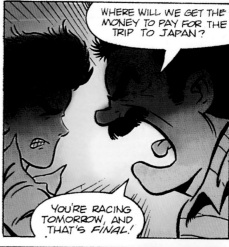

WHERE WILL WE GET THE MONEY TO PAY FOR THE TRIP TO JAPAN?

YOU'RE RACING TOMORROW, AND THAT'S FINAL!

FTER POPS STORMS OFF...

OPS IS RIGHT... WE O NEED THE MONEY. UT IF I DO WIN FIRST PLACE...

... MAYBE I CAN ONATE SOMETHING TO THE DEFENSE FUND!

POPS IS SO UPSET, IT WOULDN'T BE A GOOD TIME TO TELL HIM ABOUT REX!

BUT I CAN'T PUT IT OFF MUCH LONGER...

HE FOLLOWING DAY...

KAUAI ROAD RACE
SPONSORED BY KALALAU ESTATES

WHAT DO YOU WANT?

HI, RED-- ER, UH-- SHIRLEY.

I JUST WANTED TO WISH YOU LUCK! MAY THE BEST RACER WIN!

I'M THE BEST RACER--

--AND I'M GOING TO WIN!

A SHORT DISTANCE AWAY--

ARE YOU SURE YOU WON'T LET SPRIDLE WATCH THE RACE WITH US?

THANKS BUT HE'LL G INTO LESS TROUBLE DOWN HERE

MOMENTS LATER, THE RACE IS UNDERWAY...

I'M NOT SURE WHY, BUT I CAN'T STOP THINKING ABOUT THE RED RACER! I'VE GOT TO PUT HER OUT OF MY MIND...

KALALA

...AND CONCENTRATE ON WINNING THE RACE

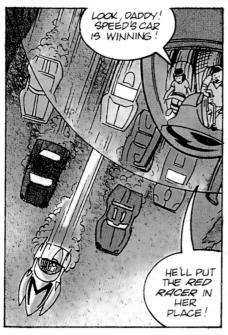

LOOK, DADDY! SPEED'S CAR IS WINNING!

HE'LL PUT THE RED RACER IN HER PLACE!

MINUTES LATER...

HOLD TIGHT, WAILANA! WE'VE CAUGHT AN UPDRAFT!

C-CAN'T GET THE CONTROL TO RESPOND -

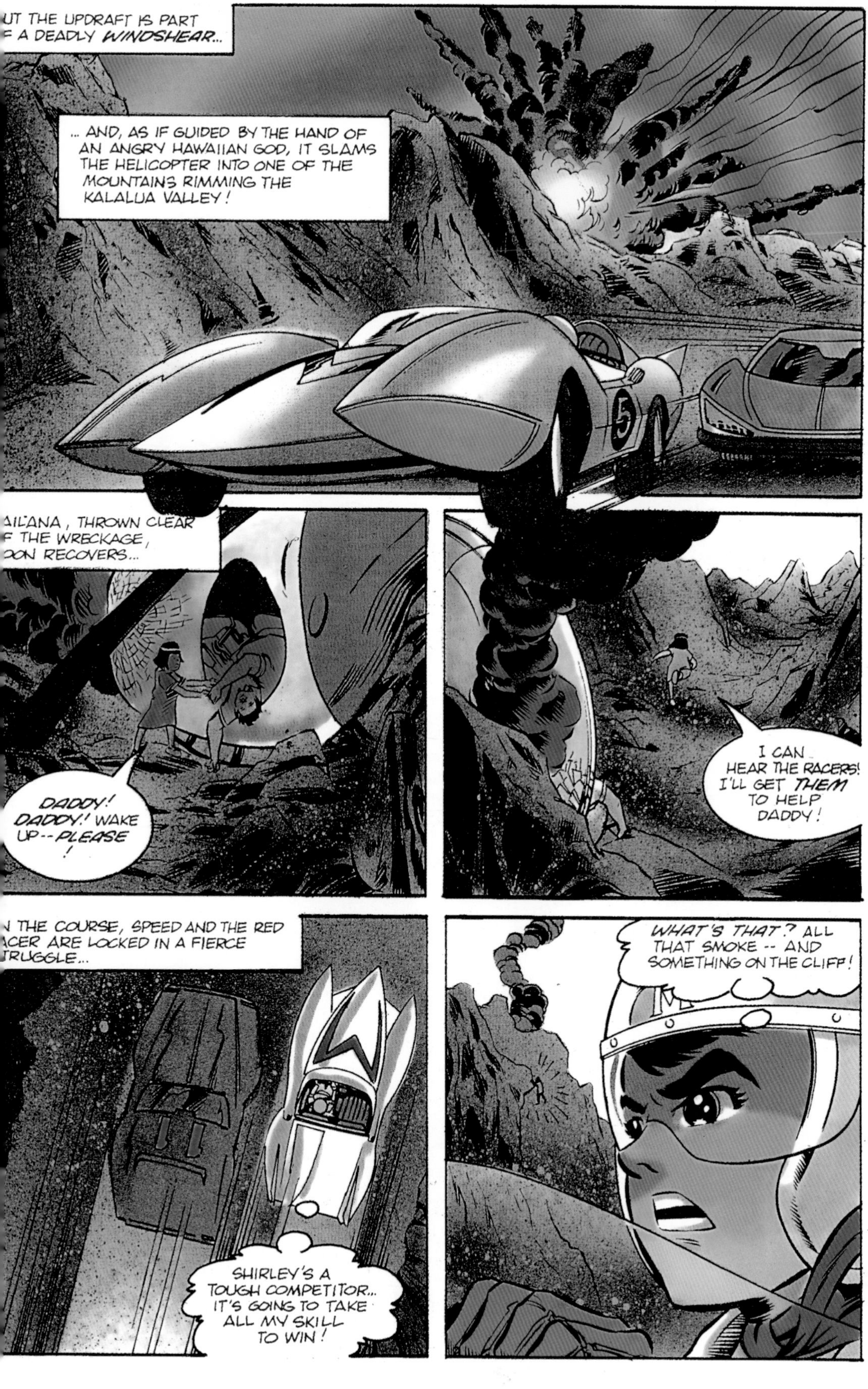
UT THE UPDRAFT IS PART
F A DEADLY WINDSHEAR...
... AND, AS IF GUIDED BY THE HAND OF AN ANGRY HAWAIIAN GOD, IT SLAMS THE HELICOPTER INTO ONE OF THE MOUNTAINS RIMMING THE KALALUA VALLEY!
AILANA, THROWN CLEAR
F THE WRECKAGE,
OON RECOVERS...
DADDY! DADDY! WAKE UP-- PLEASE!
I CAN HEAR THE RACERS! I'LL GET THEM TO HELP DADDY!
N THE COURSE, SPEED AND THE RED
ACER ARE LOCKED IN A FIERCE
TRUGGLE...
SHIRLEY'S A TOUGH COMPETITOR... IT'S GOING TO TAKE ALL MY SKILL TO WIN!
WHAT'S THAT? ALL THAT SMOKE -- AND SOMETHING ON THE CLIFF!

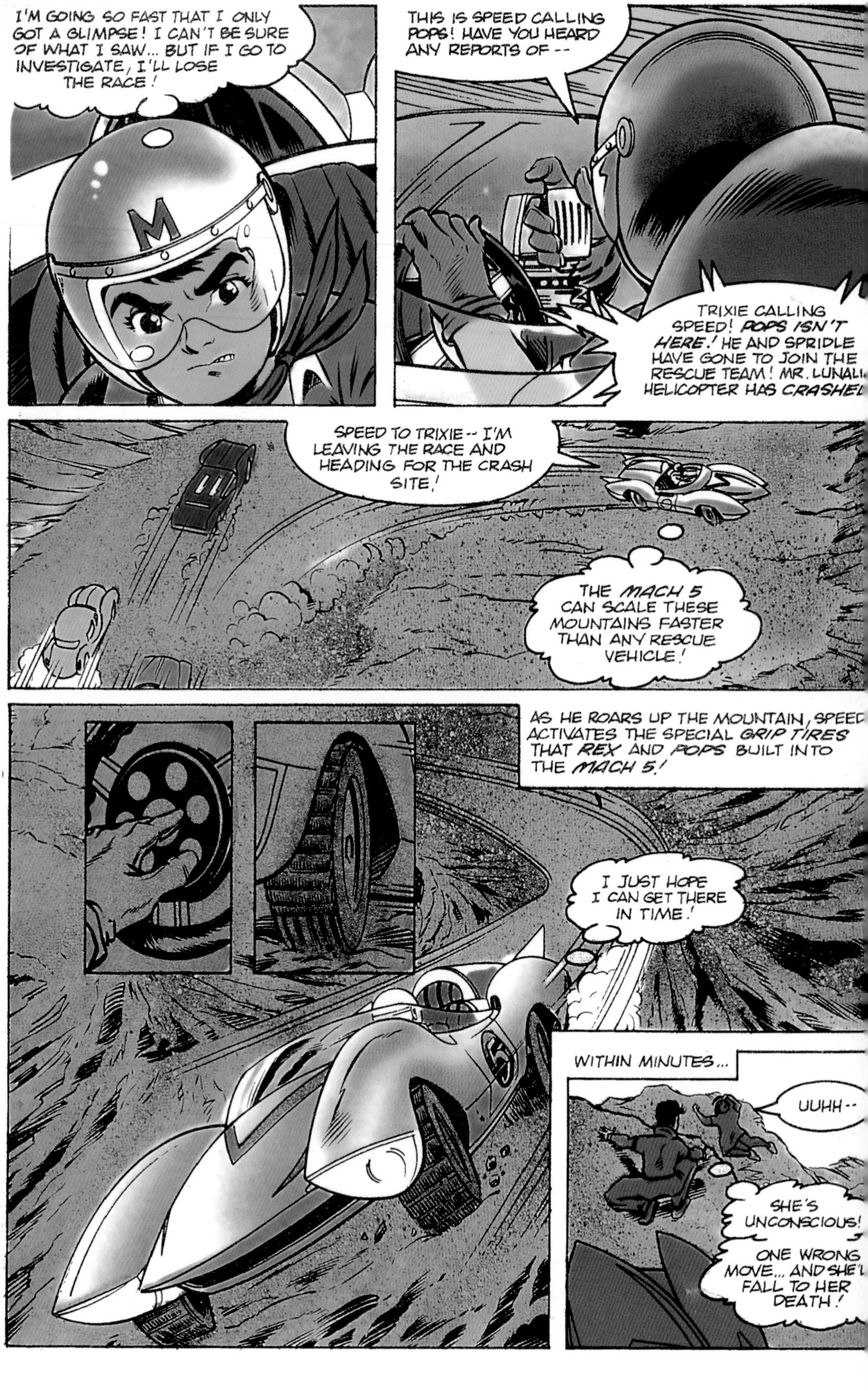
I'M GOING SO FAST THAT I ONLY GOT A GLIMPSE! I CAN'T BE SURE OF WHAT I SAW... BUT IF I GO TO INVESTIGATE, I'LL LOSE THE RACE!
THIS IS SPEED CALLING POPS! HAVE YOU HEARD ANY REPORTS OF --
TRIXIE CALLING SPEED! POPS ISN'T HERE! HE AND SPRIDLE HAVE GONE TO JOIN THE RESCUE TEAM! MR. LUNALI HELICOPTER HAS CRASHEL
SPEED TO TRIXIE -- I'M LEAVING THE RACE AND HEADING FOR THE CRASH SITE!
THE MACH 5 CAN SCALE THESE MOUNTAINS FASTER THAN ANY RESCUE VEHICLE!
AS HE ROARS UP THE MOUNTAIN, SPEEC ACTIVATES THE SPECIAL GRIP TIRES THAT REX AND POPS BUILT INTO THE MACH 5!
I JUST HOPE I CAN GET THERE IN TIME!
WITHIN MINUTES...
UUHH--
SHE'S UNCONSCIOUS!
ONE WRONG MOVE... AND SHE'L FALL TO HER DEATH!

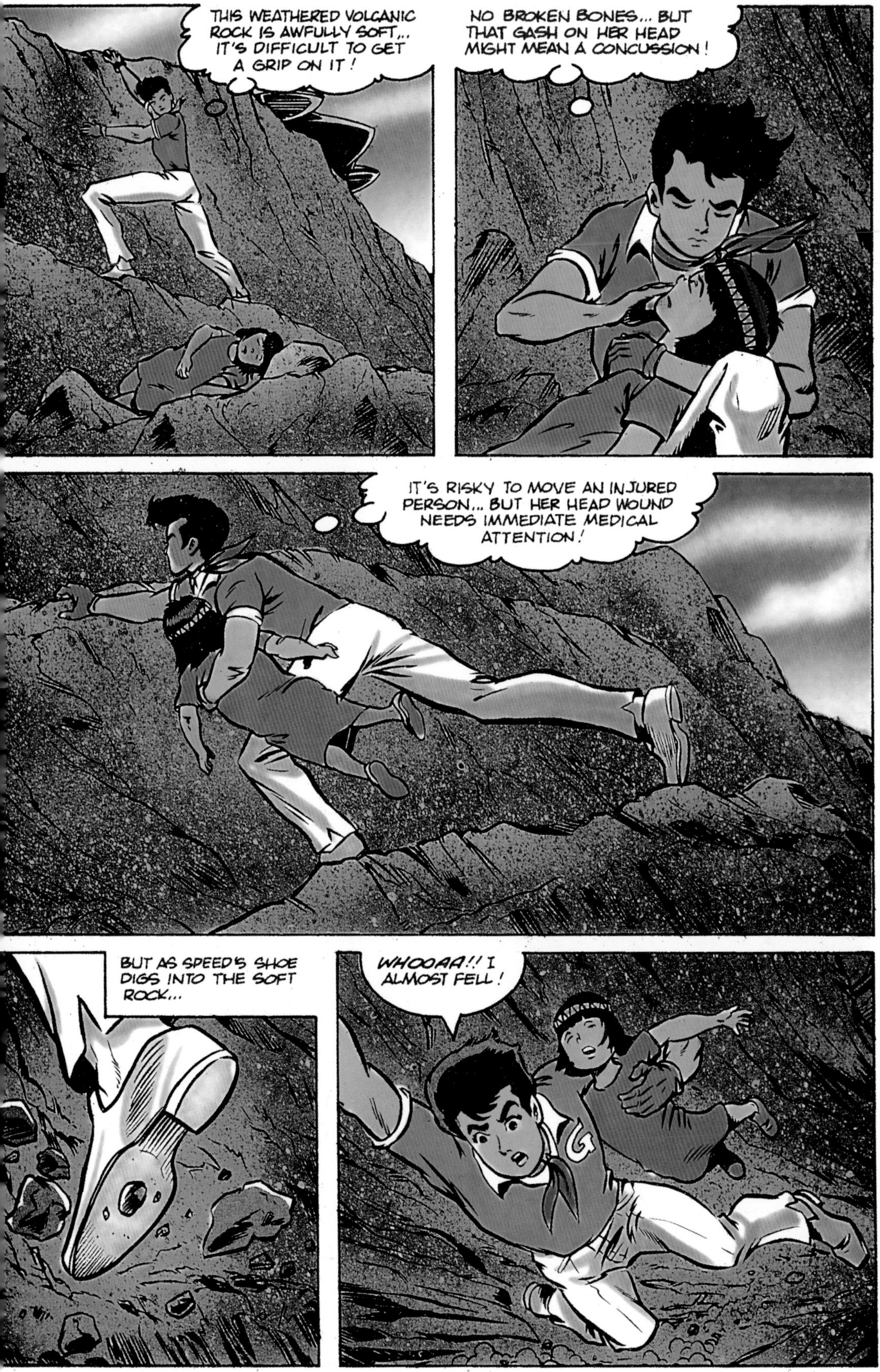

THIS WEATHERED VOLCANIC ROCK IS AWFULLY SOFT... IT'S DIFFICULT TO GET A GRIP ON IT!
NO BROKEN BONES... BUT THAT GASH ON HER HEAD MIGHT MEAN A CONCUSSION!
IT'S RISKY TO MOVE AN INJURED PERSON... BUT HER HEAD WOUND NEEDS IMMEDIATE MEDICAL ATTENTION!
BUT AS SPEED'S SHOE DIGS INTO THE SOFT ROCK...
WHOOAA!! I ALMOST FELL!

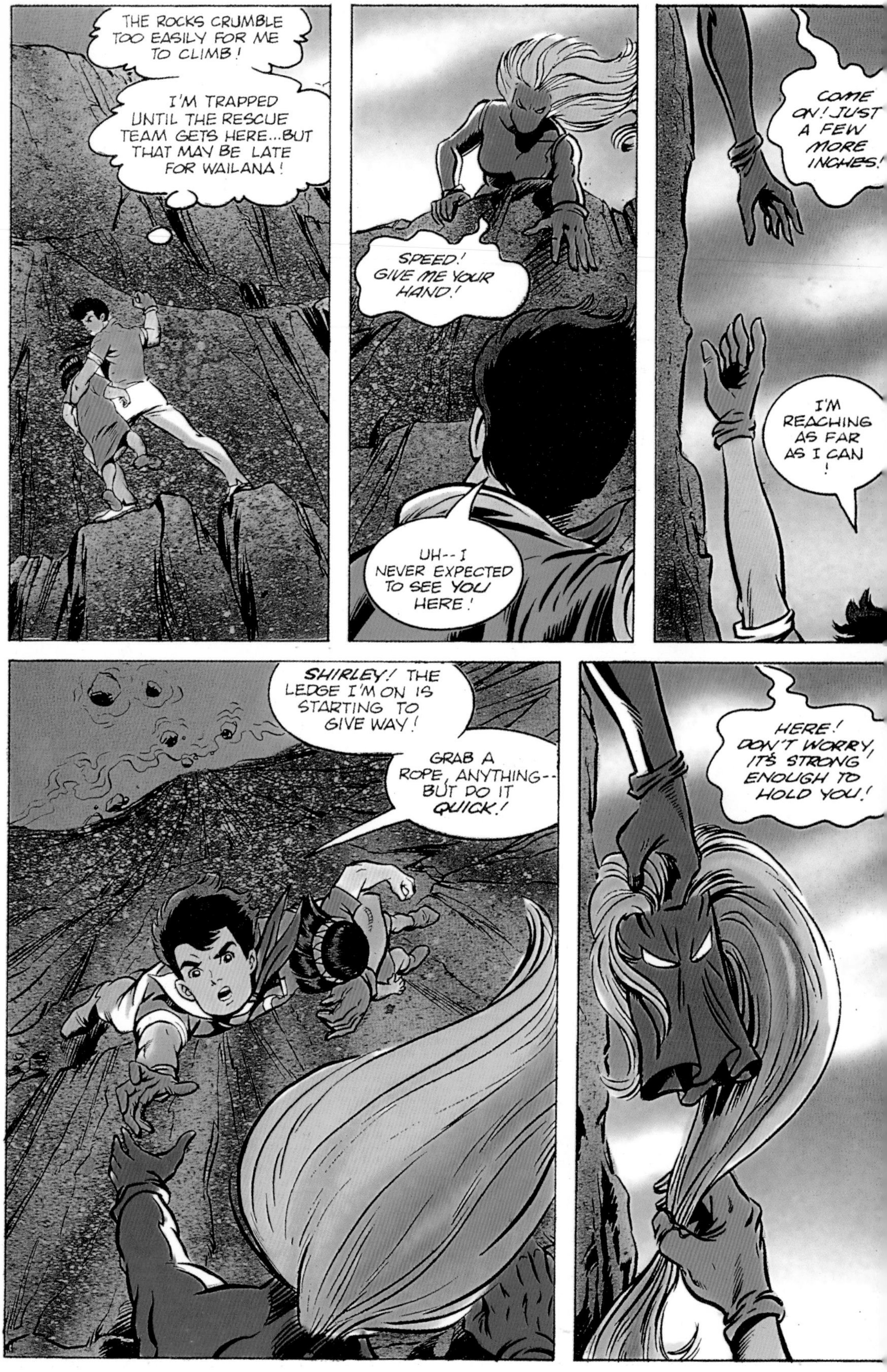
THE ROCKS CRUMBLE TOO EASILY FOR ME TO CLIMB!
I'M TRAPPED UNTIL THE RESCUE TEAM GETS HERE...BUT THAT MAY BE LATE FOR WAILANA!
SPEED! GIVE ME YOUR HAND!
UH--I NEVER EXPECTED TO SEE YOU HERE!
COME ON! JUST A FEW MORE INCHES!
I'M REACHING AS FAR AS I CAN!
SHIRLEY! THE LEDGE I'M ON IS STARTING TO GIVE WAY!
GRAB A ROPE, ANYTHING--BUT DO IT QUICK!
HERE! DON'T WORRY, IT'S STRONG ENOUGH TO HOLD YOU!

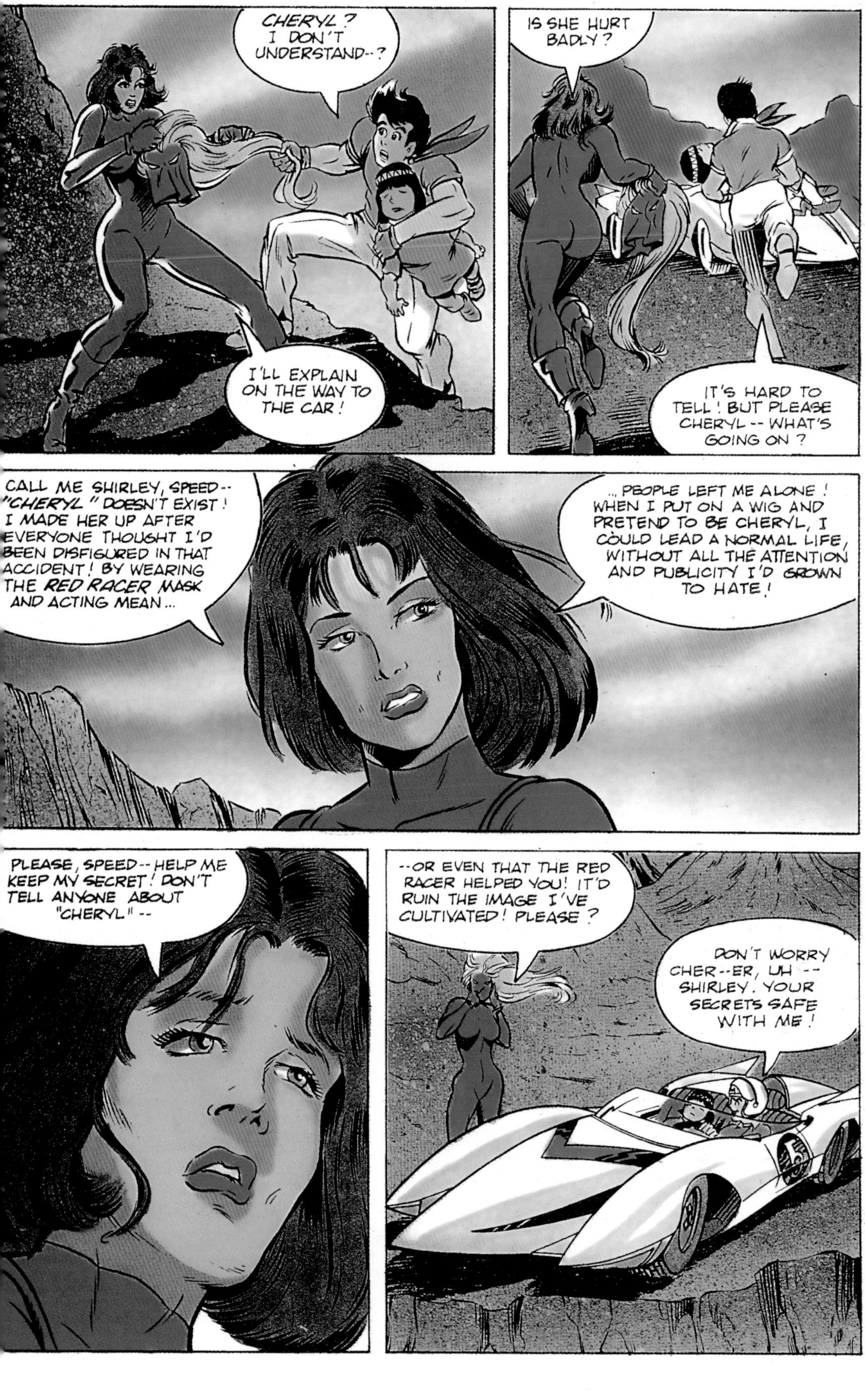
CHERYL? I DON'T UNDERSTAND--?
I'LL EXPLAIN ON THE WAY TO THE CAR!
IS SHE HURT BADLY?
IT'S HARD TO TELL! BUT PLEASE CHERYL -- WHAT'S GOING ON?
CALL ME SHIRLEY, SPEED-- "CHERYL" DOESN'T EXIST! I MADE HER UP AFTER EVERYONE THOUGHT I'D BEEN DISFIGURED IN THAT ACCIDENT! BY WEARING THE RED RACER MASK AND ACTING MEAN...
...PEOPLE LEFT ME ALONE! WHEN I PUT ON A WIG AND PRETEND TO BE CHERYL, I COULD LEAD A NORMAL LIFE, WITHOUT ALL THE ATTENTION AND PUBLICITY I'D GROWN TO HATE!
PLEASE, SPEED-- HELP ME KEEP MY SECRET! DON'T TELL ANYONE ABOUT "CHERYL" --
--OR EVEN THAT THE RED RACER HELPED YOU! IT'D RUIN THE IMAGE I'VE CULTIVATED! PLEASE?
DON'T WORRY CHER--ER, UH -- SHIRLEY. YOUR SECRETS SAFE WITH ME!

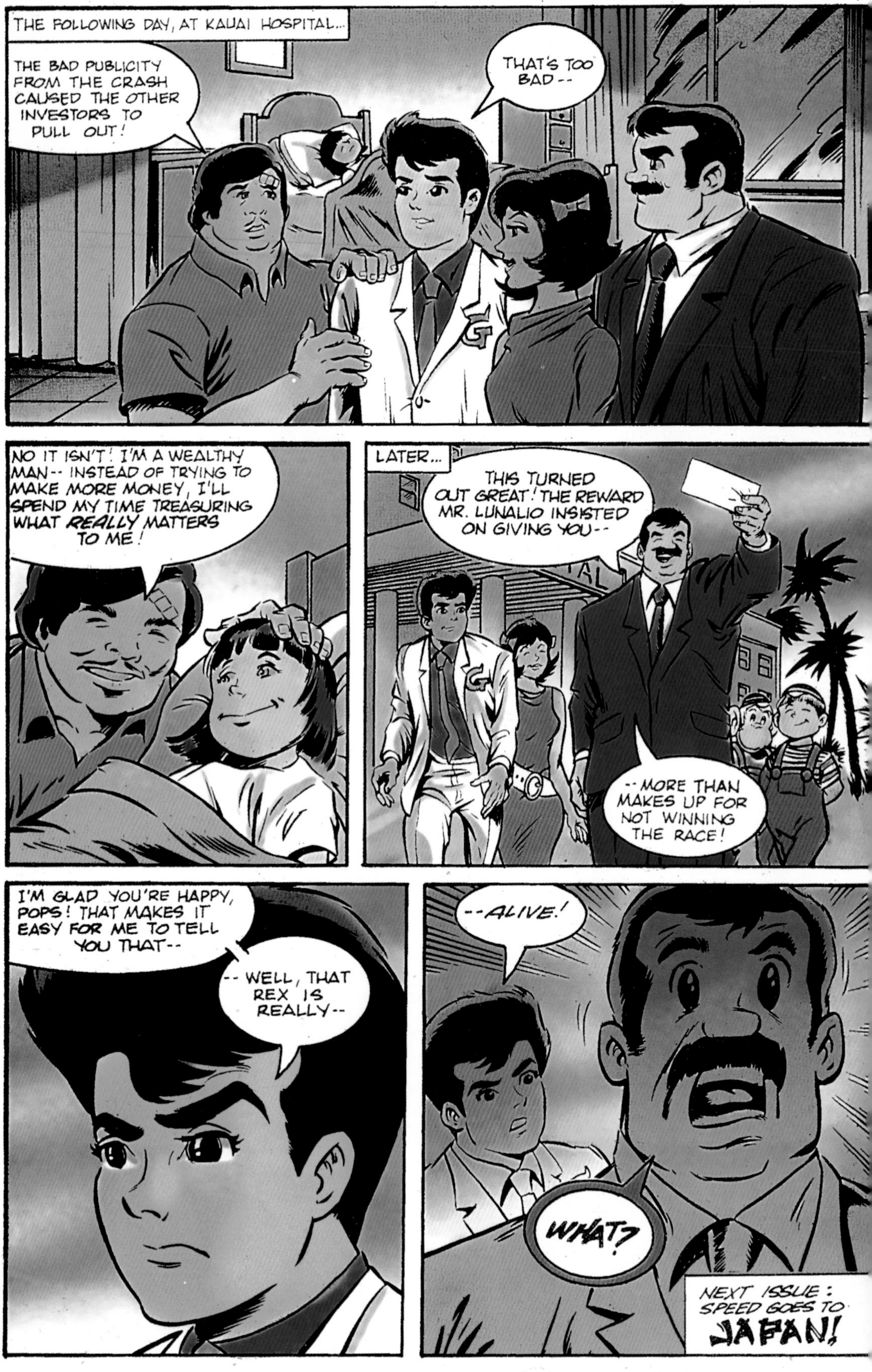
THE FOLLOWING DAY, AT KAUAI HOSPITAL...
THE BAD PUBLICITY FROM THE CRASH CAUSED THE OTHER INVESTORS TO PULL OUT!
THAT'S TOO BAD --
NO IT ISN'T! I'M A WEALTHY MAN -- INSTEAD OF TRYING TO MAKE MORE MONEY, I'LL SPEND MY TIME TREASURING WHAT REALLY MATTERS TO ME!
LATER...
THIS TURNED OUT GREAT! THE REWARD MR. LUNALIO INSISTED ON GIVING YOU --
-- MORE THAN MAKES UP FOR NOT WINNING THE RACE!
I'M GLAD YOU'RE HAPPY, POPS! THAT MAKES IT EASY FOR ME TO TELL YOU THAT --
-- WELL, THAT REX IS REALLY --
-- ALIVE!
WHAT?
NEXT ISSUE: SPEED GOES TO JAPAN!

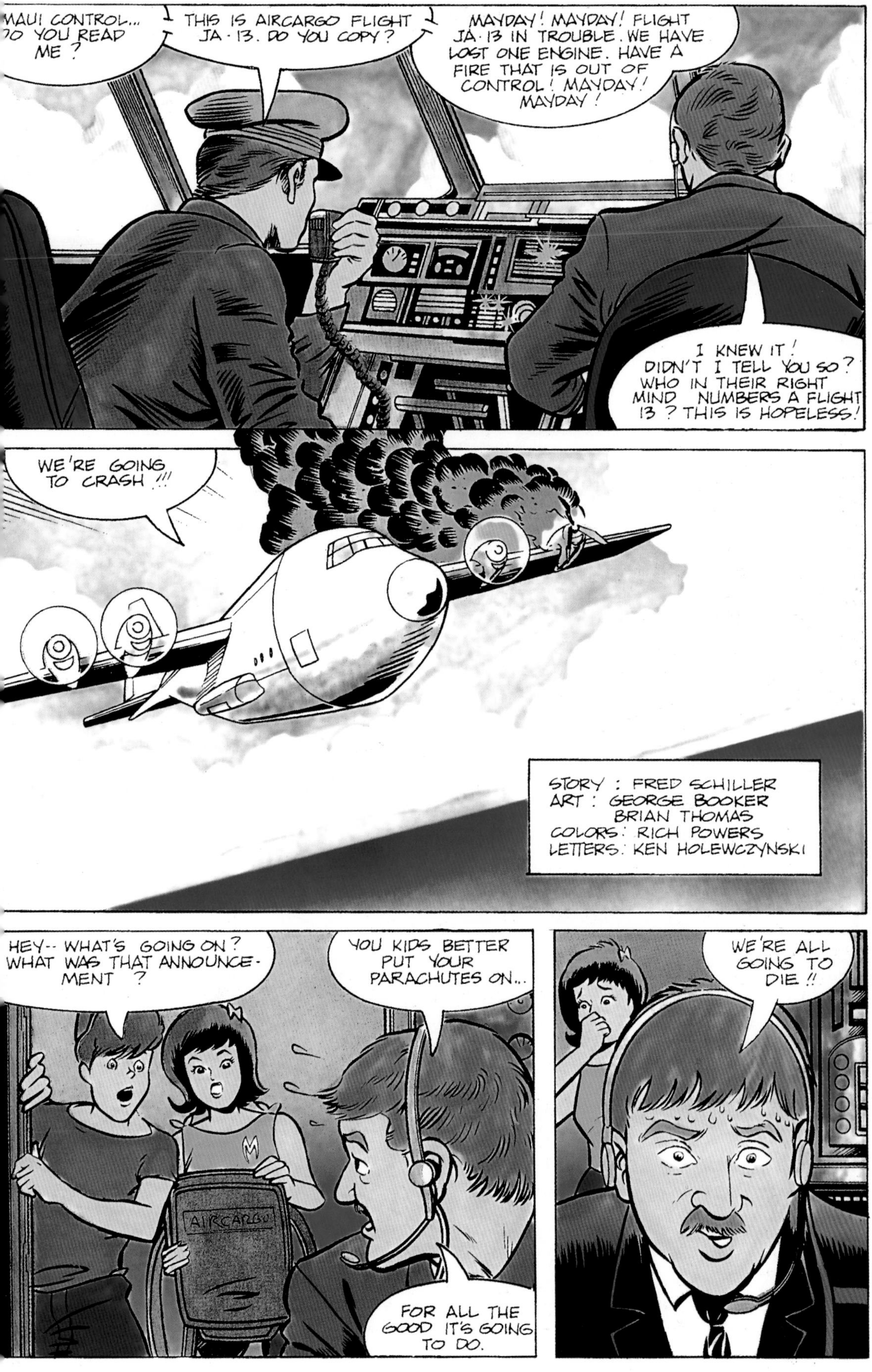
MAUI CONTROL... DO YOU READ ME ?
THIS IS AIRCARGO FLIGHT JA·13. DO YOU COPY ?
MAYDAY! MAYDAY! FLIGHT JA·13 IN TROUBLE. WE HAVE LOST ONE ENGINE. HAVE A FIRE THAT IS OUT OF CONTROL! MAYDAY! MAYDAY!
I KNEW IT! DIDN'T I TELL YOU SO? WHO IN THEIR RIGHT MIND NUMBERS A FLIGHT 13 ? THIS IS HOPELESS!
WE'RE GOING TO CRASH !!!
STORY : FRED SCHILLER
ART : GEORGE BOOKER
BRIAN THOMAS
COLORS: RICH POWERS
LETTERS: KEN HOLEWCZYNSKI
HEY-- WHAT'S GOING ON? WHAT WAS THAT ANNOUNCE-MENT ?
YOU KIDS BETTER PUT YOUR PARACHUTES ON...
AIRCARGO
FOR ALL THE GOOD IT'S GOING TO DO.
WE'RE ALL GOING TO DIE !!

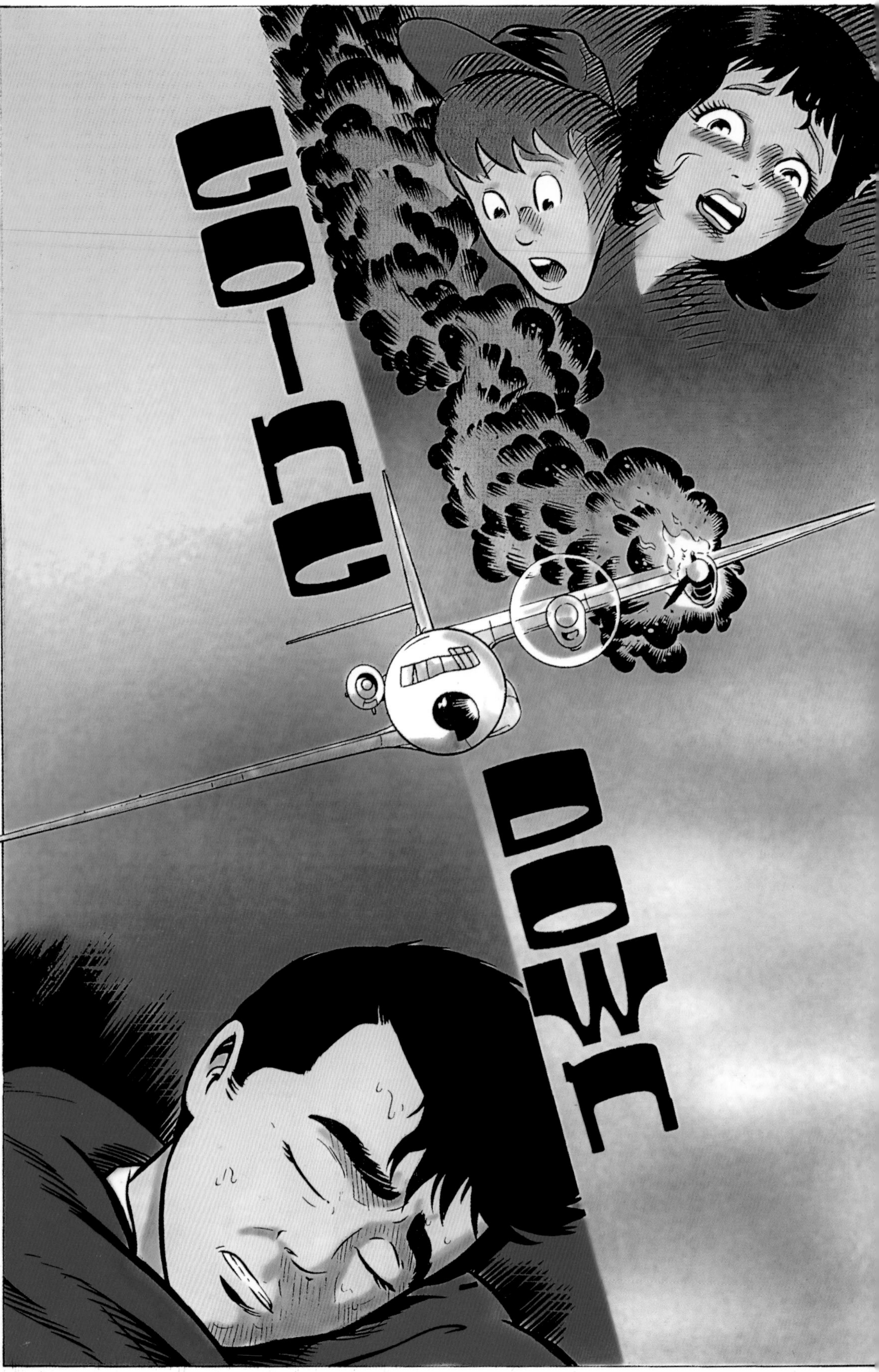
GOING
DOWN

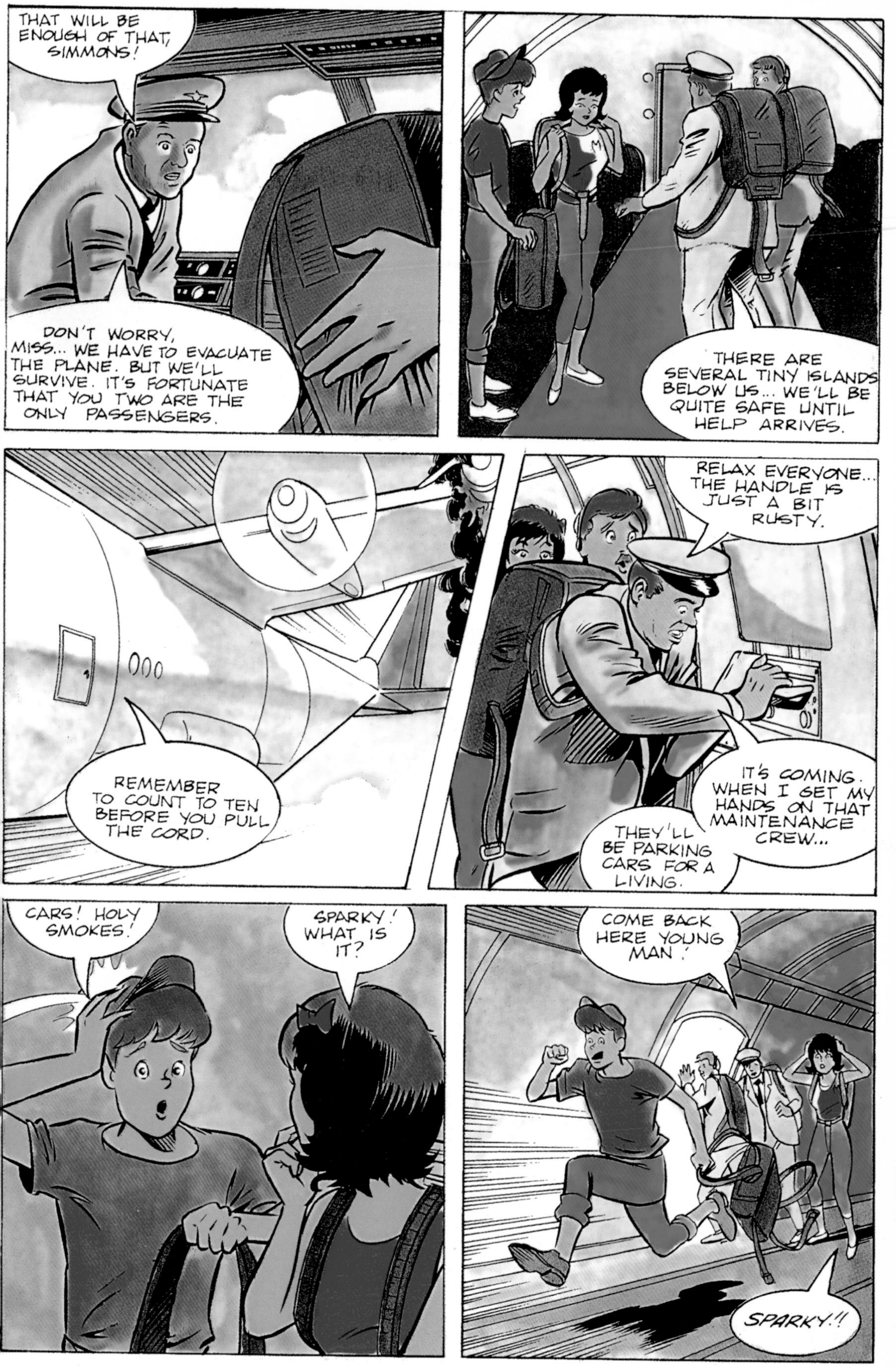
THAT WILL BE ENOUGH OF THAT, SIMMONS!
DON'T WORRY, MISS... WE HAVE TO EVACUATE THE PLANE. BUT WE'LL SURVIVE. IT'S FORTUNATE THAT YOU TWO ARE THE ONLY PASSENGERS.
THERE ARE SEVERAL TINY ISLANDS BELOW US... WE'LL BE QUITE SAFE UNTIL HELP ARRIVES.
REMEMBER TO COUNT TO TEN BEFORE YOU PULL THE CORD.
RELAX EVERYONE... THE HANDLE IS JUST A BIT RUSTY.
IT'S COMING. WHEN I GET MY HANDS ON THAT MAINTENANCE CREW...
THEY'LL BE PARKING CARS FOR A LIVING.
CARS! HOLY SMOKES!
SPARKY! WHAT IS IT?
COME BACK HERE YOUNG MAN!
SPARKY!!

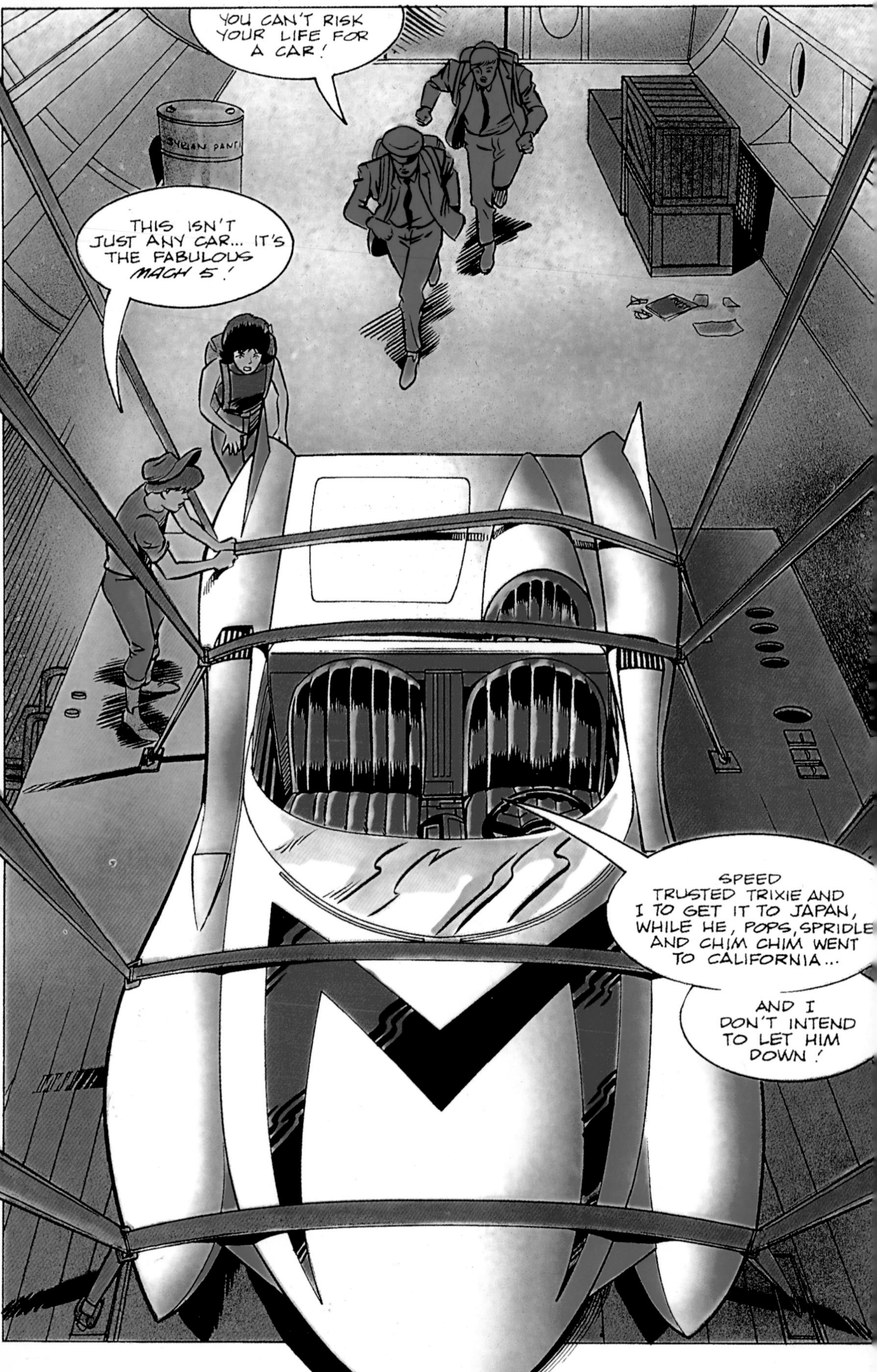
YOU CAN'T RISK YOUR LIFE FOR A CAR!
THIS ISN'T JUST ANY CAR... IT'S THE FABULOUS *MACH 5*!
SPEED TRUSTED TRIXIE AND I TO GET IT TO JAPAN, WHILE HE, POPS, SPRIDLE AND CHIM CHIM WENT TO CALIFORNIA...
AND I DON'T INTEND TO LET HIM DOWN!

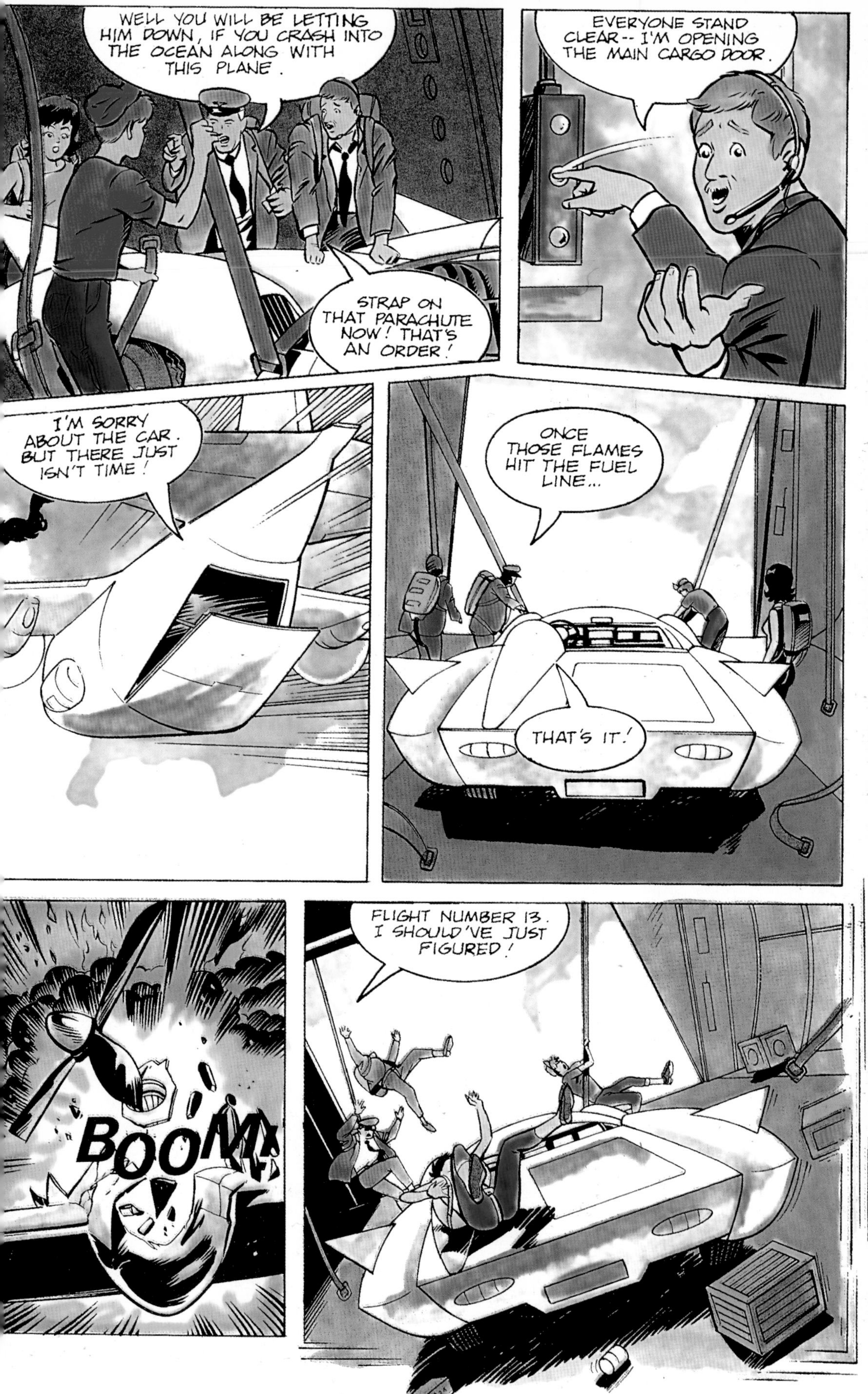
WELL YOU WILL BE LETTING HIM DOWN, IF YOU CRASH INTO THE OCEAN ALONG WITH THIS PLANE.
STRAP ON THAT PARACHUTE NOW! THAT'S AN ORDER!
EVERYONE STAND CLEAR-- I'M OPENING THE MAIN CARGO DOOR.
I'M SORRY ABOUT THE CAR. BUT THERE JUST ISN'T TIME!
ONCE THOSE FLAMES HIT THE FUEL LINE...
THAT'S IT!
BOOM!
FLIGHT NUMBER 13. I SHOULD'VE JUST FIGURED!

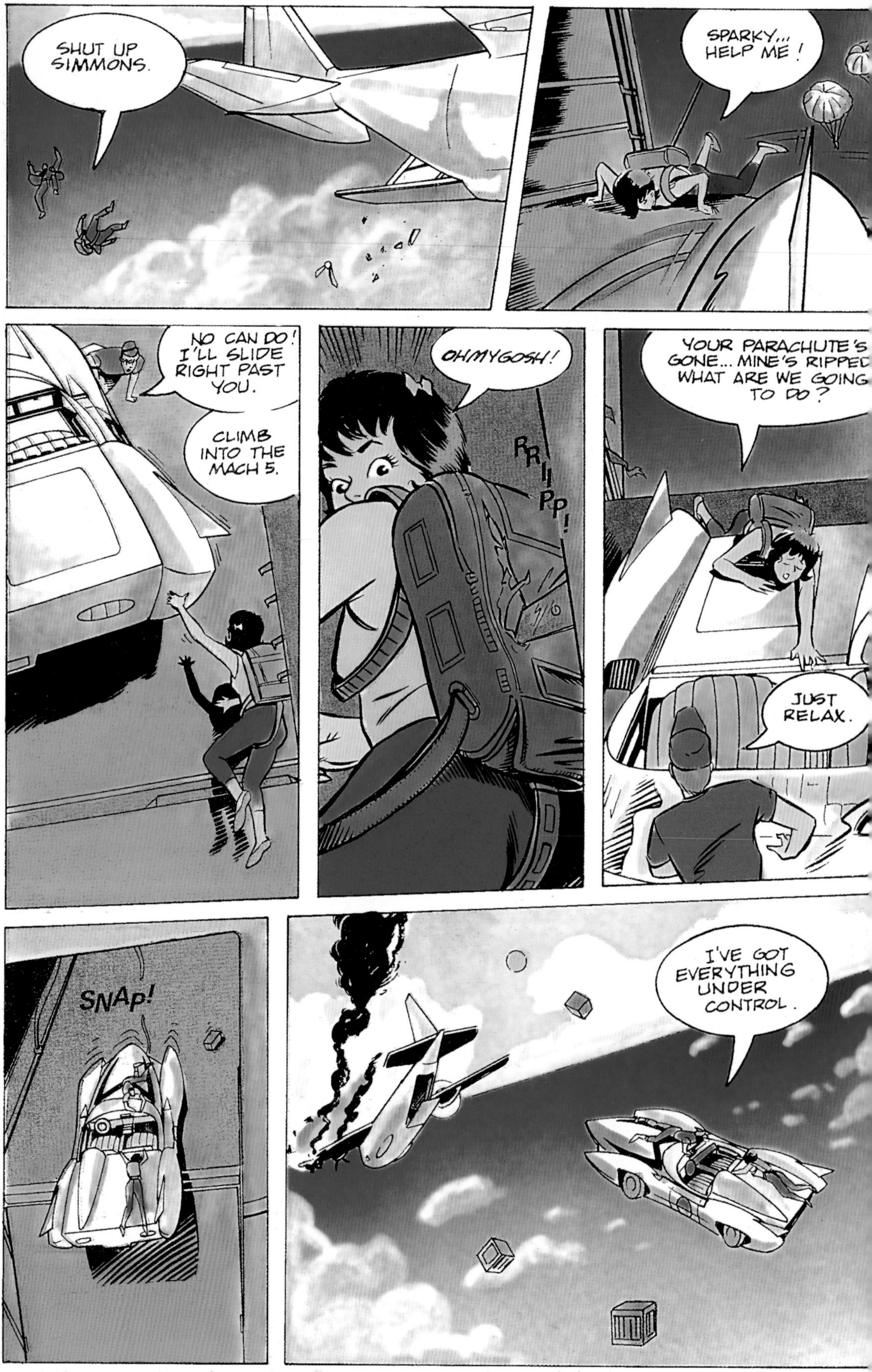
SHUT UP SIMMONS.
SPARKY,.. HELP ME!
NO CAN DO! I'LL SLIDE RIGHT PAST YOU.
CLIMB INTO THE MACH 5.
OHMYGOSH!
RRIIPP!
YOUR PARACHUTE'S GONE... MINE'S RIPPED WHAT ARE WE GOING TO DO?
JUST RELAX.
SNAP!
I'VE GOT EVERYTHING UNDER CONTROL.

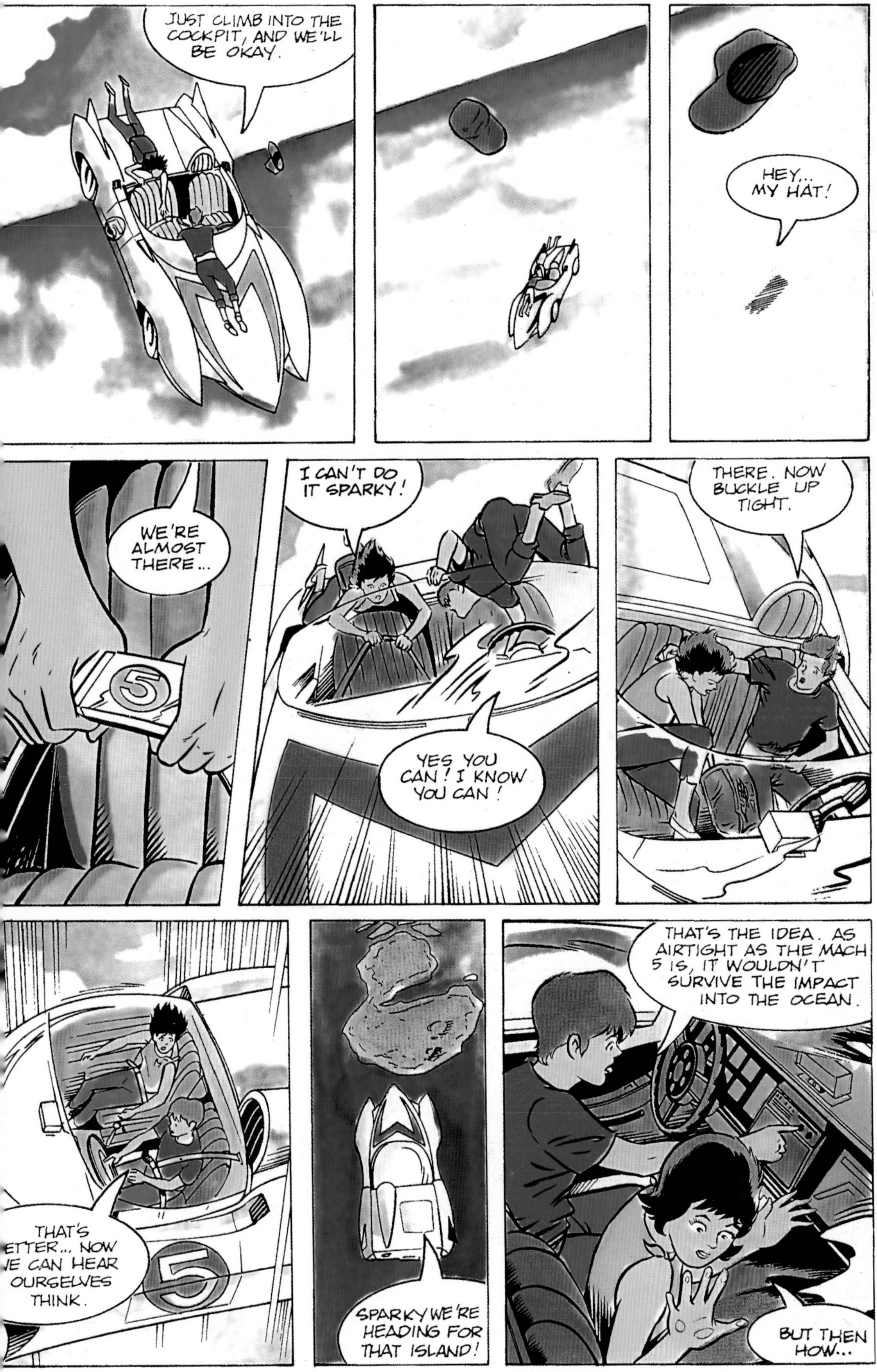
JUST CLIMB INTO THE COCKPIT, AND WE'LL BE OKAY.
HEY... MY HAT!
WE'RE ALMOST THERE...
I CAN'T DO IT SPARKY!
YES YOU CAN! I KNOW YOU CAN!
THERE. NOW BUCKLE UP TIGHT.
THAT'S ETTER... NOW E CAN HEAR OURSELVES THINK.
SPARKY WE'RE HEADING FOR THAT ISLAND!
THAT'S THE IDEA. AS AIRTIGHT AS THE MACH 5 IS, IT WOULDN'T SURVIVE THE IMPACT INTO THE OCEAN.
BUT THEN HOW...

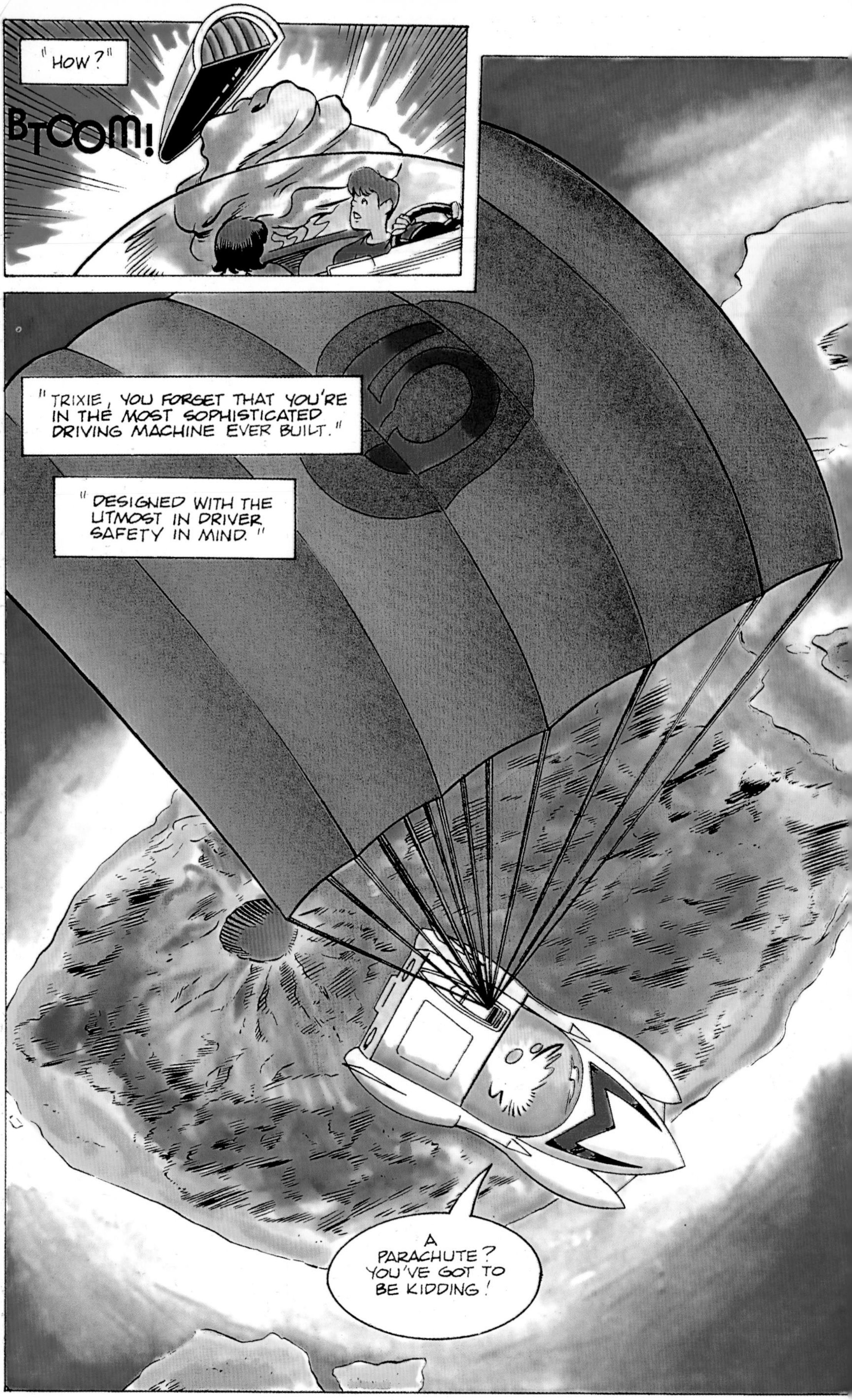
"HOW?"
BTOOM!
"TRIXIE, YOU FORGET THAT YOU'RE IN THE MOST SOPHISTICATED DRIVING MACHINE EVER BUILT."
"DESIGNED WITH THE UTMOST IN DRIVER SAFETY IN MIND."
A PARACHUTE? YOU'VE GOT TO BE KIDDING!

OPS AND I INSTALLED, IN CASE THE BRAKING SYSTEMS EVER FAILED. WASN'T DESIGNED FOR THIS TYPE OF PUNISHMENT, THOUGH.

HEY! THE PILOTS ARE LANDING ON THAT OTHER ISLAND.

SNAP!

DON'T WORRY ABOUT THEM! WHAT ABOUT US? HOW ARE WE GOING TO LAND?

" WOULD YOU RELAX ? "

VREEE!

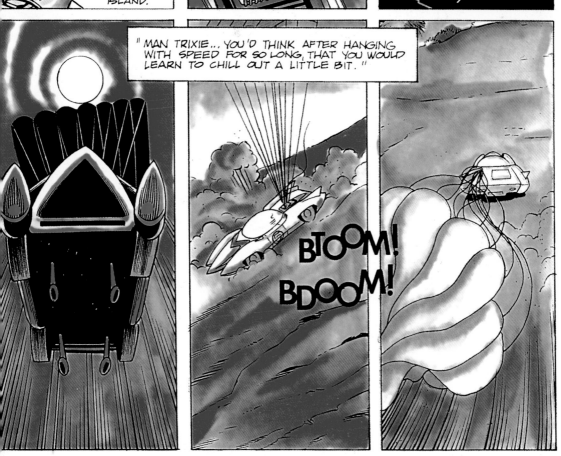

" MAN TRIXIE... YOU'D THINK AFTER HANGING WITH SPEED FOR SO LONG, THAT YOU WOULD LEARN TO CHILL OUT A LITTLE BIT. "

BTOOM!

BDOOM!

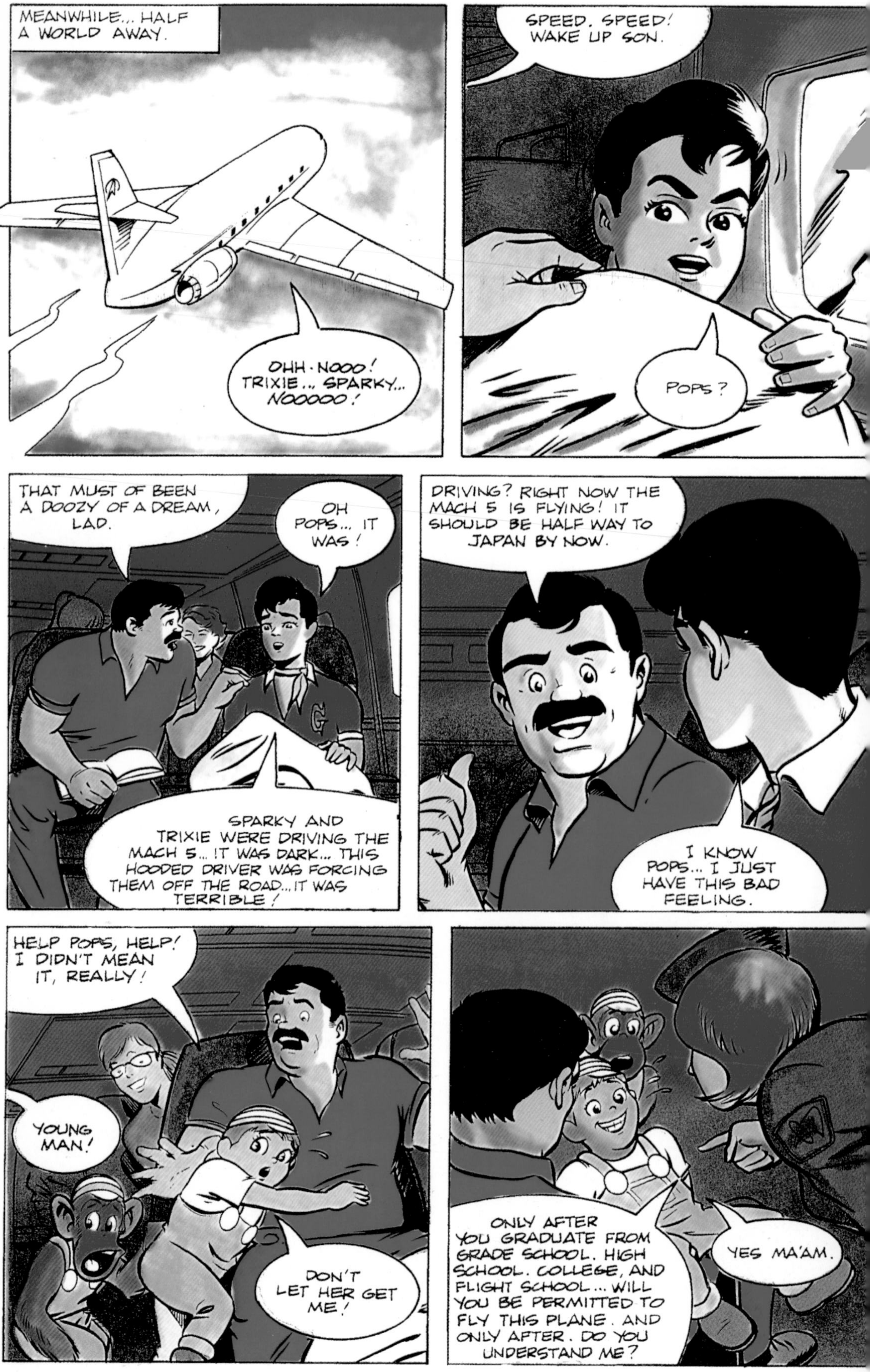
MEANWHILE... HALF A WORLD AWAY.
OHH · NOOO! TRIXIE... SPARKY... NOOOOO!
SPEED. SPEED! WAKE UP SON.
POPS?
THAT MUST OF BEEN A DOOZY OF A DREAM, LAD.
OH POPS... IT WAS!
SPARKY AND TRIXIE WERE DRIVING THE MACH 5... IT WAS DARK... THIS HOODED DRIVER WAS FORCING THEM OFF THE ROAD... IT WAS TERRIBLE!
DRIVING? RIGHT NOW THE MACH 5 IS FLYING! IT SHOULD BE HALF WAY TO JAPAN BY NOW.
I KNOW POPS... I JUST HAVE THIS BAD FEELING.
HELP POPS, HELP! I DIDN'T MEAN IT, REALLY!
YOUNG MAN!
DON'T LET HER GET ME!
ONLY AFTER YOU GRADUATE FROM GRADE SCHOOL. HIGH SCHOOL. COLLEGE, AND FLIGHT SCHOOL... WILL YOU BE PERMITTED TO FLY THIS PLANE. AND ONLY AFTER. DO YOU UNDERSTAND ME?
YES MA'AM.

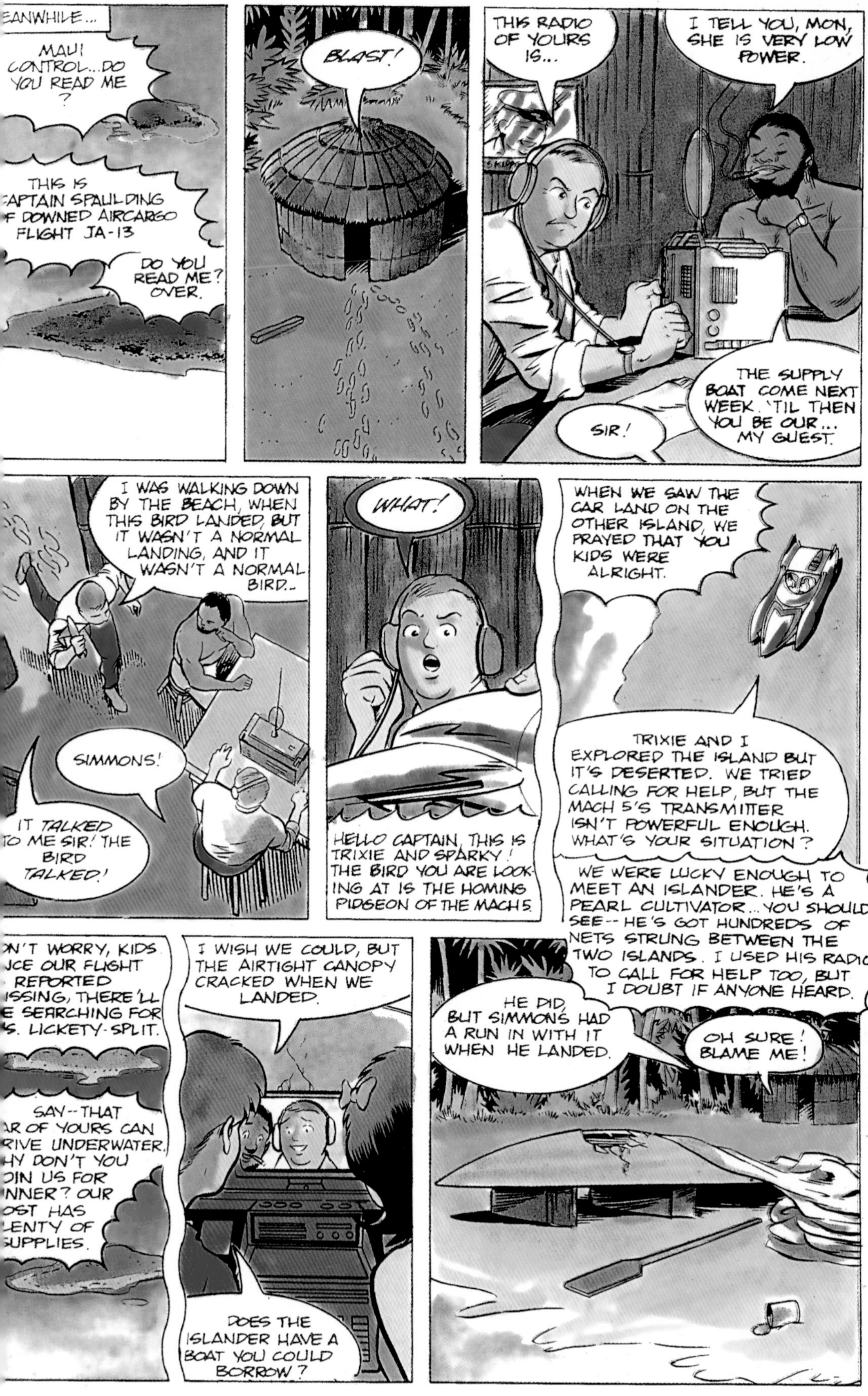
EANWHILE...
MAUI CONTROL...DO YOU READ ME?
THIS IS CAPTAIN SPAULDING F DOWNED AIRCARGO FLIGHT JA-13
DO YOU READ ME? OVER.
BLAST!
THIS RADIO OF YOURS IS...
I TELL YOU, MON, SHE IS VERY LOW POWER.
SIR!
THE SUPPLY BOAT COME NEXT WEEK. 'TIL THEN YOU BE OUR... MY GUEST.
I WAS WALKING DOWN BY THE BEACH, WHEN THIS BIRD LANDED, BUT IT WASN'T A NORMAL LANDING, AND IT WASN'T A NORMAL BIRD..
SIMMONS!
IT TALKED TO ME SIR! THE BIRD TALKED!
WHAT!
HELLO CAPTAIN, THIS IS TRIXIE AND SPARKY! THE BIRD YOU ARE LOOKING AT IS THE HOMING PIDGEON OF THE MACH 5.
WHEN WE SAW THE CAR LAND ON THE OTHER ISLAND, WE PRAYED THAT YOU KIDS WERE ALRIGHT.
TRIXIE AND I EXPLORED THE ISLAND BUT IT'S DESERTED. WE TRIED CALLING FOR HELP, BUT THE MACH 5'S TRANSMITTER ISN'T POWERFUL ENOUGH. WHAT'S YOUR SITUATION?
WE WERE LUCKY ENOUGH TO MEET AN ISLANDER. HE'S A PEARL CULTIVATOR... YOU SHOULD SEE-- HE'S GOT HUNDREDS OF NETS STRUNG BETWEEN THE TWO ISLANDS. I USED HIS RADIO TO CALL FOR HELP TOO, BUT I DOUBT IF ANYONE HEARD.
N'T WORRY, KIDS. NCE OUR FLIGHT REPORTED ISSING, THERE'LL E SEARCHING FOR S. LICKETY-SPLIT.
SAY--THAT AR OF YOURS CAN RIVE UNDERWATER. HY DON'T YOU OIN US FOR NNER? OUR OST HAS LENTY OF SUPPLIES.
I WISH WE COULD, BUT THE AIRTIGHT CANOPY CRACKED WHEN WE LANDED.
DOES THE ISLANDER HAVE A BOAT YOU COULD BORROW?
HE DID, BUT SIMMONS HAD A RUN IN WITH IT WHEN HE LANDED.
OH SURE! BLAME ME!

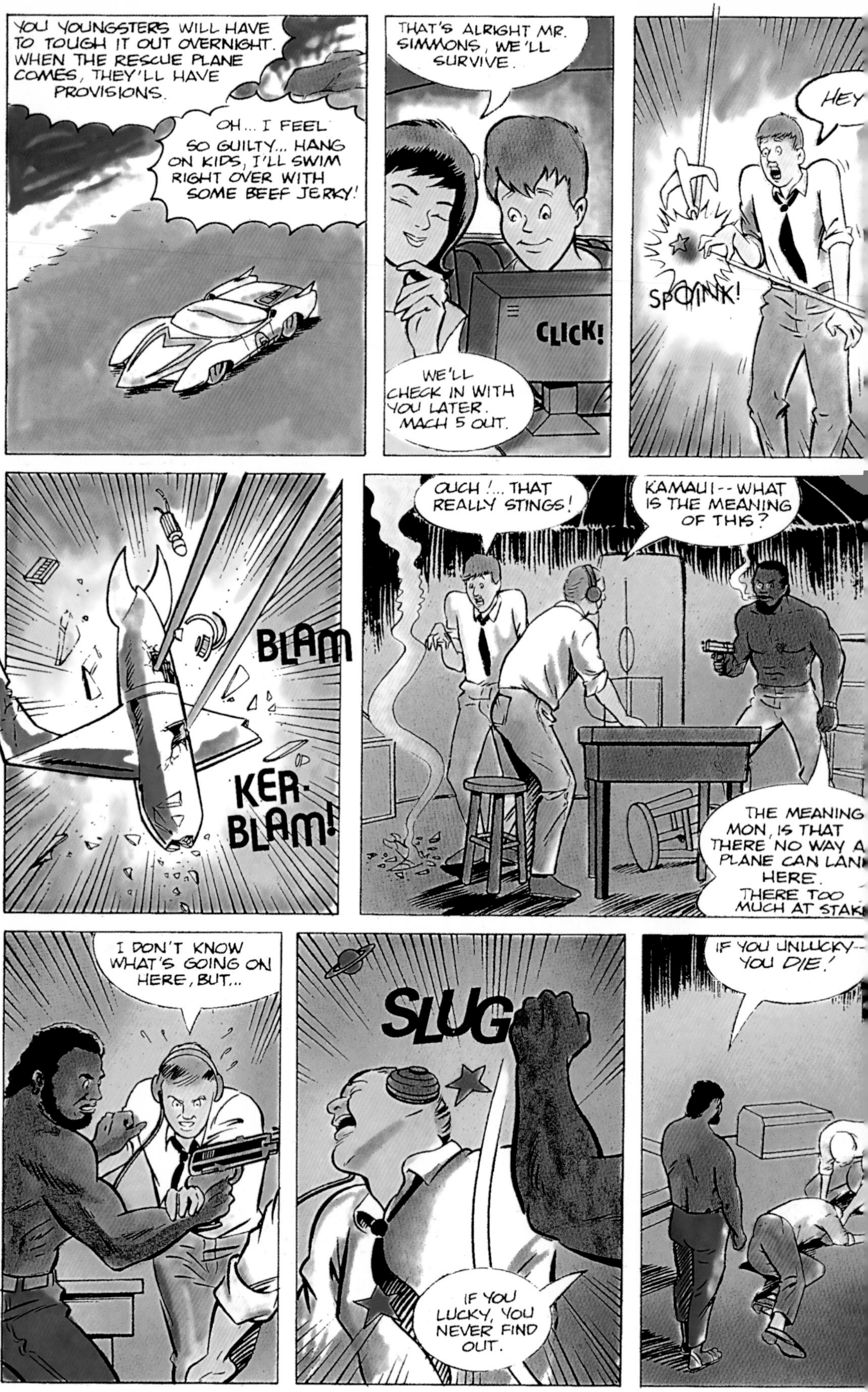
YOU YOUNGSTERS WILL HAVE TO TOUGH IT OUT OVERNIGHT. WHEN THE RESCUE PLANE COMES, THEY'LL HAVE PROVISIONS.
OH... I FEEL SO GUILTY... HANG ON KIDS, I'LL SWIM RIGHT OVER WITH SOME BEEF JERKY!
THAT'S ALRIGHT MR. SIMMONS, WE'LL SURVIVE.
CLICK!
WE'LL CHECK IN WITH YOU LATER. MACH 5 OUT.
HEY
SPOINK!
BLAM
KER-BLAM!
OUCH!... THAT REALLY STINGS!
KAMAUI-- WHAT IS THE MEANING OF THIS?
THE MEANING MON, IS THAT THERE NO WAY A PLANE CAN LAN HERE. THERE TOO MUCH AT STAK
I DON'T KNOW WHAT'S GOING ON HERE, BUT...
SLUG
IF YOU LUCKY, YOU NEVER FIND OUT.
IF YOU UNLUCKY-- YOU DIE!

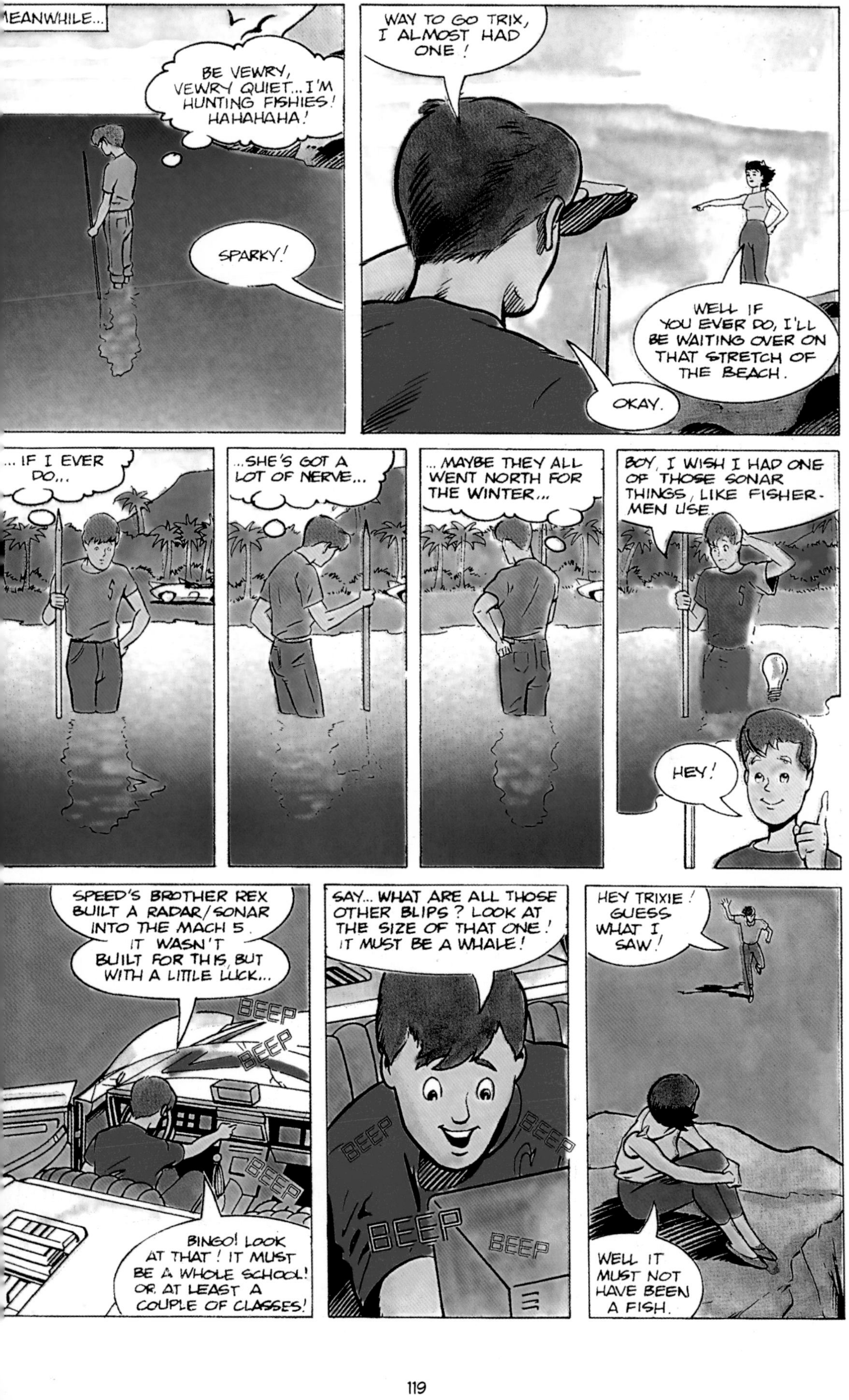

MEANWHILE...
BE VEWRY, VEWRY QUIET... I'M HUNTING FISHIES! HAHAHAHA!
SPARKY!
WAY TO GO TRIX, I ALMOST HAD ONE!
WELL IF YOU EVER DO, I'LL BE WAITING OVER ON THAT STRETCH OF THE BEACH.
OKAY.
... IF I EVER DO...
...SHE'S GOT A LOT OF NERVE...
... MAYBE THEY ALL WENT NORTH FOR THE WINTER...
BOY, I WISH I HAD ONE OF THOSE SONAR THINGS, LIKE FISHER-MEN USE.
HEY!
SPEED'S BROTHER REX BUILT A RADAR/SONAR INTO THE MACH 5. IT WASN'T BUILT FOR THIS, BUT WITH A LITTLE LUCK...
BEEP
BEEP
BEEP
BINGO! LOOK AT THAT! IT MUST BE A WHOLE SCHOOL! OR, AT LEAST A COUPLE OF CLASSES!
SAY... WHAT ARE ALL THOSE OTHER BLIPS? LOOK AT THE SIZE OF THAT ONE! IT MUST BE A WHALE!
BEEP
BEEP
BEEP
BEEP
HEY TRIXIE! GUESS WHAT I SAW!
WELL IT MUST NOT HAVE BEEN A FISH.

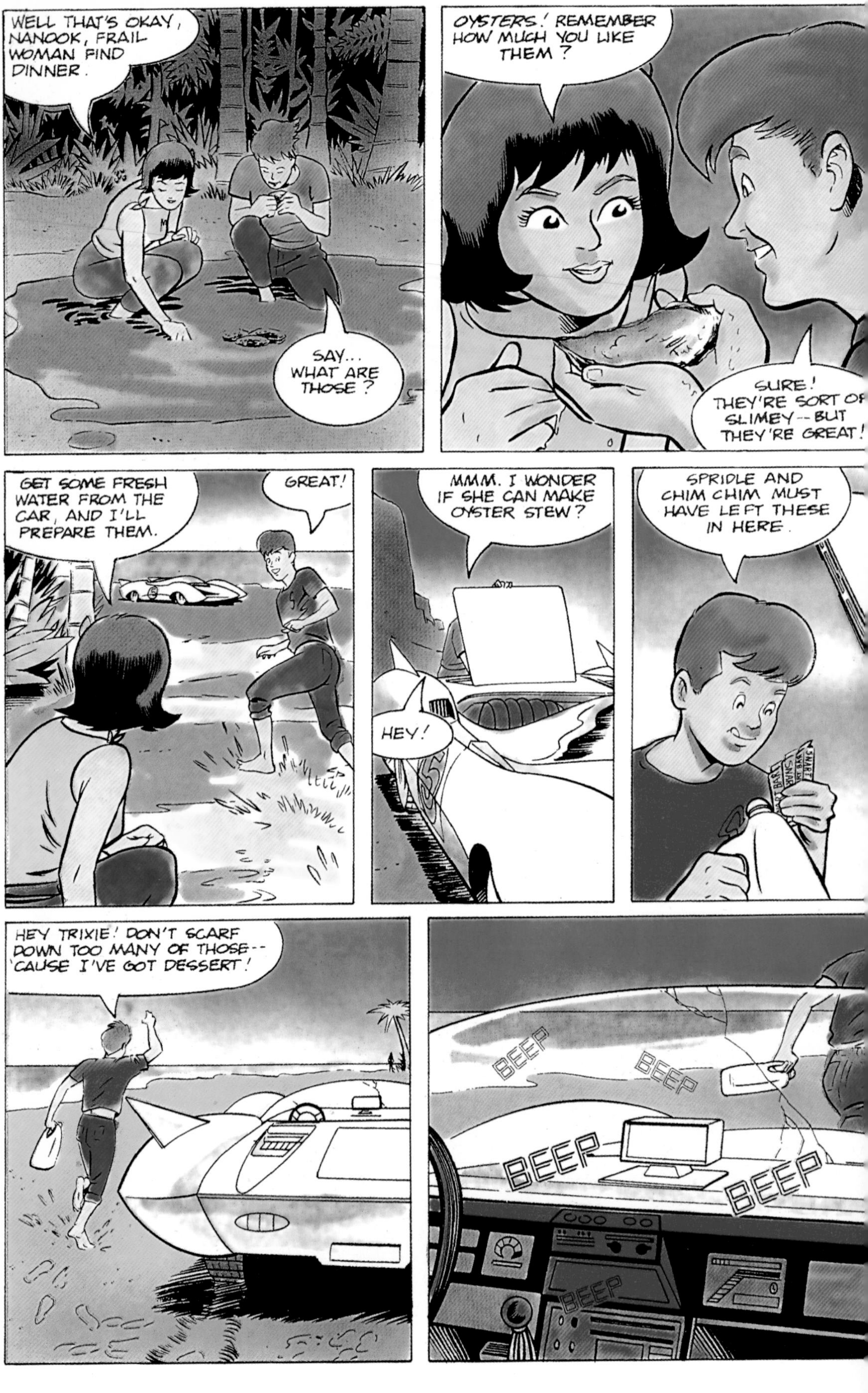

WELL THAT'S OKAY, NANOOK, FRAIL WOMAN FIND DINNER.
SAY... WHAT ARE THOSE?
OYSTERS! REMEMBER HOW MUCH YOU LIKE THEM?
SURE! THEY'RE SORT OF SLIMEY-- BUT THEY'RE GREAT!
GET SOME FRESH WATER FROM THE CAR, AND I'LL PREPARE THEM.
GREAT!
MMM. I WONDER IF SHE CAN MAKE OYSTER STEW?
HEY!
SPRIDLE AND CHIM CHIM MUST HAVE LEFT THESE IN HERE.
HEY TRIXIE! DON'T SCARF DOWN TOO MANY OF THOSE-- 'CAUSE I'VE GOT DESSERT!
BEEP
BEEP
BEEP
BEEP
BEEP

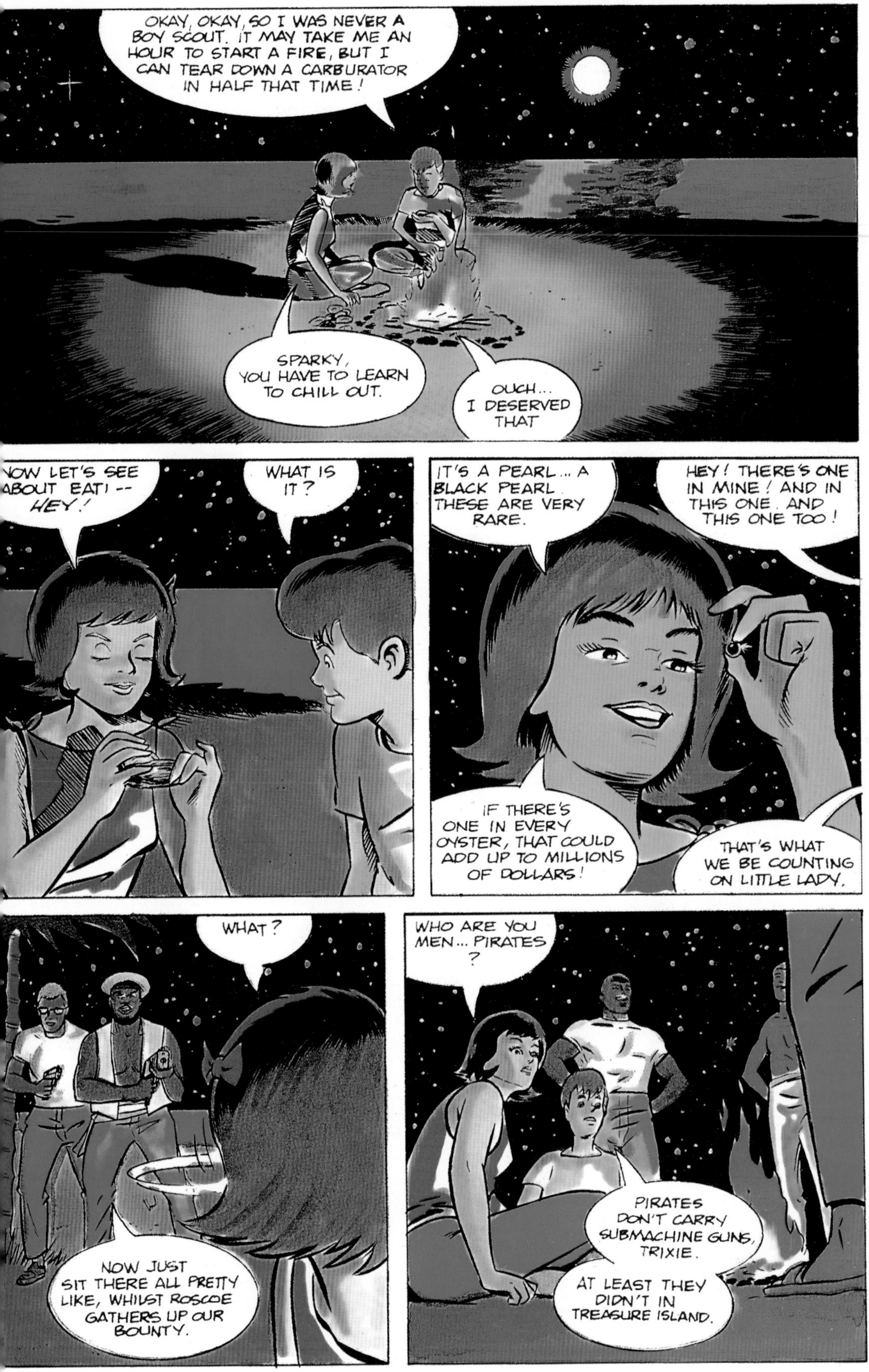
OKAY, OKAY, SO I WAS NEVER A BOY SCOUT. IT MAY TAKE ME AN HOUR TO START A FIRE, BUT I CAN TEAR DOWN A CARBURATOR IN HALF THAT TIME!
SPARKY, YOU HAVE TO LEARN TO CHILL OUT.
OUCH... I DESERVED THAT
NOW LET'S SEE ABOUT EATI -- HEY!
WHAT IS IT?
IT'S A PEARL... A BLACK PEARL. THESE ARE VERY RARE.
HEY! THERE'S ONE IN MINE! AND IN THIS ONE. AND THIS ONE TOO!
IF THERE'S ONE IN EVERY OYSTER, THAT COULD ADD UP TO MILLIONS OF DOLLARS!
THAT'S WHAT WE BE COUNTING ON LITTLE LADY.
WHAT?
NOW JUST SIT THERE ALL PRETTY LIKE, WHILST ROSCOE GATHERS UP OUR BOUNTY.
WHO ARE YOU MEN... PIRATES?
PIRATES DON'T CARRY SUBMACHINE GUNS, TRIXIE.
AT LEAST THEY DIDN'T IN TREASURE ISLAND.

OWW! THAT HURTS!

TIE THEM SECURELY, LADS.

WE DON'T WANT THEM SIGNALING FOR HELP, WHEN THAT RESCUE PLANE GETS HERE IN THE MORNING.

SAY... I KNOW WHAT YOU FELLOWS ARE UP TO. WHEN WE CRASHED HERE, WE CAUGHT YOU IN THE MIDDLE OF RAIDING THOSE OYSTER NETS.

YOU ARE A SMART ONE, LAD. RIGHT YOU ARE.

THE BOYS AND ME WAITED FIVE LONG YEARS, UNTIL THE OYSTER HAD TIME TO DO ITS MAGIC.

BUT THE CASH THEY'LL BRING IN, WILL MAKE THE WAIT WORTHWHILE.

IF YOU MEN HAD TAKEN HONEST JOBS WHILE YOU WERE WAITING, YOU WOULDN'T HAVE TO STEAL!

WORK?

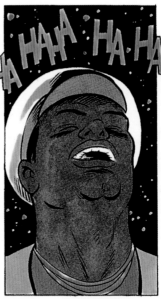

HA HAA HA HA

UFFF!

HEY MY HAT! BOY IT SURE TOOK ITS TIME COMING DOWN.

GIGGLE.

YOU'LL PAY FOR THAT.

OUR LAUNCH ISN'T BIG ENOUGH TO CARRY IT, SO WE'LL SEND THEM TO MEET DAVEY JONES IN THAT FANCY CAR OF THEIRS.

DAVY JONES OF THE MONKEYS?

SPARKY!

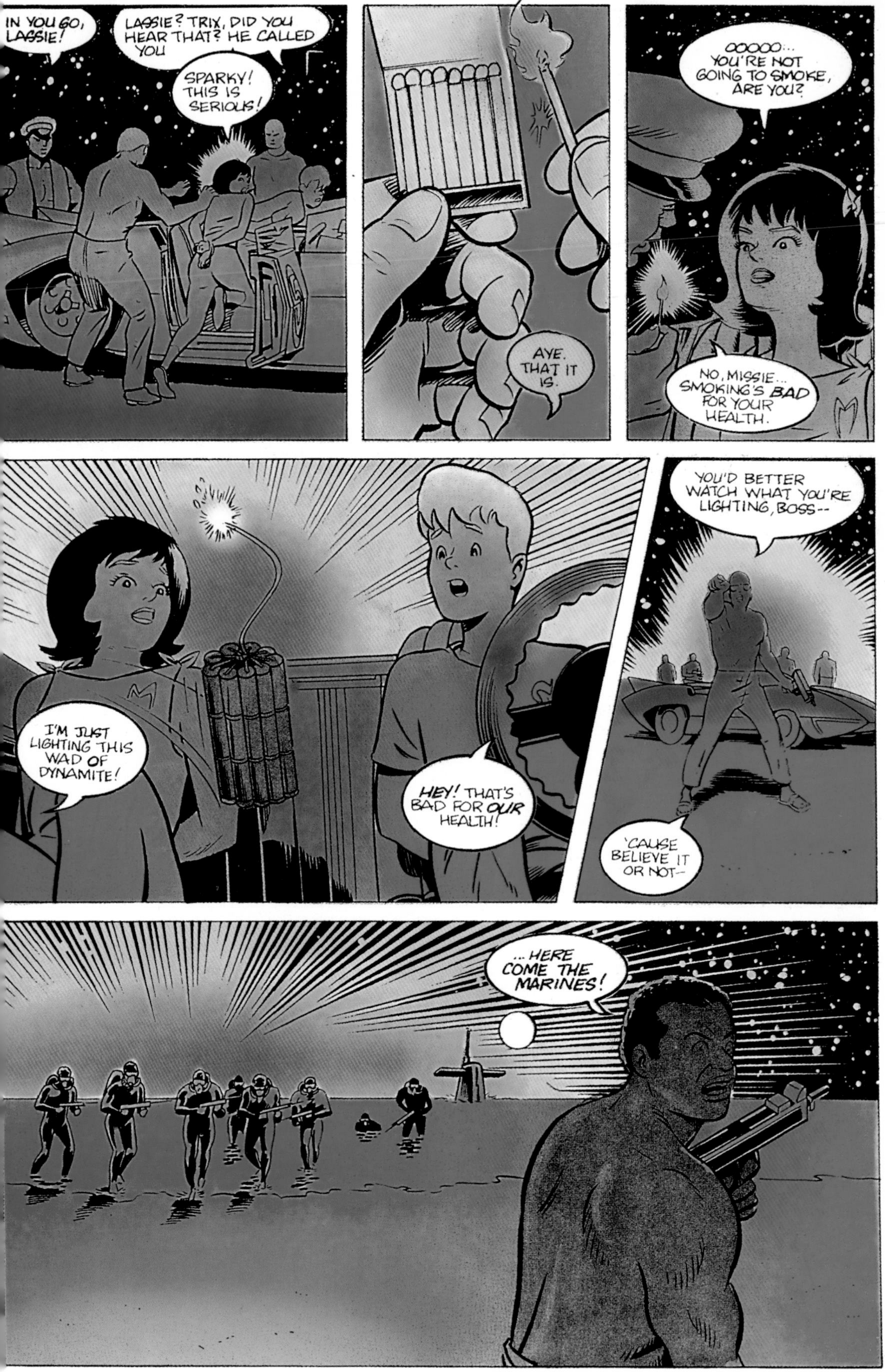
IN YOU GO, LASSIE!
LASSIE? TRIX, DID YOU HEAR THAT? HE CALLED YOU
SPARKY! THIS IS SERIOUS!
AYE. THAT IT IS.
OOOOO... YOU'RE NOT GOING TO SMOKE, ARE YOU?
NO, MISSIE... SMOKING'S BAD FOR YOUR HEALTH.
I'M JUST LIGHTING THIS WAD OF DYNAMITE!
HEY! THAT'S BAD FOR OUR HEALTH!
YOU'D BETTER WATCH WHAT YOU'RE LIGHTING, BOSS--
'CAUSE BELIEVE IT OR NOT--
...HERE COME THE MARINES!

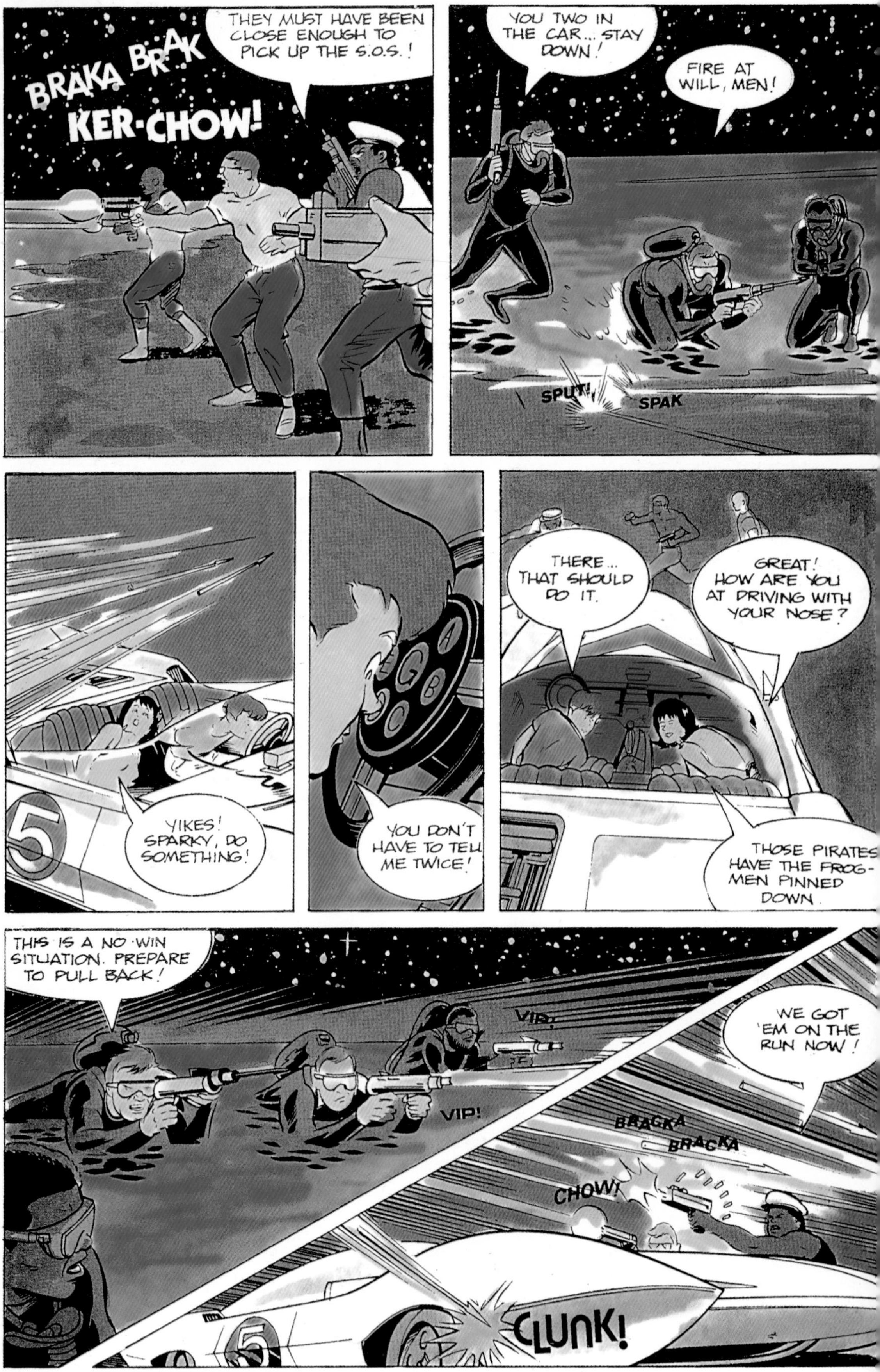
BRAKA BRAK
KER-CHOW!
THEY MUST HAVE BEEN CLOSE ENOUGH TO PICK UP THE S.O.S.!
YOU TWO IN THE CAR... STAY DOWN!
FIRE AT WILL, MEN!
SPUT!
SPAK
YIKES! SPARKY, DO SOMETHING!
YOU DON'T HAVE TO TELL ME TWICE!
THERE... THAT SHOULD DO IT.
GREAT! HOW ARE YOU AT DRIVING WITH YOUR NOSE?
THOSE PIRATES HAVE THE FROG-MEN PINNED DOWN.
THIS IS A NO-WIN SITUATION. PREPARE TO PULL BACK!
VIP!
VIP!
WE GOT 'EM ON THE RUN NOW!
BRACKA
BRACKA
CHOW!
CLUNK!

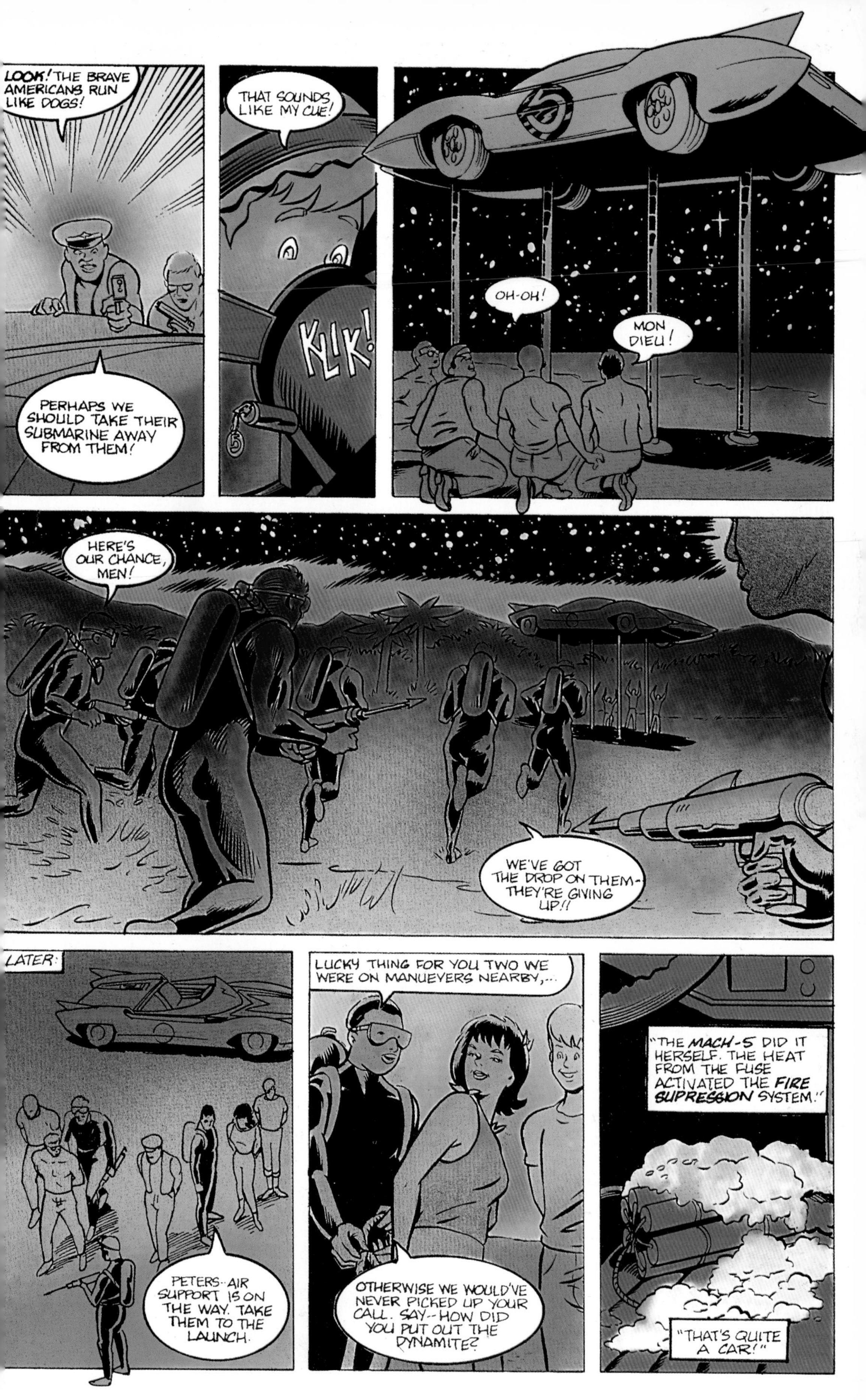
LOOK! THE BRAVE AMERICANS RUN LIKE DOGS!
PERHAPS WE SHOULD TAKE THEIR SUBMARINE AWAY FROM THEM!
THAT SOUNDS LIKE MY CUE!
KLIK!
OH-OH!
MON DIEU!
HERE'S OUR CHANCE, MEN!
WE'VE GOT THE DROP ON THEM-- THEY'RE GIVING UP!!
LATER:
PETERS-- AIR SUPPORT IS ON THE WAY. TAKE THEM TO THE LAUNCH.
LUCKY THING FOR YOU TWO WE WERE ON MANUEVERS NEARBY,...
OTHERWISE WE WOULD'VE NEVER PICKED UP YOUR CALL. SAY-- HOW DID YOU PUT OUT THE DYNAMITE?
"THE MACH-5 DID IT HERSELF. THE HEAT FROM THE FUSE ACTIVATED THE FIRE SUPRESSION SYSTEM."
"THAT'S QUITE A CAR!"

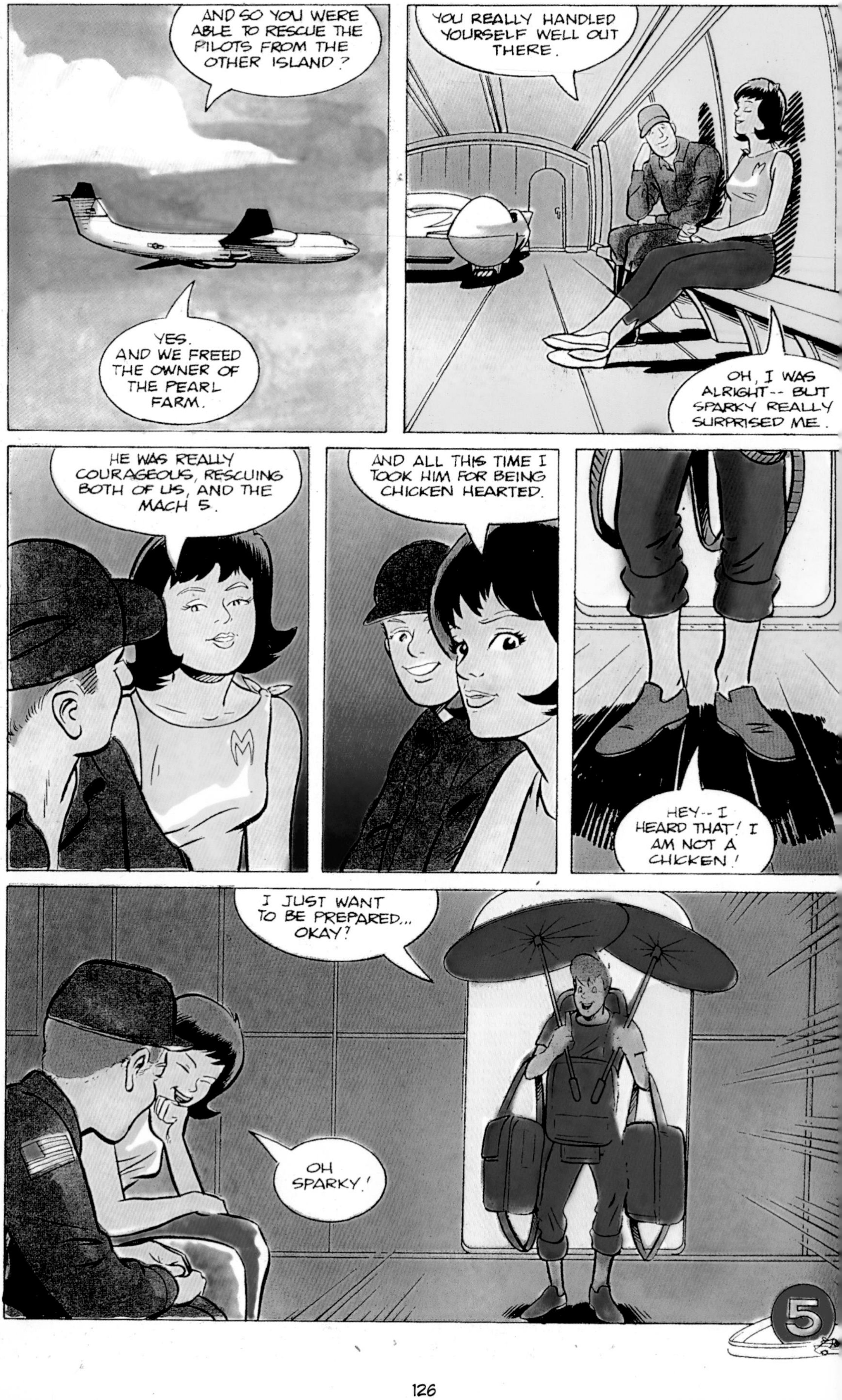
AND SO YOU WERE ABLE TO RESCUE THE PILOTS FROM THE OTHER ISLAND?
YES. AND WE FREED THE OWNER OF THE PEARL FARM.
YOU REALLY HANDLED YOURSELF WELL OUT THERE.
OH, I WAS ALRIGHT-- BUT SPARKY REALLY SURPRISED ME.
HE WAS REALLY COURAGEOUS, RESCUING BOTH OF US, AND THE MACH 5.
AND ALL THIS TIME I TOOK HIM FOR BEING CHICKEN HEARTED.
HEY-- I HEARD THAT! I AM NOT A CHICKEN!
I JUST WANT TO BE PREPARED... OKAY?
OH SPARKY!
5

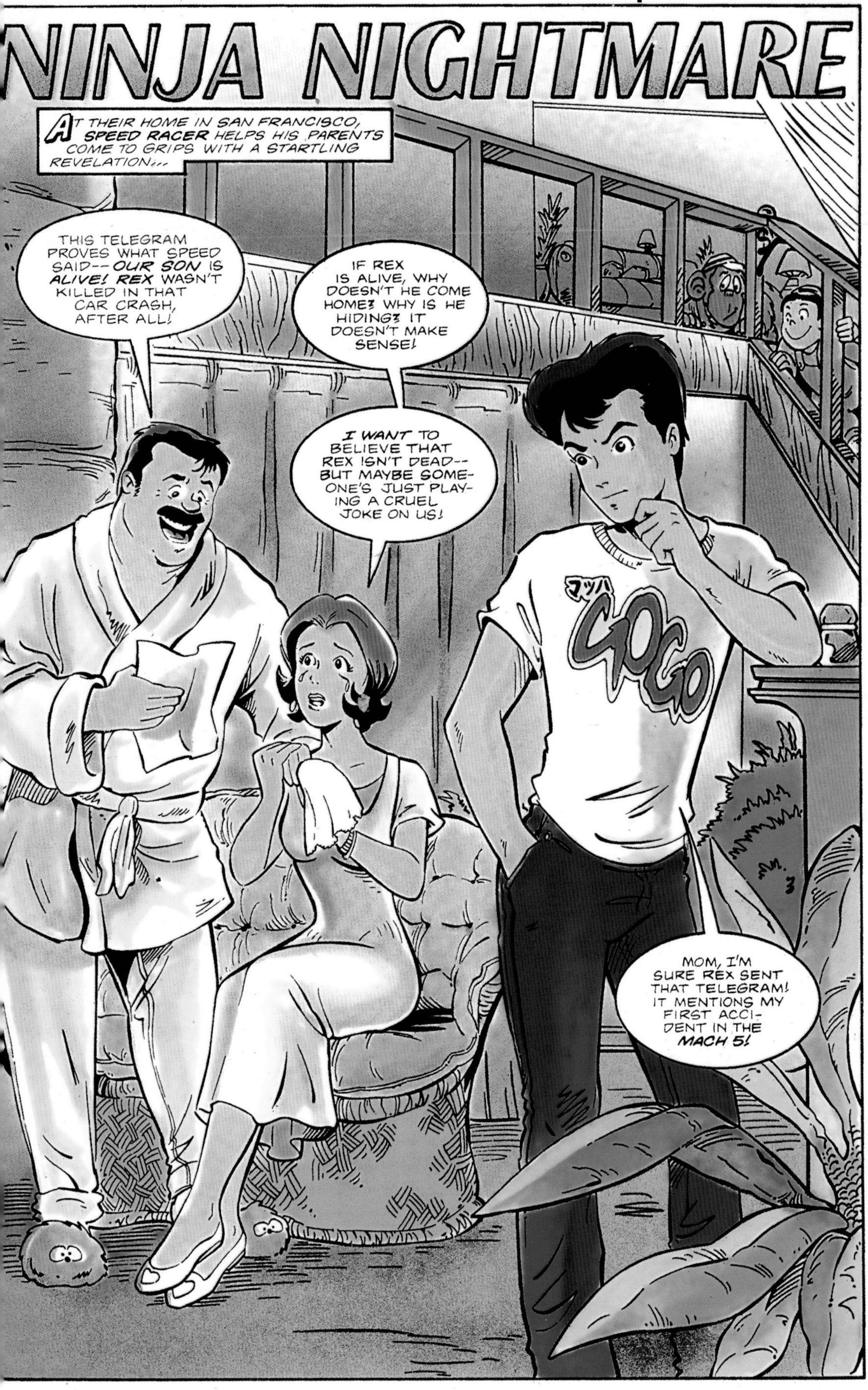
NINJA NIGHTMARE
AT THEIR HOME IN SAN FRANCISCO, SPEED RACER HELPS HIS PARENTS COME TO GRIPS WITH A STARTLING REVELATION...
THIS TELEGRAM PROVES WHAT SPEED SAID--OUR SON IS ALIVE! REX WASN'T KILLED IN THAT CAR CRASH, AFTER ALL!
IF REX IS ALIVE, WHY DOESN'T HE COME HOME? WHY IS HE HIDING? IT DOESN'T MAKE SENSE!
I WANT TO BELIEVE THAT REX ISN'T DEAD--BUT MAYBE SOME-ONE'S JUST PLAY-ING A CRUEL JOKE ON US!
MOM, I'M SURE REX SENT THAT TELEGRAM! IT MENTIONS MY FIRST ACCI-DENT IN THE MACH 5!
マッハ
GOGO

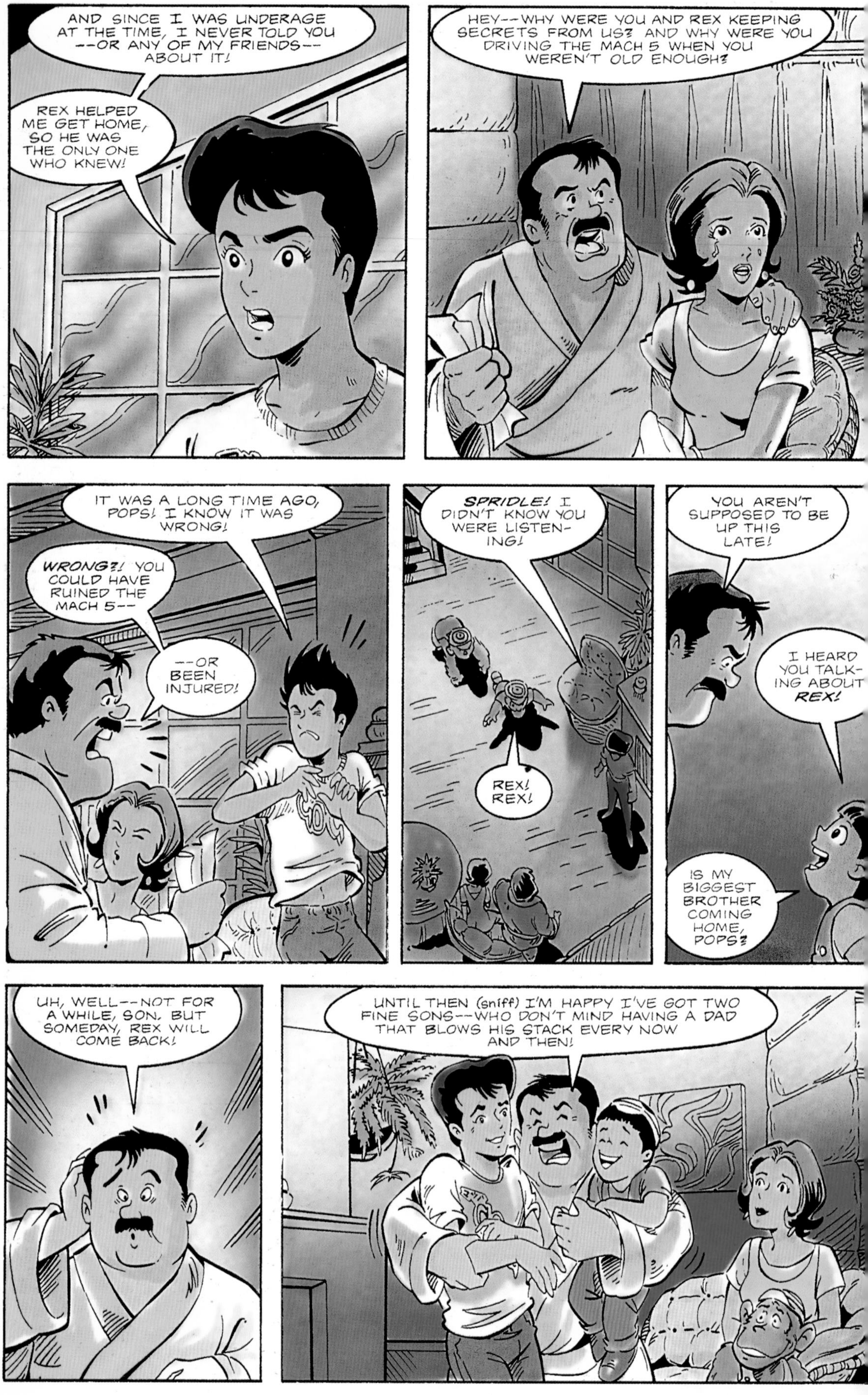
AND SINCE I WAS UNDERAGE AT THE TIME, I NEVER TOLD YOU --OR ANY OF MY FRIENDS-- ABOUT IT!
REX HELPED ME GET HOME, SO HE WAS THE ONLY ONE WHO KNEW!
HEY--WHY WERE YOU AND REX KEEPING SECRETS FROM US? AND WHY WERE YOU DRIVING THE MACH 5 WHEN YOU WEREN'T OLD ENOUGH?
IT WAS A LONG TIME AGO, POPS! I KNOW IT WAS WRONG!
WRONG?! YOU COULD HAVE RUINED THE MACH 5--
--OR BEEN INJURED!
SPRIDLE! I DIDN'T KNOW YOU WERE LISTENING!
REX! REX!
YOU AREN'T SUPPOSED TO BE UP THIS LATE!
I HEARD YOU TALKING ABOUT REX!
IS MY BIGGEST BROTHER COMING HOME, POPS?
UH, WELL--NOT FOR A WHILE, SON. BUT SOMEDAY, REX WILL COME BACK!
UNTIL THEN (sniff) I'M HAPPY I'VE GOT TWO FINE SONS--WHO DON'T MIND HAVING A DAD THAT BLOWS HIS STACK EVERY NOW AND THEN!

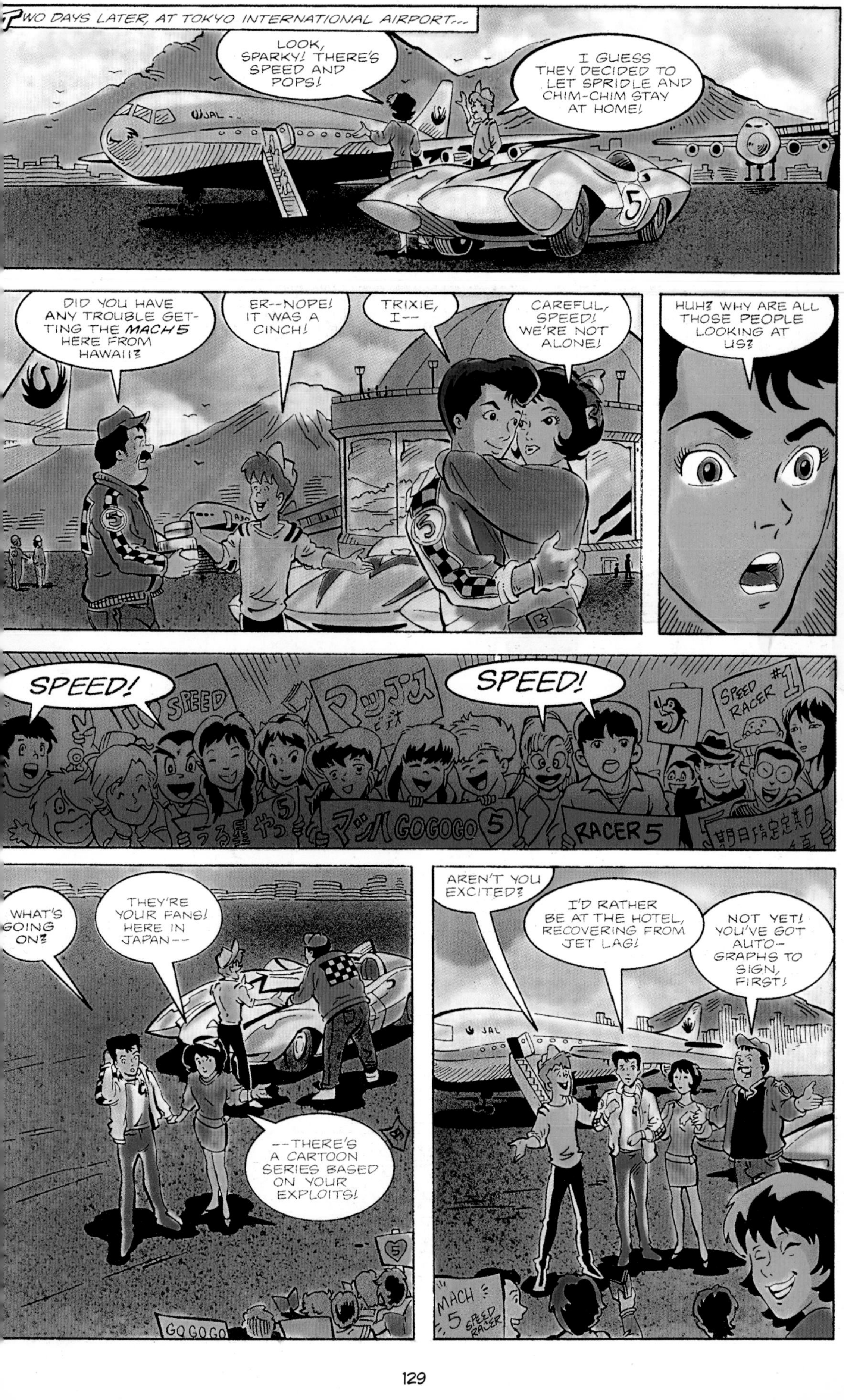
TWO DAYS LATER, AT TOKYO INTERNATIONAL AIRPORT...
LOOK, SPARKY! THERE'S SPEED AND POPS!
I GUESS THEY DECIDED TO LET SPRIDLE AND CHIM-CHIM STAY AT HOME!
DID YOU HAVE ANY TROUBLE GETTING THE MACH 5 HERE FROM HAWAII?
ER--NOPE! IT WAS A CINCH!
TRIXIE, I--
CAREFUL, SPEED! WE'RE NOT ALONE!
HUH? WHY ARE ALL THOSE PEOPLE LOOKING AT US?
SPEED!
SPEED!
SPEED
SPEED RACER #1
マッハGOGOGO 5
RACER 5
WHAT'S GOING ON?
THEY'RE YOUR FANS! HERE IN JAPAN--
--THERE'S A CARTOON SERIES BASED ON YOUR EXPLOITS!
GOGOGO
AREN'T YOU EXCITED?
I'D RATHER BE AT THE HOTEL, RECOVERING FROM JET LAG!
NOT YET! YOU'VE GOT AUTOGRAPHS TO SIGN, FIRST!
MACH 5 SPEED RACER

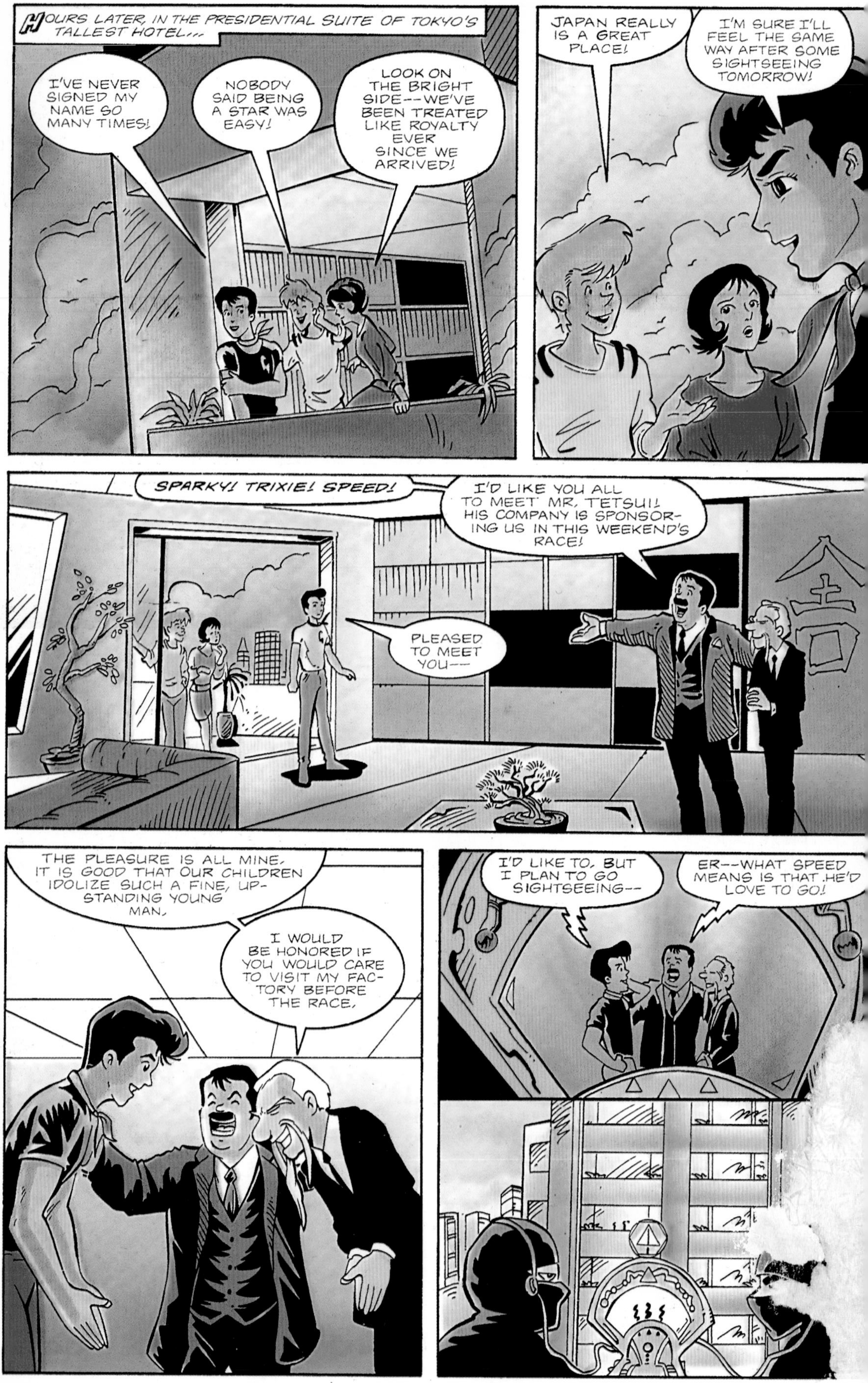
HOURS LATER, IN THE PRESIDENTIAL SUITE OF TOKYO'S TALLEST HOTEL...
I'VE NEVER SIGNED MY NAME SO MANY TIMES!
NOBODY SAID BEING A STAR WAS EASY!
LOOK ON THE BRIGHT SIDE--WE'VE BEEN TREATED LIKE ROYALTY EVER SINCE WE ARRIVED!
JAPAN REALLY IS A GREAT PLACE!
I'M SURE I'LL FEEL THE SAME WAY AFTER SOME SIGHTSEEING TOMORROW!
SPARKY! TRIXIE! SPEED!
I'D LIKE YOU ALL TO MEET MR. TETSUI! HIS COMPANY IS SPONSORING US IN THIS WEEKEND'S RACE!
PLEASED TO MEET YOU--
THE PLEASURE IS ALL MINE. IT IS GOOD THAT OUR CHILDREN IDOLIZE SUCH A FINE, UPSTANDING YOUNG MAN.
I WOULD BE HONORED IF YOU WOULD CARE TO VISIT MY FACTORY BEFORE THE RACE.
I'D LIKE TO, BUT I PLAN TO GO SIGHTSEEING--
ER--WHAT SPEED MEANS IS THAT HE'D LOVE TO GO!

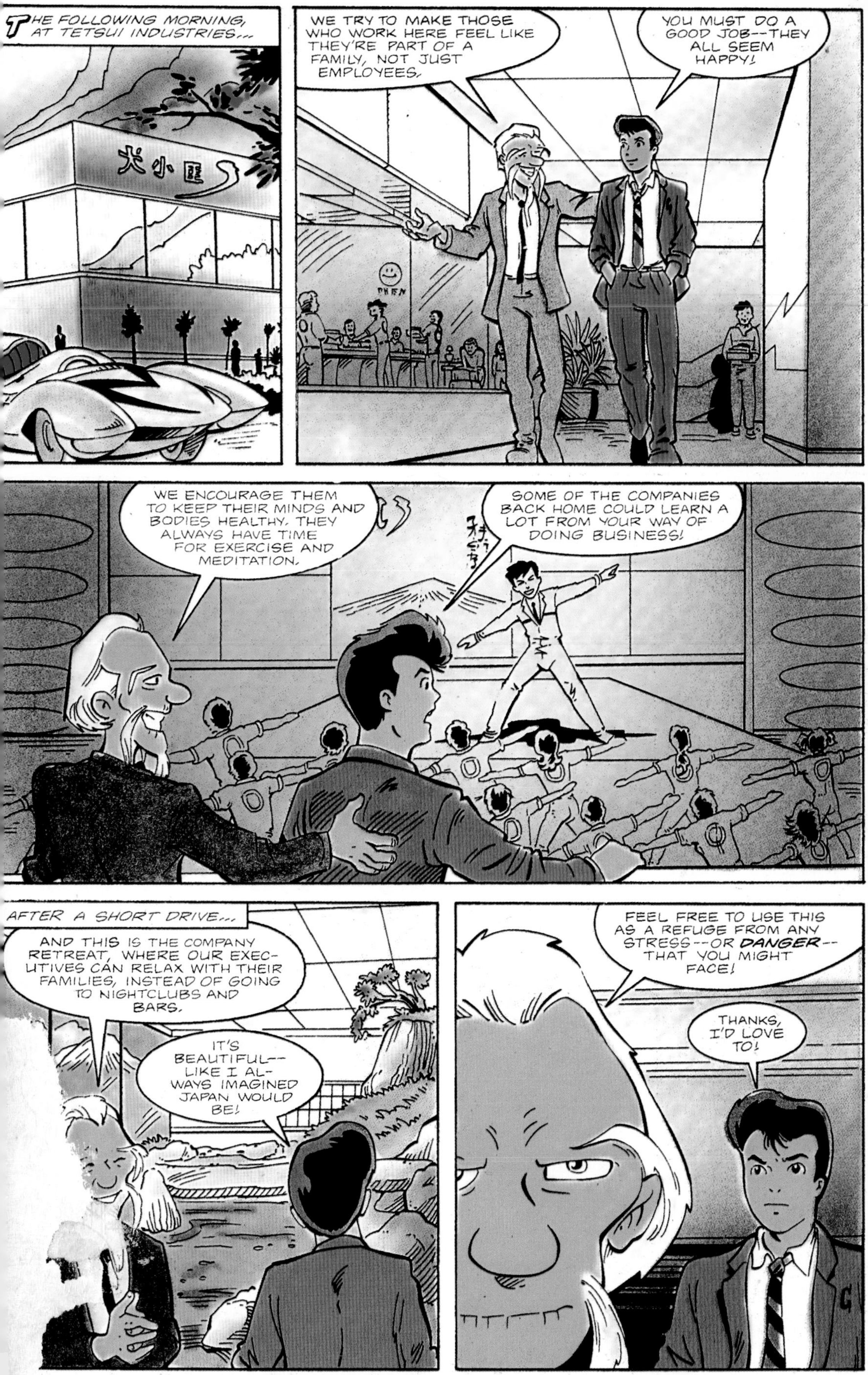
THE FOLLOWING MORNING, AT TETSUI INDUSTRIES...
WE TRY TO MAKE THOSE WHO WORK HERE FEEL LIKE THEY'RE PART OF A FAMILY, NOT JUST EMPLOYEES.
YOU MUST DO A GOOD JOB--THEY ALL SEEM HAPPY!
WE ENCOURAGE THEM TO KEEP THEIR MINDS AND BODIES HEALTHY. THEY ALWAYS HAVE TIME FOR EXERCISE AND MEDITATION.
SOME OF THE COMPANIES BACK HOME COULD LEARN A LOT FROM YOUR WAY OF DOING BUSINESS!
AFTER A SHORT DRIVE...
AND THIS IS THE COMPANY RETREAT, WHERE OUR EXEC-UTIVES CAN RELAX WITH THEIR FAMILIES, INSTEAD OF GOING TO NIGHTCLUBS AND BARS.
IT'S BEAUTIFUL--LIKE I AL-WAYS IMAGINED JAPAN WOULD BE!
FEEL FREE TO USE THIS AS A REFUGE FROM ANY STRESS--OR DANGER--THAT YOU MIGHT FACE!
THANKS, I'D LOVE TO!

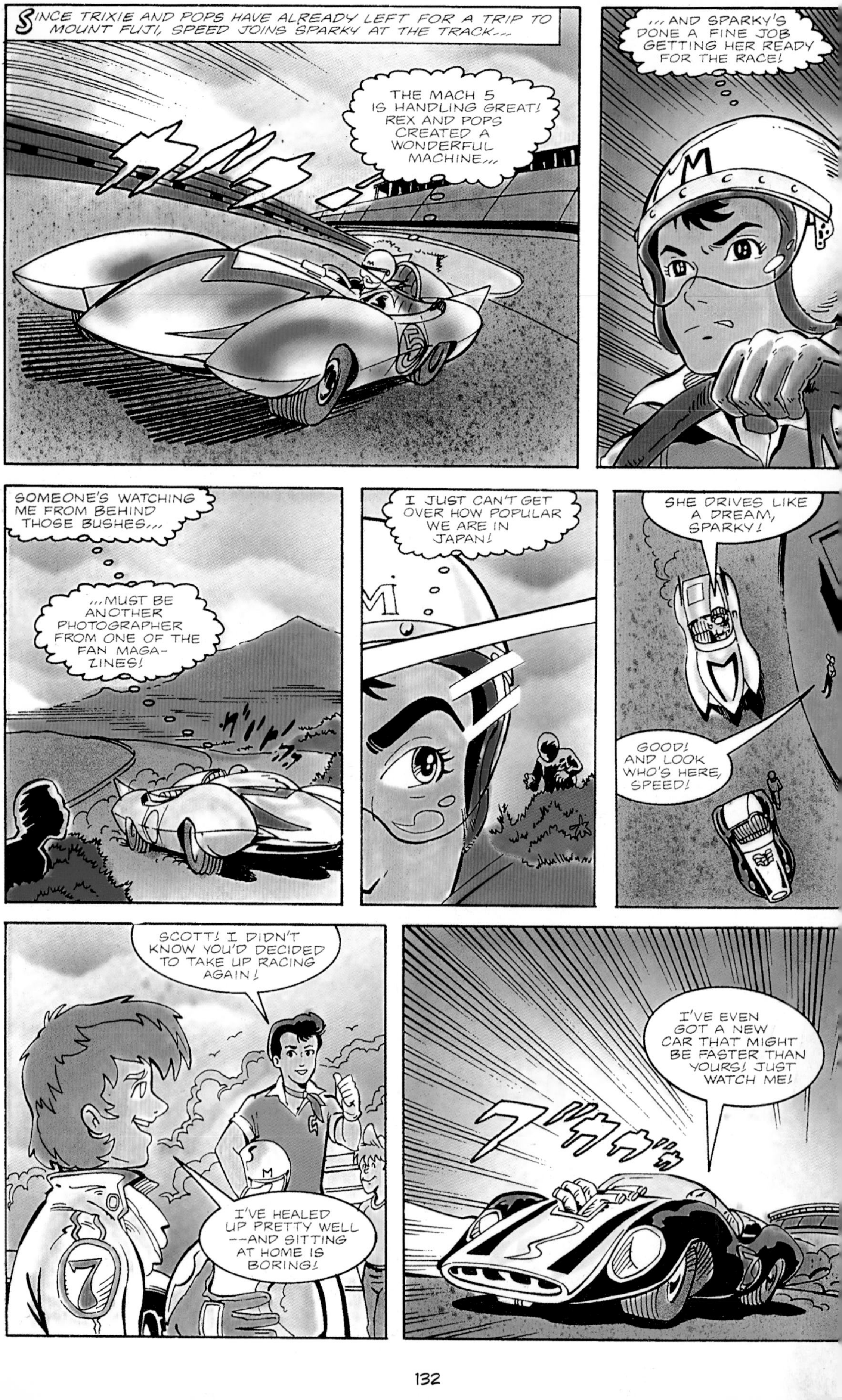

SINCE TRIXIE AND POPS HAVE ALREADY LEFT FOR A TRIP TO MOUNT FUJI, SPEED JOINS SPARKY AT THE TRACK...
THE MACH 5 IS HANDLING GREAT! REX AND POPS CREATED A WONDERFUL MACHINE...
...AND SPARKY'S DONE A FINE JOB GETTING HER READY FOR THE RACE!
SOMEONE'S WATCHING ME FROM BEHIND THOSE BUSHES...
...MUST BE ANOTHER PHOTOGRAPHER FROM ONE OF THE FAN MAGA-ZINES!
I JUST CAN'T GET OVER HOW POPULAR WE ARE IN JAPAN!
SHE DRIVES LIKE A DREAM, SPARKY!
GOOD! AND LOOK WHO'S HERE, SPEED!
SCOTT! I DIDN'T KNOW YOU'D DECIDED TO TAKE UP RACING AGAIN!
I'VE HEALED UP PRETTY WELL --AND SITTING AT HOME IS BORING!
I'VE EVEN GOT A NEW CAR THAT MIGHT BE FASTER THAN YOURS! JUST WATCH ME!

...UT AFTER ONLY A FEW SECONDS...

OH NO! MY TIRE!

SKOOK!!

I'M LOSING CONTROL—— STARTING TO FLIP OVER!

SCOTT'S IN TROUBLE, SPARKY! LET'S GO!

SKIDDDD

KAABLAMM!!

LATER...

I JUST DON'T UNDER-STAND IT!

THAT'S THE THIRD MYSTERIOUS ACCIDENT THIS WEEK!

REALLY?

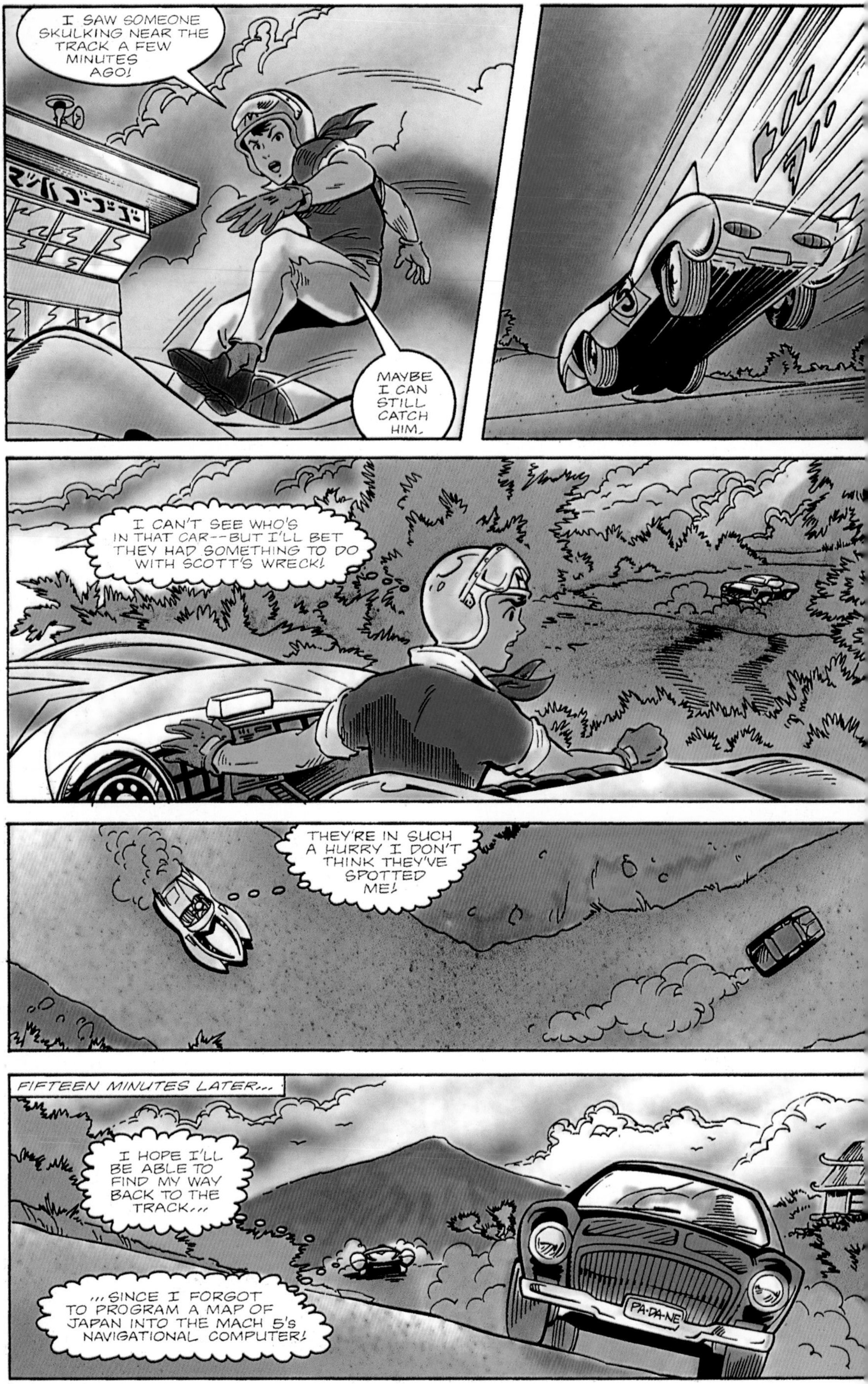
I SAW SOMEONE SKULKING NEAR THE TRACK A FEW MINUTES AGO!
MAYBE I CAN STILL CATCH HIM.
I CAN'T SEE WHO'S IN THAT CAR--BUT I'LL BET THEY HAD SOMETHING TO DO WITH SCOTT'S WRECK!
THEY'RE IN SUCH A HURRY I DON'T THINK THEY'VE SPOTTED ME!
FIFTEEN MINUTES LATER...
I HOPE I'LL BE ABLE TO FIND MY WAY BACK TO THE TRACK...
...SINCE I FORGOT TO PROGRAM A MAP OF JAPAN INTO THE MACH 5's NAVIGATIONAL COMPUTER!
PA-DA-NE

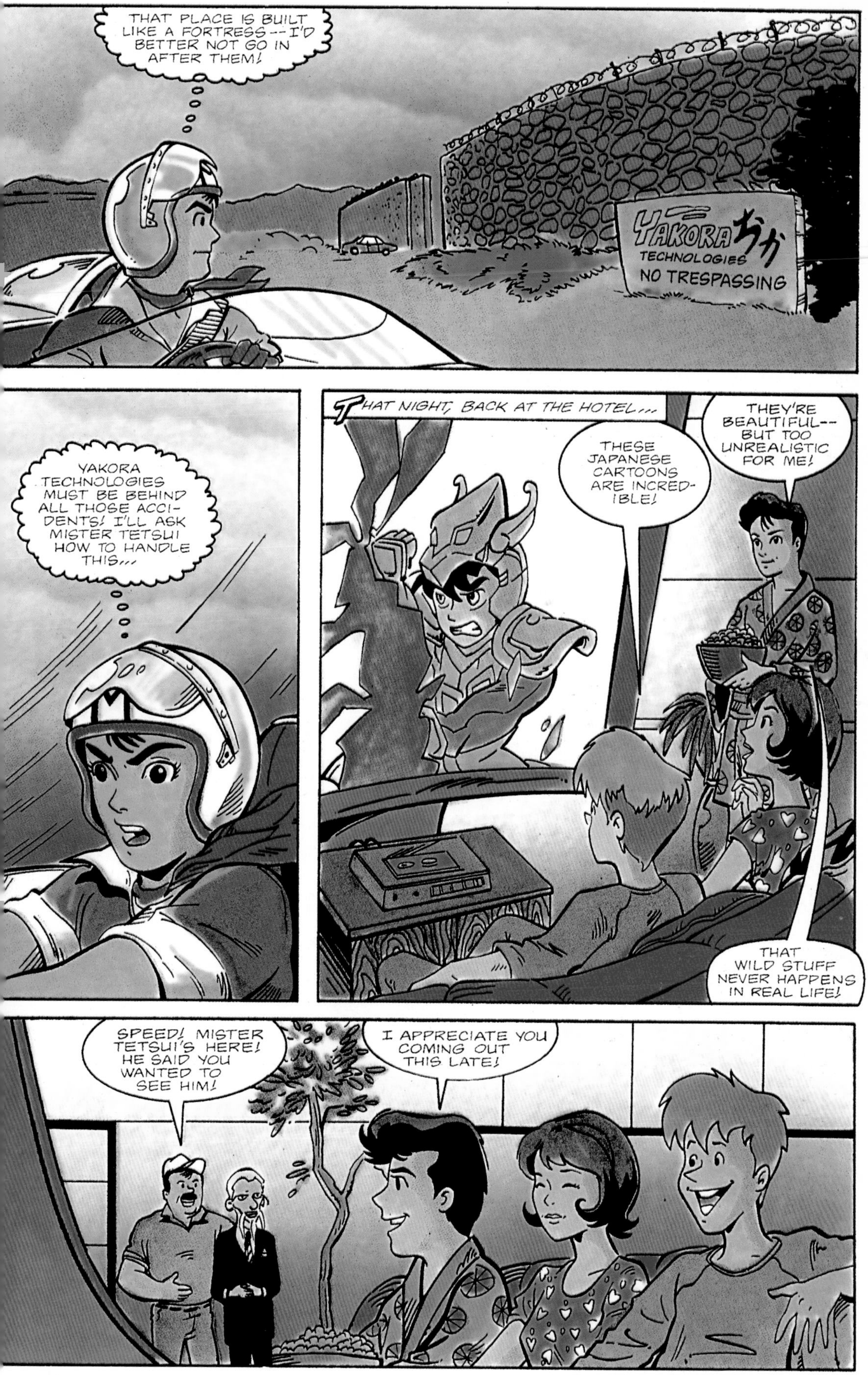

THAT PLACE IS BUILT LIKE A FORTRESS--I'D BETTER NOT GO IN AFTER THEM!
YAKORA TECHNOLOGIES
NO TRESPASSING
YAKORA TECHNOLOGIES MUST BE BEHIND ALL THOSE ACCI-DENTS! I'LL ASK MISTER TETSUI HOW TO HANDLE THIS...
THAT NIGHT, BACK AT THE HOTEL...
THESE JAPANESE CARTOONS ARE INCRED-IBLE!
THEY'RE BEAUTIFUL--BUT TOO UNREALISTIC FOR ME!
THAT WILD STUFF NEVER HAPPENS IN REAL LIFE!
SPEED! MISTER TETSUI'S HERE! HE SAID YOU WANTED TO SEE HIM!
I APPRECIATE YOU COMING OUT THIS LATE!

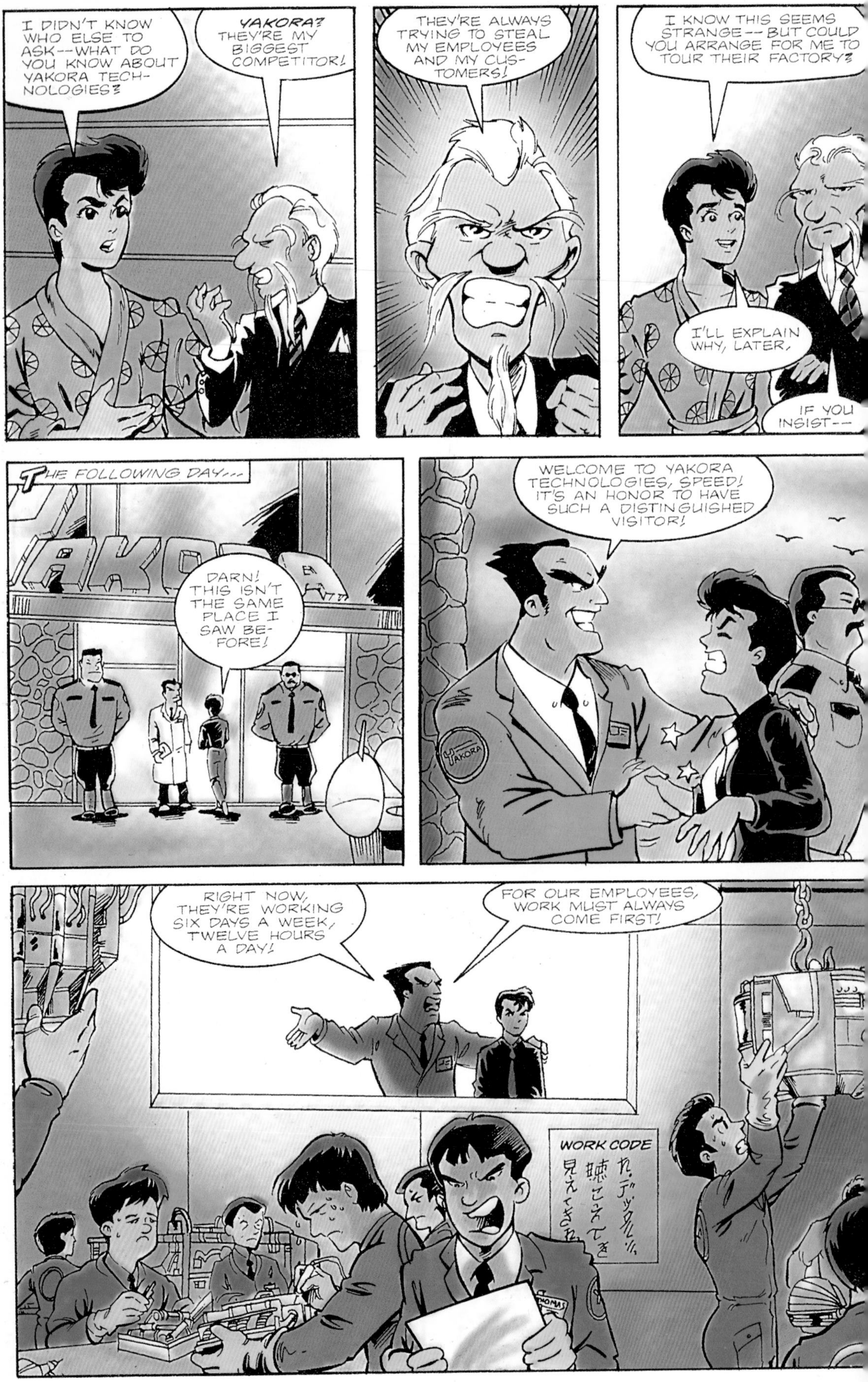
I DIDN'T KNOW WHO ELSE TO ASK--WHAT DO YOU KNOW ABOUT YAKORA TECH-NOLOGIES?
YAKORA? THEY'RE MY BIGGEST COMPETITOR!
THEY'RE ALWAYS TRYING TO STEAL MY EMPLOYEES AND MY CUS-TOMERS!
I KNOW THIS SEEMS STRANGE--BUT COULD YOU ARRANGE FOR ME TO TOUR THEIR FACTORY?
I'LL EXPLAIN WHY, LATER.
IF YOU INSIST--
THE FOLLOWING DAY...
DARN! THIS ISN'T THE SAME PLACE I SAW BE-FORE!
WELCOME TO YAKORA TECHNOLOGIES, SPEED! IT'S AN HONOR TO HAVE SUCH A DISTINGUISHED VISITOR!
YAKORA
RIGHT NOW, THEY'RE WORKING SIX DAYS A WEEK, TWELVE HOURS A DAY!
FOR OUR EMPLOYEES, WORK MUST ALWAYS COME FIRST!
WORK CODE
THOMAS

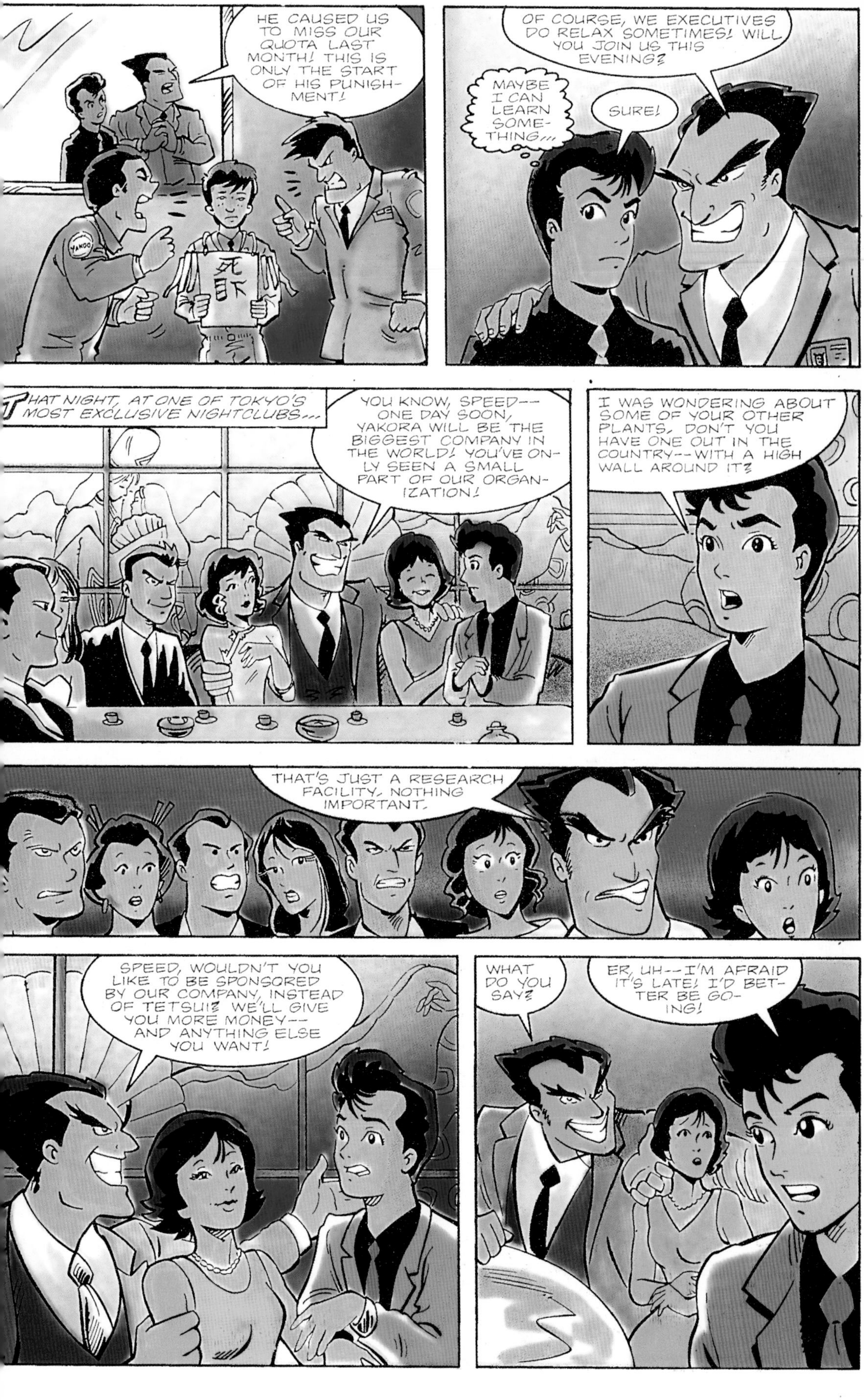
HE CAUSED US TO MISS OUR QUOTA LAST MONTH! THIS IS ONLY THE START OF HIS PUNISHMENT!
OF COURSE, WE EXECUTIVES DO RELAX SOMETIMES! WILL YOU JOIN US THIS EVENING?
MAYBE I CAN LEARN SOMETHING...
SURE!
THAT NIGHT, AT ONE OF TOKYO'S MOST EXCLUSIVE NIGHTCLUBS...
YOU KNOW, SPEED-- ONE DAY SOON, YAKORA WILL BE THE BIGGEST COMPANY IN THE WORLD! YOU'VE ONLY SEEN A SMALL PART OF OUR ORGANIZATION!
I WAS WONDERING ABOUT SOME OF YOUR OTHER PLANTS. DON'T YOU HAVE ONE OUT IN THE COUNTRY--WITH A HIGH WALL AROUND IT?
THAT'S JUST A RESEARCH FACILITY. NOTHING IMPORTANT.
SPEED, WOULDN'T YOU LIKE TO BE SPONSORED BY OUR COMPANY, INSTEAD OF TETSUI? WE'LL GIVE YOU MORE MONEY-- AND ANYTHING ELSE YOU WANT!
WHAT DO YOU SAY?
ER, UH--I'M AFRAID IT'S LATE! I'D BETTER BE GOING!

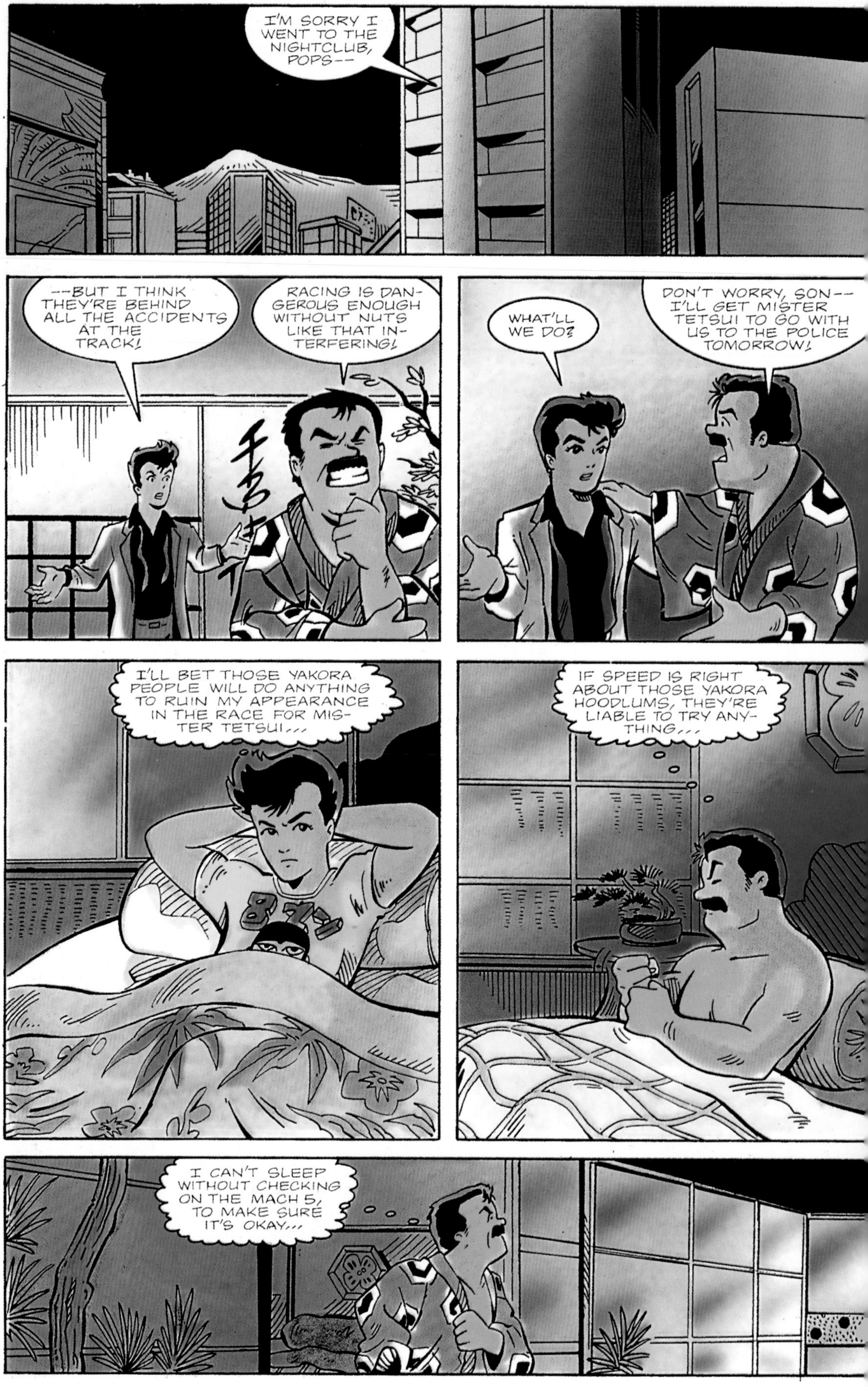
I'M SORRY I WENT TO THE NIGHTCLUB, POPS--
--BUT I THINK THEY'RE BEHIND ALL THE ACCIDENTS AT THE TRACK!
RACING IS DANGEROUS ENOUGH WITHOUT NUTS LIKE THAT INTERFERING!
WHAT'LL WE DO?
DON'T WORRY, SON-- I'LL GET MISTER TETSUI TO GO WITH US TO THE POLICE TOMORROW!
I'LL BET THOSE YAKORA PEOPLE WILL DO ANYTHING TO RUIN MY APPEARANCE IN THE RACE FOR MISTER TETSUI...
IF SPEED IS RIGHT ABOUT THOSE YAKORA HOODLUMS, THEY'RE LIABLE TO TRY ANYTHING...
I CAN'T SLEEP WITHOUT CHECKING ON THE MACH 5, TO MAKE SURE IT'S OKAY...

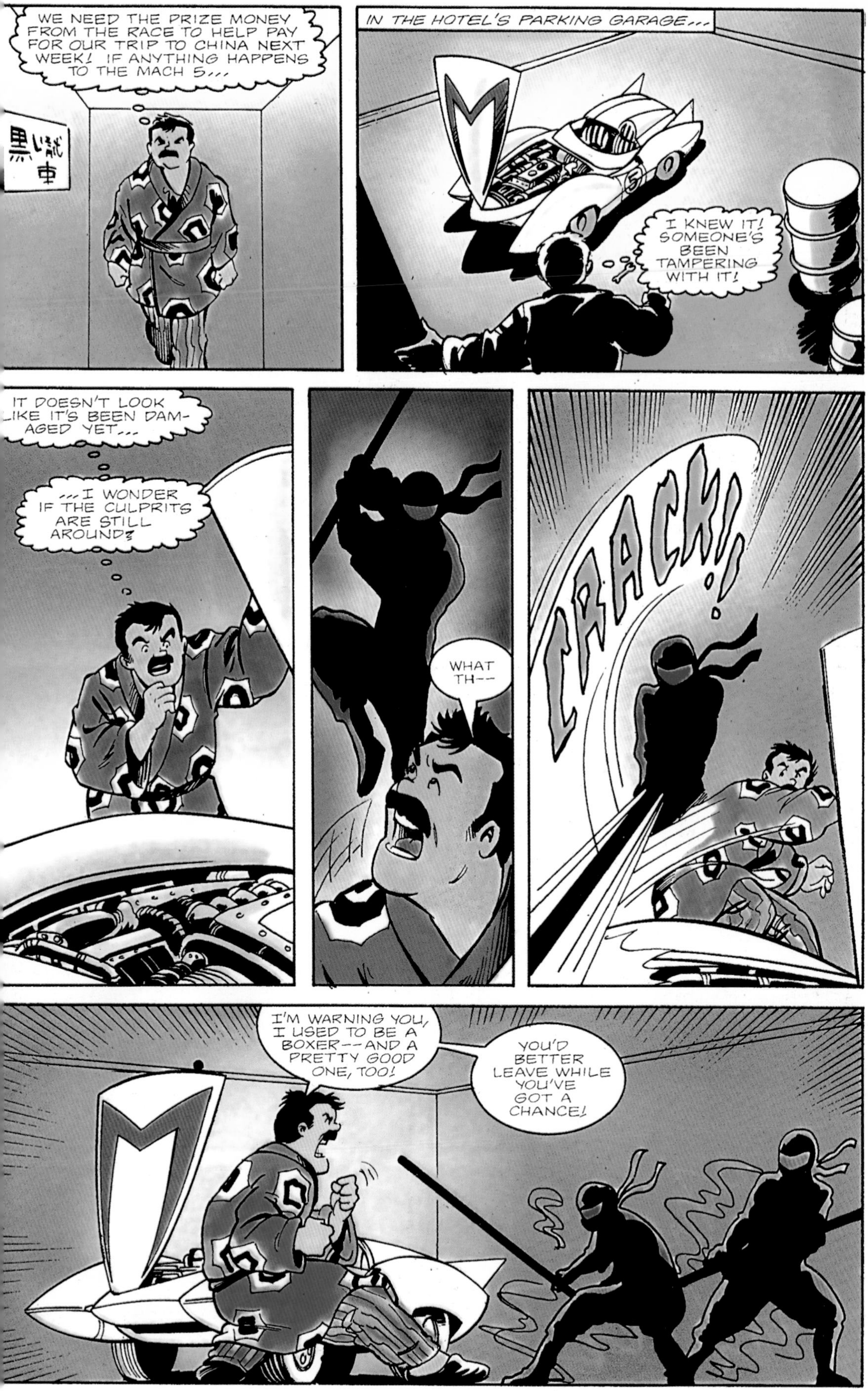

WE NEED THE PRIZE MONEY FROM THE RACE TO HELP PAY FOR OUR TRIP TO CHINA NEXT WEEK! IF ANYTHING HAPPENS TO THE MACH 5...
IN THE HOTEL'S PARKING GARAGE...
I KNEW IT! SOMEONE'S BEEN TAMPERING WITH IT!
IT DOESN'T LOOK LIKE IT'S BEEN DAM-AGED YET...
...I WONDER IF THE CULPRITS ARE STILL AROUND?
WHAT TH--
CRACK!!
I'M WARNING YOU, I USED TO BE A BOXER--AND A PRETTY GOOD ONE, TOO!
YOU'D BETTER LEAVE WHILE YOU'VE GOT A CHANCE!

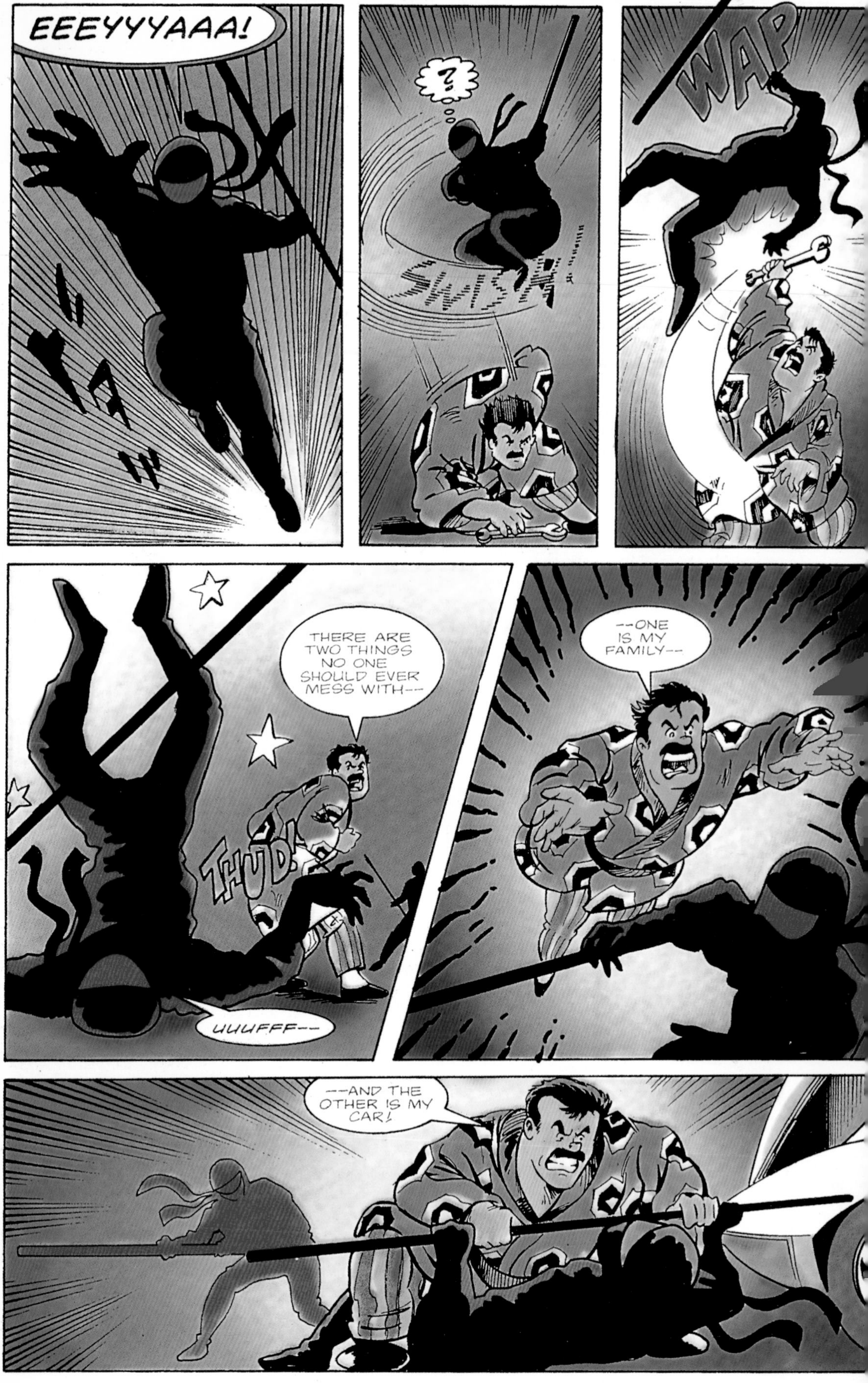
EEEYYYAAA!
YA!!
?
SWISH
WAP
THERE ARE TWO THINGS NO ONE SHOULD EVER MESS WITH--
THUD!
UUUFFF--
--ONE IS MY FAMILY--
--AND THE OTHER IS MY CAR!

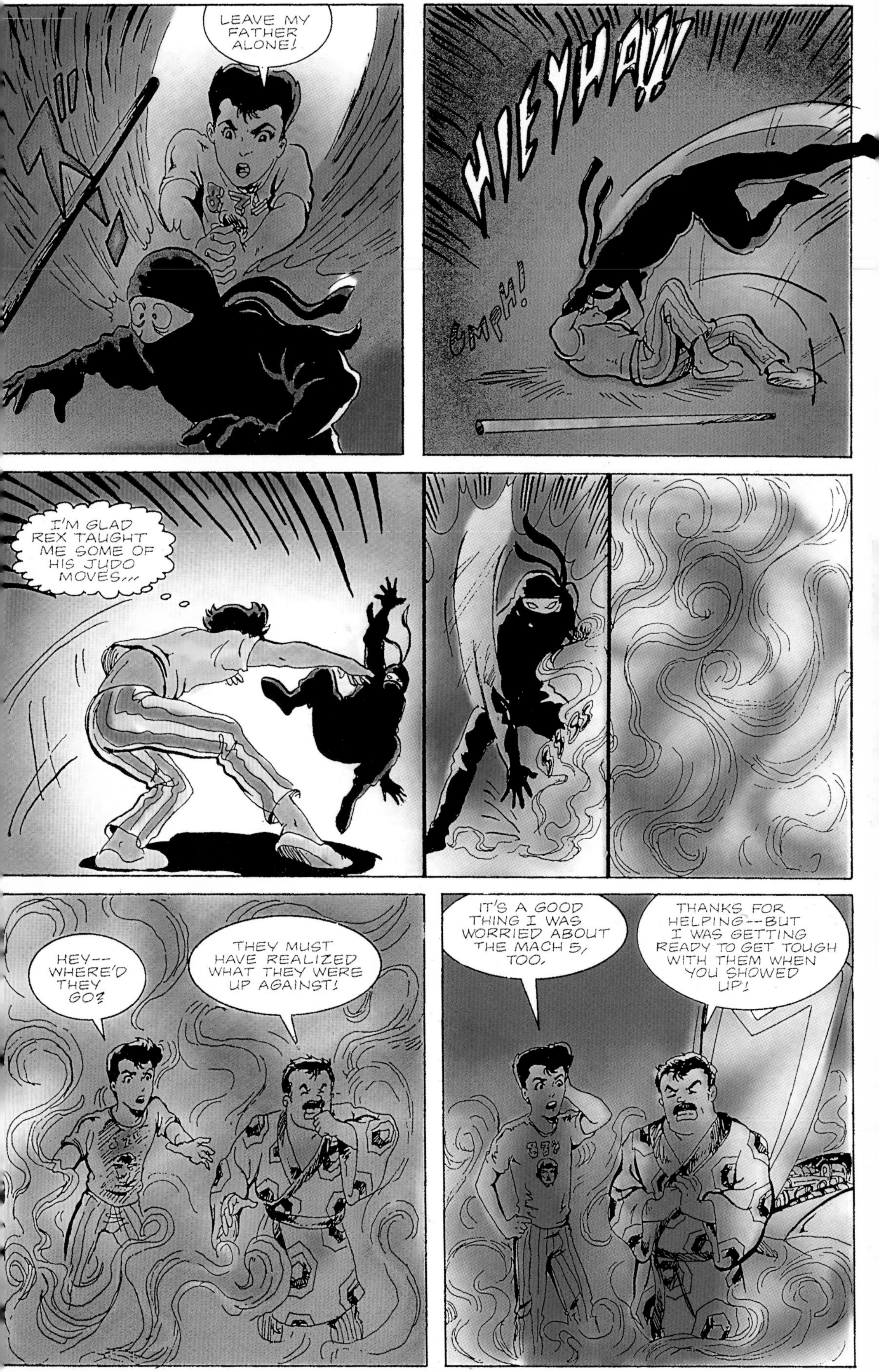
LEAVE MY FATHER ALONE!
HIEYHA!!
UMPH!
I'M GLAD REX TAUGHT ME SOME OF HIS JUDO MOVES...
HEY-- WHERE'D THEY GO?
THEY MUST HAVE REALIZED WHAT THEY WERE UP AGAINST!
IT'S A GOOD THING I WAS WORRIED ABOUT THE MACH 5, TOO.
THANKS FOR HELPING--BUT I WAS GETTING READY TO GET TOUGH WITH THEM WHEN YOU SHOWED UP!

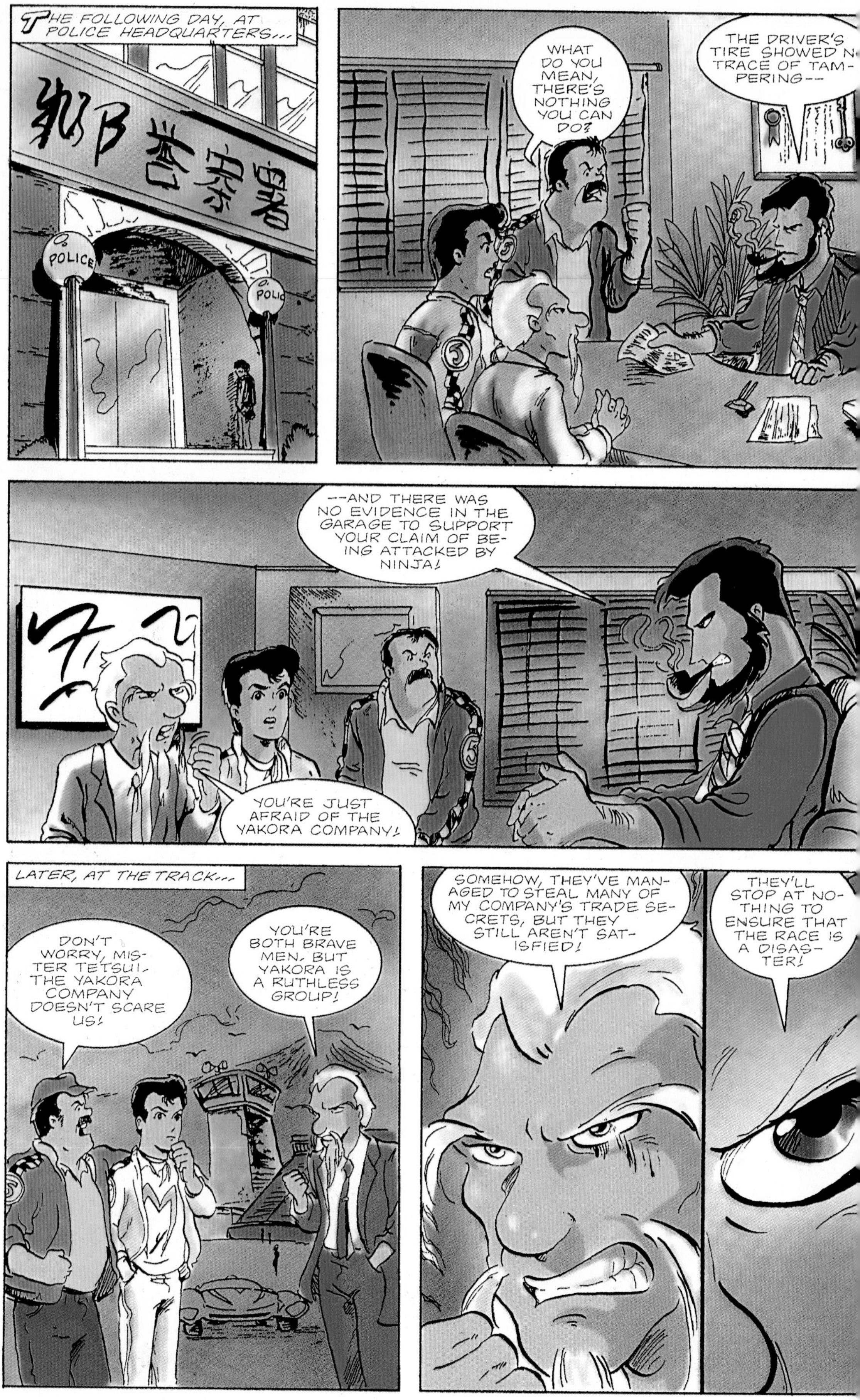
THE FOLLOWING DAY, AT POLICE HEADQUARTERS...
POLICE
POLIC
WHAT DO YOU MEAN, THERE'S NOTHING YOU CAN DO?
THE DRIVER'S TIRE SHOWED NO TRACE OF TAMPERING--
--AND THERE WAS NO EVIDENCE IN THE GARAGE TO SUPPORT YOUR CLAIM OF BEING ATTACKED BY NINJA!
YOU'RE JUST AFRAID OF THE YAKORA COMPANY!
LATER, AT THE TRACK...
DON'T WORRY, MISTER TETSUI. THE YAKORA COMPANY DOESN'T SCARE US!
YOU'RE BOTH BRAVE MEN, BUT YAKORA IS A RUTHLESS GROUP!
SOMEHOW, THEY'VE MANAGED TO STEAL MANY OF MY COMPANY'S TRADE SECRETS, BUT THEY STILL AREN'T SATISFIED!
THEY'LL STOP AT NOTHING TO ENSURE THAT THE RACE IS A DISASTER!

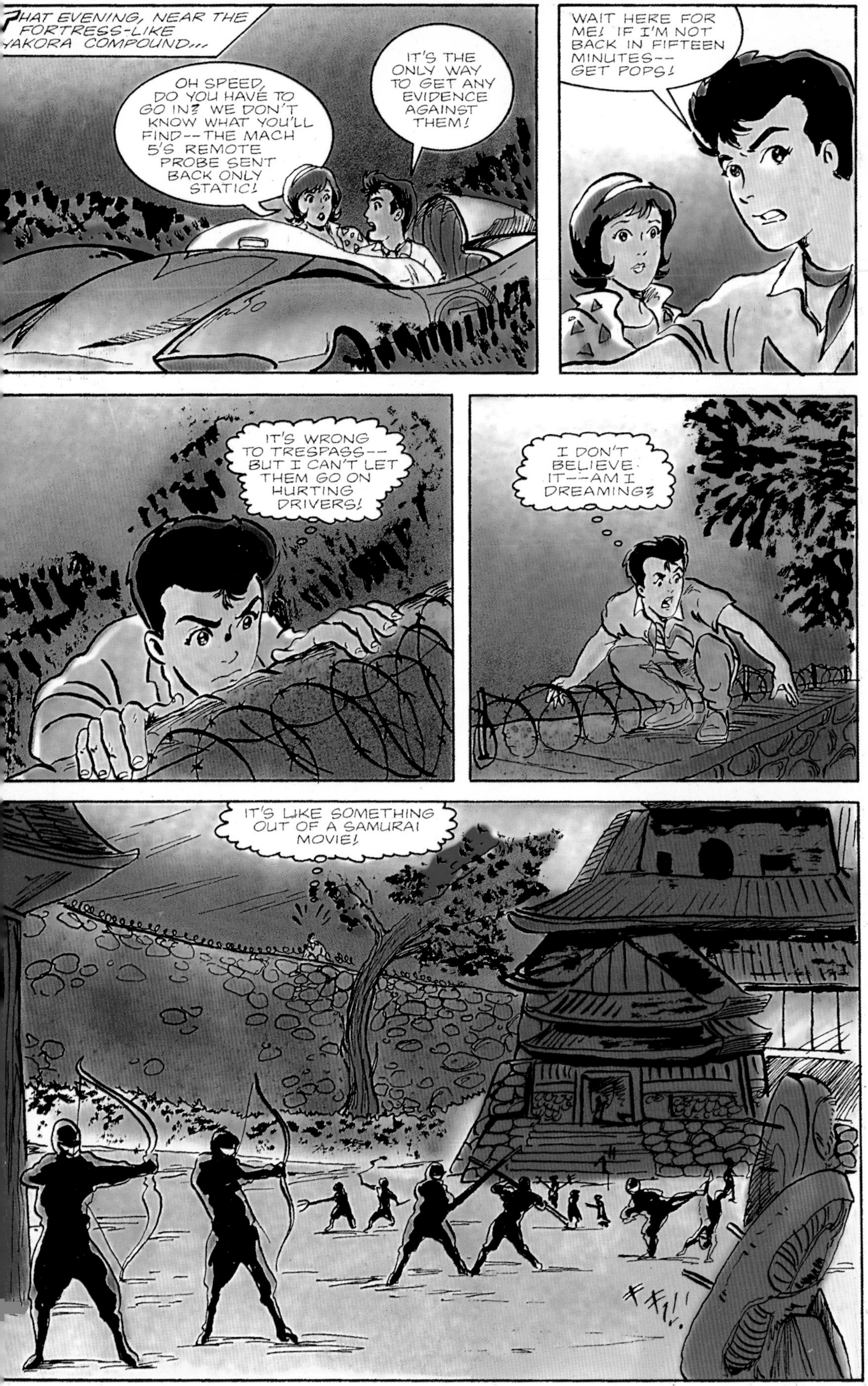
THAT EVENING, NEAR THE FORTRESS-LIKE YAKORA COMPOUND...
OH SPEED, DO YOU HAVE TO GO IN? WE DON'T KNOW WHAT YOU'LL FIND--THE MACH 5'S REMOTE PROBE SENT BACK ONLY STATIC!
IT'S THE ONLY WAY TO GET ANY EVIDENCE AGAINST THEM!
WAIT HERE FOR ME! IF I'M NOT BACK IN FIFTEEN MINUTES-- GET POPS!
IT'S WRONG TO TRESPASS-- BUT I CAN'T LET THEM GO ON HURTING DRIVERS!
I DON'T BELIEVE IT--AM I DREAMING?
IT'S LIKE SOMETHING OUT OF A SAMURAI MOVIE!

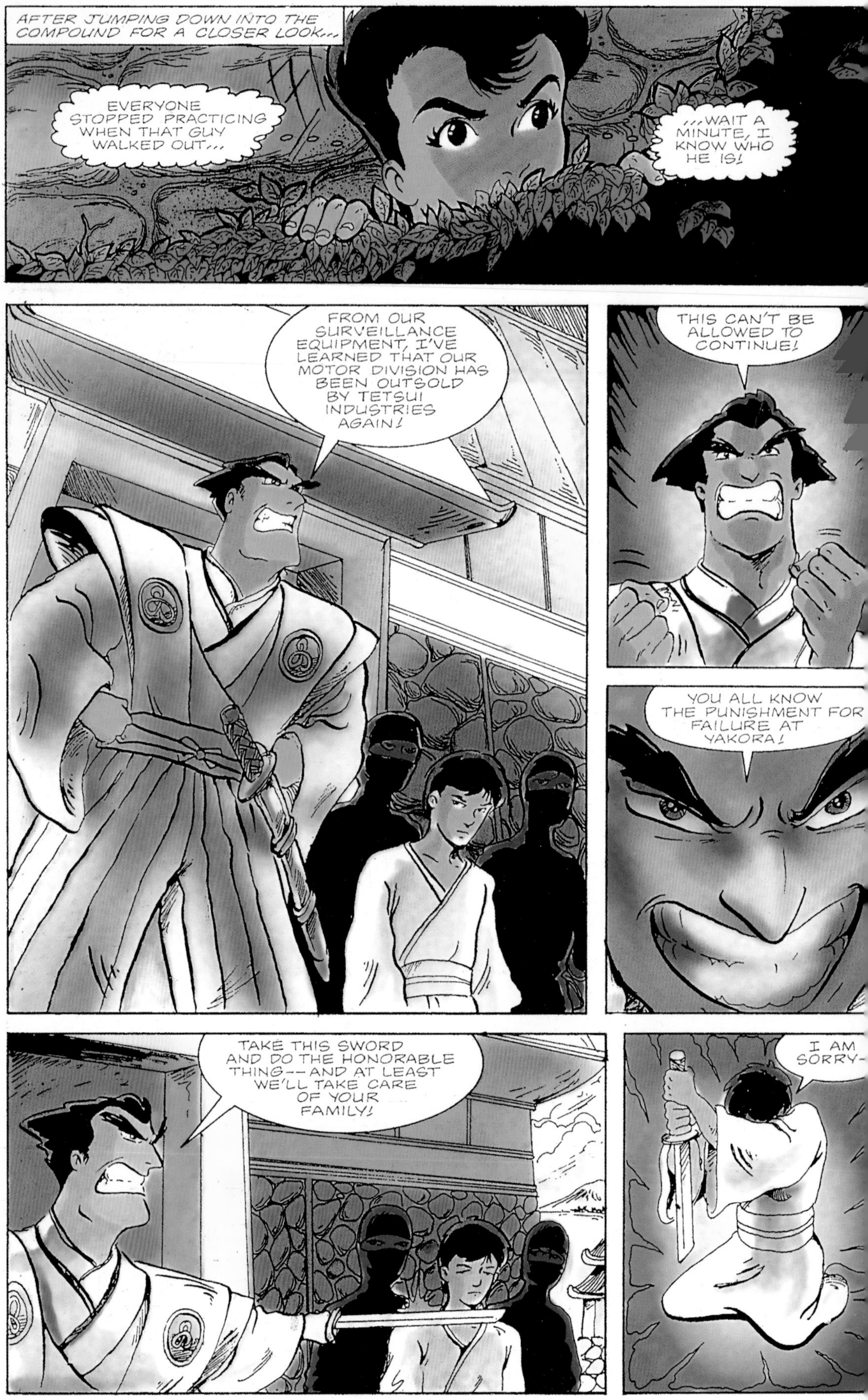
AFTER JUMPING DOWN INTO THE COMPOUND FOR A CLOSER LOOK...
EVERYONE STOPPED PRACTICING WHEN THAT GUY WALKED OUT...
...WAIT A MINUTE, I KNOW WHO HE IS!
FROM OUR SURVEILLANCE EQUIPMENT, I'VE LEARNED THAT OUR MOTOR DIVISION HAS BEEN OUTSOLD BY TETSUI INDUSTRIES AGAIN!
THIS CAN'T BE ALLOWED TO CONTINUE!
YOU ALL KNOW THE PUNISHMENT FOR FAILURE AT YAKORA!
TAKE THIS SWORD AND DO THE HONORABLE THING--AND AT LEAST WE'LL TAKE CARE OF YOUR FAMILY!
I AM SORRY-

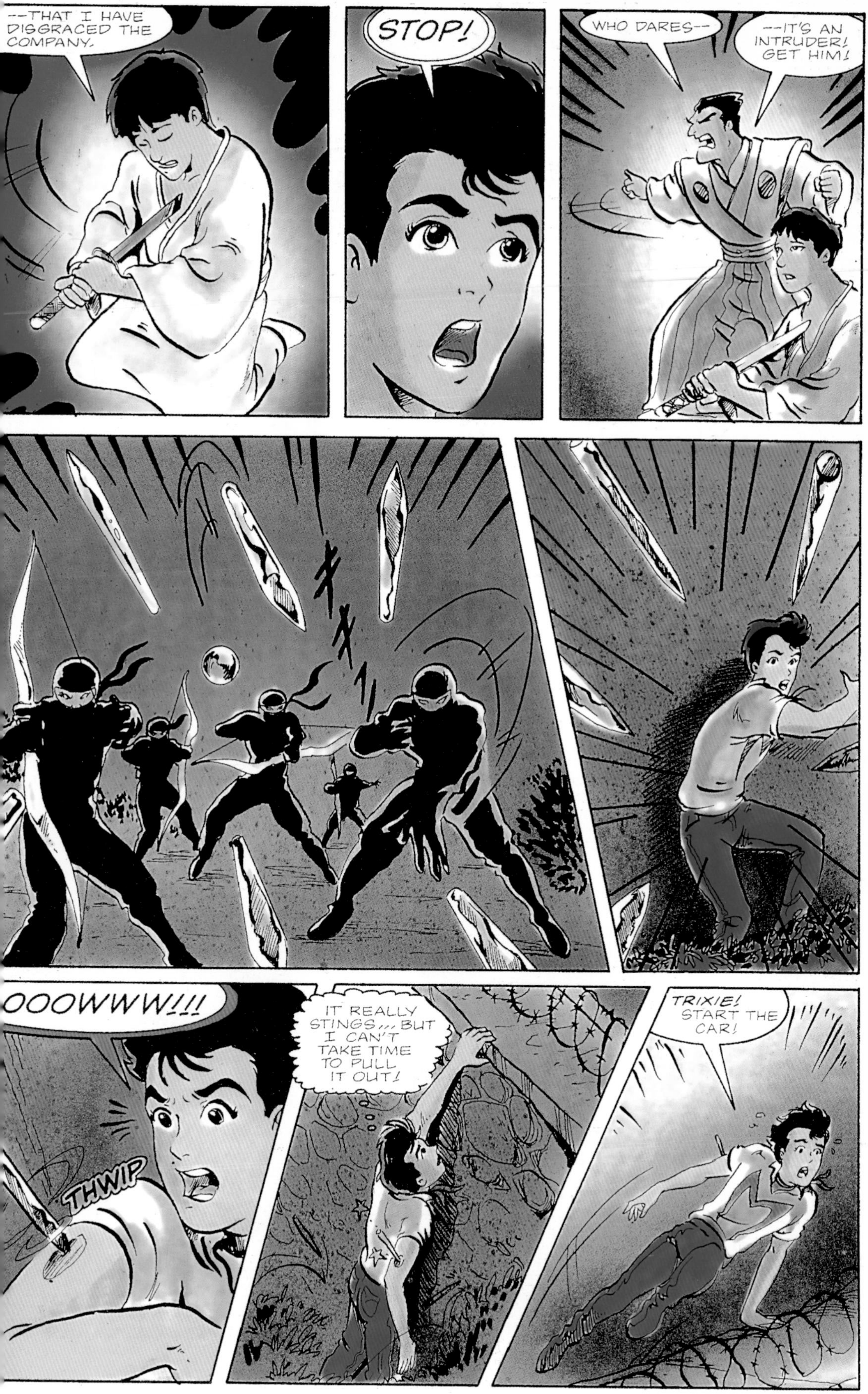
--THAT I HAVE DISGRACED THE COMPANY.
STOP!
WHO DARES--
--IT'S AN INTRUDER! GET HIM!
OOOWWW!!!
THWIP
IT REALLY STINGS... BUT I CAN'T TAKE TIME TO PULL IT OUT!
TRIXIE! START THE CAR!

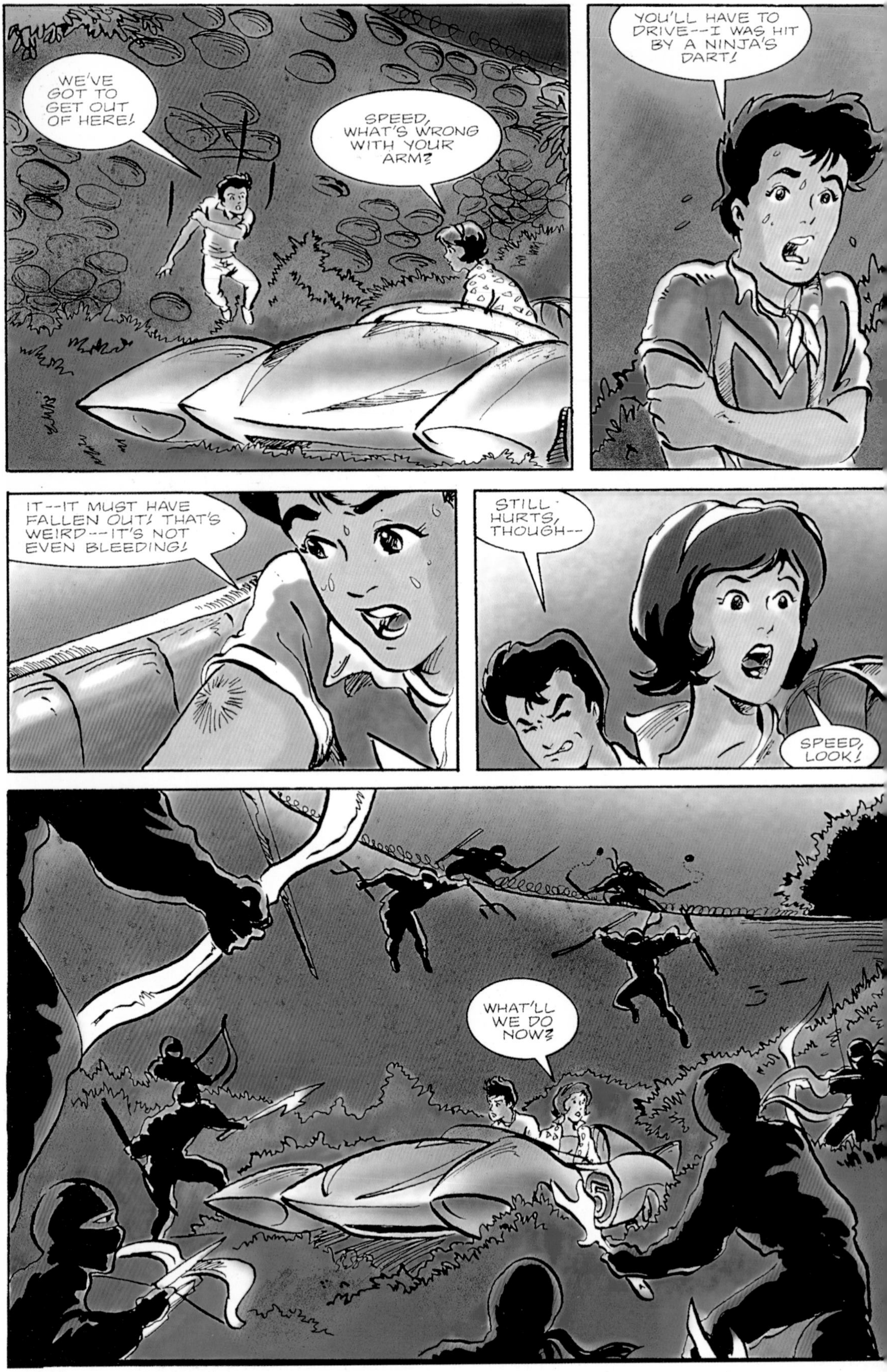
WE'VE GOT TO GET OUT OF HERE!
SPEED, WHAT'S WRONG WITH YOUR ARM?
YOU'LL HAVE TO DRIVE--I WAS HIT BY A NINJA'S DART!
IT--IT MUST HAVE FALLEN OUT! THAT'S WEIRD--IT'S NOT EVEN BLEEDING!
STILL HURTS, THOUGH--
SPEED, LOOK!
WHAT'LL WE DO NOW?

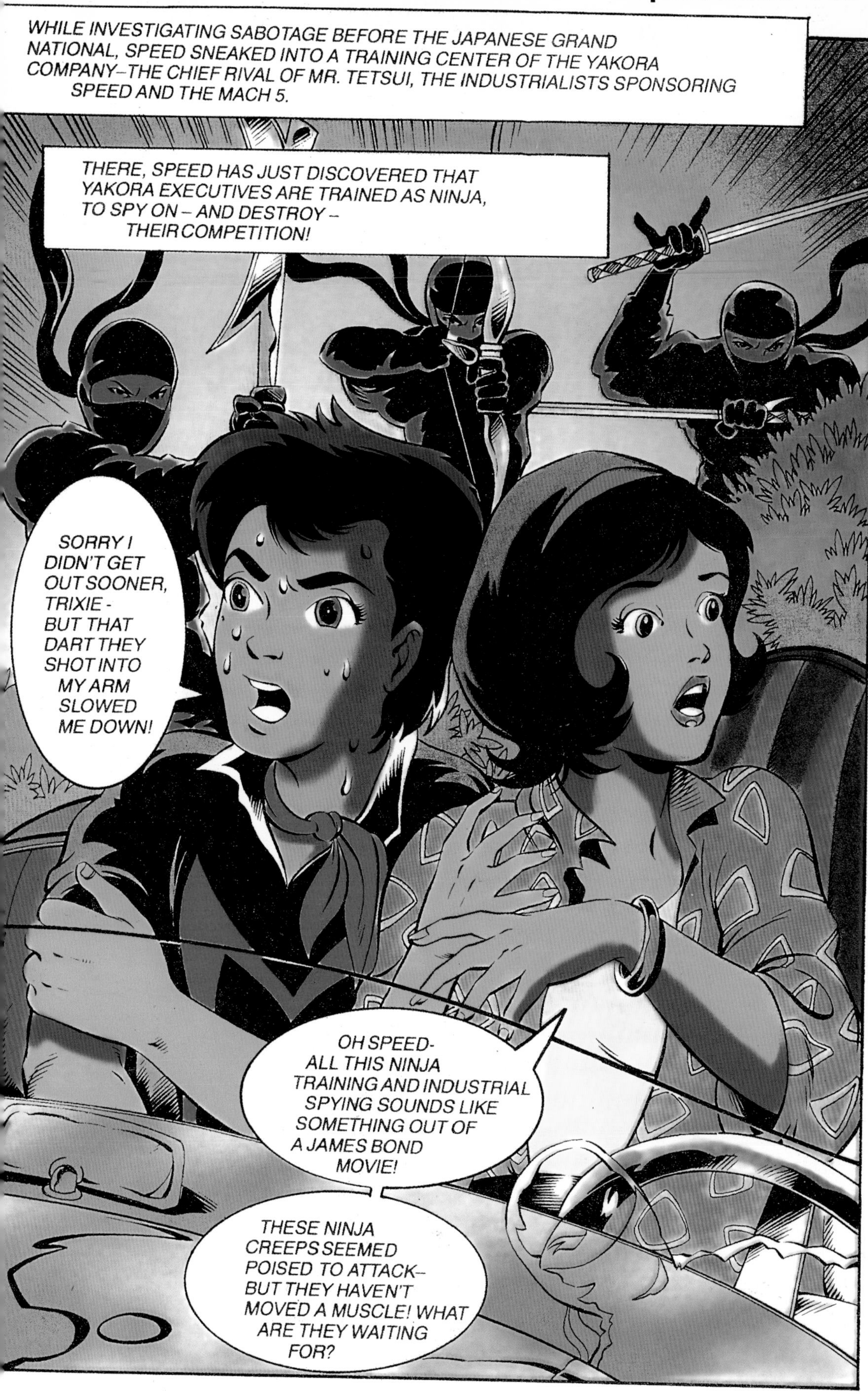
WHILE INVESTIGATING SABOTAGE BEFORE THE JAPANESE GRAND NATIONAL, SPEED SNEAKED INTO A TRAINING CENTER OF THE YAKORA COMPANY–THE CHIEF RIVAL OF MR. TETSUI, THE INDUSTRIALISTS SPONSORING SPEED AND THE MACH 5.
THERE, SPEED HAS JUST DISCOVERED THAT YAKORA EXECUTIVES ARE TRAINED AS NINJA, TO SPY ON – AND DESTROY – THEIR COMPETITION!
SORRY I DIDN'T GET OUT SOONER, TRIXIE - BUT THAT DART THEY SHOT INTO MY ARM SLOWED ME DOWN!
OH SPEED- ALL THIS NINJA TRAINING AND INDUSTRIAL SPYING SOUNDS LIKE SOMETHING OUT OF A JAMES BOND MOVIE!
THESE NINJA CREEPS SEEMED POISED TO ATTACK– BUT THEY HAVEN'T MOVED A MUSCLE! WHAT ARE THEY WAITING FOR?

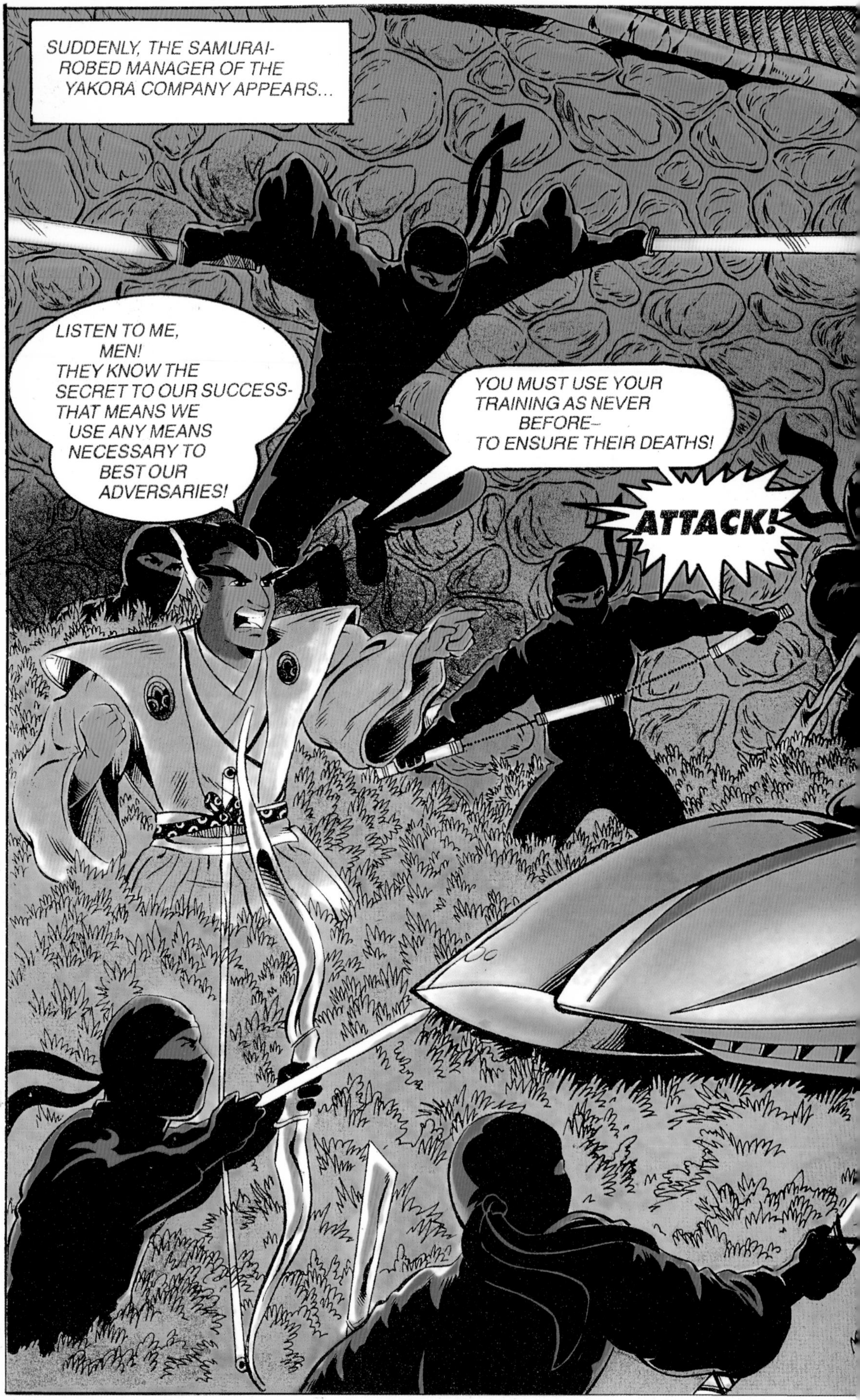
SUDDENLY, THE SAMURAI-ROBED MANAGER OF THE YAKORA COMPANY APPEARS...
LISTEN TO ME, MEN! THEY KNOW THE SECRET TO OUR SUCCESS-THAT MEANS WE USE ANY MEANS NECESSARY TO BEST OUR ADVERSARIES!
YOU MUST USE YOUR TRAINING AS NEVER BEFORE-TO ENSURE THEIR DEATHS!
ATTACK!

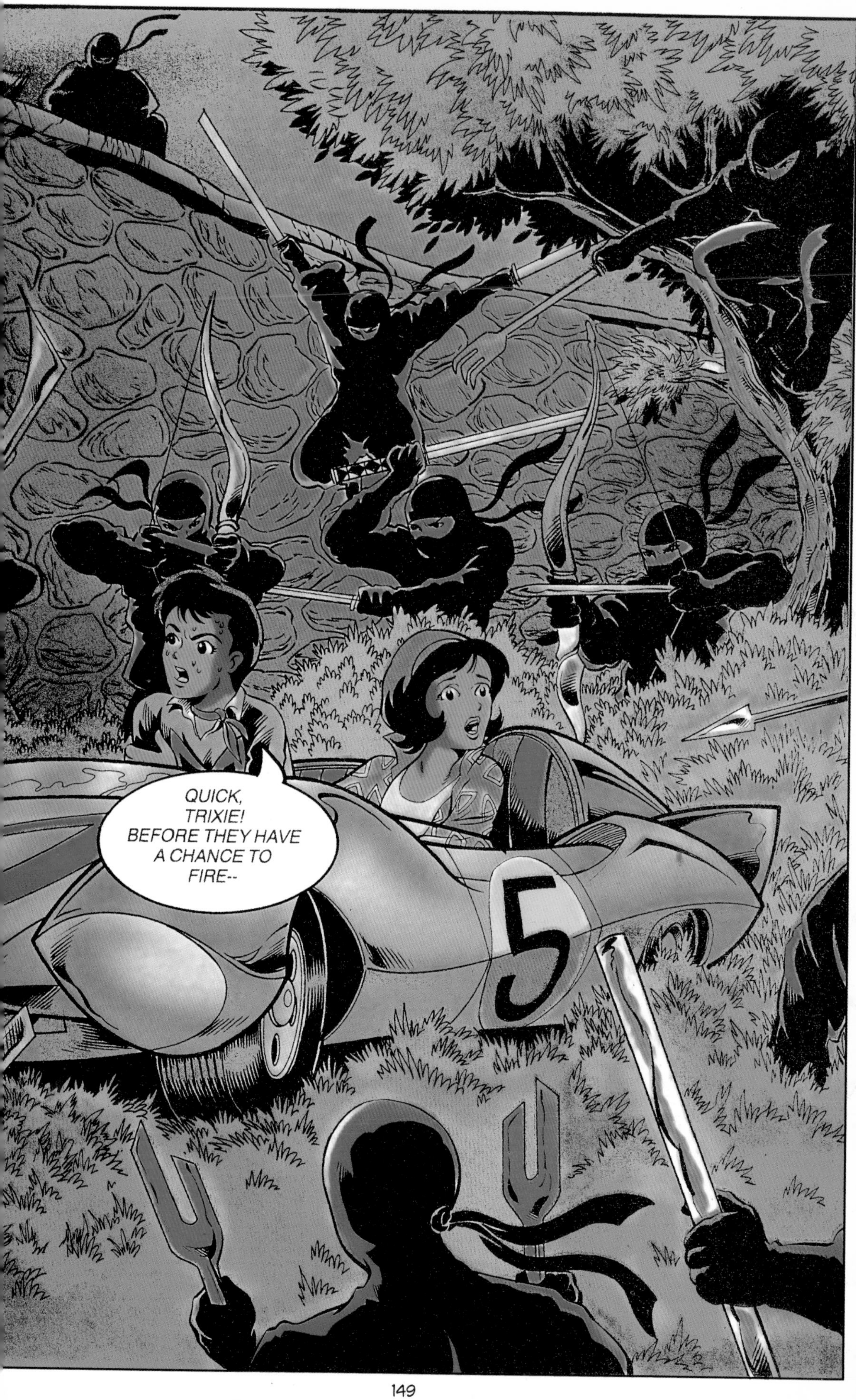
QUICK, TRIXIE! BEFORE THEY HAVE A CHANCE TO FIRE--

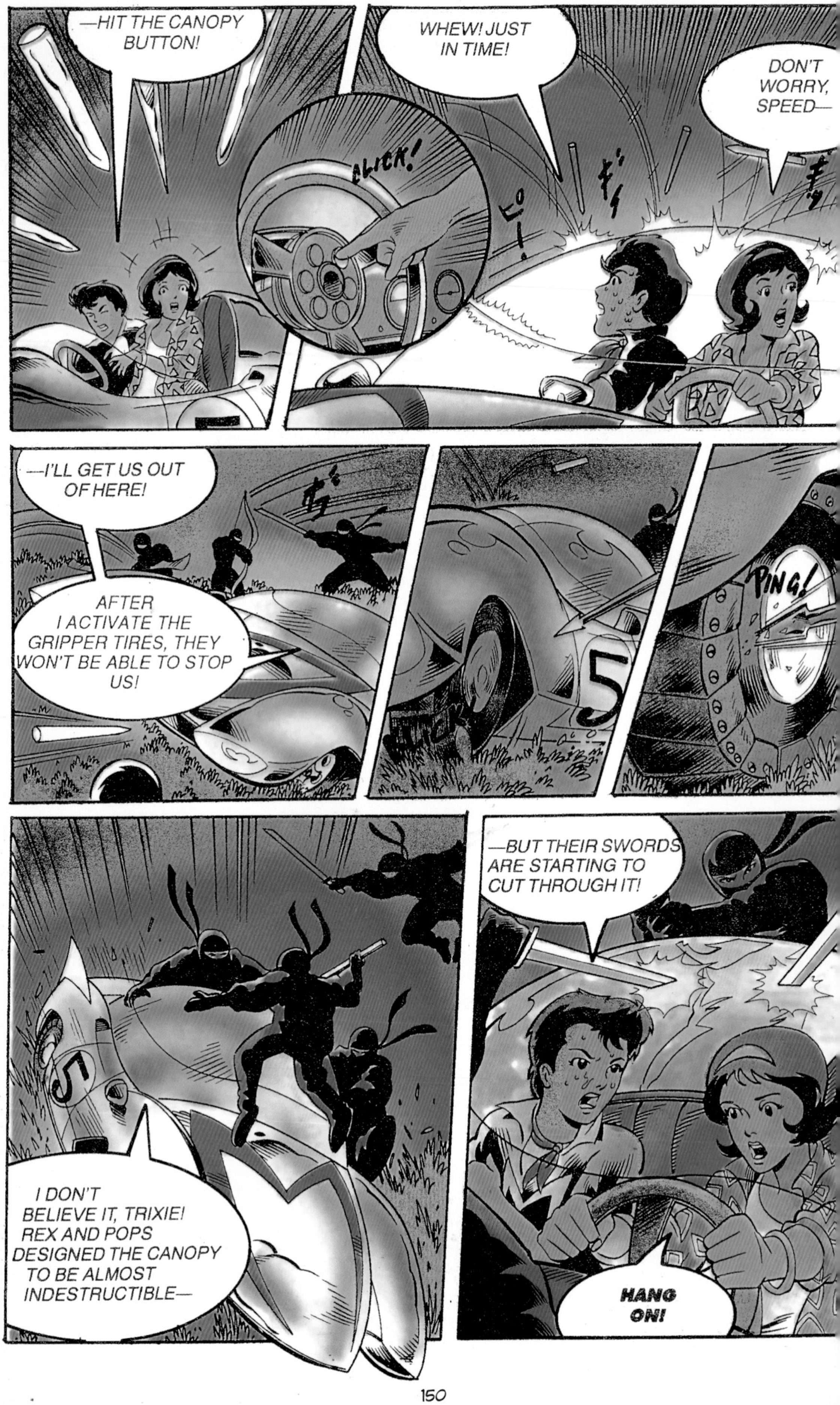
—HIT THE CANOPY BUTTON!
CLICK!
WHEW! JUST IN TIME!
DON'T WORRY, SPEED—
—I'LL GET US OUT OF HERE!
AFTER I ACTIVATE THE GRIPPER TIRES, THEY WON'T BE ABLE TO STOP US!
PING!
I DON'T BELIEVE IT, TRIXIE! REX AND POPS DESIGNED THE CANOPY TO BE ALMOST INDESTRUCTIBLE—
—BUT THEIR SWORDS ARE STARTING TO CUT THROUGH IT!
HANG ON!

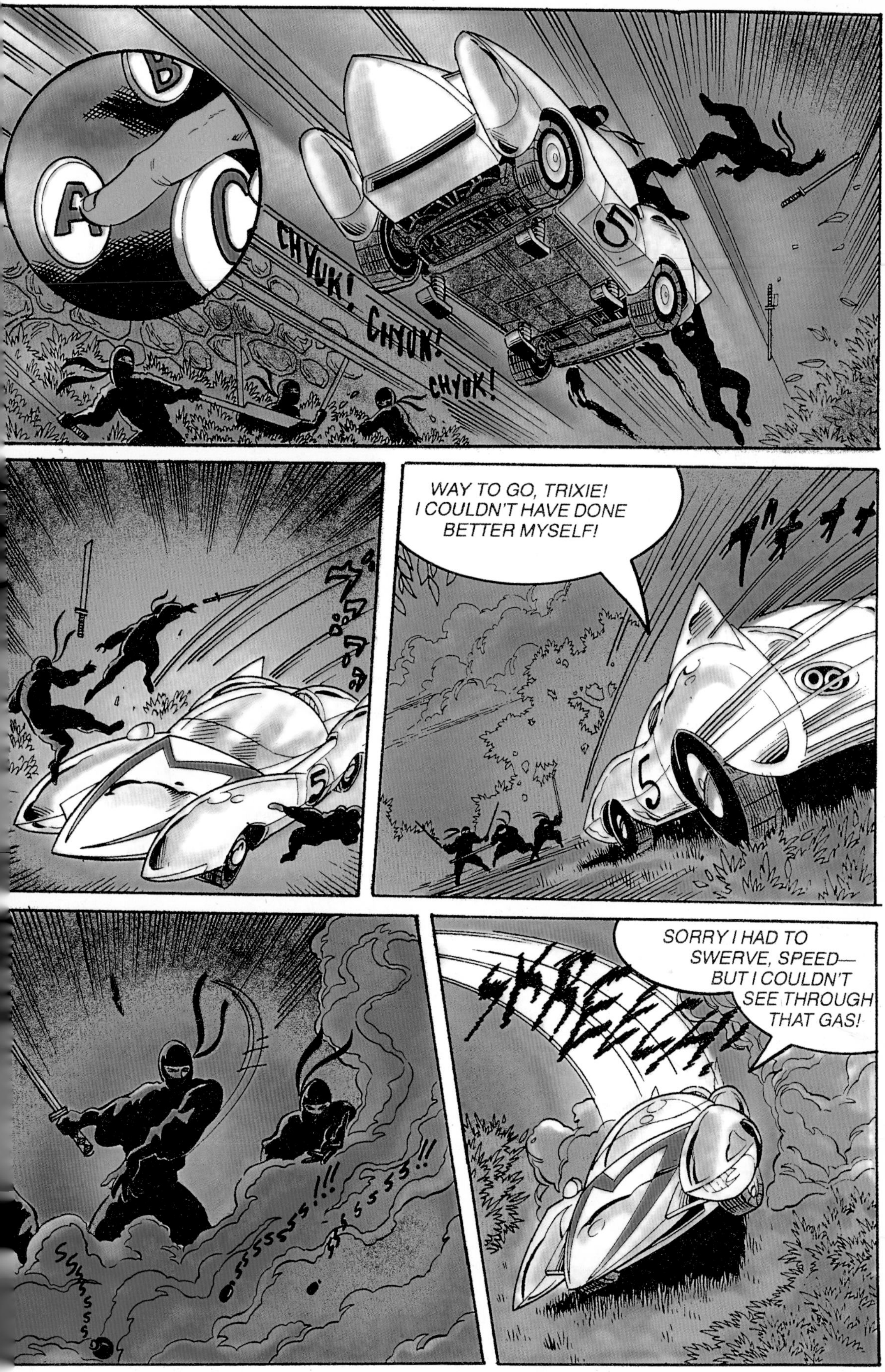
CHYUK!
CHYUK!
CHYOK!
WAY TO GO, TRIXIE!
I COULDN'T HAVE DONE
BETTER MYSELF!
SKREEECH!
SORRY I HAD TO
SWERVE, SPEED—
BUT I COULDN'T
SEE THROUGH
THAT GAS!

BLAM!

BOOM!

BOOM!

TRIXIE, THEY'RE IN THE TREES— FIRING EXPLOSIVES!

I KNOW JUST HOW TO CUT THEM DOWN TO SIZE, SPEED!

WHIRR!!

WHIRR!!

BUZZZ!!

BUZZZ!!

EEEYAAA!

ZOOM!!

BZZZ!!

SNAP!

YOU DID IT, TRIXIE! WE'RE HOME FREE!

MAYBE I SHOULD DRIVE MORE OFTEN, SPEED!

AN HOUR LATER, AT THEIR HOTEL IN DOWNTOWN TOKYO...

WHAT YOU DID WASN'T JUST DANGEROUS! IT WAS ALSO **ILLEGAL!**

BUT POPS--

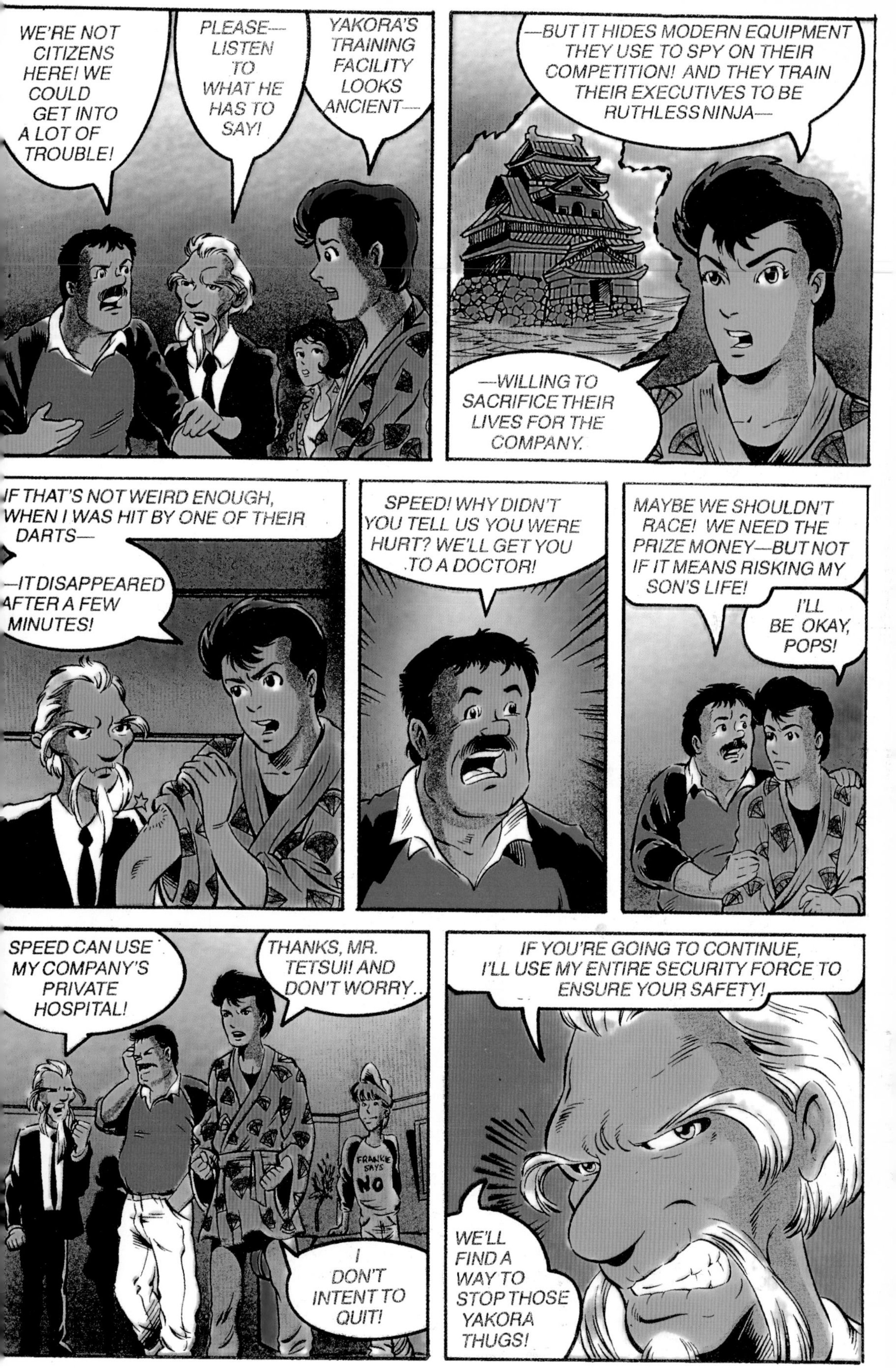

WE'RE NOT CITIZENS HERE! WE COULD GET INTO A LOT OF TROUBLE!
PLEASE— LISTEN TO WHAT HE HAS TO SAY!
YAKORA'S TRAINING FACILITY LOOKS ANCIENT—
—BUT IT HIDES MODERN EQUIPMENT THEY USE TO SPY ON THEIR COMPETITION! AND THEY TRAIN THEIR EXECUTIVES TO BE RUTHLESS NINJA—
—WILLING TO SACRIFICE THEIR LIVES FOR THE COMPANY.
IF THAT'S NOT WEIRD ENOUGH, WHEN I WAS HIT BY ONE OF THEIR DARTS—
—IT DISAPPEARED AFTER A FEW MINUTES!
SPEED! WHY DIDN'T YOU TELL US YOU WERE HURT? WE'LL GET YOU TO A DOCTOR!
MAYBE WE SHOULDN'T RACE! WE NEED THE PRIZE MONEY—BUT NOT IF IT MEANS RISKING MY SON'S LIFE!
I'LL BE OKAY, POPS!
SPEED CAN USE MY COMPANY'S PRIVATE HOSPITAL!
THANKS, MR. TETSUI! AND DON'T WORRY...
I DON'T INTENT TO QUIT!
FRANKIE SAYS NO
IF YOU'RE GOING TO CONTINUE, I'LL USE MY ENTIRE SECURITY FORCE TO ENSURE YOUR SAFETY!
WE'LL FIND A WAY TO STOP THOSE YAKORA THUGS!

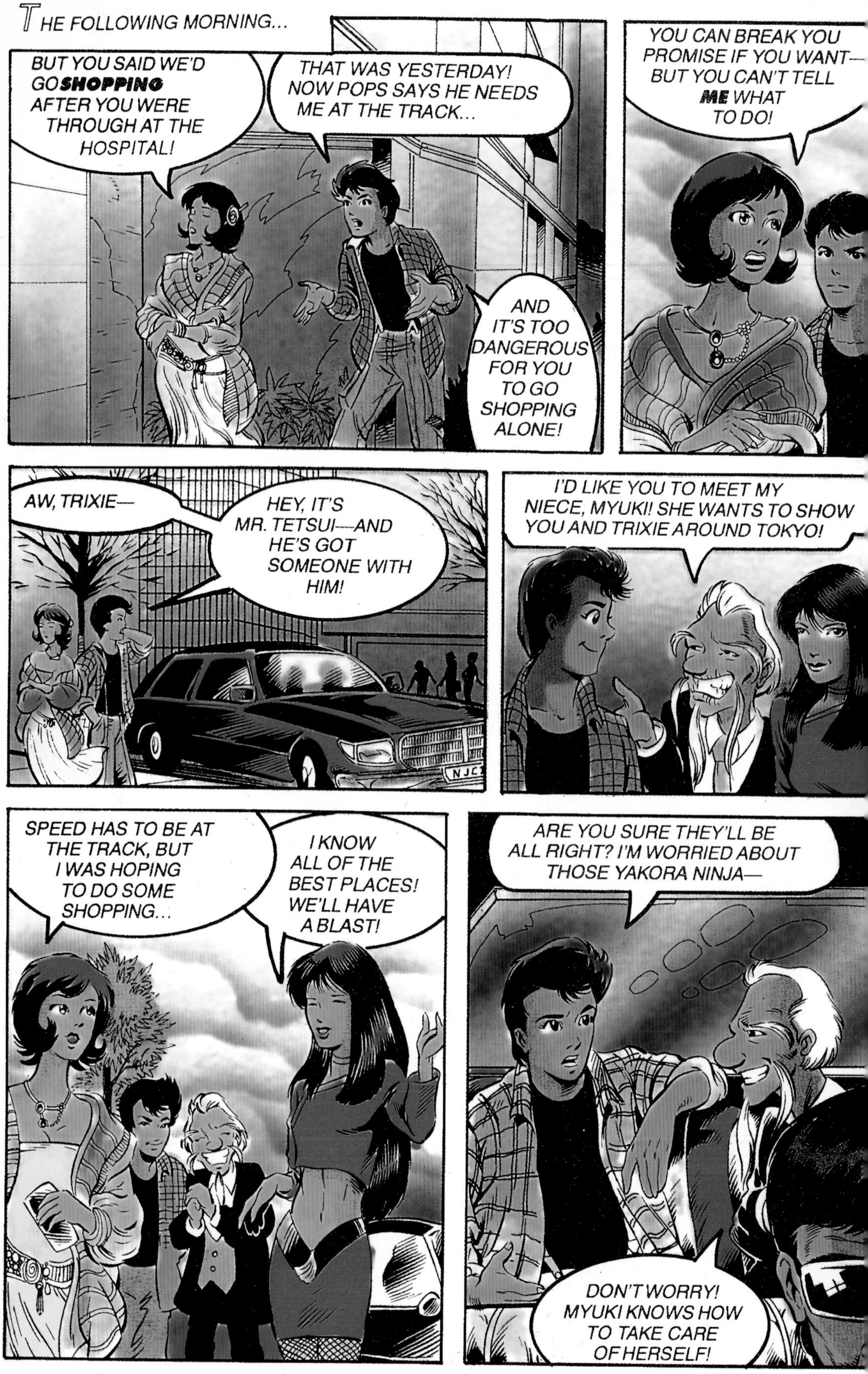
THE FOLLOWING MORNING...
BUT YOU SAID WE'D GO SHOPPING AFTER YOU WERE THROUGH AT THE HOSPITAL!
THAT WAS YESTERDAY! NOW POPS SAYS HE NEEDS ME AT THE TRACK...
AND IT'S TOO DANGEROUS FOR YOU TO GO SHOPPING ALONE!
YOU CAN BREAK YOU PROMISE IF YOU WANT—BUT YOU CAN'T TELL ME WHAT TO DO!
AW, TRIXIE—
HEY, IT'S MR. TETSUI—AND HE'S GOT SOMEONE WITH HIM!
I'D LIKE YOU TO MEET MY NIECE, MYUKI! SHE WANTS TO SHOW YOU AND TRIXIE AROUND TOKYO!
SPEED HAS TO BE AT THE TRACK, BUT I WAS HOPING TO DO SOME SHOPPING...
I KNOW ALL OF THE BEST PLACES! WE'LL HAVE A BLAST!
ARE YOU SURE THEY'LL BE ALL RIGHT? I'M WORRIED ABOUT THOSE YAKORA NINJA—
DON'T WORRY! MYUKI KNOWS HOW TO TAKE CARE OF HERSELF!

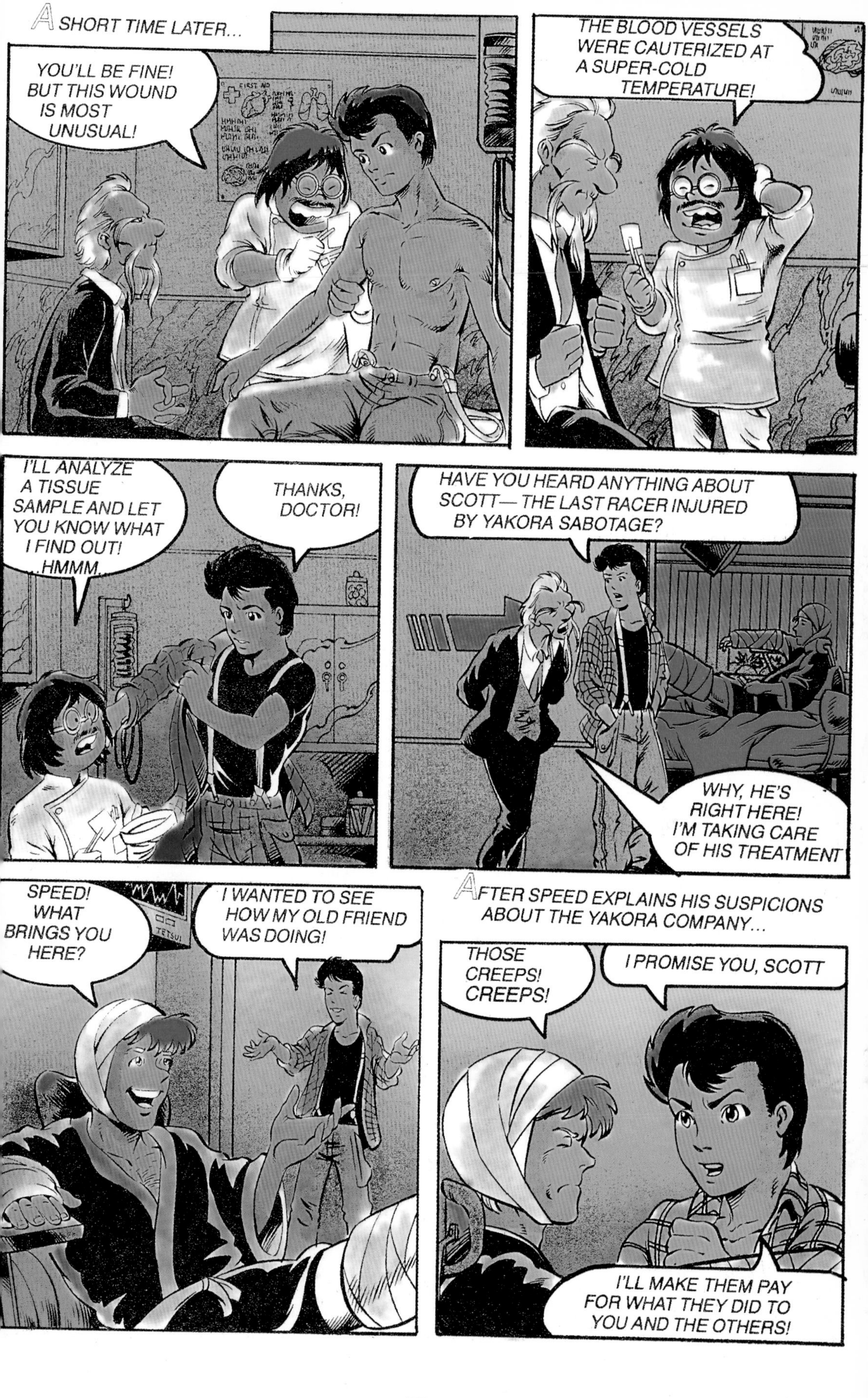
A SHORT TIME LATER...
YOU'LL BE FINE! BUT THIS WOUND IS MOST UNUSUAL!
THE BLOOD VESSELS WERE CAUTERIZED AT A SUPER-COLD TEMPERATURE!
I'LL ANALYZE A TISSUE SAMPLE AND LET YOU KNOW WHAT I FIND OUT! ..HMMM..
THANKS, DOCTOR!
HAVE YOU HEARD ANYTHING ABOUT SCOTT— THE LAST RACER INJURED BY YAKORA SABOTAGE?
WHY, HE'S RIGHT HERE! I'M TAKING CARE OF HIS TREATMENT
SPEED! WHAT BRINGS YOU HERE?
I WANTED TO SEE HOW MY OLD FRIEND WAS DOING!
AFTER SPEED EXPLAINS HIS SUSPICIONS ABOUT THE YAKORA COMPANY...
THOSE CREEPS! CREEPS!
I PROMISE YOU, SCOTT
I'LL MAKE THEM PAY FOR WHAT THEY DID TO YOU AND THE OTHERS!

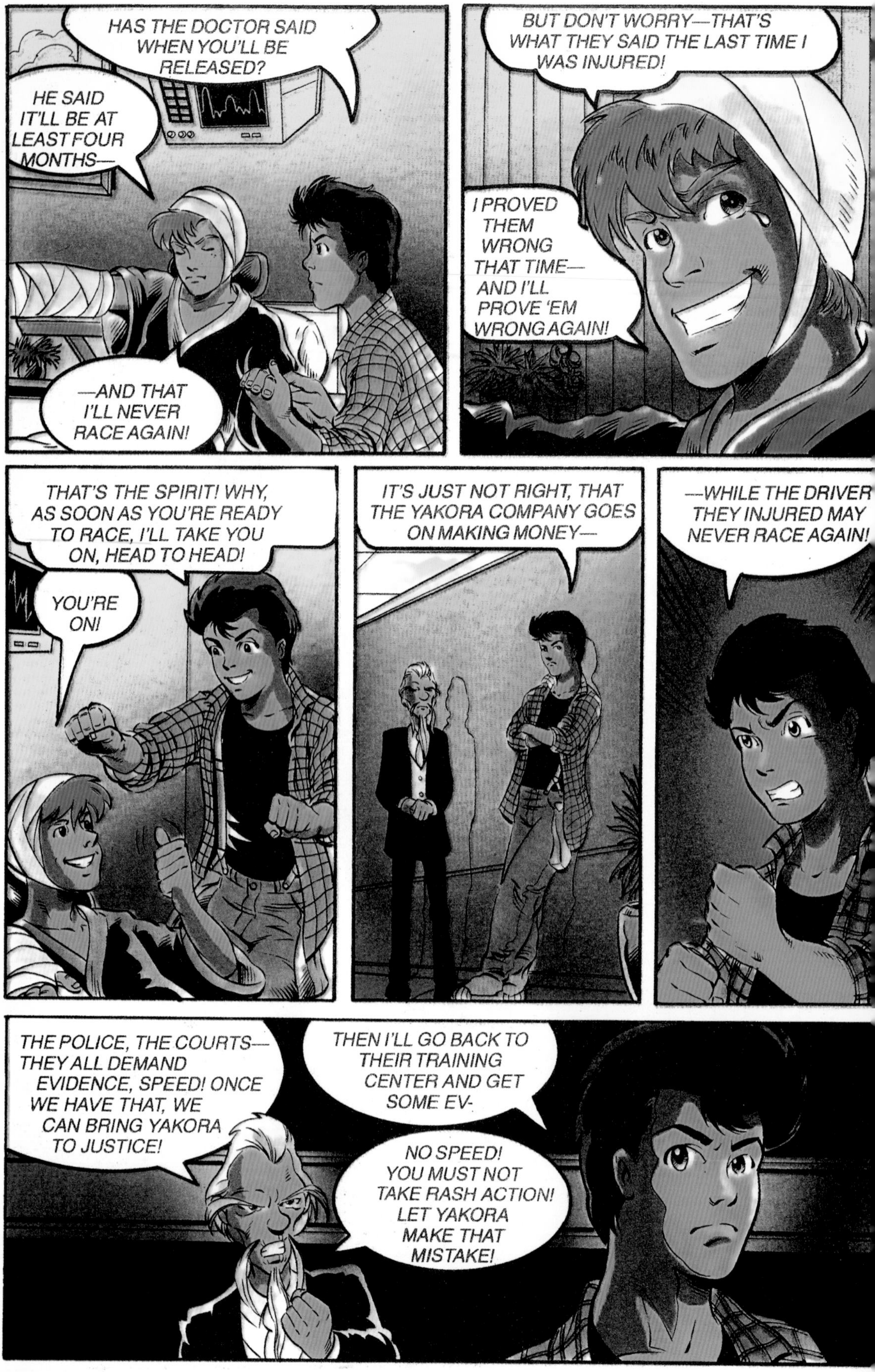
HAS THE DOCTOR SAID WHEN YOU'LL BE RELEASED?
HE SAID IT'LL BE AT LEAST FOUR MONTHS—
—AND THAT I'LL NEVER RACE AGAIN!
BUT DON'T WORRY—THAT'S WHAT THEY SAID THE LAST TIME I WAS INJURED!
I PROVED THEM WRONG THAT TIME— AND I'LL PROVE 'EM WRONG AGAIN!
THAT'S THE SPIRIT! WHY, AS SOON AS YOU'RE READY TO RACE, I'LL TAKE YOU ON, HEAD TO HEAD!
YOU'RE ON!
IT'S JUST NOT RIGHT, THAT THE YAKORA COMPANY GOES ON MAKING MONEY—
—WHILE THE DRIVER THEY INJURED MAY NEVER RACE AGAIN!
THE POLICE, THE COURTS— THEY ALL DEMAND EVIDENCE, SPEED! ONCE WE HAVE THAT, WE CAN BRING YAKORA TO JUSTICE!
THEN I'LL GO BACK TO THEIR TRAINING CENTER AND GET SOME EV-
NO SPEED! YOU MUST NOT TAKE RASH ACTION! LET YAKORA MAKE THAT MISTAKE!

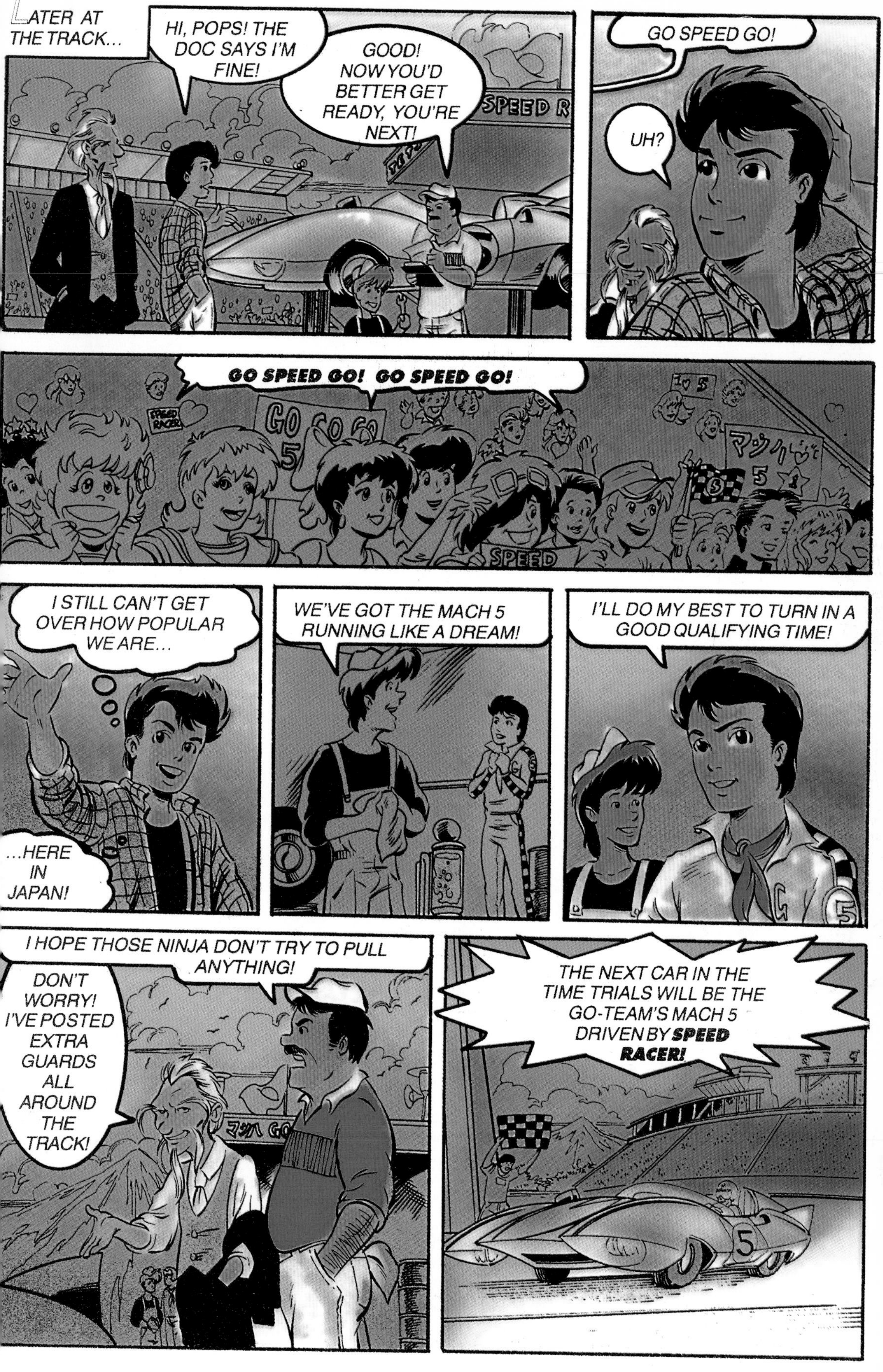
LATER AT THE TRACK...
HI, POPS! THE DOC SAYS I'M FINE!
GOOD! NOW YOU'D BETTER GET READY, YOU'RE NEXT!
GO SPEED GO!
UH?
GO SPEED GO! GO SPEED GO!
I STILL CAN'T GET OVER HOW POPULAR WE ARE...
...HERE IN JAPAN!
WE'VE GOT THE MACH 5 RUNNING LIKE A DREAM!
I'LL DO MY BEST TO TURN IN A GOOD QUALIFYING TIME!
I HOPE THOSE NINJA DON'T TRY TO PULL ANYTHING!
DON'T WORRY! I'VE POSTED EXTRA GUARDS ALL AROUND THE TRACK!
THE NEXT CAR IN THE TIME TRIALS WILL BE THE GO-TEAM'S MACH 5 DRIVEN BY **SPEED RACER!**

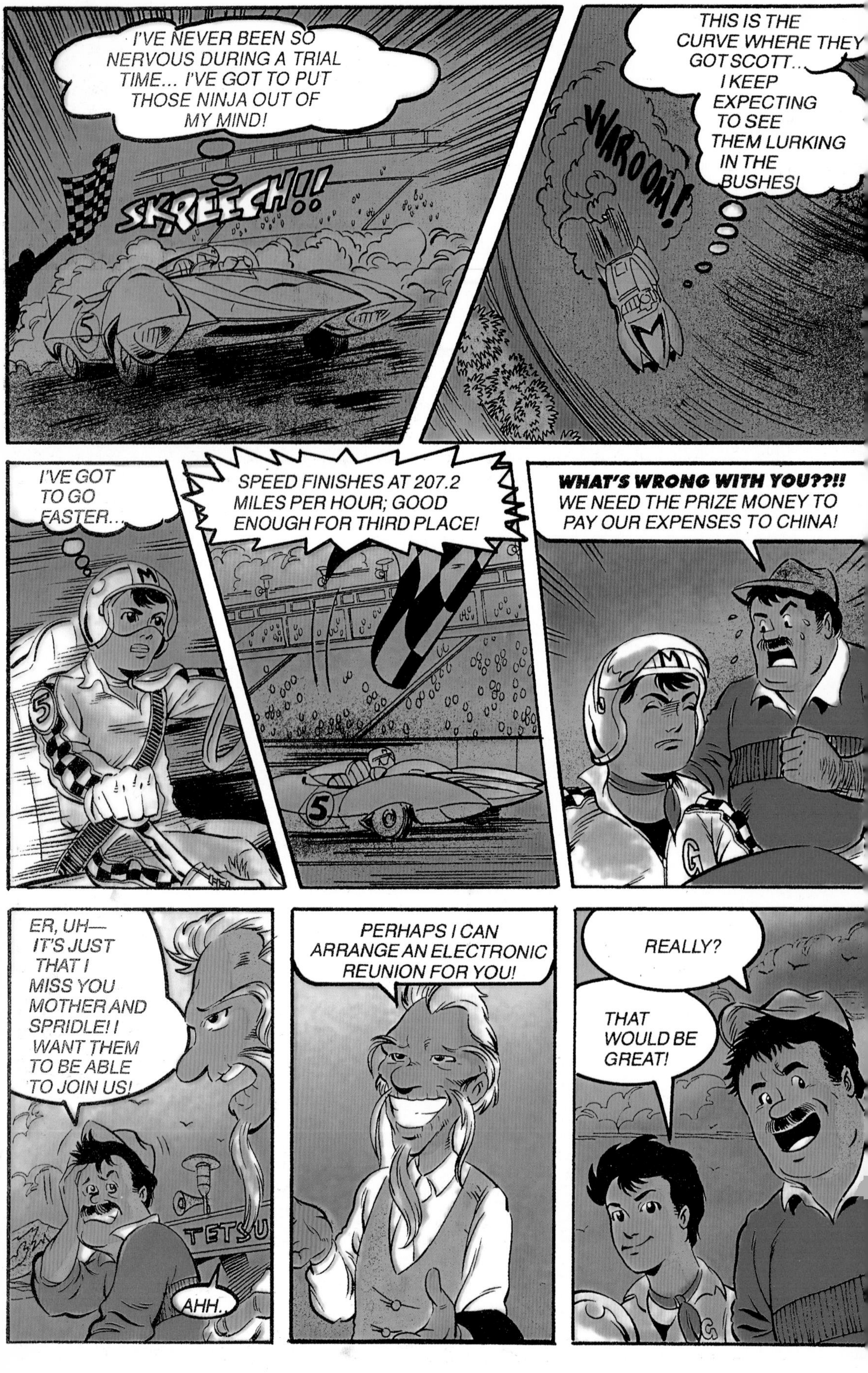
I'VE NEVER BEEN SO NERVOUS DURING A TRIAL TIME... I'VE GOT TO PUT THOSE NINJA OUT OF MY MIND!
SKREECH!!
VVAROOOM!
THIS IS THE CURVE WHERE THEY GOT SCOTT... I KEEP EXPECTING TO SEE THEM LURKING IN THE BUSHES!
I'VE GOT TO GO FASTER...
SPEED FINISHES AT 207.2 MILES PER HOUR; GOOD ENOUGH FOR THIRD PLACE!
WHAT'S WRONG WITH YOU??!! WE NEED THE PRIZE MONEY TO PAY OUR EXPENSES TO CHINA!
ER, UH— IT'S JUST THAT I MISS YOU MOTHER AND SPRIDLE! I WANT THEM TO BE ABLE TO JOIN US!
TETSU
AHH..
PERHAPS I CAN ARRANGE AN ELECTRONIC REUNION FOR YOU!
REALLY?
THAT WOULD BE GREAT!

THAT EVENING AT THEIR HOTEL...

REALLY, MOM—YOU WOULDN'T BELIEVE HOW WELL WE'RE BEING TREATED!

I'M SO GLAD TO HEAR THAT YOU'RE ALL HAVING SUCH A GOOD TIME!

IT'S NOT AS GOOD AS IT'LL BE WHEN WE'RE ALL TOGETHER AGAIN!

I'M GETTING THINGS PACKED FOR CHINA! LET ME KNOW WHEN YOU HAVE MONEY FOR THE PLANE TICKETS! GOODBYE!

IT WAS NICE OF MR. TETSUI TO ARRANGE THAT—I'VE REALLY MISSED THEM!

IF ONLY IT WERE AS EASY TO CONTACT REX—

KLICK!

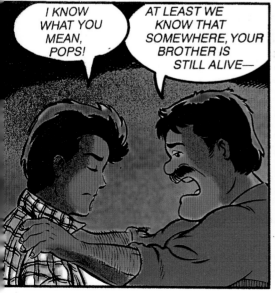

I KNOW WHAT YOU MEAN, POPS!

AT LEAST WE KNOW THAT SOMEWHERE, YOUR BROTHER IS STILL ALIVE—

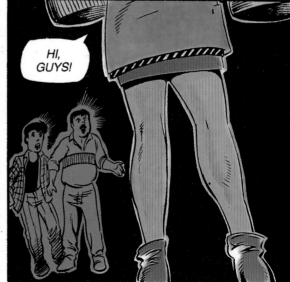

HI, GUYS!

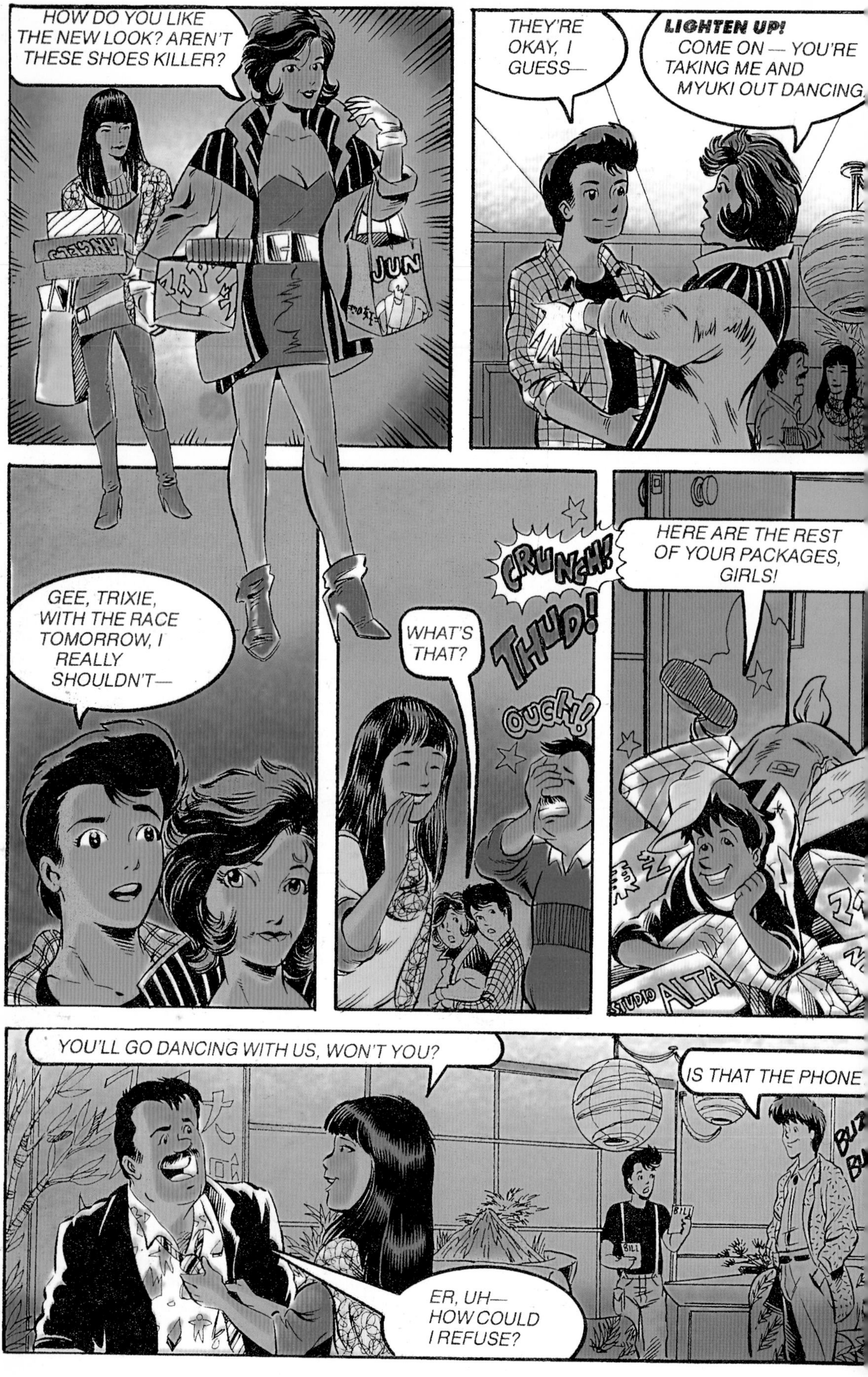
HOW DO YOU LIKE THE NEW LOOK? AREN'T THESE SHOES KILLER?
JUN
THEY'RE OKAY, I GUESS—
LIGHTEN UP! COME ON — YOU'RE TAKING ME AND MYUKI OUT DANCING
GEE, TRIXIE, WITH THE RACE TOMORROW, I REALLY SHOULDN'T—
WHAT'S THAT?
CRUNCH!
THUD!
OUCH!
HERE ARE THE REST OF YOUR PACKAGES, GIRLS!
STUDIO ALTA
YOU'LL GO DANCING WITH US, WON'T YOU?
IS THAT THE PHONE
BILL
ER, UH— HOW COULD I REFUSE?

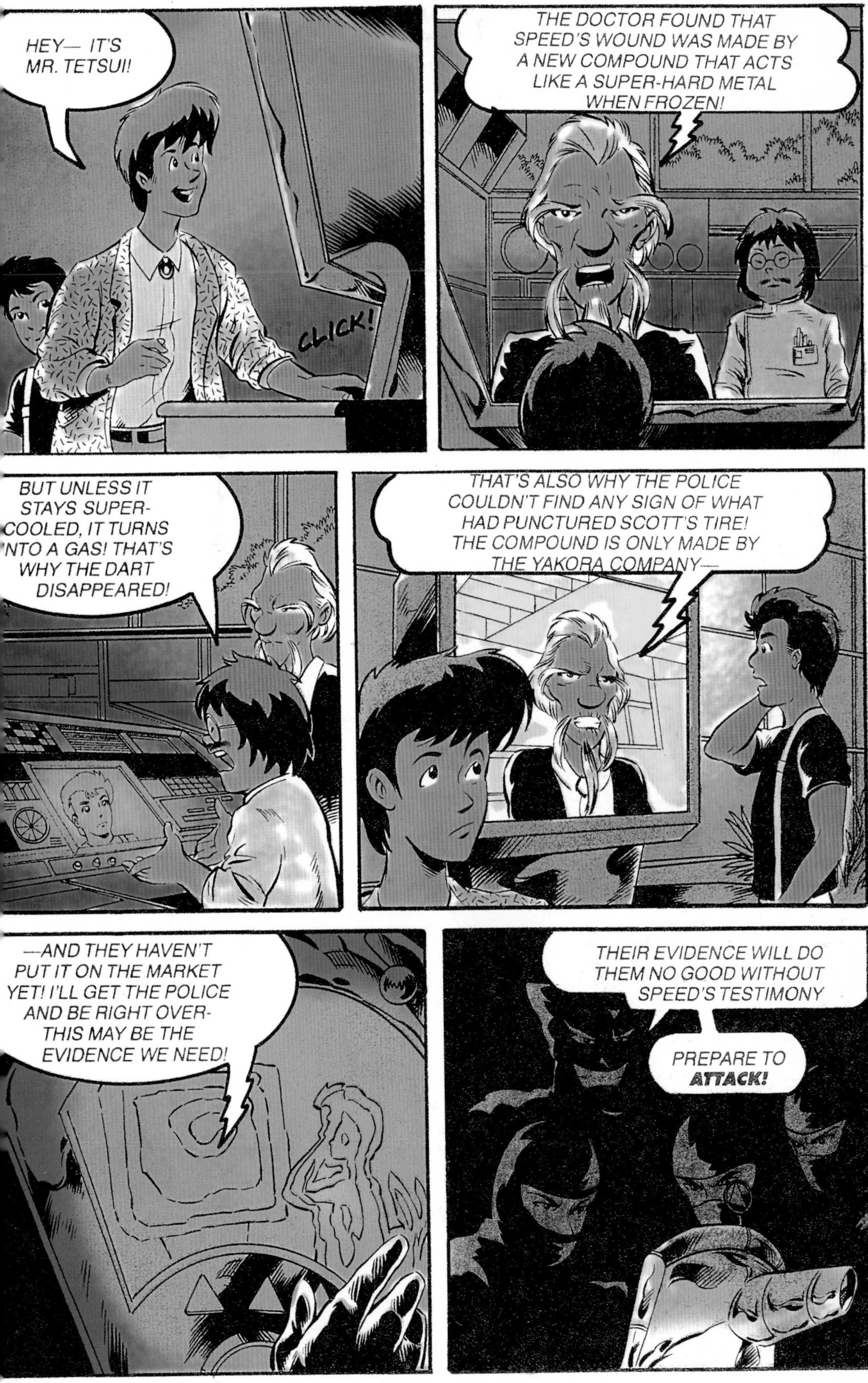
HEY— IT'S MR. TETSUI!
CLICK!
THE DOCTOR FOUND THAT SPEED'S WOUND WAS MADE BY A NEW COMPOUND THAT ACTS LIKE A SUPER-HARD METAL WHEN FROZEN!
BUT UNLESS IT STAYS SUPER-COOLED, IT TURNS INTO A GAS! THAT'S WHY THE DART DISAPPEARED!
THAT'S ALSO WHY THE POLICE COULDN'T FIND ANY SIGN OF WHAT HAD PUNCTURED SCOTT'S TIRE! THE COMPOUND IS ONLY MADE BY THE YAKORA COMPANY—
—AND THEY HAVEN'T PUT IT ON THE MARKET YET! I'LL GET THE POLICE AND BE RIGHT OVER- THIS MAY BE THE EVIDENCE WE NEED!
THEIR EVIDENCE WILL DO THEM NO GOOD WITHOUT SPEED'S TESTIMONY
PREPARE TO ATTACK!

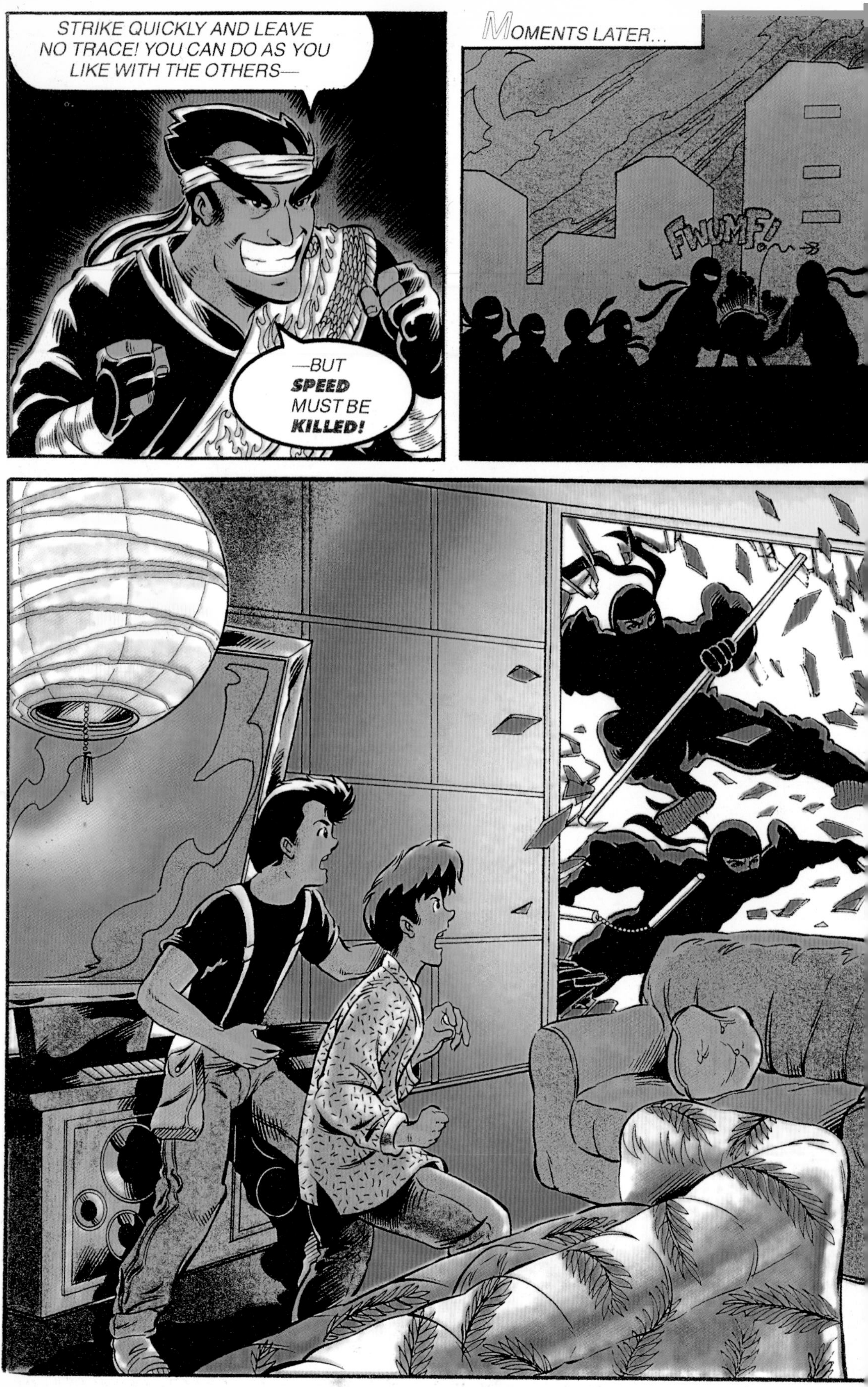
STRIKE QUICKLY AND LEAVE NO TRACE! YOU CAN DO AS YOU LIKE WITH THE OTHERS—
—BUT **SPEED** MUST BE **KILLED!**
MOMENTS LATER...
FWUMF!

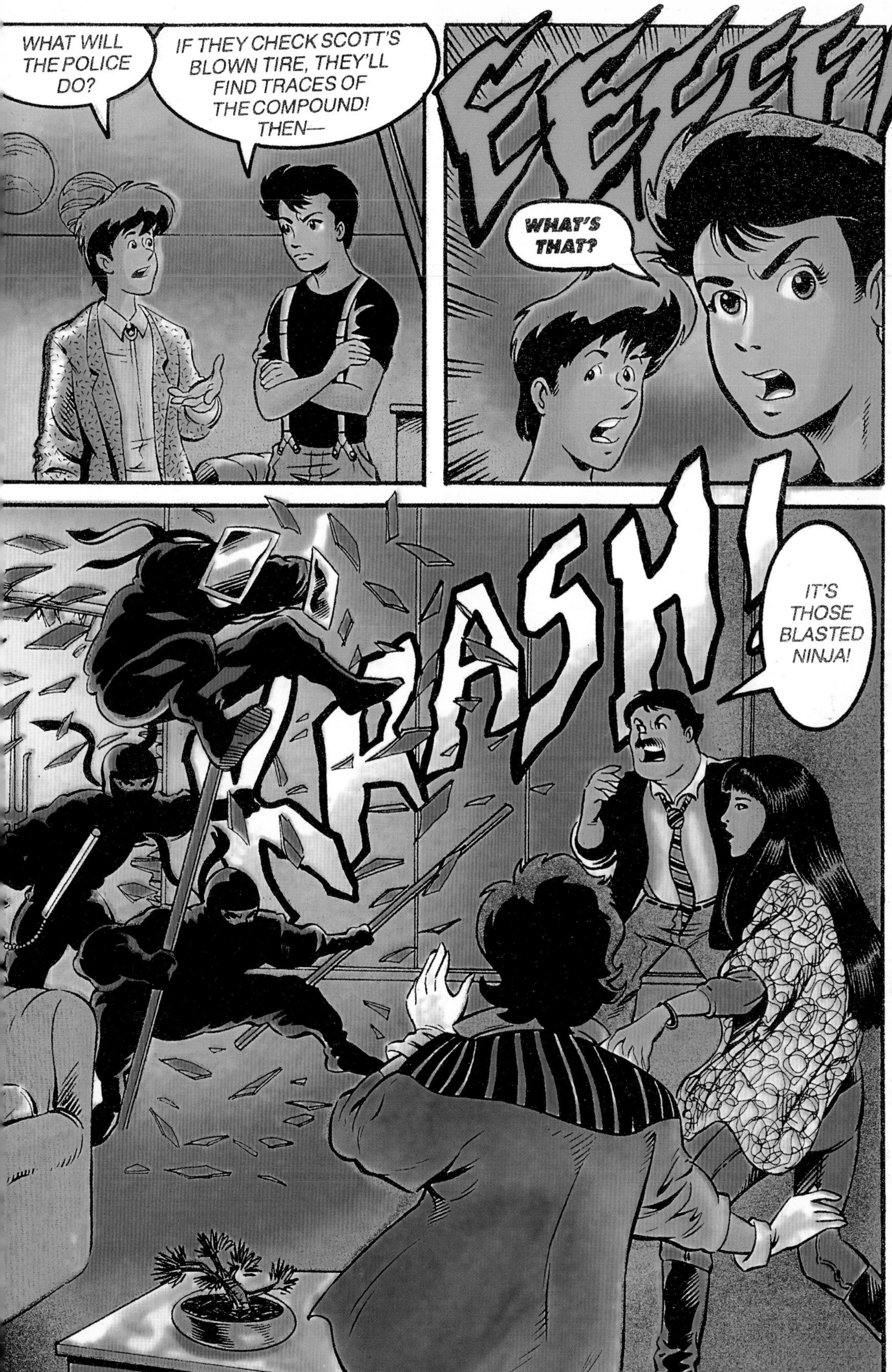
WHAT WILL THE POLICE DO?
IF THEY CHECK SCOTT'S BLOWN TIRE, THEY'LL FIND TRACES OF THE COMPOUND! THEN—
EEEEE!!
WHAT'S THAT?
KRASH!
IT'S THOSE BLASTED NINJA!

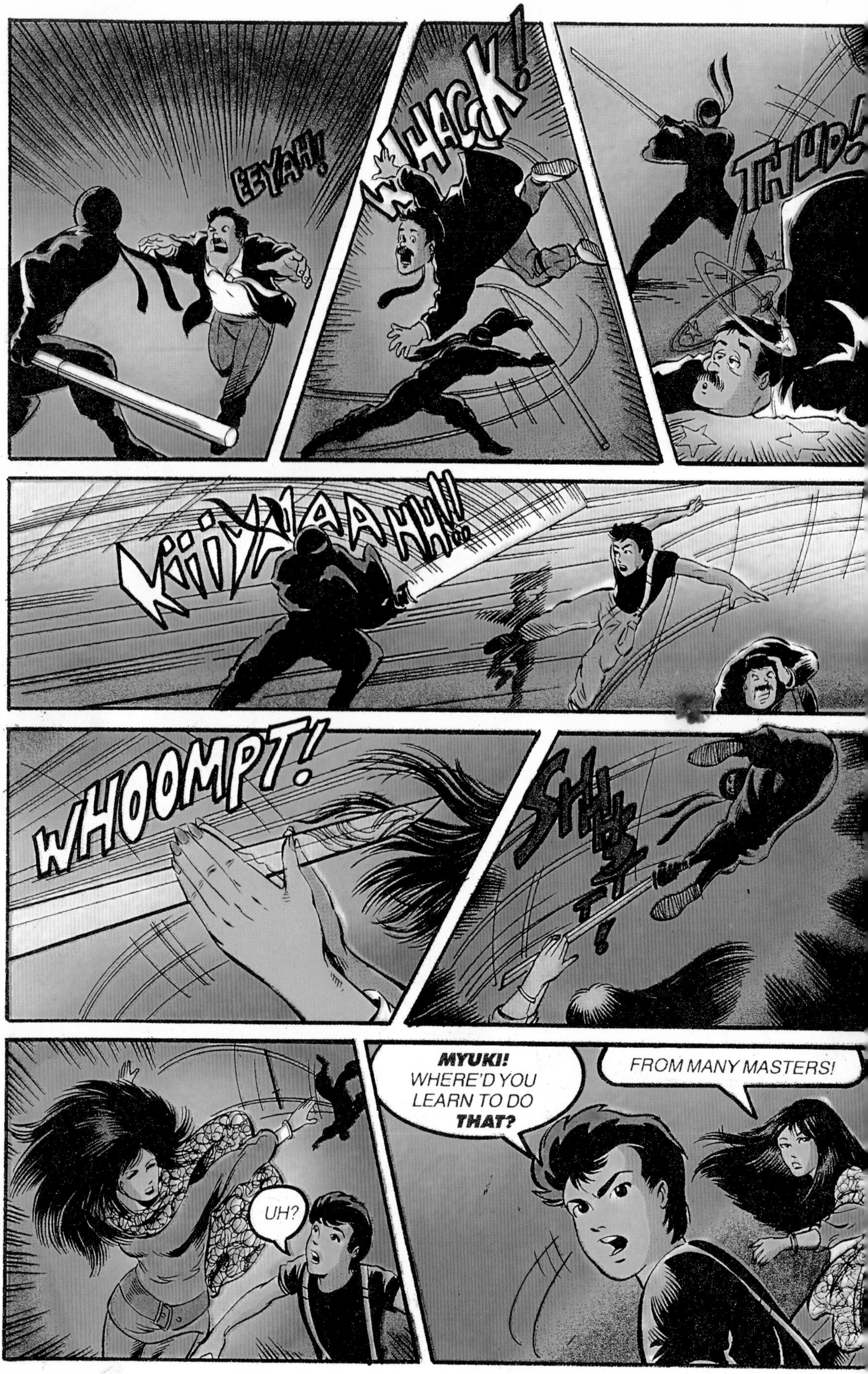

EEYAH!
WHACCK!
THUD!
KIIYAAAHH!!
WHOOMPT!
UH?
MYUKI! WHERE'D YOU LEARN TO DO THAT?
FROM MANY MASTERS!

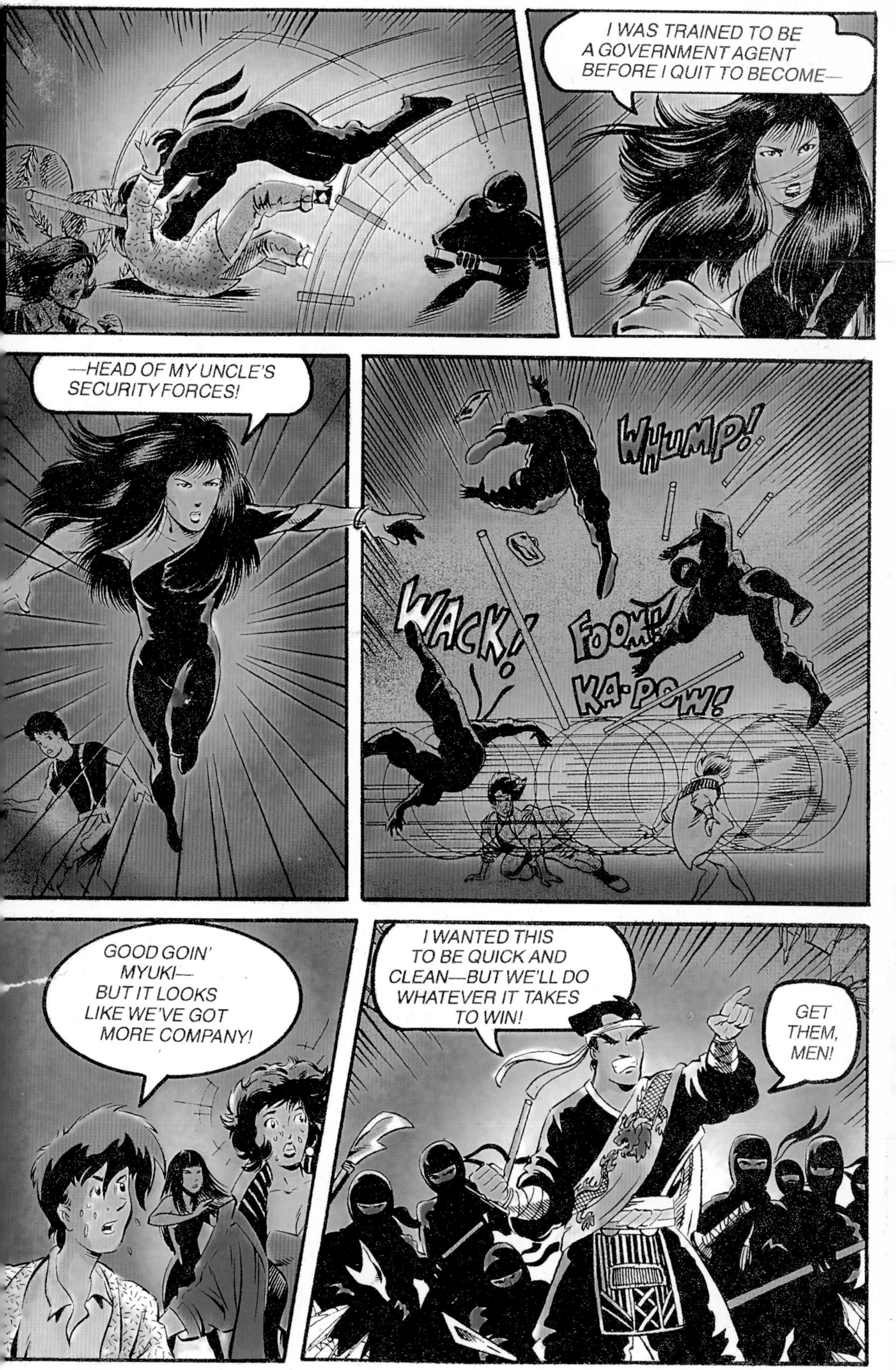
I WAS TRAINED TO BE A GOVERNMENT AGENT BEFORE I QUIT TO BECOME—
—HEAD OF MY UNCLE'S SECURITY FORCES!
WHUMP!
WACK!
FOOM!
KA-POW!
GOOD GOIN' MYUKI— BUT IT LOOKS LIKE WE'VE GOT MORE COMPANY!
I WANTED THIS TO BE QUICK AND CLEAN—BUT WE'LL DO WHATEVER IT TAKES TO WIN!
GET THEM, MEN!

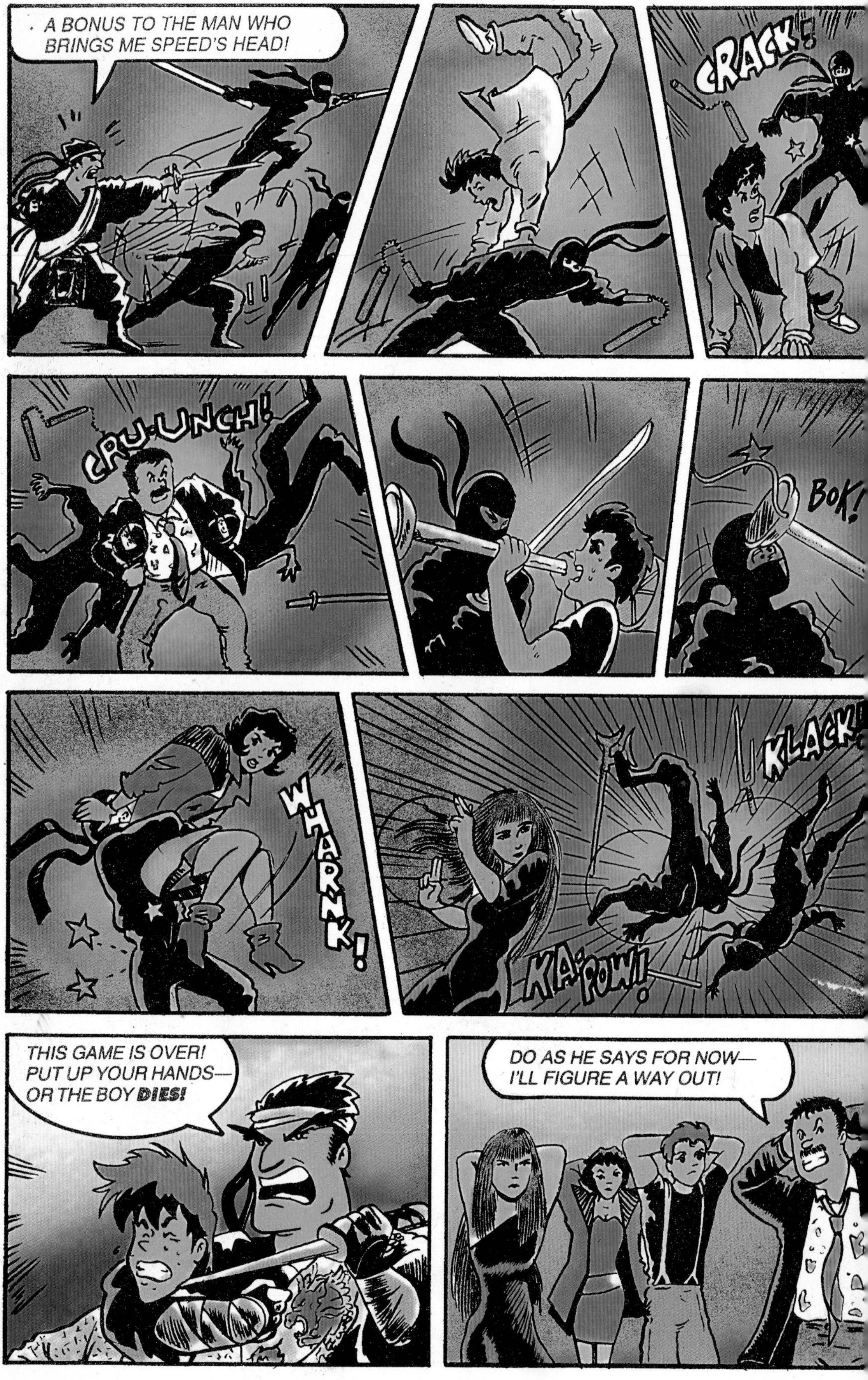
. A BONUS TO THE MAN WHO BRINGS ME SPEED'S HEAD!
CRACK!
CRU-UNCH!
BOK!
WHARNK!
KLACK!
KA-POW!
THIS GAME IS OVER! PUT UP YOUR HANDS— OR THE BOY DIES!
DO AS HE SAYS FOR NOW— I'LL FIGURE A WAY OUT!

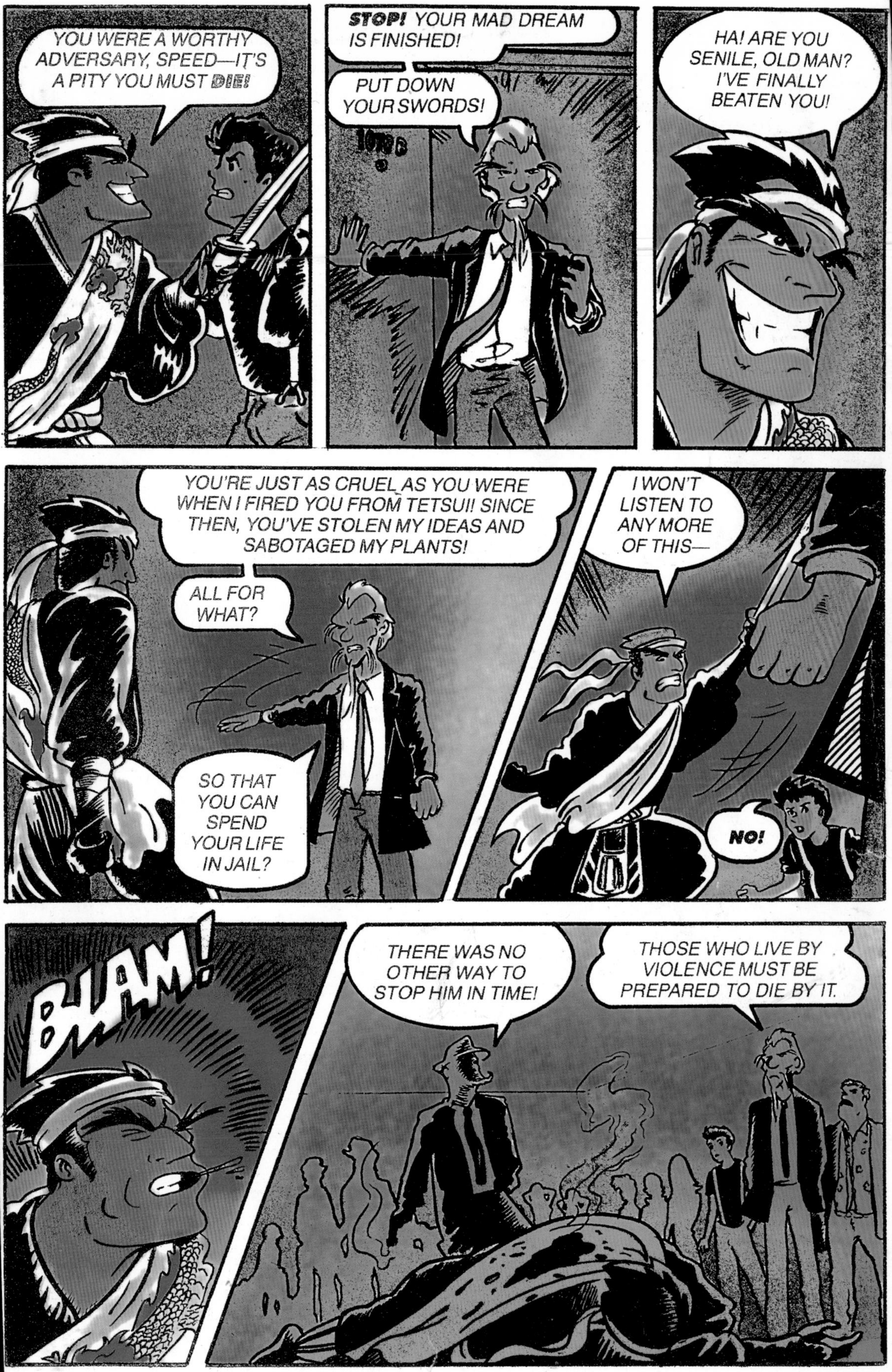
YOU WERE A WORTHY ADVERSARY, SPEED—IT'S A PITY YOU MUST DIE!
STOP! YOUR MAD DREAM IS FINISHED!
PUT DOWN YOUR SWORDS!
HA! ARE YOU SENILE, OLD MAN? I'VE FINALLY BEATEN YOU!
YOU'RE JUST AS CRUEL AS YOU WERE WHEN I FIRED YOU FROM TETSUI! SINCE THEN, YOU'VE STOLEN MY IDEAS AND SABOTAGED MY PLANTS!
ALL FOR WHAT?
SO THAT YOU CAN SPEND YOUR LIFE IN JAIL?
I WON'T LISTEN TO ANY MORE OF THIS—
NO!
BLAM!
THERE WAS NO OTHER WAY TO STOP HIM IN TIME!
THOSE WHO LIVE BY VIOLENCE MUST BE PREPARED TO DIE BY IT.

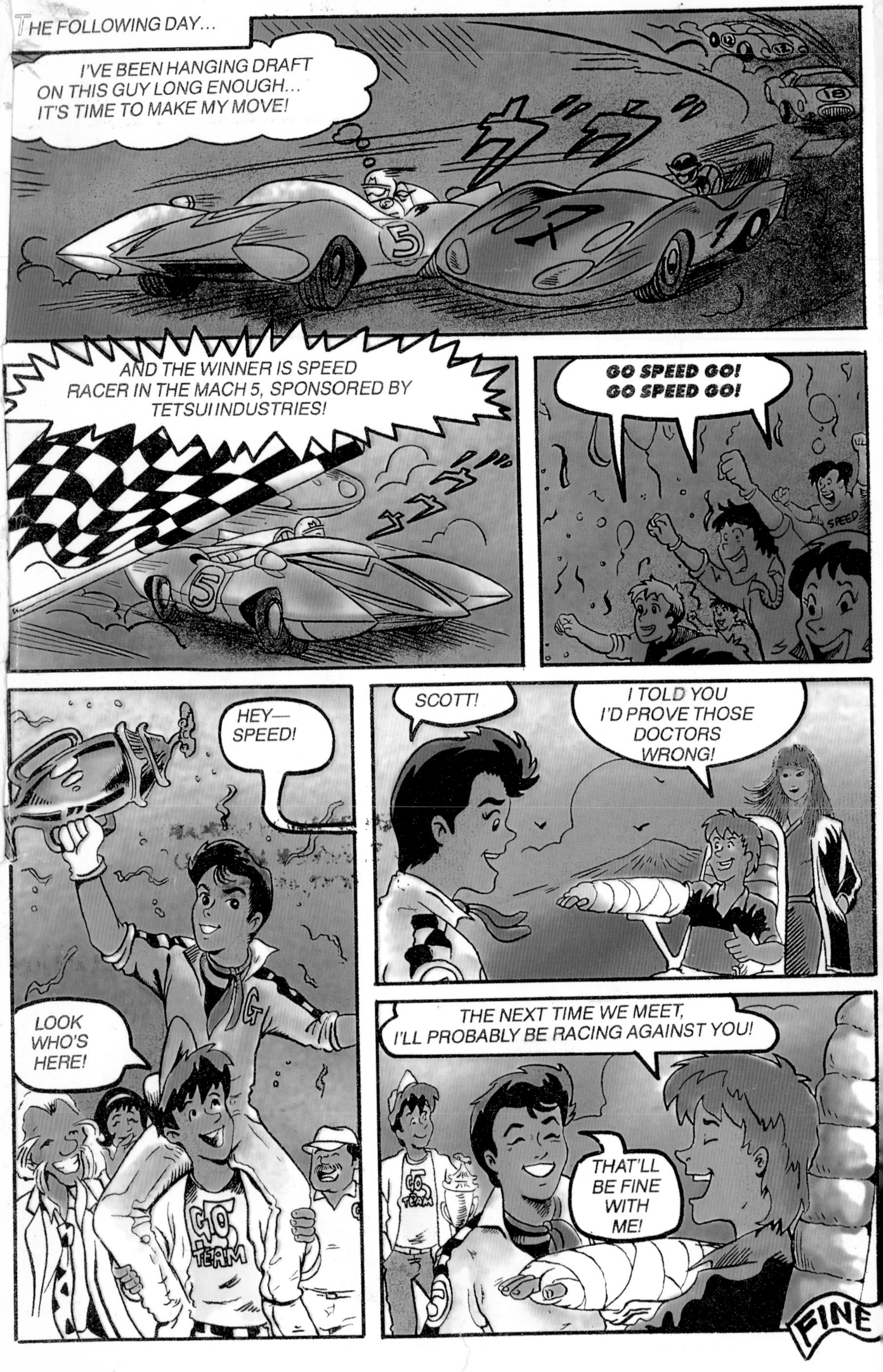
THE FOLLOWING DAY...
I'VE BEEN HANGING DRAFT ON THIS GUY LONG ENOUGH... IT'S TIME TO MAKE MY MOVE!
AND THE WINNER IS SPEED RACER IN THE MACH 5, SPONSORED BY TETSUI INDUSTRIES!
GO SPEED GO! GO SPEED GO!
HEY— SPEED!
LOOK WHO'S HERE!
SCOTT!
I TOLD YOU I'D PROVE THOSE DOCTORS WRONG!
THE NEXT TIME WE MEET, I'LL PROBABLY BE RACING AGAINST YOU!
THAT'LL BE FINE WITH ME!
FINE